Copyright 2020 by Greg Bales -All rights reserved.

No part of this book may be reproduced or transmitted in any form or by any means, electronic or mechanical, including photocopying and recording, or by any information storage and retrieval system, without permission in writing from the publisher. This is a work of fiction. Names, places, characters and incidents are either the product of the author's imagination or are used fictitiously, and any resemblance to any actual persons, living or dead, organizations, events or locales is entirely coincidental. The unauthorized reproduction or distribution of this copyrighted work is ilegal.

Disclaimer Notice:

Please note the information contained within this document is for educational and entertainment purposes only. All effort has been executed to present accurate, up to date, reliable, complete information. No warranties of any kind are declared or implied. Readers acknowledge that the author is not engaged in the rendering of legal, financial, medical, or professional advice. The content within this book has been derived from various sources. Please consult a licensed professional before attempting any techniques outlined in this book.

By reading this document, the reader agrees that under no circumstances is the author responsible for any losses, direct or indirect, that are incurred as a result of the use of the information contained within this document, including, but not limited to, errors, omissions, or inaccuracies.

CONTENTS

INTRODUCTION 7
    Ketogenic Diet and Your Keto Pantry 7
    Top Three Benefits of the Ketogenic Diet....... 7
    How You'll Benefit from Your Instant Pot 8
    A Word about Our Recipe Collection................ 9
POULTRY 10
    1. Chicken Legs with Piquant Mayo Sauce....... 10
    2. Herbes de Provence Chicken Drumettes..... 10
    3. Hot Spicy Chicken Soup.............................. 10
    4. Cheesy and Creamy Chicken Fillets............ 11
    5. Chicken Drumsticks in Creamy Butter Sauce 11
    6. Chicken Parm Chowder 11
    7. Roasted Turkey Breast Tenderloins 12
    8. Turkey Soup with Swiss Chard 12
    9. Two-Cheese Chicken Drumsticks 12
    10. Hot Chicken Wingettes with Cilantro Dip 13
    11. Greek-Style Chicken Wraps...................... 13
    12. Chicken Wings with Paprika Mayo 13
    13. Chicken Fillets with Keto Sauce 13
    14. The Best Chicken Tacos 14
    15. Country Chicken Stew 14
    16. One Pot Chicken Teriyaki.......................... 14
    17. Quick and Easy Chicken Carnitas 15
    18. Sensational Turkey Legs............................ 15
    19. Traditional Hungarian Paprikash............... 15
    20. Chicken Medley with White Mushrooms.. 16
    21. The Best Ever Chicken Goulash................ 16
    22. Italian-Style Turkey Meatloaf.................... 16
    23. Cheesy Chicken and Mushroom Casserole 17
    24. Gruyère and Turkey Au Gratin.................. 17
    25. Chicken Liver Pâté 17
    26. Grandma's Chunky Turkey Soup 18
    27. Thai Coconut Chicken............................... 18
    28. Kid-Friendly Chicken Meatballs................ 18
    29. Winter Chicken Salad................................ 19
    30. Creamy Turkey Breasts with Mushrooms 19
    31. Family Cheese and Chicken Sandwiches .. 19
    32. Easy Roasted Chicken Drumettes.............. 20
    33. Peppery Spicy Ground Chicken................. 20
    34. Chicken Roulade with Kale and Cheese ... 20
    35. Chicken Legs in Mustard Curry Sauce 21
    36. Holiday Stuffed Turkey Breasts 21
    37. Budget-Friendly Turkey Salad 21
    38. Chicken Legs with Salsa............................ 22
    39. Ground Chicken and Zucchini Casserole .. 22
    40. Chicken Philly Cheese Steak..................... 22
    41. Saucy Chicken Drumettes with Squashsta 23
    42. Cheesy Chicken Stuffed Peppers............... 23
    43. Two-Cheese Turkey Bake 23
    44. Creamy Cauliflower and Chicken Soup 23
    45. Easy One-Pot Mexican Chili 24
    46. Asian-Style Turkey Meatballs.................... 24
    47. Turkey Breasts with Homemade Pesto...... 24
    48. Chinese Meatball Soup.............................. 25
    49. Holiday Chicken Wrapped in Prosciutto .. 25
    50. Thanksgiving Turkey with Mushroom Gravy... 25
PORK 27
    51. Barbecue Spare Ribs 27
    52. Hungarian-Style Pork Goulash Soup......... 27
    53. Family Pork Roast...................................... 27
    54. The Best Pork Chile Verde 27
    55. Pork Meatballs alla Parmigiana 28
    56. Five-Star Zoddles Bolognese..................... 28
    57. Tender Pulled Pork..................................... 28
    58. Sausages with Cremini Mushrooms 29
    59. Sloppy Joes with Homemade Oopsies...... 29
    60. Traditional Keema with Cauliflower......... 29
    61. Za'atar-Rubbed Pork Shank 30
    62. Pork Belly Cooked in Milk........................ 30
    63. Greek-Style Pork Stew............................... 30
    64. Malaysian Bak-Kut-The Soup................... 31
    65. Pork Cutlets with Porcini Mushroom Sauce 31
    66. Pork Loin Sliders....................................... 31
    67. Pork Roast with Avocado and Garlic Mayo 31
    68. Pork Chops with Winter Squash Salad...... 32
    69. Pork Loin with Goat-Cheese Sauce 32
    70. Tender Pork Cutlets in Mustard Sauce...... 32
    71. Easy Curried Pork Steak 33
    72. Blade Pork Steaks with Sausages and Sauerkraut... 33
    73. Beer Braised Boston-Style Butt................. 33
    74. Elegant Pork Shank with Cauliflower 34
    75. Japanese-Style Sirloin Pork Roast............. 34
    76. Old-Fashioned Pork Chili 34
    77. Pork and Bacon Chowder.......................... 35
    78. Pork Carnitas Burrito Bowl....................... 35
    79. Peperonata with Pork Sausages 36
    80. Traditional Greek Youvarlakia 36
    81. Noodle-less Classic Lasagna..................... 36
    82. Quick and Easy Albóndigas Sinaloenses... 37
    83. Pork Tenderloin "Rosa di Parma" 37
    84. Tender Pork Steaks with Pico de Gallo 37
    85. Cheesy Salsa Meatloaf............................... 38
    86. Summer Barbecue Baby Back Ribs........... 38
    87. Tamarind Pork Spare Ribs......................... 38
    88. Delicious Provolone-Stuffed Meatballs 38
    89. Hunter's Pork Roast................................... 39
    90. Easy Pork Tortilla Soup 39
    91. Pork Shoulder with Herb Dijon Sauce 39
    92. Ground Pork Taco Bowl............................ 40
    93. Country-Style Pork Loin Ribs 40
    94. Indian Pork Vindaloo 40
    95. Thai Shredded Pork Salad......................... 41
    96. Smoky Marinated Pork Ribs..................... 41
    97. Ground Pork Taco Casserole..................... 41
    98. Ruby Port-Braised Pork with Mustard Greens... 42
    99. Buffalo Thick Pork Soup 42

100. Mediterranean Pork Cutlets 42

BEEF 43

101. Beef Stew with a Twist 43
102. Blade Roast with Béarnaise Sauce 43
103. Mexican-Style Beef Brisket 43
104. Thick Flank Steak Chili 44
105. Beer-Braised Shredded Beef 44
106. Beef Medley with Sausage 44
107. Silky Beef al Sangiovese 44
108. Aromatic Beef Curry 45
109. Juicy Beef Shoulder Roast 45
110. Beef Shawarma Bowls 45
111. Beef Salad with a Twist 46
112. Winter Beef Soup 46
113. Ground Beef Chili with Kale 46
114. Father's Day Beef Cheeseburgers 47
115. Hearty Swiss Meatball Casserole 47
116. Italian-Style Beef and Cauliflower 47
117. Spring Spicy Meatloaf 48
118. Zucchini Keto Lasagna 48
119. Steak with Cheese and Porcini Mushroom Sauce 48
120. Quick and Easy Korean Beef Bowl 49
121. Family Beef and Cabbage Stew 49
122. Favorite Beef Paprikash 49
123. Cheesy Beef and Cauliflower Soup 50
124. Chili Hot Dog Bake 50
125. Rich Pepperoni Pizza Bake 50
126. Cozy Peasant Chowder 51
127. Spaghetti Squash with Meat Sauce 51
128. Polska Kielbasa with Winter Squash 51
129. Beef, Bacon and Spinach Chili 52
130. Beef Steak with Rainbow Noodles 52
131. Zettuccini with Pepperoni and Cheese Sauce 52
132. Sinfully Delicious Cheeseburger Soup 52
133. Hamburgers with Kale and Cheese 53
134. Beef Stroganoff with a Twist 53
135. Spicy Broccoli, Leek and Beef Soup 53
136. Red Wine Stew with Smoked Cheddar Cheese 54
137. Bottom Eye Roast in Hoisin Sauce 54
138. Festive Bayrischer Gulasch 54
139. Garbure Gersoise Soup 55
140. Spezzatino di Manzo 55
141. German Leberkäse with Sauerkraut 55
142. Christmas Bacon Meatloaf 56
143. Perfect Filet Mignon in Beer Sauce 56
144. Restaurant-Style Oxtail Soup 56
145. Extraordinary Steak Sandwiches 57
146. Top Blade Roast with Horseradish Sauce 57
147. Chipolatas with Spinach and Cheese 57
148. Herbed Mustard Beef Shanks 58
149. Beef and Yogurt Curry 58
150. Beef Short Ribs with Cilantro Cream 58

FISH & SEAFOOD 59

151. Tilapia Fillets with Arugula 59
152. Cod Fillets with Sautéed Vegetables 59
153. The Best Jambalaya Ever 59
154. Classic Mussel Stew with Asiago Cheese 60
155. Creamy Cheesy Shrimp Salad 60
156. Halászlé Hungarian Fisherman's Soup ... 60
157. Mom's Halibut Stew 60
158. Creamed Seafood Chowder with Bacon . 61
159. Herbed Cod Steaks 61
160. Zingy Shrimp Salad 61
161. Warm Tuna Salad 62
162. Chinese-Style Snapper Soup 62
163. Trout Casserole with Pepper-Jack Cheese 62
164. Prawn Salad in Portobello "Buns" 63
165. Buttery and Lemony Tuna Fillets 63
166. Greek-Style Fish and Vegetable Bake 63
167. Easy Scallops with Parsley and Wine 64
168. Oysters with Chive-Mayo Sauce 64
169. Aromatic Mahi-Mahi Filets with Peppers 64
170. Chunky Fish Paprikash 64
171. Simple Garlicky Halibut Steak 65
172. Malabar Fish Curry 65
173. Faster-than-Fast-Food Salmon Burgers . 65
174. Snapper in Aromatic Tomato Sauce 65
175. Basil Wine Scallops 66
176. Poached Salmon with Bok Choy 66
177. Foil-Packet Haddock with Veggies 66
178. Hot Oyster Stew with Sour Cream 67
179. Favorite Monkfish Stew 67
180. Carp Steaks with Homemade Aioli 67
181. Creole Lobster with Lime Cream Sauce .. 68
182. Ahi Tuna Salad To-Go 68
183. Beer-Poached Alaskan Cod 68
184. The Best Fish Chili 69
185. Haddock and Cheese Stuffed Peppers 69
186. Swai with Port Wine Sauce 69
187. Authentic Garam Masala Fish 69
188. Easy Party Seafood Dip 70
189. Red Curry Perch Fillets 70
190. Milky Mackerel Chowder 70
191. Bluefish in Tarragon-Vermouth Sauce ... 71
192. Grouper with Mushrooms and Smoked Sausage 71
193. King Crab with Baby Bellas 71
194. Rainbow Trout with Buttery Mixed Greens 71
195. Simply Creole Sea Scallops 72
196. Tuna and Parmesan Stuffed Zucchini 72
197. Salmon Steaks with Garlic Yogurt 72
198. Spicy Chanterelles and Scampi Boil 72
199. Hangover Seafood Bowl 73
200. Tiger Prawns with Herbed Butter Sauce 73

VEGETABLES & SIDE DISHES 74

201. Easy Cheesy Artichokes 74
202. Chinese Bok Choy 74
203. Green Cabbage with Bacon 74
204. Warm Broccoli Salad Bowl 74
205. Creamed Spinach with Cheese 75
206. Turnip Greens with Sausage 75
207. Asparagus with Colby Cheese 75
208. Mediterranean Aromatic Zucchini 75

209. Chanterelles with Cheddar Cheese 76
210. Family Cauliflower Soup 76
211. Cauliflower and Kohlrabi Mash 76
212. Old-Fashioned Stuffed Peppers 76
213. Aromatic Tomato Soup 77
214. Bok Choy with Tofu 77
215. Braised Garlicky Endive 77
216. Italian Pancetta and Cabbage Soup 77
217. Buttery and Garlicky Fennel 78
218. Vegetables à la Grecque 78
219. Caramelized Endive with Goat Cheese ... 78
220. Loaded Tuscan Rapini Soup 79
221. Nopales with Sour Cream 79
222. Swiss Chard with Ham Hock 79
223. Green Beans with Canadian Bacon 79
224. Cauliflower Soup with Blue Cheese 80
225. Balkan Autumn Satarash 80
226. Vegetable Medley with Pork Sausage 80
227. Southern-Style Sausage Gumbo 80
228. Braised Sauerkraut with Bacon 81
229. Aromatic Okra with Pancetta 81
230. Hearty Root Vegetable Soup 81
231. Paprika Kohlrabi with Asiago 82
232. French-Style Cauliflower with Bacon 82
233. Lazy Sunday Bok Choy Soup 82
234. Savoy Cabbage Soup with Cabécou Cheese 82
235. Spicy Crimini Mushroom and Asparagus Soup 83
236. Broccoli Medley with Bacon and Colby Cheese 83
237. Cabbage and Turkey Delight 83
238. Warm Eggplant and Chicken Bowl 84
239. Celery Soup with Salsiccia 84
240. Chinese-Style Warm Pe-Tsai Salad 84
241. Asparagus alla Fontina 84
242. Chunky Cabbage and Capocollo Soup 85
243. Rich and Easy Portobello Mushroom Casserole 85
244. Zucchini with Green Peppercorn Sauce . 85
245. Spicy Collards with Caciocavallo 86
246. Traditional Caramelized Onion Soup 86
247. The Best Mushroom Ragoût 86
248. Cheesy Leek and Chorizo Soup 87
249. The Best Italian Zuppa Ever 87
250. Simple Steamed Tomato Salad 87

FAST SNACKS & APPETIZERS 88
251. Easy Buttery Brussels Sprouts 88
252. Easy Spinach Dip 88
253. Asparagus with Chervil Dip 88
254. Cheesy Mustard Greens Dip 88
255. Asian-Style Cocktail Sausage 88
256. Colorful Stuffed Mushrooms 89
257. Dad's Cocktail Meatballs 89
258. Herbed and Caramelized Mushrooms 89
259. Colby Cheese Dip with Peppers 90
260. Party Chicken Drumettes 90
261. Cheesy Cauliflower Balls 90
262. Crave-Worthy Balsamic Baby Carrots 90
263. Super Bowl Pizza Dip 91
264. Minty Party Meatballs 91
265. Chicken Wings Italiano 91
266. Amazing Cauliflower Tots 91
267. Mexican-Style Broccoli Balls Ole 92
268. Gruyère, Rutabaga and Bacon Bites 92
269. Shrimp Cocktail Salad on a Stick 92
270. Spring Deviled Eggs 92
271. Easy Cheesy Taco Dip 93
272. Cheese-Stuffed Cocktail Meatballs 93
273. Chorizo and Halloumi Fat Bombs 93
274. Bacon Wrapped Cocktail Wieners 94
275. Brussels Sprouts with Aioli 94
276. Creole Egg and Pancetta Balls 94
277. Umami Party Chicken Wings 94
278. Chicken Salad Skewers 95
279. Zucchini Loaded Meatballs 95
280. Queso Fundido Dip 95
281. Asian-Style Appetizer Ribs 95
282. Two-Cheese Artichoke Dip 96
283. Easy Party Mushrooms 96
284. Herbed Party Shrimp 96
285. Crispy and Yummy Beef Bites 96
286. Asparagus with Greek Aioli 97
287. Carrot Sticks with Blue-Cheese Sauce 97
288. Zingy Zucchini Bites 97
289. Kohlrabi Sticks with Hungarian Mayo ... 97
290. Bok Choy Boats with Shrimp Salad 98
291. Game Day Sausage Dip 98
292. Stuffed Baby Bell Peppers 98
293. Party Garlic Prawns 98
294. Barbecue Lil Smokies 99
295. Two-Cheese and Caramelized Onion Dip 99
296. Hot Lager Chicken Wings 99
297. Braised Spring Kale Appetizer 99
298. Wax Beans with Pancetta 100
299. Middle-Eastern Eggplant Dip 100
300. Cheesy Cauliflower Bites 100

EGGS & DAIRY 101
301. Kale and Tomato Frittata 101
302. Tyrolese Egg Salad 101
303. Mom's Cheesy Soup 101
304. Asian-Style Savory Egg Custard 101
305. Fluffy Scrambled Eggs 102
306. Golden Cheddar Muffins with Chard 102
307. Broccoli with Asiago Cheese 102
308. The Best Homemade Cheese Ever 102
309. Scamorza Open Tart 103
310. Bacon and Pepper Casserole with Goat Cheese 103
311. Savory Muffins with Canadian Bacon ... 103
312. Swiss Cheese and Celery Soup 103
313. Peppery and Cheesy Deviled Eggs 104
314. Spicy Stuffed Avocado Boats 104
315. Three-Cheese and Beer Dip 104
316. Breakfast Lettuce Wraps 105
317. Indian Egg Muffins 105
318. Egg and Bell Pepper "Sandwich" 105
319. Manchego, Sausage and Vegetable Bake 105

- 320. Goat Cheese, Avocado and Egg Muffins 106
- 321. Ooey Gooey, Cheesy Pizza 106
- 322. Zingy Habanero Eggs................................. 106
- 323. Egg Salad with Poppy Seed Dressing.... 106
- 324. Fat Bombs with Peppers and Manchego 107
- 325. Egg Curry in a Hurry................................. 107
- 326. Italian Sausage and Fontina Bake 107
- 327. Egg Drop Soup with Gorgonzola 108
- 328. Family Taco Casserole 108
- 329. Kid-Friendly Mini Frittatas 108
- 330. Breakfast Egg Salad Bowl 108
- 331. Asparagus and Colby Cheese Frittatas. 109
- 332. Special Breakfast Eggs 109
- 333. Two-Cheese and Mustard Green Dip.... 109
- 334. Paneer and Cauliflower Dipping Sauce 109
- 335. Portobello Mushrooms Baked Eggs and Cheese 110
- 336. Eggs, Cheese, and Mortadella Roll-Ups 110
- 337. Eggs with Peppers in Tomato Sauce..... 110
- 338. Tocino and Egg Cups 110
- 339. Mélange with Spanish Chorizo 111
- 340. Italian Great-Grandmother Eggs........... 111
- 341. Ground Meat and Cheese Dip................. 111
- 342. Italian-Style Greens with Eggs and Cheese 112
- 343. B.E.L.T – Bacon, Egg, Lettuce Tomato... 112
- 344. Mini Meatloaves with Cheese.................. 112
- 345. Green Beans with Cheese and Eggs....... 113
- 346. Eggs with Green Cabbage 113
- 347. Indian Egg Bhurji....................................... 113
- 348. Garden Omelet with Colby Cheese 113
- 349. Winter Bacon and Leek Quiche 114
- 350. Weeknight Meat and Egg Muffins.......... 114

VEGAN.. 115
- 351. Aromatic Garlicky Zucchini..................... 115
- 352. Thai-Style Tempeh Curry 115
- 353. Tangy Green Cabbage Stew 115
- 354. Vegan Mushroom Stroganoff.................. 115
- 355. Braised Kale with Red Wine 116
- 356. Indian-Style Cauliflower 116
- 357. Saucy King Oysters.................................... 116
- 358. Sauerkraut and Mushroom Casserole.. 116
- 359. Korean Kimchi and Tofu Stew 117
- 360. Spinach with Almond Cheese 117
- 361. Porridge with Coconut and Seeds.......... 117
- 362. Raspberry and Walnut Granola 117
- 363. Zucchini Lasagna with Cashew-Spinach Cream 118
- 364. The Best Sunday Tacos Ever................... 118
- 365. Creamed Asparagus and Mushroom Soup 119
- 366. Mushrooms with Barbecue Sauce 119
- 367. Zoodles with Mediterranean Sauce and Avocado... 119
- 368. Asian-Style Vegan Stew 119
- 369. Easy Chunky Autumn Soup.................... 120
- 370. Cauliflower Medley with Spinach 120
- 371. Rum Coconut Granola.............................. 120
- 372. Zucchini "Tagliatelle" with Almond Butter 121
- 373. Winter One-Pot-Wonder......................... 121
- 374. Vegan Cream of Tomato Soup................ 121
- 375. Zucchini and Leek Soup........................... 121
- 376. Cabbage Medley with Tempeh............... 122
- 377. Easy Brussels Sprouts with Peppers 122
- 378. Superb Teriyaki Mushrooms................... 122
- 379. Broccoli Bake with Vegan Béchamel 122
- 380. Sunday Sweet Porridge 123
- 381. Everyday Italian Pepperonata 123
- 382. Luxurious Cauliflower Parmigiana 123
- 383. Favorite Winter Noatmeal....................... 124
- 384. Green Beans with Scallions and Mushrooms... 124
- 385. One-Pot Mushroom and Tofu Curry 124
- 386. Croatian Blitva with Dry Sherry............ 124
- 387. Broccoli, Artichoke and Spinach Dip 125
- 388. Indian Peppers with Coconut Flour Naan 125
- 389. Tofu with Zhoug Sauce 125
- 390. Classic Vegan Cauliflower Soup............. 126
- 391. Thai Cream of Celery Soup...................... 126
- 392. Ranch Broccoli Dip.................................... 126
- 393. Spanish-Style Carrot Dip......................... 127
- 394. Onion and Tofu Dipping Sauce 127
- 395. Summer Veggie Kabobs........................... 127
- 396. French-Style Broccoli Rabe Soup........... 127
- 397. Traditional Sunday Ratatouille.............. 128
- 398. Piri-Piri Tofu... 128
- 399. Party Cauliflower Balls 128
- 400. Sriracha Carrot and Chard Purée........... 129

DESSERTS... 130
- 401. Raspberry Upside-Down Cake 130
- 402. Chocolate Dream Cheesecake 130
- 403. Grandma's Orange Cheesecake.............. 130
- 404. Star Anise Raspberry Curd..................... 131
- 405. Yummy and Easy Chocolate Mousse 131
- 406. Luscious Tropical Dream Dessert.......... 131
- 407. Almond and Chocolate Crème................ 132
- 408. Vanilla Rum Flan.. 132
- 409. Navel Orange Cheesecake....................... 132
- 410. Sunday Butterscotch Custard................. 132
- 411. Fabulous Blackberry Brownies 133
- 412. Blueberry Dessert Porridge.................... 133
- 413. Coconut and Lemon Squares 133
- 414. Zucchini and Peanut Cake 134
- 415. Sophisticated Lavender Brownies......... 134
- 416. Romantic Rosewater Dessert Porridge 134
- 417. Coconut and Raspberry Cupcakes......... 134
- 418. Mixed Berry Mini Cheesecakes............... 135
- 419. Chocolate and Hazelnut Birthday Cake 135
- 420. Party Blueberry Cobbler.......................... 135
- 421. Easy Mexican-Style Flan.......................... 136
- 422. Almond and Blackberry Crisp................ 136
- 423. Mom's Red Velvet Cheesecake............... 136
- 424. Traditional Carrot Cake........................... 137
- 425. Brownie Squares with Blackberry-Goat Cheese Swirl.. 137

426. Triple-Berry and Bourbon Granola Crisp 137
427. Coconut and Chocolate Fudge 138
428. Orange-White Chocolate Mini Lava Cakes 138
429. Blueberry and Cinnamon Muffins 138
430. Zucchini Bundt Cake with Cream Cheese Frosting 139
431. Peanut and Chocolate Chip Cupcakes .. 139
432. Crêpe with Cinnamon-Cream Cheese Topping 139
433. White Peanut Butter and Chocolate Fudge 140
434. Key Lime Curd 140
435. Chunky Walnut Mini Cheesecakes 140
436. Mint and Coconut Mousse 141
437. Espresso Molten Cake 141
438. Cherry Baby Cakes 141
439. Raspberry and Chocolate Lava Muffins 142
440. Hazelnut and Cranberry Cookies 142
441. Slow Cooker Cranberry Delight 142
442. Cappuccino Chocolate Pudding 142
443. Peanut Butter and Chocolate Mousse .. 143
444. French-Style Pots de Crème 143
445. Exotic Coconut Idli 143
446. Orange Dessert with White Chocolate . 144
447. Grandma's Zucchini Cake 144
448. Peanut and White Chocolate Chip Cookies 144
449. Fudge with Nuts and Neufchatel 145
450. Light and Fluffy Lemon Cookies 145

OTHER KETO FAVORITES 146
451. Apple Pie Granola 146
452. Spinach and Cheese Muffins 146
453. Shirred Eggs with Peppers and Scallions 146
454. Homemade Blueberry Yogurt 146
455. Breakfast Meatloaf Cups 147
456. Breakfast Casserole with Zucchini and Bacon 147
457. Spicy and Cheesy Chard Quiche 147
458. Bacon Frittata Muffins 147
459. Hungarian Hot Pot 148
460. Spring Avocado Eggs 148
461. Dilled Cauliflower Purée with Au Jus Gravy 148
462. Aromatic Cheesy and Kale Bake 149
463. Coconut Porridge with Berries 149
464. Cauliflower "Mac and Cheese" 149
465. Zucchini Sloppy Joe's 149
466. Delicious Homemade Burgers 150
467. Fluffy Berry Cupcakes 150
468. Mediterranean-Style Savory Tart 150
469. Salmon and Ricotta Fat Bombs 151
470. Pork and Green Bean Casserole 151
471. Greek-Style Mushroom Muffins 151
472. Pancakes with Cottage Cheese Topping 151
473. Sichuan-Style Duck Breast 152
474. Classic Chicken Gumbo 152
475. Chia and Blackberry Jam 152
476. Mushroom and Cream Cheese Pâté 153
477. Japanese-Style Savory Custard 153
478. Zucchini Cardamom Bread 153
479. Creamy Breakfast "Cereals" 153
480. Old-Fashioned Cherry Jam 154
481. Spicy Mushroom Hot Pot 154
482. Egg Balls in Marinara Sauce 154
483. Lobster and Cheese Dip 154
484. Party-Style Cheeseburger Dip 155
485. Cauliflower Breakfast Cups 155
486. Mexican-Style Stuffed Peppers 155
487. Goat Cheese and Cauliflower Pancake . 155
488. Lasagna Cupcakes with Zucchini and Mozzarella 156
489. Dad's Chorizo Dip 156
490. Easy Pizza Cups 156
491. Favorite Lettuce Wraps 156
492. Classic Turkey Sandwiches 157
493. Tacos with Pulled Pork and Pico de Gallo 157
494. Canapés with a Twist 157
495. Egg Salad "Sandwich" 157
496. Mexican Beef Taco Lettuce Wraps 158
497. Summer Picnic Fish Sandwiches 158
498. Mexican-Style Muffins 158
499. Savory Cheese Biscuits with Bacon 159
500. Chicken Liver Mousse 159

INTRODUCTION

Most of us think that cooking can be fast or gourmet, and there is no third possibility. On the other hand, the majority of people think that food cannot be healthy and delicious all at the same time. Yes, we are right; there are recipes that require hours of preparation. If you don't have extra time on your hands and you are feeling a little overwhelmed, it can be daunting for you. This is the main reason why we rather opt for a take-out food. If we have to follow a specific diet, it makes things even more difficult!

Notwithstanding this truth, there is a practical solution out there. It's time for a paradigm shift that will make a change in your life! An Instant Pot offers delicious, healthy, gourmet and quick meals at one time. Furthermore, if you follow a ketogenic diet, you can cook your favorite food in the Instant Pot easily and effortlessly. You can get benefits of the ketogenic diet and pressure cooking plus the extra time for your loved ones. It is a win-win situation!

Ketogenic Diet and Your Keto Pantry

A KETOGENIC DIET is a low-carbohydrate, high-fat, and moderate-protein eating plan. During this diet, your body makes ketones and uses them as the main source of energy. It means that your body burns fats rather than carbs. Say goodbye to pizza and pie and hello to burgers and fat!

The main goal of this diet is to get into a state of ketosis, which is a natural process that occurs when our calorie intake is lower than calorie burn. In this manner, you will be able to lose weight, stay healthy, and feel amazing, while boosting mental and physical performances.

A low-carb dietary regimen is easy to follow but there are some major points you should know. What foods are included in the ketogenic diet?

Meat & Seafood – pork, beef, poultry, fish, and seafood;
Dairy Products – raw whole milk, full-fat and hard cheese, sour cream, heavy cream, full-fat unsweetened yogurt or kefir, butter, ghee;
Eggs;
Oils & Fats – olive, coconut, hemp, flaxseed, and avocado oil;
Sweeteners – Splenda, yacon sweetener, xylitol, stevia, erythritol, and monk fruit powder;
Above ground vegetables – cauliflower, cabbage, broccoli, celery, mushrooms, peppers, greens, arugula, green beans, tomato, asparagus, onions, leek, bok choy, and Brussels sprouts. Canned and pickled vegetables, especially homemade versions, are allowed too;
Nuts and seeds;
Fruit – avocado and berries;
Condiments and seasonings – herbs, soy sauce, mustard, vinegar, unsweetened cocoa powder, coconut aminos, and low-carb sauces.

This is not a full list of keto foods, but we included as many ingredients as possible to give you a visual guide to what to eat on a keto dietary regimen. These items will be essential for your ketogenic pantry, and, of course, you should be able to purchase them easily.

Some good example of keto meals could include chicken drumsticks with cheese (approximately 4.8 grams of carbs per serving); chicken liver pâté (approximately 2.3 grams of carbs per serving); pork stew with keto vegetables (approximately 5.1 grams of carbs per serving); zucchini keto lasagna (approximately 6 grams of carbs per serving); egg muffins (approximately 4.7 grams of carbs per serving). As you can see for yourself, you do not need to make radical changes in your lifestyle.

Foods that are strictly off-limits include grains, sugar, dry beans, cereals, grain flour, starchy fruits such as bananas, and root vegetables. The main foods to stay away from to achieve all benefits of the keto diet are foods that are processed and foods that contain carbohydrates.

It is not rocket science, is it? Therefore, it should be easy for you to start the ketogenic diet and achieve fabulous results. What to expect on a ketogenic diet? Although it doesn't work the same for everyone, listed below are the most common benefits of the ketogenic diet.

Top Three Benefits of the Ketogenic Diet

1. The ketogenic diet can help you lose weight in a healthy way

If you want to lose weight without starving and putting your health at risk, it is imperative to adopt healthy eating habits. Finding a good diet plan is easier said than done because there is too much information out there. It may be difficult to stick to a certain diet and find motivation in the long run. Difficult, but not impossible! Research suggests that by following the guidelines of the keto diet, you'll not only lose your weight but also significantly improve the quality of your life.

"When a person goes on a keto diet, they lose a lot of weight. That's just what happens," says the New York City–based dietitian Kristen Mancinelli, RD. As a matter of fact, if you try this eating approach, you will find it easy to follow. Your keto meal plan for weight loss should include all kinds of hunger-curbing foods such as hearty soups, nutritious poultry stews, melt-in-your-mouth meat, lip-smacking sauces, and other nutrient-dense foods. For instance, you can prepare an omelet or scrambled eggs for breakfast; then, you can make fish fillets for lunch and serve them with fresh salad. When it comes to dinner, the most popular options include stuffed mushrooms, low-carb quiche, chicken casseroles, etc. Do not forget that any successful keto diet plan includes healthy and smart snacking. Choose hard-boiled eggs, chicken wings, or cheese balls; these smart choices will help you stay on track!

Generally, you should create a calorie deficit to lose weight. Reducing your intake of carbs consequently decreases your calorie intake. You can achieve this by simply avoiding starchy foods, sugar and grains, and eating a protein food, healthy fats, and vegetables that grow above ground. It is highly recommended to use a reliable carb gram counter in order to track the carbohydrate amounts in your daily meal plan.

To achieve the best results, you should eat all major types of nutrients: protein, carbohydrates, and fats. The human body needs the three major macronutrients to function properly. You need to get 15–30 percent of calories from protein, 60–75 percent of your calories from fat, 5–10 percent of calories from carbs. These daily requirements are based on your body weight. Use these recommendations as a guideline and your body will become a fat-burning machine!

2. Health benefits of the ketogenic diet

Losing weight and staying healthy without going on a diet sounds like a dream, isn't it? Needless to say that a well-balanced eating plan is a key factor that contributes to a healthy lifestyle. As with any healthy eating program, the ketogenic diet is more about your good eating habits rather than obsessing over a rigid diet plan. Healthy fats and proteins are encouraged on this diet so you can enjoy fish, avocado, meat, eggs, and cheese on a daily basis. You can enhance the flavor of your meals by adding herbs, spices, and low-carb condiments. You need to drink plenty of water, tea, coffee, tea, low-carb smoothies, and even hard liquor, light beer, and unsweetened wines in moderation.

Cutting out your intake of calorie-dense carbs can have amazing benefits to your body. It can provide health benefits in blood sugar regulation and decrease insulin levels. A ketogenic diet can help fight and control diabetes naturally. Another influencing factor is that a low-carb diet can also improve your cognitive health as well as boost your mood naturally. Moreover, this diet is routinely prescribed as a treatment for people with epilepsy.

On a ketogenic diet, we are aiming to eat wholesome and unprocessed, preferably homemade food. You should eat healthy fats from nuts, seeds, avocados and olive oil on a regular basis. Further, include fish, seafood and, pasture-raised chicken in your diet and opt for high-quality protein such as eggs, unsweetened milk, tofu, and mushrooms. Unhealthy low-carb foods like artificial sugar, fast food and processed food with additives are forbidden on the ketogenic diet.

Almost without exception, if you make your own meals, you will avoid the temptation to eat unhealthy foods and ensure your ongoing success with the ketogenic diet. Healthy food choices lead to a longer life that is free of chronic diseases related to stress and weight gain.

3. Crave-worthy meals

People often eat boring and bland food when they are on a diet. Surprisingly, healthy cooking doesn't mean giving up good flavors.

The ketogenic diet is not restrictive so you'll be able to enjoy a wide variety of tasty foods. You just need to focus on a natural, unprocessed, and low-carb food. Compared with other more restrictive diets, you can eat most of your favorite foods on the ketogenic diet so it's easier to stick to the diet in the long-term. Your social life will not suffer for food and diet because you can sit at the family table and enjoy a leisurely meal every day. Because of a variety of food, the whole family will be able to enjoy the ketogenic recipes!

Here are some affordable food swaps that are easy to make. Instead of a store-bought jam with sugar, make your own homemade jam with a keto sweetener. Instead of pasta, you can make veggie noodles using zucchini, celery or cucumbers. Instead of a traditional pilaf, you can serve "riced" cauliflower. The possibilities are actually endless!

How You'll Benefit from Your Instant Pot

For so long home cooks have been searching for a cooking method to make healthy tasty foods. Pressure cooking became one of the hottest new culinary trends nowadays while the Instant Pot has come to offer new ideas by providing better and healthier food options. The Instant Pot electric pressure cooker is a multifunctional programmable kitchen appliance that can do the job of a slow cooker, rice maker, a steamer, a sautéing pan, a warming pot, and yogurt maker.

Now, we can pose the question: Which Instant Pot button to use? Listed below are the Instant Pot smart cooking programs:

Sauté function is the perfect flavor-enhancing technique. You will be able to sauté your veggies before pressure cooking as well as sear and brown the meat without an additional pan.

Manual is an all-purpose button. You can actually adjust the time and temperature and cook almost every meal using this function.
Meat/Stew is the perfect program for cooking red meats and old-fashioned stews.
Poultry is an excellent choice for chicken, turkey, and duck.
Porridge is a function designed for cooking grains.
Rice, as the name indicates, is designed to cook all types of rice.
Soup is the fully automated function for cooking the best homemade soups and chowders quickly and effortlessly.
Bean/Chili is the program for making your favorite chilies.
Slow cook is the perfect option if you want to have a warm meal ready when you arrive home.
Multigrain is designed for cooking grains.
Yogurt is a two-step program for making a homemade yogurt.
Keep Warm/Cancel is a very practical feature. Once cooking is complete, you need to push the "Cancel" button; otherwise, the warming function is automatically activated.
If you are a fan of one-pot meals, keep in mind these obvious benefits of using an Instant Pot.
1) Cook fast and eat well. Do you think that cooking at home is time-consuming? Do all these cookware and appliances make you feel uncomfortable in the kitchen? We've got news for you – you probably don't have the right kitchen tools. The Instant Pot is an intelligent, third-generation cooker so you don't need to stand by the stove, watching and stirring your food. In addition to speed, you will save your time by cooking an entire meal in the Instant Pot.
Instant Pot cooks your food as much as 70 percent quicker than other conventional cookware. You will love its hands-off functionality! Simply choose your favorite ketogenic recipe, set up the Instant Pot, sit back, relax and try to spend quality time out of the kitchen!
The Instant Pot has proven to be the efficient home appliance of everyone who does not want to spend all day slaving over a hot stove but eager to start cooking for his/her families. The Instant Pot cooks our food way faster than conventional cookers and pots, which makes it the perfect choice for busy households.
2) Palatability and succulence are the main goals. Obviously, a high-temperature cooking produces more flavor in your meals. This cooking method requires very little fat and other flavor enhancers so that your food retains most of their natural flavors and nutrients. It provides a good balance of flavors because it is practically impossible to overdo food in the Instant Pot and end up with a wishy-washy food.
3) Health is the greatest wealth. It may sound like a cliché, but everything begins with you. Your own health and your values. This is a logical reason why you need to cook your food properly.
As a modern-day pressure cooker, the Instant Pot utilizes short cooking time, high temperature and pressure to cook food efficiently without nutrient loss. Since liquids do not evaporate in your Instant Pot, you can cook very lean meats because they remain succulent, juicy and buttery tender. Moreover, the Instant Pot is an eco-friendly gadget because it uses two to three times less energy than much other cookware.

A Word about Our Recipe Collection

This cookbook includes proven strategies on how to maximize the use of your Instant Pot for better ketogenic meals. These recipes will guide you every step of the way in order to make the perfect meals without the fuss. Once you decided to go on the ketogenic diet, you, your Instant Pot and this cookbook are sure to become "best friends"!
Once you get to know Ketogenic Instant Pot Recipes, it opens up a completely new perspective on dieting and cooking. Thus, you can serve your favorite food without the guilt that often comes with it. This cookbook is chock-full of various ketogenic recipes that are easy to follow and fun to eat. They will help you unlock the "mysteries" of the ketogenic diet, pressure cooking, and home-cooked food. You will find unique combinations, clever alternatives, and inventive twists on traditional recipes. We will share with you 500 recipes that will provide you with a huge selection of options to improve your eating habits and meet your diet goals. Each recipe is accompanied by nutritional analyses so you'll know how to create your meal plan.
The vast majority of these absolutely scrumptious recipes can be prepared in a fraction of the time. In other words, with the Instant Pot and these recipes, you will be able to take a shortcut in preparing your favorite ketogenic meals. You will experience increased feelings of well-being thanks to this healthy lifestyle. Welcome to innovative, healthy, and delightful Ketogenic Instant Pot meals!

POULTRY

1. Chicken Legs with Piquant Mayo Sauce

(Ready in about 25 minutes | Servings 4)

Sriracha, the fiery Thai-descended ketchup, is a great addition to this dipping sauce; it goes wonderfully with these extraordinary chicken legs. Good substitutions for Sriracha include Tabasco sauce, Tapatio or Jerk sauce; just be careful with your total daily intake of carbohydrates.

Per serving: 484 Calories; 42.6g Fat; 2.4g Carbs; 22.3g Protein; 0.5g Sugars

Ingredients
4 chicken legs, bone-in, skinless
2 garlic cloves, peeled and halved
1/2 teaspoon coarse sea salt
1/4 teaspoon ground black pepper, or more to taste
1/2 teaspoon red pepper flakes, crushed
1 tablespoon olive oil
1/4 cup chicken broth
Dipping Sauce:
3/4 cup mayonnaise
2 tablespoons stone ground mustard
1 teaspoon fresh lemon juice
1/2 teaspoon Sriracha
Topping:
1/4 cup fresh cilantro, roughly chopped

Directions
Rub the chicken legs with garlic halves; then, season with salt, black pepper, and red pepper flakes. Press the "Sauté" button.
Once hot, heat the oil and sauté chicken legs for 4 to 5 minutes, turning once during cooking time. Add a splash of chicken broth to deglaze the bottom of the pan.
Secure the lid. Choose "Manual" mode and High pressure; cook for 14 minutes. Once cooking is complete, use a natural pressure release; carefully remove the lid.
Meanwhile, mix all ingredients for the dipping sauce; place in the refrigerator until ready to serve.
Garnish chicken legs with cilantro. Serve with the piquant mayo sauce on the side. Bon appétit!

2. Herbes de Provence Chicken Drumettes

(Ready in about 15 minutes | Servings 6)

When you're looking for just the right thing to serve for Sunday lunch, simply toss the chicken with a classic herb mix that's reminiscent of the south of France and cook it with fresh tomatoes.

Per serving: 346 Calories; 18.3g Fat; 2.7g Carbs; 40.5g Protein; 0.9g Sugars

Ingredients
2 tablespoons olive oil
2 ½ pounds chicken drumettes, trimmed of fat
1 tomato, chopped
2 garlic cloves, sliced
1 tablespoon Herbes de Provence
Sea salt, to taste
1/3 teaspoon ground black pepper
1/2 teaspoon paprika
1 cup water
2/3 cup mayonnaise
2 tablespoons Dijon mustard
1/2 lemon, cut into slices

Directions
Press the "Sauté" button. Heat the oil and brown chicken drumettes for 2 to 3 minutes on each side. Add tomato, garlic, Herbes de Provence, salt, black pepper, paprika, and water.
Secure the lid. Choose "Manual" mode and High pressure; cook for 10 minutes. Once cooking is complete, use a natural pressure release; carefully remove the lid.
Serve with mayonnaise, mustard, and lemon slices. Bon appétit!

3. Hot Spicy Chicken Soup

(Ready in about 20 minutes | Servings 5)

In this recipe, you can use a homemade, low-sodium beef or vegetable broth. Remaining soup can be refrigerated for up to 4 days. It freezes well, too.

Per serving: 238 Calories; 17g Fat; 5.4g Carbs; 16.4g Protein; 2.6g Sugars

Ingredients
2 tablespoons grapeseed oil
2 banana shallots, chopped
4 cloves garlic, minced
1 cup Cremini mushrooms, sliced
2 bell peppers, seeded and sliced
1 serrano pepper, seeded and sliced
2 ripe tomatoes, pureed
1 teaspoon porcini powder
2 tablespoons dry white wine
Sea salt and ground black pepper, to your liking
1 teaspoon dried basil
1/2 teaspoon dried dill weed
5 cups broth, preferably homemade
4 chicken wings

Directions
Press the "Sauté" button and heat the oil. Once hot, sauté the shallots until just tender and aromatic. Add the garlic, mushrooms, and peppers; cook an additional 3 minutes or until softened.
Now, stir in tomatoes, porcini powder, white wine, salt, and black pepper. Add the remaining ingredients and stir to combine.

Secure the lid. Choose "Manual" mode and High pressure; cook for 18 minutes. Once cooking is complete, use a quick pressure release.

Make sure to release any remaining steam and carefully remove the lid. Remove the chicken wings from the Instant Pot. Discard the bones and chop the meat.

Add the chicken meat back to the Instant Pot. Ladle into individual bowls and serve warm. Bon appétit!

4. Cheesy and Creamy Chicken Fillets

(Ready in about 25 minutes | Servings 6)

Stunning cooking aromas are coming from your kitchen… Everyone can become an awesome cook with an Instant Pot electric pressure cooker!

Per serving: 450 Calories; 24.1g Fat; 2.5g Carbs; 53.6g Protein; 0.2g Sugars

Ingredients

1 ¼ cups water
10 ounces Ricotta cheese, crumbled
6 chicken fillets
Salt, to taste
1/2 teaspoon cayenne pepper
6 tablespoons bacon crumbles
4 ounces Monterey-Jack cheese
1 tablespoon chicken bouillon granules

Directions

Add water to the bottom of the Instant Pot. Add Ricotta cheese and chicken fillets; sprinkle with salt and cayenne pepper.

Secure the lid. Choose "Manual" mode and High pressure; cook for 18 minutes. Once cooking is complete, use a quick pressure release.

Now, shred the chicken with two forks and return it back to the Instant Pot. Stir in bacon crumbles, cheese, and chicken bouillon granules.

Place the lid back on the Instant Pot, press the "Sauté" button and cook an additional 4 minutes. Divide among serving plates and serve immediately. Bon appétit!

5. Chicken Drumsticks in Creamy Butter Sauce

(Ready in about 20 minutes | Servings 6)

Chicken drumsticks go well with a butter-based sauces like this one. In this recipe, you can use chili peppers to spice it up.

Per serving: 351 Calories; 15.7g Fat; 7g Carbs; 43.5g Protein; 3.3g Sugars

Ingredients

2 ripe tomatoes, chopped
1/2 cup roasted vegetable broth, preferably homemade
1 red onion, chopped
1 red bell pepper, seeded and chopped
1 green bell pepper, seeded and chopped
4 cloves garlic
1 teaspoon curry powder
1/2 teaspoon paprika
1/4 teaspoon ground black pepper
Sea salt, to taste
A pinch of grated nutmeg
1/2 teaspoon ground cumin
2 pounds chicken drumsticks, boneless, skinless
2 tablespoons butter
1/3 cup double cream
1 tablespoon flaxseed meal

Directions

Add tomatoes, vegetable broth, onion, peppers, garlic, curry powder, paprika, black pepper, salt, grated nutmeg, and ground cumin to the bottom of your Instant Pot.

Add chicken drumsticks. Secure the lid. Choose "Manual" mode and High pressure; cook for 12 minutes. Once cooking is complete, use a natural pressure release.

Allow it to cool completely and reserve the chicken. In a mixing dish, whisk the remaining ingredients and add this mixture to the Instant Pot; press the "Sauté" button and bring it to a boil.

Now, add the chicken back to the cooking liquid. Press the "Cancel" button and serve immediately. Bon appétit!

6. Chicken Parm Chowder

(Ready in about 40 minutes | Servings 6)

You can't go wrong with this combination of Parm chicken, full-fat milk, cottage cheese and whole chicken. Cooked with carrot, shallots and spices, each bite packs a punch of deliciousness.

Per serving: 405 Calories; 18.4g Fat; 6.6g Carbs; 50.1g Protein; 1.1g Sugars

Ingredients

2 pounds whole chicken, cut into pieces
3 ounces full-fat milk
1 teaspoon fresh lemon juice
1/2 teaspoon fresh ginger, grated
2 garlic cloves, minced
4 ounces cottage cheese, at room temperature
2 banana shallots, peeled and chopped
1 carrot, chopped
2 tablespoons butter
1 tablespoon dried rosemary
1/4 teaspoon ground black pepper
Sea salt, to taste
4 cups chicken stock, low-sodium
1/2 cup Parmesan cheese, preferably freshly grated
1 tablespoon fresh parsley, chopped

Directions

In a mixing bowl, place the chicken pieces, milk, lemon juice, ginger, and garlic; let it marinate for 1 hour in the refrigerator.

Add the chicken, along with the marinade, to your Instant Pot. Add cottage cheese, shallots, carrot, butter, rosemary, black pepper, salt, and chicken stock.

Secure the lid. Press the "Soup" button and cook for 35 minutes. Once cooking is complete, use a quick pressure release.

Remove the chicken from the cooking liquid. Discard the bones and add the chicken back to the Instant Pot. Add freshly grated Parmesan cheese to the hot cooking liquid; stir until it is melted and everything is well combined. Ladle into individual serving bowls, garnish with fresh parsley and enjoy!

7. Roasted Turkey Breast Tenderloins

(Ready in about 40 minutes | Servings 6)
Make this family-pleasing turkey tenderloin for Thanksgiving as a good alternative to roasting a whole bird. It is a great idea for a small dinner party as well.
Per serving: 255 Calories; 7.1g Fat; 0.7g Carbs; 49.7g Protein; 0g Sugars
Ingredients
6 turkey breast tenderloins
4 cloves garlic, halved
2 tablespoons grapeseed oil
1/2 teaspoon paprika
1/2 teaspoon dried basil
1/2 teaspoon dried oregano
1/2 teaspoon dried marjoram
1 cup water
Sea salt, to taste
1/4 teaspoon ground black pepper, or more to taste
Directions
Rub turkey fillets with garlic halves. Now, massage 1 tablespoon of oil into your turkey and season it with paprika, basil, oregano, marjoram, water, salt, and black pepper.
Press the "Sauté" button and add another tablespoon of oil. Brown the turkey fillets for 3 to 4 minutes per side.
Add the rack to the Instant Pot; lower the turkey onto the rack.
Secure the lid. Choose the "Manual" setting and cook for 30 minutes. Once cooking is complete, use a natural pressure release; carefully remove the lid.
Serve right away. Bon appétit!

8. Turkey Soup with Swiss Chard

(Ready in about 35 minutes | Servings 6)
Who said a good soup can't be ketogenic? You won't miss noodles in your soup, just use leafy greens like Swiss chard or kale.
Per serving: 188 Calories; 9.2g Fat; 8.9g Carbs; 17.7g Protein; 3.2g Sugars
Ingredients
1 tablespoon canola oil
1 pound turkey thighs
1 carrot, trimmed and chopped
1 leek, chopped
1 parsnip, chopped
2 garlic cloves, minced
1 ½ quarts turkey broth
2 star anise pods
Sea salt, to taste
1/4 teaspoon ground black pepper, or more to taste
1 bay leaf
1 bunch fresh Thai basil
1/4 teaspoon dried dill
1/2 teaspoon turmeric powder
2 cups Swiss chard, torn into pieces
Directions
Press the "Sauté" button and heat the canola oil. Now, brown turkey thighs for 2 to 3 minutes on each side; reserve.
Add a splash of turkey broth to scrape up any browned bits from the bottom.
Then, add the carrot, leek, parsnip and garlic to the Instant Pot. Sauté until they are softened.
Add remaining turkey broth, star anise pods, salt, black pepper, bay leaf, Thai basil, dill, and turmeric powder.
Secure the lid. Choose the "Soup" setting and cook for 30 minutes. Once cooking is complete, use a natural pressure release; carefully remove the lid.
Stir in Swiss chard while still hot to wilt leaves. Enjoy!

9. Two-Cheese Chicken Drumsticks

(Ready in about 25 minutes | Servings 5)
Chicken drumsticks have been seared to gain a deep brown color and rich flavor, then, pressure cooked in the Instant Pot. Perfect!
Per serving: 409 Calories; 23.8g Fat; 4.8g Carbs; 41.7g Protein; 2.4g Sugars
Ingredients
1 tablespoon olive oil
5 chicken drumsticks
1/2 teaspoon marjoram
1/2 teaspoon thyme
1 teaspoon shallot powder
2 garlic cloves, minced
1/2 cup chicken stock
1/4 cup dry white wine
1/4 cup full-fat milk
6 ounces ricotta cheese
4 ounces cheddar cheese
1/4 teaspoon ground black pepper
1/2 teaspoon cayenne pepper
Sea salt, to taste
Directions
Press the "Sauté" button and heat the oil. Once hot, brown chicken drumsticks for 3 minutes; turn the chicken over and cook an additional 3 minutes, Now, add marjoram, thyme, shallot powder, garlic, chicken stock, wine, and milk.
Secure the lid. Choose the "Manual" setting and cook for 15 minutes. Once cooking is complete, use a natural pressure release; carefully remove the lid.
Shred the chicken meat and return to the Instant Pot. Press the "Sauté" button and stir in ricotta cheese, cheddar cheese, black pepper, and cayenne pepper. Cook for a couple of minutes longer or until the cheese melts and everything is heated through.
Season with sea salt, taste and adjust the seasonings. Bon appétit!

10. Hot Chicken Wingettes with Cilantro Dip

(Ready in about 1 hour 15 minutes | Servings 6)

You don't have to use cayenne peppers, any fresh or dried chili peppers will work. Add more or fewer peppers depending on how spicy you like your food.

Per serving: 296 Calories; 22.5g Fat; 11.3g Carbs; 10.8g Protein; 4.3g Sugars

Ingredients
10 fresh cayenne peppers, trimmed and chopped
3 garlic cloves, minced
1 ½ cups white vinegar
1/2 teaspoon black pepper
1 teaspoon sea salt
1 teaspoon onion powder
12 chicken wingettes
2 tablespoons olive oil
Dipping Sauce:
1/2 cup mayonnaise
1/2 cup sour cream
1/2 cup cilantro, chopped
2 cloves garlic, minced
1 teaspoon smoked paprika

Directions
Place cayenne peppers, 3 garlic cloves, white vinegar, black pepper, salt, and onion powder in a container. Add chicken wingettes, and let them marinate, covered, for 1 hour in the refrigerator.
Add the chicken wingettes, along with the marinade and olive oil to the Instant Pot.
Secure the lid. Choose the "Manual" setting and cook for 6 minutes. Once cooking is complete, use a quick pressure release; carefully remove the lid.
In a mixing bowl, thoroughly combine mayonnaise, sour cream, cilantro, garlic, and smoked paprika. Serve warm chicken with the dipping sauce on the side. Bon appétit!

11. Greek-Style Chicken Wraps

(Ready in about 20 minutes | Servings 6)

If you crave tortilla wraps or tacos, try this recipe immediately. These Greek-inspired wraps are ready in twenty minutes and they are endlessly delicious.

Per serving: 238 Calories; 9.5g Fat; 9.1g Carbs; 29.1g Protein; 6.1g Sugars

Ingredients
1 ½ pounds chicken tenderloin, cut into 1/2-inch pieces
Salt and black pepper, to taste
1 teaspoon dried oregano
1/2 teaspoon dried basil
1/2 teaspoon ground cumin
1 cup water
2 ripe tomatoes, pureed
2 garlic cloves, minced
1 tablespoon golden Greek peppers, minced
1 tablespoon freshly squeezed lemon juice
1 large-sized head lettuce
6 ounces Feta cheese, cubed
1 ounce Kalamata olives, pitted and sliced
2 Florina peppers, seeded and chopped

Directions
Add the chicken, salt, black pepper, oregano, basil, cumin, and water to your Instar Pot.
Secure the lid. Choose the "Manual" setting and High pressure; cook for 10 minutes. Once cooking is complete, use a natural pressure release; carefully remove the lid. Reserve the chicken.
Then, add tomatoes, garlic, and Greek peppers to the Instant Pot.
Press the "Sauté" button and cook for 6 minutes at Low pressure. Add the shredded chicken back into the Instant Pot.
To serve, divide the chicken mixture among lettuce leaves. Top with Feta cheese, olives, and Florina peppers. Roll up in taco-style, serve and enjoy!

12. Chicken Wings with Paprika Mayo

(Ready in about 45 minutes | Servings 6)

Delicious and juicy, these chicken wings are served with a flavored mayo for dipping. It's an easy dish that you'll want to make again and again.

Per serving: 301 Calories; 19g Fat; 3.5g Carbs; 27.4g Protein; 2.1g Sugars

Ingredients
1 ½ pounds chicken wings, bone-in, skin-on
1 tablespoon olive oil
1 tablespoon balsamic vinegar
1 tablespoon Shoyu sauce
2 tablespoons ketchup
1 cup water
Sea salt, to taste
1/2 teaspoon cayenne pepper
1 cup mayonnaise
1 tablespoon sweet paprika

Directions
Place chicken wings, olive oil, balsamic vinegar, Shoyu sauce, ketchup, water, salt and cayenne pepper, and granulated garlic in a mixing dish.
Let it marinate for 30 minutes in the refrigerator. Secure the lid.
Now, press the "Manual" button. Cook the chicken wings along with their marinade for 14 minutes under High pressure.
Once cooking is complete, use a natural pressure release; carefully remove the lid.
In the meantime, mix mayonnaise with sweet paprika until it is well incorporated. Serve chicken wings with the paprika mayo for dipping. Bon appétit!

13. Chicken Fillets with Keto Sauce

(Ready in about 15 minutes | Servings 4)

Entertaining your family during the holiday season doesn't have to leave you stuck in the kitchen all day long. The Instant Pot is here to help!

Per serving: 314 Calories; 20.3g Fat; 1.7g Carbs; 29.9g Protein; 1.5g Sugars

Ingredients
1 tablespoon peanut oil

1 pound chicken fillets
Salt and freshly ground black pepper, to taste
1/2 teaspoon dried basil
1 cup broth, preferably homemade
Cheese Sauce:
3 teaspoons butter, at room temperature
1/3 cup double cream
1/3 cup Neufchâtel cheese, at room temperature
1/3 cup Gruyère cheese, preferably freshly grated
3 tablespoons milk
1/2 teaspoon granulated garlic
1 teaspoon shallot powder
Directions
Press the "Sauté" button and add peanut oil. Once hot, sear the chicken fillets for 3 minutes per side.
Season the chicken fillets with salt, black pepper, and basil; pour in the broth.
Secure the lid. Choose the "Manual" setting and cook for 6 minutes. Once cooking is complete, use a natural pressure release; carefully remove the lid.
Clean the Instant Pot and press the "Sauté" button.
Now, melt the butter and add double cream, Neufchâtel cheese, Gruyère cheese and milk; add granulated garlic and shallot powder.
Cook until everything is heated through. Bon appétit!

14. The Best Chicken Tacos

(Ready in about 30 minutes | Servings 6)
Anything pork can do, poultry can do better! Seriously, Instant Pot chicken with keto tortillas will blow your mind!
Per serving: 443 Calories; 17.3g Fat; 4.6g Carbs; 63.7g Protein; 1.7g Sugars
Ingredients
Low Carb Tortillas:
2 ounces pork rinds, crushed into a powder
A pinch of baking soda
A pinch of salt
2 ounces ricotta cheese
3 eggs
1/4 cup water
Nonstick cooking spray
Chicken:
1 ½ pounds chicken legs, skinless
4 cloves garlic, pressed or chopped
1/2 cup scallions, chopped
1 teaspoon dried basil
1/2 teaspoon dried thyme
1/2 teaspoon dried rosemary
1 teaspoon dried oregano
Sea salt, to your liking
1/3 teaspoon ground black pepper
1/4 cup freshly squeezed lemon juice
1 cup water
1/4 cup dry white wine
1/2 cup salsa, preferably homemade
Directions
To make low carb tortillas, add pork rinds, baking soda, and salt to your food processor; pulse a few times.
Now, fold in the cheese and eggs; mix until well combined. Add the water and process until smooth and uniform.
Spritz a pancake pan with a nonstick cooking spray. Preheat the pancake pan over moderate heat.
Now, pour the batter into the pan and prepare like you would a tortilla. Reserve keeping the tortillas warm.
Then, press the "Sauté" button and cook chicken legs for 2 to 4 minutes per side; reserve. Add the garlic and scallions and cook until aromatic.
Add the remaining ingredients, except for salsa. Return the chicken legs back to the Instant Pot.
Secure the lid. Choose the "Poultry" setting and cook for 15 minutes. Once cooking is complete, use a quick pressure release; carefully remove the lid.
Shred the chicken with two forks and discard the bones; serve with prepared tortillas and salsa. Enjoy!

15. Country Chicken Stew

(Ready in about 25 minutes | Servings 6)
Here's a rich and flavorful chicken stew your guests will love for sure! A dollop of sour cream is the perfect addition that compliments this chicken dish.
Per serving: 453 Calories; 22.6g Fat; 5.9g Carbs; 53.6g Protein; 2.6g Sugars
Ingredients
2 slices bacon
6 chicken legs, skinless and boneless
3 cups water
2 chicken bouillon cubes
1 leek, chopped
1 carrot, trimmed and chopped
4 garlic cloves, minced
1/2 teaspoon dried thyme
1/2 teaspoon dried basil
1 teaspoon Hungarian paprika
1 bay leaf
1 cup double cream
1/2 teaspoon ground black pepper
Directions
Press the "Sauté" button to heat up your Instant Pot. Now, cook the bacon, crumbling it with a spatula; cook until the bacon is crisp and reserve.
Now, add the chicken legs and cook until browned on all sides.
Add the water, bouillon cubes, leeks, carrot, garlic, thyme, basil, paprika, and bay leaf; stir to combine.
Secure the lid. Choose the "Poultry" setting and cook for 15 minutes at High pressure. Once cooking is complete, use a natural pressure release; carefully remove the lid.
Fold in the cream and allow it to cook in the residual heat, stirring continuously. Ladle into individual bowls, sprinkle each serving with freshly grated black pepper and serve warm. Bon appétit!

16. One Pot Chicken Teriyaki

(Ready in about 15 minutes | Servings 6)

With a wonderful teriyaki sauce and spices, this chicken teriyaki is super addicting! You can substitute cornstarch for arrowroot starch and skip the alcohol if desired.
Per serving: 326 Calories; 13.2g Fat; 3.1g Carbs; 45.6g Protein; 0.7g Sugars
Ingredients
1/3 cup coconut aminos
1/4 cup rice wine vinegar
3 tablespoons Mirin
8 drops liquid stevia
1 tablespoon cornstarch
1/3 cup water
2 tablespoons olive oil
2 pounds chicken legs, boneless and skinless
1 teaspoon garlic powder
1 teaspoon ginger powder
Sea salt and black pepper, to taste
1/2 teaspoon sweet paprika
2/3 cup chicken stock
Directions
Press the "Sauté" button to heat up your Instant Pot. Now, add the coconut aminos, vinegar, Mirin, liquid stevia, and cornstarch; whisk to combine well.
Now, pour in water and cook, bringing to a boil; cook until the liquid is thickened; reserve teriyaki sauce.
Wipe down the Instant Pot with a damp cloth; then, heat olive oil and cook the chicken until browned.
Add garlic powder and ginger powder.
Season with salt, black pepper, and paprika.
Add chicken stock and 2/3 of teriyaki sauce; stir to combine. Secure the lid. Choose the "Manual" setting and cook for 10 minutes.
Once cooking is complete, use a natural pressure release; carefully remove the lid. Serve with the remaining 1/3 of teriyaki sauce and enjoy!

17. Quick and Easy Chicken Carnitas
(Ready in about 20 minutes | Servings 8)
Prepare chicken carnitas in advance for the whole week or make it for a festive dinner party. For even better results, you can crisp up your chicken under the broiler.
Per serving: 294 Calories; 15.4g Fat; 2.8g Carbs; 35.2g Protein; 1.3g Sugars
Ingredients
3 pounds whole chicken, cut into pieces
3 cloves garlic, pressed
1 guajillo chili, minced
1 tablespoon avocado oil
1/3 cup roasted vegetable broth
Sea salt, to taste
1/2 teaspoon ground bay leaf
1/3 teaspoon cayenne pepper
1/2 teaspoon paprika
1/3 teaspoon black pepper
1 cup crème fraiche, to serve
2 heaping tablespoons fresh coriander, chopped
Directions
Place all of the above ingredients, except for crème fraiche and fresh coriander, in the Instant Pot. Secure the lid. Choose the "Poultry" setting and cook for 15 minutes. Once cooking is complete, use a quick pressure release; carefully remove the lid.
Shred the chicken with two forks and discard the bones. Add a dollop of crème fraiche to each serving and garnish with fresh coriander. Enjoy!

18. Sensational Turkey Legs
(Ready in about 40 minutes | Servings 6)
These turkey legs are a cinch to make! They pair wonderfully with a tangy low-carb cauliflower salad.
Per serving: 339 Calories; 19.3g Fat; 1.3g Carbs; 37.7g Protein; 0.4g Sugars
Ingredients
3 tablespoons sesame oil
2 pounds turkey legs
Sea salt and ground black pepper, to your liking
A bunch of scallions, roughly chopped
1 ½ cups turkey broth
Directions
Press the "Sauté" button and heat the sesame oil. Now, brown turkey legs on all sides; season with salt and black pepper.
Add the scallions and broth.
Secure the lid. Choose the "Manual" setting and cook for 35 minutes. Once cooking is complete, use a natural pressure release; carefully remove the lid.
You can thicken the cooking liquid on the "Sauté" setting if desired. Serve warm.

19. Traditional Hungarian Paprikash
(Ready in about 25 minutes | Servings 6)
A one-pot traditional recipe that features tomato, peppers, paprika, and chicken thighs. This is something worth trying!
Per serving: 402 Calories; 31.7g Fat; 8.1g Carbs; 21g Protein; 3.4g Sugars
Ingredients
1 tablespoon lard, at room temperature
1 ½ pounds chicken thighs
1/2 cup tomato puree
1 ½ cups water
1 yellow onion, chopped
1 large-sized carrot, sliced
1 celery stalk, diced
2 garlic cloves, minced
2 bell peppers, seeded and chopped
1 Hungarian wax pepper, seeded and minced
1 teaspoon cayenne pepper
1 tablespoon Hungarian paprika
1 teaspoon coarse salt
1/2 teaspoon ground black pepper
1/2 teaspoon poultry seasoning
6 ounces sour cream
1 tablespoon arrowroot powder
1 cup water
Directions

Press the "Sauté" button to heat up the Instant Pot. Now, melt the lard until hot; sear the chicken thighs for 2 to 3 minutes per side.
Add the tomato puree, 1 ½ cups of water, onion, carrot, celery, garlic, peppers, and seasonings.
Secure the lid. Choose the "Manual" setting and cook for 20 minutes at High pressure. Once cooking is complete, use a quick pressure release; carefully remove the lid.
In the meantime, thoroughly combine sour cream, arrowroot powder and 1 cup of water; whisk to combine well.
Add the sour cream mixture to the Instant Pot to thicken the cooking liquid. Cook for a couple of minutes on the residual heat.
Ladle into individual bowls and serve immediately.

20. Chicken Medley with White Mushrooms

(Ready in about 20 minutes | Servings 8)
You don't need to be an expert chef to make this tasty, gourmet chicken medley. Chicken breasts go wonderfully with white mushrooms and cook perfectly in the Instant Pot.
Per serving: 222 Calories; 12g Fat; 2.5g Carbs; 24.6g Protein; 1g Sugars
Ingredients
2 teaspoons olive oil
2 pounds chicken breast halves, cubed
1 teaspoon cayenne pepper
1 teaspoon onion powder
1/2 teaspoon porcini powder
Sea salt, to taste
1/4 teaspoon freshly ground black pepper, or more to taste
1 cup white mushrooms, thinly sliced
1 parsnip, chopped
4 garlic cloves, minced
2 cups vegetable broth
2 bay leaves
1/2 cup half-and-half cream
2 heaping tablespoons fresh cilantro
Directions
Press the "Sauté" button to heat up the Instant Pot. Now, heat the oil until sizzling. Then, cook the chicken breast for 4 to 6 minutes, turning them over a few times.
Add cayenne pepper, onion powder, porcini powder, salt, black pepper, and white mushrooms. Continue to sauté until they are fragrant.
Now, stir in parsnip, garlic, broth, and bay leaves.
Secure the lid. Choose the "Manual" setting and cook for 10 minutes at High pressure. Once cooking is complete, use a quick pressure release; carefully remove the lid.
Add half-and-half cream and stir until the cooking liquid is slightly thickened. Serve garnished with fresh cilantro. Bon appétit!

21. The Best Ever Chicken Goulash

(Ready in about 25 minutes | Servings 6)
Winter is the perfect time of the year to enjoy a hearty chicken goulash. However, a traditional goulash makes a perfect lunch all year round. Serve over cauli rice.
Per serving: 353 Calories; 19.5g Fat; 7.5g Carbs; 34.3g Protein; 4.9g Sugars
Ingredients
1 tablespoon olive oil
2 pounds chicken breast halves, boneless and skinless
2 small-sized shallots, chopped
1 teaspoon garlic paste
1 cup milk
2 ripe tomatoes, chopped
1 teaspoon curry powder
1 tablespoon tamari sauce
1 tablespoon balsamic vinegar
2 tablespoons vermouth
Sea salt, to taste
1/2 teaspoon cayenne pepper
1/3 teaspoon black pepper
1/2 teaspoon hot paprika
1/2 teaspoon ginger, freshly grated
1 celery stalk with leaves, chopped
1 bell pepper, chopped
1 tablespoon flaxseed meal
Directions
Press the "Sauté" button to heat up the Instant Pot. Now, add olive oil. Once hot, sear the chicken breast halves for 3 to 4 minutes per side.
Add the shallots, garlic, milk, tomatoes, curry powder, tamari sauce, vinegar, vermouth, salt, cayenne pepper, black pepper, hot paprika, ginger, celery and bell pepper to the Instant Pot; stir to combine well.
Secure the lid. Choose the "Meat/Stew" setting and cook for 20 minutes at High pressure. Once cooking is complete, use a quick pressure release; carefully remove the lid.
Add flaxseed meal and continue stirring in the residual heat. Ladle into serving bowls and enjoy!

22. Italian-Style Turkey Meatloaf

(Ready in about 35 minutes | Servings 6)
Everyone loves a meatloaf! This rich, cheesy turkey meatloaf, gently cooked in an electric pressure cooker, is guaranteed to hit the spot!
Per serving: 449 Calories; 29.7g Fat; 8.1g Carbs; 36.2g Protein; 3.7g Sugars
Ingredients
2 pounds ground turkey
2/3 cup pork rind crumbs
1/2 cup Parmigiano-Reggiano, grated
1 tablespoon coconut aminos
2 eggs, chopped
Sea salt, to taste
1/4 teaspoon ground black pepper
1 yellow onion, peeled and chopped
2 garlic cloves, minced
4 ounces tomato paste

1 tablespoon Italian seasoning
1/2 cup tomato sauce
1 cup water
1 teaspoon mustard powder
1/2 teaspoon chili powder
Directions
Prepare your Instant Pot by adding a metal rack and 1 ½ cups of water to the bottom of the inner pot.
In a large mixing bowl, thoroughly combine ground turkey with pork rind crumbs, Parmigiano-Reggiano, coconut aminos, eggs, salt, black pepper, onion, garlic, tomato paste, Italian seasoning.
Shape this mixture into a meatloaf; lower your meatloaf onto the metal rack.
Then, in a mixing bowl, thoroughly combine tomato sauce with water, mustard and chili powder. Spread this mixture over the top of your meatloaf.
Secure the lid. Choose the "Meat/Stew" setting and cook for 20 minutes at High pressure. Once cooking is complete, use a natural pressure release; carefully remove the lid.
Afterwards, place your meatloaf under the preheated broiler for 5 minutes. Allow the meatloaf to rest for 6 to 8 minutes before slicing and serving. Bon appétit!

23. Cheesy Chicken and Mushroom Casserole
(Ready in about 15 minutes | Servings 4)
Minimal work and maximum pay-off! This chicken casserole is perfect for your next dinner party or a lazy Sunday lunch at home with your family.
Per serving: 469 Calories; 32.3g Fat; 8.1g Carbs; 36.3g Protein; 4.2g Sugars
Ingredients
1 tablespoon lard
1 pound chicken breasts, cubed
10 ounces button mushrooms, thinly sliced
2 cloves garlic, smashed
1/2 cup yellow onion, chopped
1/2 teaspoon turmeric powder
1/2 teaspoon shallot powder
1/2 teaspoon dried sage
1/2 teaspoon dried basil
Kosher salt, to taste
1/2 teaspoon cayenne pepper
1/3 teaspoon ground black pepper
1 cup chicken broth
1/2 cup double cream
1 cup Colby cheese, shredded
Directions
Press the "Sauté" button to heat up the Instant Pot.
Now, melt lard and cook chicken, mushrooms, garlic, and onion; cook until the vegetables are softened.
Add turmeric powder, shallot powder, sage, basil, salt, cayenne pepper, black pepper, and broth.
Secure the lid. Choose the "Meat/Stew" setting and cook for 6 minutes at High pressure. Once cooking is complete, use a natural pressure release; carefully remove the lid.

Now, add double cream and cook in the residual heat until thoroughly heated.
Top with cheese and bake in the preheated oven at 390 degrees F until cheese is bubbling. Serve right away.

24. Gruyère and Turkey Au Gratin
(Ready in about 40 minutes | Servings 4)
Turkey legs and Gruyère cheese is a luxurious combination. Don't forget to add a pinch of chili powder for some extra oomph!
Per serving: 540 Calories; 35g Fat; 2.9g Carbs; 51.8g Protein; 1.8g Sugars
Ingredients
1 tablespoon canola oil
1 pound turkey legs, boneless and skinless
6 ounces smoked deli ham
8 ounces Cottage cheese
1/2 teaspoon mustard powder
1/3 teaspoon cayenne pepper, or more to taste
1 cup water
2 cups Gruyère cheese, shredded
Salt and ground black pepper, to taste
Directions
Press the "Sauté" button to heat up the Instant Pot.
Now, heat the oil and cook the turkey legs until no longer pink.
Add ham, Cottage cheese, mustard powder, cayenne pepper, and water; gently stir to combine.
Secure the lid. Choose the "Meat/Stew" setting and cook for 35 minutes under High pressure. Once cooking is complete, use a natural pressure release; carefully remove the lid.
Add shredded Gruyère cheese and continue to cook in the residual heat until the cheese has melted completely.
Season with salt and black pepper; taste, adjust the seasonings and serve. Bon appétit!

25. Chicken Liver Pâté
(Ready in about 15 minutes | Servings 8)
Chicken liver pâté is a sophisticated and delicious snack, perfect for Sunday afternoon or a holiday dinner party. Serve with ketogenic flatbread.
Per serving: 109 Calories; 6.5g Fat; 2.3g Carbs; 10g Protein; 0.3g Sugars
Ingredients
1 pound chicken livers
1/2 cup leeks, chopped
2 garlic cloves, crushed
2 tablespoons olive oil
1 tablespoon poultry seasonings
1 teaspoon dried rosemary
1/2 teaspoon dried marjoram
1/4 teaspoon dried dill weed
1/2 teaspoon paprika
1/2 teaspoon red pepper flakes
Salt, to taste
1/2 teaspoon ground black pepper
1 cup water

1 tablespoon stone ground mustard
Directions
Press the "Sauté" button to heat up the Instant Pot. Now, heat the oil.
Once hot, sauté the chicken livers until no longer pink.
Add the remaining ingredients, except for the mustard, to your Instant Pot.
Secure the lid. Choose the "Manual" setting and cook for 10 minutes at High pressure. Once cooking is complete, use a quick pressure release; carefully remove the lid.
Transfer the cooked mixture to a food processor; add stone ground mustard. Process until smooth and uniform. Bon appétit!

26. Grandma's Chunky Turkey Soup

(Ready in about 20 minutes | Servings 4)
Here's a vintage-style, grandma's favorite comfort food recipe. This mouthwatering soup is full of flavor and can be served on any occasion.
Per serving: 429 Calories; 26.2g Fat; 6.7g Carbs; 40.2g Protein; 3.1g Sugars
Ingredients
2 teaspoons coconut oil
2 onions, chopped
2 garlic cloves, finely chopped
1/2 teaspoon freshly grated ginger
2 tomatoes, chopped
1 celery stalk with leaves, chopped
1 teaspoon dried basil
1/2 teaspoon dried rosemary
1 bay leaf
1/4 teaspoon freshly ground black pepper
1/2 teaspoon red pepper flakes, crushed
Sea salt, to taste
3 turkey thighs
4 cups roasted vegetable broth
1/4 cup fresh parsley, finely minced
Directions
Press the "Sauté" button to heat up the Instant Pot. Now, heat the oil. Cook the onion and garlic until softened and aromatic.
Add grated ginger, tomatoes, celery, basil, rosemary, bay leaf, black pepper, red pepper, salt, turkey thighs and vegetable broth.
Secure the lid. Choose the "Manual" setting and cook for 15 minutes at High pressure. Once cooking is complete, use a quick pressure release; carefully remove the lid.
Remove turkey thighs from the soup; discard the bones, shred the meat and return it to the Instant Pot.
Add fresh parsley and stir well. Serve in individual bowls. Bon appétit!

27. Thai Coconut Chicken

(Ready in about 15 minutes | Servings 4)
Don't forget to add Thai chili for some extra oomph. Thai chili, also sold as Bird's eye chili, is available jarred or dried in supermarkets.
Per serving: 192 Calories; 7.5g Fat; 5.4g Carbs; 25.2g Protein; 2.2g Sugars
Ingredients
1 tablespoon coconut oil
1 pound chicken, cubed
1 shallot, peeled and chopped
2 cloves garlic, minced
1 teaspoon fresh ginger root, julienned
1/3 teaspoon cumin powder
1 teaspoon Thai chili, minced
1 cup vegetable broth, preferably homemade
1 tomato, peeled and chopped
1/3 cup coconut milk, unsweetened
1 teaspoon Thai curry paste
2 tablespoons tamari sauce
1/2 cup sprouts
Salt and freshly ground black pepper, to taste
Directions
Press the "Sauté" button to heat up the Instant Pot. Now, heat the coconut oil. Cook the chicken for 2 to 3 minutes, stirring frequently; reserve.
Then, in pan drippings, cook the shallot and garlic until softened; add a splash of vegetable broth, if needed.
Add ginger, cumin powder and Thai chili and cook until aromatic or 1 minute more.
Now, stir in vegetable broth, tomato, coconut milk, Thai curry paste, and tamari sauce.
Secure the lid. Choose the "Manual" setting and cook for 10 minutes under High pressure. Once cooking is complete, use a quick pressure release; carefully remove the lid.
Afterwards, add sprouts, salt, and black pepper and serve immediately. Bon appétit!

28. Kid-Friendly Chicken Meatballs

(Ready in about 15 minutes | Servings 6)
Here's your go-to meatball recipe you'll never want to be without – cheddar tucked inside each meatball! Kids of all ages will be amazed!
Per serving: 470 Calories; 34.1g Fat; 7.8g Carbs; 31.5g Protein; 4.1g Sugars
Ingredients
1 ½ pounds ground chicken
2 eggs
2 tablespoons scallions, finely chopped
1 teaspoon garlic, minced
1/2 cup pork rind crumbs
1 teaspoon cayenne pepper
Kosher salt and freshly ground black pepper, to taste
1/4 teaspoon ground bay leaf
1/4 teaspoon dried marjoram
1/4 teaspoon dried oregano
6 ounces cheddar cheese, cubed
2 tablespoons olive oil
3/4 cup tomato sauce
1/2 cup water

Directions
In a mixing dish, thoroughly combine ground chicken, eggs, scallions, garlic, pork rind crumbs, and seasonings; mix until everything is well incorporated. Now, shape the mixture into balls. Press 1 cheese cube into center of each meatball, sealing it inside. Press the "Sauté" button and heat the olive oil. Sear the meatballs for a couple of minutes or until browned on all sides. Add the tomato sauce and water.

Secure the lid. Choose the "Manual" setting and cook for 8 minutes under High pressure. Once cooking is complete, use a quick pressure release; carefully remove the lid.

Serve your meatballs with the sauce. Bon appétit!

29. Winter Chicken Salad

(Ready in about 15 minutes + chilling time | Servings 8)

Many people can't imagine holidays without a good chicken salad. It's so easy to prepare with an Instant Pot. You don't need to be an expert chef to make this gourmet chicken salad.

Per serving: 343 Calories; 26.2g Fat; 1.6g Carbs; 24.9g Protein; 0.3g Sugars

Ingredients
2 pounds chicken
1 cup vegetable broth
2 sprigs fresh thyme
1 teaspoon onion powder
1 teaspoon granulated garlic
1/2 teaspoon black pepper, ground
1 bay leaf
1 cup mayonnaise
1 teaspoon Dijon mustard
1 teaspoon fresh lemon juice
2 stalks celery, chopped
2 tablespoons fresh chives, chopped
1/2 teaspoon coarse sea salt

Directions
Place the chicken, broth, thyme, onion powder, garlic, black pepper, and bay leaf in your Instant Pot.

Secure the lid. Choose the "Poultry" setting and cook for 12 minutes under High pressure. Once cooking is complete, use a natural pressure release; carefully remove the lid.

Remove the chicken from the Instant Pot; allow it to cool slightly.

Now, cut the chicken breasts into strips and transfer it to a salad bowl. Add the remaining ingredients and gently stir until everything is well combined. Serve well-chilled and enjoy!

30. Creamy Turkey Breasts with Mushrooms

(Ready in about 15 minutes | Servings 6)

Cozy up to a bowl of delicious, creamy turkey breasts with mushrooms. This is something worth trying!

Per serving: 248 Calories; 13.9g Fat; 3.3g Carbs; 26.1g Protein; 1.6g Sugars

Ingredients
3 teaspoons butter
1 ½ pounds turkey breasts, cubed
1 cup white mushrooms, thinly sliced
2 cloves garlic, minced
1/2 leek, chopped
1/2 cup broth, preferably homemade
Salt and black pepper, to taste
1/4 teaspoon ground allspice
1/2 teaspoon basil
1/2 teaspoon dried parsley flakes
1 teaspoon porcini powder
1/2 cup double cream

Directions
Press the "Sauté" button and melt the butter. Now, sear the turkey for 3 to 4 minutes, stirring constantly; set aside.

Add the mushrooms, garlic and leeks and cook in pan drippings until aromatic and just tender. Add broth and aromatics.

Now, secure the lid. Choose the "Manual" setting and cook for 8 minutes under High pressure. Once cooking is complete, use a quick pressure release; carefully remove the lid.

Add double cream and cook in the residual heat until thoroughly warmed.

Ladle into serving bowls and serve immediately. Enjoy!

31. Family Cheese and Chicken Sandwiches

(Ready in about 20 minutes | Servings 4)

These sandwich rolls are grain-free, low-carb, and flavorful. You can toast them to add a little crunch to your sandwiches if desired.

Per serving: 500 Calories; 37.4g Fat; 2.2g Carbs; 36.9g Protein; 0.6g Sugars

Ingredients
4 chicken drumsticks, boneless
Celery salt, to taste
1/2 teaspoon ground black pepper
1/2 teaspoon cayenne pepper
2 bay leaves
1/3 cup vegetable stock
1 cup water
1/2 cup almond flour
3/4 teaspoon baking powder
A pinch of table salt
1/2 teaspoon granulated garlic
2 eggs, whisked
2 tablespoons butter
4 tablespoons mayonnaise
4 teaspoons mustard
4 (1-ounce) slices Cheddar cheese

Directions
Add the chicken drumsticks to the Instant Pot Sprinkle with celery salt, black pepper, and cayenne pepper; add bay leaves, vegetable stock, and water.

Now, secure the lid. Choose the "Poultry" setting and cook for 15 minutes under High pressure. Once

cooking is complete, use a quick pressure release; carefully remove the lid.
Then, mix almond flour with baking powder, table salt, granulated garlic, eggs, and butter in mugs; mix to combine well.
Place the mugs in your microwave; microwave for 1 minute 30 seconds on high. Split each roll into halves to make your sandwiches.
Assemble your sandwiches with chicken, mayo, mustard and cheese. Serve and enjoy!

32. Easy Roasted Chicken Drumettes

(Ready in about 2 hours 25 minutes | Servings 4)
Here's a completely new way to eat chicken drumettes! Chicken drumettes are funny, delicious and kid-friendly!
Per serving: 283 Calories; 13.9g Fat; 2.3g Carbs; 35.7g Protein; 0.3g Sugars
Ingredients
2 tablespoons olive oil
1 tablespoon tamari sauce
2 teaspoons champagne vinegar
2 garlic cloves, smashed
1/2 teaspoon turmeric powder
1 teaspoon freshly grated ginger
1/2 teaspoon sea salt
1/4 teaspoon ground black pepper
1 teaspoon paprika
1 ½ pounds chicken drumettes
1/2 cup fresh chives, roughly chopped
2 tablespoons black sesame seeds, toasted
Directions
Place all of the above ingredients, except for fresh chives and black sesame seeds, in a mixing dish; cover and let it marinate for 2 hours in your refrigerator.
Add 1 ½ cups of water and metal trivet to the Instant Pot.
Then, place the chicken on the trivet.
Now, secure the lid. Choose the "Poultry" setting and cook for 20 minutes under High pressure. Once cooking is complete, use a quick pressure release; carefully remove the lid.
Preheat your oven to broil. Place the chicken drumettes on a parchment-lined baking sheet; spoon the reserved marinade over them.
Now, broil the chicken drumettes for 3 minutes on each side or until they are crisp and browned.
Serve garnished with fresh chives and toasted sesame seeds. Enjoy!

33. Peppery Spicy Ground Chicken

(Ready in about 15 minutes | Servings 6)
A combo of bacon, ground chicken and peppers will blow your mind! It freezes and reheats well.
Per serving: 231 Calories; 13.6g Fat; 3.1g Carbs; 24.3g Protein; 1.6g Sugars
Ingredients
2 slices bacon, chopped
1 ½ pounds ground chicken
2 garlic cloves, minced
1/2 cup green onions, chopped
1 serrano pepper, chopped
1 red bell pepper, seeded and chopped
1 green bell pepper, seeded and chopped
1 tomato, chopped
1/3 cup chicken broth
1 cup water
1 teaspoon paprika
1/4 teaspoon ground allspice
1 teaspoon onion powder
Sea salt and ground black pepper, to taste
2 bay leaves
Directions
Press the "Sauté" button to heat up your Instant Pot. Now, cook the bacon until crisp; reserve.
Then, brown the ground chicken in bacon grease, crumbling it with a spatula; reserve.
Sauté the garlic, green onions, and peppers for 2 to 3 minutes until softened. Stir in the other ingredients.
Now, secure the lid. Choose the "Poultry" setting and cook for 5 minutes under High pressure.
Once cooking is complete, use a natural pressure release; carefully remove the lid. Serve over ketogenic sandwich rolls. Enjoy!

34. Chicken Roulade with Kale and Cheese

(Ready in about 15 minutes | Servings 4)
When you run out of ideas, here is the perfect solution – simply stuff butterflied chicken breasts with whatever keto ingredients you have on hand. Some other ideas include ham, bacon, asparagus, spinach and other types of cheese.
Per serving: 468 Calories; 31.8g Fat; 3.9g Carbs; 40.4g Protein; 0.9g Sugars
Ingredients
2 chicken breasts, boneless, skinless and butterflied
6 ounces kale, cooked, chopped and squeezed dry.
2 ounces Ricotta cheese, crumbled
2 ounces goat cheese, crumbled
2 ounces Colby cheese, shredded
2 cloves garlic, sliced
Kosher salt and freshly ground black pepper, to taste
2 tablespoons vegetable oil
Directions
Pat dry the chicken breasts on both sides.
Lay 2 chicken breasts flat on a cutting board.
Divide cooked kale, cheese, and garlic among chicken breasts. Now, wrap the stuffed chicken breasts and season them with salt and black pepper.
Press the "Sauté" button to heat up your Instant Pot. Heat the vegetable oil until sizzling.
Once hot, brown stuffed chicken breast for 2 minutes per side. Clean the Instant Pot and add 1 ½ cups of water and trivet to the inner pot.
Lower the stuffed chicken onto the trivet. Now, secure the lid. Choose the "Poultry" setting and cook for 5 minutes under High pressure.

Once cooking is complete, use a quick pressure release; carefully remove the lid. Cut each chicken roulade into halves, serve warm and enjoy!

35. Chicken Legs in Mustard Curry Sauce
(Ready in about 25 minutes | Servings 5)
Pancetta does not contain carbohydrates and sugars, so you can easily include this pork product into your ketogenic diet.
Per serving: 477 Calories; 26.1g Fat; 4.5g Carbs; 52.8g Protein; 1.4g Sugars
Ingredients
5 chicken legs, boneless, skin-on
2 garlic cloves, halved
Sea salt, to taste
1/4 teaspoon black pepper, preferably freshly ground
1/2 teaspoon smoked paprika
2 teaspoons olive oil
1 tablespoon yellow mustard
1 teaspoon curry paste
4 strips pancetta, chopped
1 shallot, peeled and chopped
1 cup roasted vegetable broth, preferably homemade
Directions
Rub the chicken legs with garlic halves; then, season with salt, black pepper, and smoked paprika.
Press the "Sauté" button to heat up your Instant Pot. Once hot, heat the oil and sauté chicken legs for 4 to 5 minutes, turning once during cooking. Add a splash of chicken broth to deglaze the bottom of the pan.
Spread the legs with mustard and curry paste. Add pancetta, shallot and remaining vegetable broth.
Secure the lid. Choose "Manual" mode and High pressure; cook for 14 minutes. Once cooking is complete, use a natural pressure release; carefully remove the lid. Bon appétit!

36. Holiday Stuffed Turkey Breasts
(Ready in about 25 minutes | Servings 8)
Give a turkey breast this simple but delicious makeover. Stuffing it with sausage, mushrooms, and bacon makes all the difference.
Per serving: 517 Calories; 25.3g Fat; 0.9g Carbs; 67.4g Protein; 0g Sugars
Ingredients
1 (3-pound) turkey breast, skinless, boneless and butterflied
Salt, to taste
1/4 teaspoon freshly ground black pepper, or more to taste
1/2 teaspoon cayenne pepper
6 ounces chicken sausage, removed from casing
3 ounces bacon, finely diced
1 cup button mushrooms, thinly sliced
1 teaspoon garlic, pressed
1 tablespoon fresh basil, roughly chopped
1 tablespoon fresh parsley, roughly chopped
1 tablespoon olive oil
Directions
Pat dry the turkey breast with kitchen towels. Lay the turkey breast flat on a cutting board. Sprinkle it with salt, black pepper, and cayenne pepper.
Press the "Sauté" button to heat up your Instant Pot. Cook chicken sausage, bacon, and mushrooms for 3 to 4 minutes.
Stir in the garlic, basil, and parsley, and cook an additional minute. Spread this stuffing mixture on the turkey breast; roll the turkey around the stuffing and wrap kitchen twine around the breast.
Press the "Sauté" button again. Heat olive oil and sear turkey breasts for 2 minutes per side.
Clean the Instant Pot and add 1 ½ cups of water and trivet to the inner pot. Lower the stuffed turkey breast onto the trivet.
Secure the lid. Choose "Manual" mode and High pressure; cook for 20 minutes. Once cooking is complete, use a natural pressure release; carefully remove the lid. Bon appétit!

37. Budget-Friendly Turkey Salad
(Ready in about 25 minutes | Servings 6)
This turkey salad is inexpensive and healthy, and it tastes so divine! Best of all, you only need 25 minutes to get your family dinner ready!
Per serving: 321 Calories; 17.2g Fat; 4.4g Carbs; 35g Protein; 1.4g Sugars
Ingredients
2 pounds turkey breast, boneless and skinless
1/2 teaspoon black pepper, preferably freshly ground
1/2 teaspoon red pepper flakes, crushed
Seasoned salt, to taste
2 sprigs thyme
1 sprig sage
2 garlic cloves, pressed
1 leek, sliced
1/2 cup mayonnaise
1 ½ tablespoons Dijon mustard
1/2 cup celery, finely diced
1 cucumber, chopped
Directions
Prepare your Instant Pot by adding 1 ½ cups of water and a metal trivet to the bottom of the inner pot.
Now, sprinkle turkey breast with black pepper, red pepper, and salt. Lower the seasoned turkey breast onto the trivet. Top with thyme, sage, and garlic.
Now, secure the lid. Choose the "Poultry" setting and cook for 20 minutes under High pressure. Once cooking is complete, use a natural pressure release; carefully remove the lid.
Allow the turkey to cool completely. Slice the turkey into strips.
Add the remaining ingredients and transfer the mixture to a salad bowl. Serve well-chilled. Bon appétit!

38. Chicken Legs with Salsa
(Ready in about 15 minutes | Servings 5)
For a real and authentic Mexican flavor, make your own salsa sauce. You can make a big batch of salsa and freeze leftovers for later use.
Per serving: 355 Calories; 11.3g Fat; 8.8g Carbs; 52.2g Protein; 4.4g Sugars
Ingredients
5 chicken legs, skinless and boneless
1/2 teaspoon sea salt
Salsa Sauce:
1 cup pureed tomatoes
1 teaspoon granulated garlic
2 bell peppers, deveined and chopped
1 minced jalapeño, chopped
1 cup onion, chopped
2 tablespoons fresh cilantro, minced
3 teaspoons lime juice
Directions
Press the "Sauté" button to heat up your Instant Pot. Sear the chicken legs for 2 to 3 minutes on each side or until delicately browned. Season with sea salt.
In a mixing bowl, thoroughly combine the remaining ingredients to make your salsa. Spoon the salsa mixture over the browned chicken legs.
Secure the lid. Choose "Manual" mode and High pressure; cook for 10 minutes. Once cooking is complete, use a natural pressure release; carefully remove the lid. Bon appétit!

39. Ground Chicken and Zucchini Casserole
(Ready in about 15 minutes | Servings 4)
Here's a ridiculously simple way to make a vegetable and chicken casserole in a pressure cooker. Just keep reading the recipe.
Per serving: 459 Calories; 32.9g Fat; 6.8g Carbs; 33.8g Protein; 1.8g Sugars
Ingredients
3 teaspoons olive oil
1 pound ground chicken
1/2 cup parmesan cheese, grated
2 tablespoons pork rind crumbs
Coarse sea salt and freshly ground black pepper, to taste
2 garlic cloves, minced
1 teaspoon dried basil
1/2 teaspoon dried oregano
1/2 teaspoon dried sage
1/2 pound zucchini, thinly sliced
2 ripe tomatoes, pureed
1/2 cup water
1 teaspoon mustard powder
1 teaspoon minced jalapeño
4 ounces Monterey-Jack cheese, shredded
Directions
Press the "Sauté" button to heat up the Instant Pot. Now, heat 1 teaspoon of olive oil until sizzling. Brown ground chicken for 2 minutes, crumbling it with a wide spatula or fork. Now, add parmesan cheese, pork rind crumbs, salt, black pepper, garlic, basil, oregano, and sage.
Cook an additional minute and reserve.
Wipe down the Instant Pot with a damp cloth; spritz the inner pot with a nonstick cooking spray. Arrange 1/3 of zucchini slices on the bottom.
Spread 1/3 of meat mixture over zucchini. Repeat the layering two more times.
In a mixing bowl, whisk tomatoes with the remaining 2 teaspoons of olive oil, water, mustard powder, and jalapeno.
Pour this tomato sauce over the casserole.
Secure the lid. Choose "Manual" mode and High pressure; cook for 10 minutes. Once cooking is complete, use a quick pressure release; carefully remove the lid.
Then, top the casserole with shredded cheese; allow it to melt on the residual heat. Bon appétit!

40. Chicken Philly Cheese Steak
(Ready in about 25 minutes | Servings 4)
Philadelphia chicken cheese steak, please. This American feast comes together in under 25 minutes. Enjoy!
Per serving: 497 Calories; 37g Fat; 6.2g Carbs; 34.2g Protein; 2.2g Sugars
Ingredients
1 tablespoon bacon fat
3 chicken breast halves
Seasoned salt, to taste
1/3 teaspoon ground black pepper
1 red onion, chopped
1 bell pepper, seeded and chopped
1 habanero pepper, seeded and chopped
1/2 cup chicken broth
1/2 cup water
1/2 teaspoon dried basil
1/2 teaspoon celery seeds
1/2 teaspoon mustard seeds
1/2 cup mayonnaise
1 cup cheddar cheese, shredded
1 cup provolone cheese, sliced
Directions
Press the "Sauté" button to heat up the Instant Pot. Now, warm bacon fat.
Once hot, sear the chicken breasts for 2 to 3 minutes on each side; season with salt and ground black pepper; set aside.
In pan drippings, cook the onion and peppers until softened. Add the reserved chicken, along with broth, water, basil, celery seeds, and mustard seeds.
Wipe down the Instant Pot with a damp cloth. Add 1 ½ cups of water and metal trivet to the bottom of your Instant Pot.
Spoon the chicken mixture into a lightly greased casserole dish; top with mayo and cheese.
Secure the lid. Choose "Manual" mode and High pressure; cook for 20 minutes. Once cooking is complete, use a quick pressure release; carefully remove the lid. Bon appétit!

41. Saucy Chicken Drumettes with Squashsta

(Ready in about 55 minutes | Servings 8)

A big bowl of spaghetti and chicken on a keto diet? Use spaghetti squash to make this super easy, fun and delicious keto pasta.

Per serving: 224 Calories; 9.4g Fat; 7g Carbs; 26.4g Protein; 1.1g Sugars

Ingredients
2 tablespoons grapeseed oil
8 chicken drumettes
2 cloves garlic, minced
Sea salt and ground black pepper, to taste
2 ripe tomatoes, pureed
2 tablespoons capers, rinsed and drained
1 cup broth, preferably homemade
1 tablespoon flaxseed meal
1 (3-pound) spaghetti squash, halved
1 tablespoon olive oil
Coarse sea salt, to taste

Directions
Press the "Sauté" button to heat up the Instant Pot. Heat the grapeseed oil.
Brown the chicken drumettes for 2 to 3 minutes per side.
Add the garlic, salt, black pepper, tomatoes, capers, and broth.
Secure the lid. Choose "Manual" mode and High pressure; cook for 10 minutes. Once cooking is complete, use a natural pressure release; carefully remove the lid.
Reserve the chicken drumettes. Press the "Sauté" button again and add the flaxseed meal to the Instant Pot.
Thicken the tomato sauce for a couple of minutes or until your desired thickness is achieved.
Preheat your oven to 380 degrees F. Place squash halves, cut-side down on a lightly greased baking pan. Drizzle olive oil over them and sprinkle with sea salt. Roast for 40 minutes. Afterwards, scrape the flesh to create "spaghetti". Serve with warm chicken drumettes and tomato sauce. Enjoy!

42. Cheesy Chicken Stuffed Peppers

(Ready in about 20 minutes | Servings 5)

Stuffed with ground chicken and plenty of goat cheese and served with sour cream, these stuffed peppers will win your heart!

Per serving: 335 Calories; 19.6g Fat; 8.9g Carbs; 30g Protein; 3.9g Sugars

Ingredients
1 tablespoon butter, at room temperature
1 pound chicken, ground
1/2 cup scallions, chopped
1/2 teaspoon chili powder
1/2 teaspoon sea salt
1/3 teaspoon paprika
1/4 teaspoon shallot powder
1/3 teaspoon ground cumin
6 ounces goat cheese, crumbled
5 bell peppers, tops, membrane and seeds removed
1/2 cup sour cream

Directions
Press the "Sauté" button to heat up the Instant Pot. Melt the butter.
Once hot, cook the chicken and scallions for 2 to 3 minutes. Add chili powder, salt, paprika, shallot powder, and cumin; stir to combine. Now, add crumbled goat cheese, stir, and reserve.
Then, clean your Instant Pot and add 1 ½ cups of water and a metal trivet to the bottom of the inner pot.
Fill bell peppers with enough of the meat/scallion mixture; don't pack the peppers too tightly.
Place the peppers on the trivet and secure the lid. Choose "Poultry" mode and High pressure; cook for 15 minutes.
Once cooking is complete, use a natural pressure release; carefully remove the lid. Serve with a dollop of sour cream and enjoy!

43. Two-Cheese Turkey Bake

(Ready in about 30 minutes | Servings 8)

Here's the perfect ketogenic dinner! Turkey breasts go wonderfully with full-fat dairy products and mayonnaise.

Per serving: 472 Calories; 33g Fat; 3.2g Carbs; 38.9g Protein; 0.7g Sugars

Ingredients
2 pounds turkey breasts
2 garlic cloves, halved
Sea salt and ground black pepper, to taste
1 teaspoon paprika
1 tablespoon butter
10 slices Colby cheese, shredded
2/3 cup mayonnaise
1/3 cup sour cream
1 cup Romano cheese, preferably freshly grated

Directions
Rub the turkey breast with garlic halves; now, sprinkle with salt, black pepper, and paprika.
Press the "Sauté" button to heat up the Instant Pot. Melt the butter and sear the turkey breast for 2 to 3 minutes per side.
In a mixing bowl, combine shredded Colby cheese, mayonnaise, sour cream, 1/2 cup of grated Romano. Spread this mixture over turkey breast; top with the remaining Romano cheese.
Secure the lid. Choose "Manual" mode and High pressure; cook for 20 minutes. Once cooking is complete, use a quick pressure release; carefully remove the lid. Bon appétit!

44. Creamy Cauliflower and Chicken Soup

(Ready in about 15 minutes | Servings 4)

Nothing beats a hearty chicken soup on a winter's night. A fresh flavor of cauliflower and leeks will brighten the entire dish.
Per serving: 201 Calories; 14.1g Fat; 9.4g Carbs; 9g Protein; 4g Sugars
Ingredients
1 ½ tablespoons olive oil
4 chicken thighs
1 leek, chopped
1 teaspoon garlic, minced
1/2 pound cauliflower, broken into small florets
1 tablespoon sage, chopped
4 cups chicken broth
3 ounces mild blue cheese, crumbled
1/2 cup double cream
Directions
Press the "Sauté" button to heat up the Instant Pot. Heat the olive oil and brown chicken thigs for 2 to 3 minutes per side; reserve.
Now, cook leeks and garlic in pan drippings until softened.
Add the cauliflower, sage, and broth to the Instant Pot.
Secure the lid. Choose "Manual" mode and High pressure; cook for 6 minutes. Once cooking is complete, use a natural pressure release; carefully remove the lid.
Shred the chicken meat and discard the bones. Return the chicken meat to the Instant Pot.
Add blue cheese and double cream to the cooking liquid and continue to stir in the residual heat.
Ladle into individual bowls and serve immediately. Bon appétit!

45. Easy One-Pot Mexican Chili
(Ready in about 35 minutes | Servings 6)
This ground turkey dish might earn a permanent spot in your keto meal plan. Mexican cheese blend is a perfect addition to this surprisingly delicious chili.
Per serving: 391 Calories; 27g Fat; 8.1g Carbs; 28.4g Protein; 4.9g Sugars
Ingredients
1 tablespoon olive oil
1 pound turkey, ground
1/2 pound pork, ground
1 onion, finely chopped
2 garlic cloves, minced
2 ripe tomatoes, pureed
1 Mexican chili pepper, minced
1/2 teaspoon ground cumin
1 teaspoon red pepper flakes
Salt and ground black pepper, to taste
1 cup chicken stock
1 ½ cups Mexican cheese blend
Directions
Press the "Sauté" button to heat up the Instant Pot. Heat the olive oil and brown the turkey and pork until no longer pink or about 3 minutes.
Add the remaining ingredients, except for Mexican cheese blend, to your Instant Pot.

Secure the lid. Choose "Poultry" mode and High pressure; cook for 15 minutes. Once cooking is complete, use a natural pressure release; carefully remove the lid.
Ladle into soup bowls; top each bowl with Mexican cheese blend and serve hot.

46. Asian-Style Turkey Meatballs
(Ready in about 15 minutes | Servings 6)
Make a big batch of these meatballs to keep on hand for any occasion. You can easily freeze and reheat these meatballs; they will still be delicious and moist inside.
Per serving: 590 Calories; 50.7g Fat; 5g Carbs; 29.2g Protein; 2.4g Sugars
Ingredients
1 pound ground turkey
1/2 pound ground pork
1/2 cup Parmesan cheese, grated
2 eggs, whisked
1/2 cup green onions
2 cloves garlic, minced
1/2 teaspoon grated ginger
2 tablespoons Shaoxing wine
2 tablespoons dark soy sauce
Sea salt and ground black pepper, to taste
2 tablespoons sesame oil
1 cup tomato sauce
Directions
In a mixing dish, thoroughly combine ground turkey, pork, Parmesan cheese, eggs, green onions, garlic, ginger, Shaoxing wine, dark soy sauce, salt, and black pepper; mix until everything is well incorporated.
Press the "Sauté" button and heat the sesame oil. Sear the meatballs for a couple of minutes or until browned on all sides. Add tomato sauce.
Secure the lid. Choose the "Manual" setting and cook for 10 minutes under High pressure. Once cooking is complete, use a quick pressure release; carefully remove the lid.
Serve your meatballs with the sauce. Bon appétit!

47. Turkey Breasts with Homemade Pesto
(Ready in about 25 minutes | Servings 6)
There are so many ways to cook turkey breasts. Pressure cooking is one of the easiest and healthiest ways to do that. Serve with a homemade pesto sauce and enjoy!
Per serving: 391 Calories; 26.3g Fat; 1.8g Carbs; 34.9g Protein; 0.4g Sugars
Ingredients
2 pounds turkey breast
Sea salt and ground black pepper, to taste
1 teaspoon paprika
1 tablespoon olive oil
1 cup water
Pesto Sauce:
2 tablespoons pine nuts, toasted
1/2 cup fresh basil leaves

1/3 cup Parmesan cheese, grated
1/3 cup olive oil
1 garlic clove, halved
Salt and ground black pepper, to taste
Directions
Season turkey breast with salt, black pepper, and paprika.
Press the "Sauté" button to heat up the Instant Pot. Heat 1 tablespoon of olive oil and sear the turkey breast for 2 to 3 minutes per side.
Pour in the water and secure the lid. Choose "Poultry" mode and High pressure; cook for 20 minutes. Once cooking is complete, use a quick pressure release; carefully remove the lid.
To make the pesto sauce, add the pine nuts and fresh basil leaves to your food processor.
Add the remaining ingredients and process until everything is well incorporated. Serve the prepared turkey breast with pesto sauce. Bon appétit!

48. Chinese Meatball Soup
(Ready in about 20 minutes | Servings 6)
Chinese cabbage can help you regulate blood pressure and keep your eyes healthy. It is an excellent source of antioxidants, vitamins, and minerals. You can add a pinch of Sichuan peppercorns if desired.
Per serving: 375 Calories; 24.1g Fat; 7.8g Carbs; 31.1g Protein; 3.3g Sugars
Ingredients
Meatballs:
1 pound ground chicken
1/2 pound ground pork
1/4 cup fresh cilantro, chopped
2 tablespoons scallions, finely chopped
1 teaspoon garlic powder
1/2 Chinese Five-spice powder
1/2 teaspoon grated ginger
1 tablespoon soy sauce
Sea salt, to taste
1/2 teaspoon ground black pepper
1/2 teaspoon red pepper flakes, crushed
1 egg, well-beaten
Soup:
1 tablespoon olive oil
1 teaspoon dried rosemary
1 teaspoon dried thyme
1 tablespoon fresh dill, chopped
1/2 teaspoon cumin
1/2 cup tomato puree, sugar-free
2 celery stalks, chopped
1 ½ cups Chinese cabbage, chopped
6 cups chicken bone broth, preferably homemade
Directions
In a mixing bowl, combine all ingredients for the meatballs. Shape the meat mixture into balls; set aside.
Press the "Sauté" button to heat up the Instant Pot. Heat the olive oil and sear the meatballs on all sides until crisp and browned.
Stir in the remaining ingredients.
Secure the lid. Choose the "Poultry" setting and cook for 15 minutes under High pressure. Once cooking is complete, use a quick pressure release; carefully remove the lid. Bon appétit!

49. Holiday Chicken Wrapped in Prosciutto
(Ready in about 20 minutes | Servings 5)
These fatty wraps go perfectly with pickles or fresh vegetable salad. They are so delicious that you won't miss any bread or tortilla.
Per serving: 548 Calories; 28.4g Fat; 1.1g Carbs; 68.3g Protein; 0g Sugars
Ingredients
5 chicken breast halves, butterflied
2 garlic cloves, halved
Sea salt, to taste
1/4 teaspoon ground black pepper, or more to taste
1/2 teaspoon red pepper flakes
1 teaspoon marjoram
10 strips prosciutto
Directions
Prepare the Instant Pot by adding 1 ½ cups of water and metal trivet to the bottom.
Rub chicken breast halves with garlic. Then, season the chicken with salt, black pepper, red pepper, and marjoram.
Then, wrap each chicken breast into 2 prosciutto strips; secure with toothpicks. Arrange wrapped chicken on the metal trivet.
Secure the lid. Choose the "Poultry" setting and cook for 15 minutes under High pressure. Once cooking is complete, use a natural pressure release; carefully remove the lid. Bon appétit!

50. Thanksgiving Turkey with Mushroom Gravy
(Ready in about 30 minutes | Servings 6)
Here's a delicious and sophisticated Thanksgiving recipe. However, you'll be making this super yummy turkey dish on repeat all year long.
Per serving: 280 Calories; 12.8g Fat; 4.9g Carbs; 35.2g Protein; 1.9g Sugars
Ingredients
2 pounds turkey breast, boneless and skinless
Seasoned salt and ground black pepper, to taste
1/2 teaspoon smoked paprika
1/4 teaspoon mustard powder
1 head cauliflower, broken into small florets
1 cup scallions, chopped
2 cloves garlic, crushed
1 celery with leaves, chopped
1 bay leaf
1 ½ cups water
1 tablespoon butter
6 ounces Cremini mushrooms, chopped
Directions
Spritz your Instant Pot with a nonstick cooking spray.

Place turkey breasts on the bottom of the Instant Pot. Season them with salt, black pepper, paprika, and mustard powder.
Top with cauliflower, scallions, garlic, and celery. Afterwards, add bay leaf and water.
Secure the lid. Choose the "Poultry" setting and cook for 20 minutes under High pressure. Once cooking is complete, use a natural pressure release; carefully remove the lid.

Remove the turkey from the Instant Pot. Transfer the cooking liquid along with vegetables to your food processor; puree until silky and smooth.
Press the "Sauté" button and melt the butter. Sauté the mushrooms until fragrant, approximately 4 minutes.
Stir in pureed vegetables and continue to cook until the sauce is thickened. Spoon mushroom gravy over turkey breasts. Bon appétit!

PORK

51. Barbecue Spare Ribs

(Ready in about 35 minutes | Servings 8)

Pork ribs are one of the favorite main dishes that cook perfectly in the Instant Pot. Spare ribs and barbecue sauce combine very well so this family dish is attractive in appearance too.

Per serving: 444 Calories; 33g Fat; 4.4g Carbs; 32.5g Protein; 1.7g Sugars

Ingredients
3 pounds spare ribs
Sea salt and ground black pepper, to taste
1/2 teaspoon granulated garlic
1 teaspoon cayenne pepper
For the sauce:
3/4 cup tomato puree
A few drops of stevia
1 tablespoon balsamic vinegar
1/3 cup broth
1 cup water
1/3 teaspoon liquid smoke
1/2 teaspoon ground cloves

Directions
Season the ribs with salt, black pepper, garlic, and cayenne pepper.
Add the spare ribs to the Instant Pot.
Combine the ingredients for the sauce; whisk until everything is well mixed. Pour this sauce mixture over the spare ribs.
Secure the lid. Choose the "Meat/Stew" setting and cook for 30 minutes under High pressure. Once cooking is complete, use a natural pressure release; carefully remove the lid.
You can thicken the cooking liquid with a tablespoon or two of flaxseed meal if desired. Enjoy!

52. Hungarian-Style Pork Goulash Soup

(Ready in about 30 minutes | Servings 6)

An Instant Pot inspires us in so many ways! In this soup recipe, pork shoulder is seared in hot lard and then, cooked with aromatics and vegetables.

Per serving: 434 Calories; 28.5g Fat; 3.8g Carbs; 38.5g Protein; 1.2g Sugars

Ingredients
2 teaspoons lard, at room temperature
2 pounds pork shoulder, cubed
Kosher salt, to taste
1/3 teaspoon ground black pepper, or more to taste
1 celery with leaves, chopped
1/2 cup leeks, thinly sliced
1 teaspoon garlic, minced
1 sprig rosemary
1 sprig thyme
1 tablespoon Hungarian sweet paprika
1 tablespoon Hungarian hot paprika
3 tablespoons tomato puree
1/2 teaspoon cumin powder
1 cup chicken bone broth
1/4 cup fresh cilantro, for garnish

Directions
Press the "Sauté" button to heat up the Instant Pot. Now, melt 1 teaspoon of lard and sear the pork for 2 to 3 minutes or until it is no longer pink; season with salt and black pepper; reserve.
Next, melt the remaining teaspoon of lard; cook the celery and leeks until softened. After that, cook the garlic, rosemary and thyme until aromatic or 1 minute more.
Add paprika, tomato puree, cumin powder, and chicken bone broth.
Secure the lid. Choose the "Manual" setting and cook for 20 minutes under Low pressure. Once cooking is complete, use a quick pressure release; carefully remove the lid.
Ladle into soup bowls and serve garnished with fresh cilantro. Bon appétit!

53. Family Pork Roast

(Ready in about 30 minutes | Servings 6)

Here is a classic family recipe that you can prepare for any occasion! Use a food thermometer to check pork roast for doneness. Pork roast should be cooked between 145 and 160 degrees F

Per serving: 329 Calories; 18.2g Fat; 0g Carbs; 38.7g Protein; 0g Sugars

Ingredients
2 teaspoons peanut oil
2 pounds pork tenderloin
1 cup beef bone broth
2 bay leaves
1 teaspoon mixed peppercorns

Directions
Massage the peanut oil into the pork.
Press the "Sauté" button to heat up the Instant Pot. Heat the oil and sear the meat for 2 to 3 minute on both sides.
Add the broth, bay leaves and mixed peppercorns to the Instant Pot.
Secure the lid. Choose the "Meat/Stew" setting and cook for 20 minutes under High pressure. Once cooking is complete, use a natural pressure release; carefully remove the lid.
Serve over cauli rice. Bon appétit!

54. The Best Pork Chile Verde

(Ready in about 25 minutes | Servings 6)

As the name implies, this pork recipe is all about the chilies. You can use mild green chilies like Anaheim or Hatch.

Per serving: 358 Calories; 19.2g Fat; 4.5g Carbs; 39.7g Protein; 2.1g Sugars

Ingredients
1 tablespoon olive oil
2 pounds Boston butt, trimmed, cut into cubes
2 tomatoes, diced

1 cup water
1/2 cup mild green chilies, roasted, seeded and diced
1 red bell pepper, seeded and chopped
1/2 cup green onions, chopped
3 cloves garlic, peeled and halved
1 teaspoon cumin, ground
1 teaspoon dried Mexican oregano
Kosher salt and ground black pepper, to taste
1 teaspoon red pepper flakes
2 tablespoons fresh cilantro leaves, chopped
Directions
Press the "Sauté" button to heat up the Instant Pot. Heat the oil until sizzling. Then, sear Boston butt for 2 to 4 minutes, stirring frequently.
Add the other ingredients, except for cilantro leaves.
Secure the lid. Choose the "Meat/Stew" setting and cook for 20 minutes under High pressure. Once cooking is complete, use a natural pressure release; carefully remove the lid; reserve the pork.
Add cilantro to the cooking liquid. Blitz the mixture in your food processor until creamy and uniform.
Return the pork to the Instant Pot.
Ladle into individual bowls and serve immediately. Bon appétit!

55. Pork Meatballs alla Parmigiana
(Ready in about 15 minutes | Servings 6)
Just to be sure, make your own ketogenic tomato sauce without sugar. The key to a good homemade sauce is to find the best quality tomatoes. Everything else is easy. Add good aromatics and puree them in your food processor. Ta-da!
Per serving: 356 Calories; 17.2g Fat; 5.6g Carbs; 44.7g Protein; 1.5g Sugars
Ingredients
2 pounds lean ground pork
1 teaspoon red pepper flakes, crushed
1 cup grated parmesan cheese
1/4 cup pork rinds, crushed
1 egg
1 teaspoon garlic paste
2 tablespoons scallions, chopped
Seasoned salt and ground black pepper, to taste
1 teaspoon shallot powder
1/2 teaspoon dried basil
1/2 teaspoon dried sage, crushed
1/4 cup beef bone broth
1 tablespoon sesame oil
2 cups keto tomato sauce
4 ounces mozzarella cheese, slices
Directions
In a mixing bowl, thoroughly combine ground pork, red pepper, parmesan cheese, pork rinds, egg, garlic paste, scallions, aromatics, and beef bone broth.
Mix to combine well. Now, shape the mixture into 2-inch meatballs.
Press the "Sauté" button to heat up the Instant Pot. Heat the oil until sizzling. Now, sear the meatballs until delicately browned.
Pour the tomato sauce over the meatballs.
Secure the lid. Choose the "Manual" setting and cook for 8 minutes under High pressure. Once cooking is complete, use a quick pressure release; carefully remove the lid.
Afterwards, top the meatballs with mozzarella slices and broil them until mozzarella is golden. Bon appétit!

56. Five-Star Zoddles Bolognese
(Ready in about 15 minutes | Servings 4)
Try this refreshing, chunky pasta sauce with pressure cooked pork, zucchini noodles and tons of flavor! You can also bake or microwave your zoodles, but raw zoodles are packed with enzymes and flavors.
Per serving: 356 Calories; 17.2g Fat; 5.6g Carbs; 44.7g Protein; 1.5g Sugars
Ingredients
1 teaspoon canola oil
1 pound pork, ground
2 garlic cloves, minced
1 teaspoon dried basil
1 teaspoon dried oregano
1/2 teaspoon fresh thyme
2 tomatoes, puréed
1 cup water
2 zucchini, julienned
1/4 cup Parmesan cheese, preferably freshly grated
Directions
Press the "Sauté" button to heat up the Instant Pot. Heat the oil until sizzling. Brown the ground pork for 2 to 3 minutes, crumbling with a fork.
Add the garlic and cook an additional minute. Add dried basil, oregano, and thyme; cook for 30 seconds more or until fragrant. Add pureed tomatoes and water.
Secure the lid. Choose the "Manual" setting and cook for 5 minutes under High pressure. Once cooking is complete, use a natural pressure release; carefully remove the lid.
Spoon Bolognese sauce over fresh zucchini noodles. Top with freshly grated Parmesan cheese and serve. Enjoy!

57. Tender Pulled Pork
(Ready in about 55 minutes | Servings 6)
So tender, so flavorful, pulled pork is an ultimate comfort food. It has never been easier to prepare this pork dish.
Per serving: 434 Calories; 29.1g Fat; 1.5g Carbs; 38.6g Protein; 0.4g Sugars
Ingredients
2 pounds pork butt
Celery salt and ground black pepper, to your liking
1 tablespoon lard
4 cloves garlic, smashed
1/2 teaspoon caraway seeds
1/2 teaspoon mustard seeds
1 bay leaf
1 cup beef bone broth
1 tablespoon chile powder

1 teaspoon cayenne pepper
1/2 teaspoon hot Hungarian paprika
1/2 teaspoon onion powder
Directions
Season the pork butt with salt and ground black pepper.
Press the "Sauté" button to heat up the Instant Pot. Melt the lard and brown the pork on all sides.
Add the remaining ingredients.
Secure the lid. Choose the "Manual" setting and cook for 50 minutes under High pressure. Once cooking is complete, use a natural pressure release; carefully remove the lid.
Shred the meat with two forks and serve with keto bread rolls. Bon appétit!

58. Sausages with Cremini Mushrooms

(Ready in about 10 minutes | Servings 8)
Need a last-minute dinner for a family gathering? Serve pork sausages cooked with delicate Cremini mushrooms, tomato, and spices.
Per serving: 410 Calories; 36.2g Fat; 2.5g Carbs; 17.3g Protein; 0.9g Sugars
Ingredients
8 pork sausages, casing removed
1 cup Cremini mushrooms, chopped
2 garlic cloves, minced
1/2 yellow onion, chopped
1 ripe tomato, chopped
1 cup broth, preferably homemade
1/2 teaspoon dried basil
1/2 teaspoon dried oregano
1/2 teaspoon dried rosemary
Directions
Add all ingredients to your Instant Pot in the order listed above.
Secure the lid. Choose the "Manual" setting and cook for 8 minutes under High pressure. Once cooking is complete, use a quick pressure release; carefully remove the lid.
Serve over cauli rice and enjoy!

59. Sloppy Joes with Homemade Oopsies

(Ready in about 35 minutes | Servings 4)
Here's a fantastic way to get the taste of restaurant-style Sloppy Joes without extra carbs! In this recipe, you will learn how to make homemade Oopsie bread too.
Per serving: 524 Calories; 45g Fat; 5.5g Carbs; 27.8g Protein; 1.9g Sugars
Ingredients
Sloppy Joes
1 tablespoon olive oil
1 pound lean ground pork
1/2 yellow onion, chopped
2 cloves garlic, minced
1 tomato, puréed
1 teaspoon stone ground mustard
1 tablespoon coconut aminos
1 cup roasted vegetable broth
Sea salt and ground black pepper, to taste
Oopsies:
2 eggs, separated yolks and whites
1/4 teaspoon sea salt
3 ounces cream cheese
1/4 teaspoon baking powder
Directions
Press the "Sauté" button to heat up the Instant Pot. Heat the oil until sizzling. Brown the ground pork for 2 to 3 minutes, crumbling with a fork.
Add the other ingredients for Sloppy Joes and stir to combine well.
Secure the lid. Choose the "Manual" setting and cook for 5 minutes under High pressure. Once cooking is complete, use a quick pressure release; carefully remove the lid.
To make your oopsies, beat the egg whites together with salt until very firm peaks form.
In another bowl, thoroughly combine the egg yolks with cream cheese. Now, add the baking powder and stir well.
Next, fold the egg white mixture into the egg yolk mixture. Divide the mixture into 6 oopsies and transfer them to a silicon sheet.
Bake in the preheated oven at 290 degrees F for about 23 minutes. Serve Sloppy Joes between 2 oopsies and enjoy!

60. Traditional Keema with Cauliflower

(Ready in about 15 minutes | Servings 6)
Who said "Rich and Spicy"? This ground pork Indian-inspired dish is sure to please! Keema is a traditional dish with ground meat, potatoes and peas. We will add the cauliflower to make it low-carb and keto-friendly. Enjoy!
Per serving: 389 Calories; 29g Fat; 5.1g Carbs; 30.4g Protein; 2.5g Sugars
Ingredients
1 tablespoon sesame oil
1/2 cup yellow onion, chopped
2 garlic cloves, minced
1 (1-inch) piece fresh ginger, minced
1 jalapeño pepper, seeded and minced
1/2 teaspoon hot paprika
Sea salt and ground black pepper, to taste
1/4 teaspoon turmeric powder
1/2 teaspoon ground cumin
4 cloves, whole
1 teaspoon brown mustard seeds
1 teaspoon garam masala
1 ½ pounds ground pork
1 cup cauliflower, chopped into small florets
2 ripe tomatoes, puréed
1 cup water
Directions

Press the "Sauté" button to heat up the Instant Pot. Heat the sesame oil. Once hot, sauté yellow onion for 2 to 3 minutes or until softened and aromatic.
Then, stir in garlic and ginger; cook an additional minute. Add the remaining ingredients.
Secure the lid. Choose the "Manual" setting and cook for 5 minutes under High pressure. Once cooking is complete, use a quick pressure release; carefully remove the lid.
Afterwards, you can thicken the cooking liquid on "Sauté" setting, if desired. Serve in individual bowls. Bon appétit!

61. Za'atar-Rubbed Pork Shank

(Ready in about 45 minutes | Servings 6)
This Middle Eastern-inspired pork dish is elegant and sophisticated but so fun and easy to prepare. In addition, pork shanks are a cinch to make in the Instant Pot.
Per serving: 328 Calories; 18.1g Fat; 9g Carbs; 30.6g Protein; 2.6g Sugars
Ingredients
1 ½ pounds pork shank
Seasoned salt and ground black pepper, to taste
2 tablespoons za'atar
1 tablespoon olive oil
1 medium-sized leek, sliced
2 garlic cloves, smashed
1 carrot, chopped
1 parsnip, chopped
1 celery with leaves, chopped
1 tablespoon dark soy sauce
1/2 teaspoon mustard powder
1 cup beef bone broth
1 tablespoon flaxseed meal
Directions
Generously season the pork shank with salt and black pepper. Now, sprinkle with za'atar on all sides. Press the "Sauté" button to heat up the Instant Pot. Heat the olive oil. Once hot, sear the pork shank for 2 to 4 minute per side; reserve.
Now, sauté leeks in pan drippings for 3 minutes. After that, add the garlic, carrot parsnip, celery with leaves, soy sauce, mustard powder, and broth.
Add the pork shank back to the Instant Pot.
Secure the lid. Choose the "Meat/Stew" setting and cook for 35 minutes under High pressure. Once cooking is complete, use a natural pressure release; carefully remove the lid.
Mix flaxseed meal with 1 tablespoon of water. Add this slurry to the Instant Pot. Press the "Sauté" button again to thicken the cooking liquid. Serve warm.

62. Pork Belly Cooked in Milk

(Ready in about 50 minutes | Servings 8)
Try this succulent pork dish that is just as good with a family dinner, as it is served on holidays.
Per serving: 596 Calories; 60g Fat; 1.2g Carbs; 11.1g Protein; 0.8g Sugars
Ingredients
2 pounds pork belly, skin scored
Seasoned salt and ground black pepper, to taste
1 teaspoon cayenne pepper
1 teaspoon oyster sauce
1 teaspoon hot sauce
1/3 cup full-fat milk
1 cup water
Directions
Season the pork with salt, black pepper, and cayenne pepper. Add the remaining ingredients.
Secure the lid. Choose the "Soup/Broth" setting and cook for 40 minutes under High pressure. Once cooking is complete, use a natural pressure release; carefully remove the lid.
Then, strain cooking liquid into a saucepan. Bring to the boil over high heat. Cook, stirring occasionally, for 7 to 9 minutes or until sauce reduces.
Lastly, cut the pork into thick slices and serve accompanied with the milk sauce. Bon appétit!

63. Greek-Style Pork Stew

(Ready in about 15 minutes | Servings 8)
If you are a great believer in a tradition of family dinner, this is the right recipe for you. In this recipe, choosing a good quality pork is half way to success.
Per serving: 249 Calories; 10.1g Fat; 5.1g Carbs; 31.2g Protein; 2.7g Sugars
Ingredients
1 tablespoon olive oil
2 ½ pounds pork stew meat, cubed
1 red onion, chopped
4 cloves garlic, peeled
1 bell pepper, chopped
2 tablespoons Greek red wine
1 cup beef bone broth
1 star anise
Coarse sea salt and ground black pepper, to taste
1 teaspoon dried basil
1 teaspoon dried oregano
1/2 teaspoon dried dill weed
1 (14.5-ounce) can diced tomatoes
2 tablespoons fresh basil leaves, snipped
Directions
Press the "Sauté" button to heat up the Instant Pot. Heat the olive oil and sauté the meat until browned; reserve.
Then, in pan drippings, cook the onion, garlic, and bell pepper until softened. Add red wine to deglaze the pan.
Add beef bone broth, star anise, sea salt, black pepper, dried basil, oregano, dill and canned tomatoes.
Secure the lid. Choose the "Manual" setting and cook for 10 minutes under High pressure. Once cooking is complete, use a quick pressure release; carefully remove the lid.
Ladle into individual bowls and serve garnished with fresh basil leaves. Bon appétit!

64. Malaysian Bak-Kut-The Soup

(Ready in about 25 minutes | Servings 5)

Bak-kut-the is a popular pork dish that can be found in Malaysian cuisine. Chenpi is actually sun-dried mandarin peel that is used as a traditional seasoning and medicine.

Per serving: 316 Calories; 18.1g Fat; 4.3g Carbs; 34.3g Protein; 1.6g Sugars

Ingredients

2 tablespoons sesame oil
1 ½ pounds spare ribs, boneless and cubed
1 shallot, chopped
1 celery stalk, chopped
2 garlic cloves, minced
1 thin slice ginger
1 small piece chenpi
1/2 teaspoon fennel seeds
1/2 teaspoon cloves, whole
5 cups roasted vegetable broth
1 tablespoon light soy sauce
1 ½ cups cauliflower, chopped
1/4 teaspoon black pepper
1/2 teaspoon cayenne pepper
Seasoned salt, to taste

Directions

Press the "Sauté" button to heat up the Instant Pot. Heat the sesame oil and cook the ribs until no longer pink; reserve.
Add the shallot and celery; sauté the vegetables, adding a splash of broth, until softened.
Now, sauté garlic and ginger for 30 to 40 seconds or until aromatic. After that, stir in the other ingredients; stir to combine.
Secure the lid. Choose the "Soup/Broth" setting and cook for 20 minutes under High pressure. Once cooking is complete, use a natural pressure release; carefully remove the lid. Bon appétit!

65. Pork Cutlets with Porcini Mushroom Sauce

(Ready in about 15 minutes | Servings 4)

Two words – pork cutlets! You can experiment with this recipe and add another combo of seasonings.

Per serving: 412 Calories; 25.4g Fat; 2.1g Carbs; 41.5g Protein; 0.8g Sugars

Ingredients

2 teaspoons olive oil
4 pork cutlets
Seasoned salt to taste
1/2 teaspoon ground black pepper
1/2 teaspoon cayenne pepper
1/2 cup scallions, chopped
1 cup Porcini mushrooms, thinly sliced
1 teaspoon roasted garlic paste
1 bay leaf
1 cup broth, preferably homemade
1 tablespoon arrowroot powder + 1 tablespoon water
1/2 cup heavy cream

Directions

Press the "Sauté" button to heat up the Instant Pot; add olive oil.
Now, sear the pork cutlets until delicately browned on both sides. Season with salt, black pepper, and cayenne pepper.
Then, add the scallions, mushrooms, garlic paste, bay leaf, and broth to the Instant Pot.
Secure the lid. Choose the "Manual" setting and cook for 10 minutes under High pressure. Once cooking is complete, use a quick pressure release; carefully remove the lid.
Now, whisk the arrowroot powder with 1 tablespoon of water in a small mixing bowl. Ad this slurry along with heavy cream to the cooking liquid.
Press the "Sauté" button again to thicken the cooking liquid. Serve this sauce over pork cutlets.

66. Pork Loin Sliders

(Ready in about 20 minutes | Servings 6)

Keto sliders are easy to prepare and fun to eat! You just have to swap whole-wheat burger buns with keto bread rolls.

Per serving: 357 Calories; 17.4g Fat; 2.7g Carbs; 44.7g Protein; 1.1g Sugars

Ingredients

2 teaspoons canola oil
2 pounds pork tenderloins, trimmed
Sea salt and freshly ground pepper
1/2 teaspoon cayenne pepper
1/2 cup leek, thinly sliced
2 garlic cloves, finely chopped
1/2 cup broth, preferably homemade
1 cup water
2 sprigs thyme
1/2 teaspoon ground bay leaf
6 Oopsie bread rolls
6 leaves Iceberg lettuce
4 tablespoons mayonnaise

Directions

Press the "Sauté" button to heat up the Instant Pot; add canola oil.
Sear the pork until browned on all sides. Season with salt, black pepper, and cayenne pepper. Add the leeks, garlic, broth, water, thyme, and ground bay leaf.
Secure the lid. Choose the "Manual" setting and cook for 12 minutes under High pressure. Once cooking is complete, use a natural pressure release; carefully remove the lid.
Serve over oopsie bread rolls, garnished with lettuce and mayo!

67. Pork Roast with Avocado and Garlic Mayo

(Ready in about 35 minutes | Servings 6)

If you are looking for the best and quickest way to grill pork roast, look no further. Use your Instant Pot and watch how the magic happens.

Per serving: 390 Calories; 22.4g Fat; 3g Carbs; 42.1g Protein; 0.7g Sugars

Ingredients

Pork Roast:
1 tablespoon lard, melted
2 pounds pork roast
1 cup chicken stock
1/2 cup shallots, chopped
1 celery rib, chopped
1 tablespoon fish sauce
1 tablespoon coconut aminos
1/4 teaspoon ground black pepper
Sea salt, to your liking
Avocado and Garlic Mayo:
1/3 cup mayonnaise
1/2 avocado, pitted and peeled
2 garlic cloves, pressed
1 teaspoon lemon juice
Directions
Press the "Sauté" button to heat up the Instant Pot. Melt the lard and brown pork roast for 2 to 4 minutes. Now, add the pork roast, chicken stock, shallots, celery, fish, sauce, coconut aminos, black pepper, and sea salt to the Instant Pot.
Secure the lid. Choose the "Manual" setting and cook for 30 minutes under High pressure. Once cooking is complete, use a natural pressure release; carefully remove the lid.
In the meantime, mix all ingredients for the mayonnaise in your food processor or blender. Cut pork roast into slices and serve with Avocado and Garlic Mayo on the side. Bon appétit!

68. Pork Chops with Winter Squash Salad

(Ready in about 35 minutes | Servings 6)
Buttery chops with a refreshing winter squash salad might become your new favorite! The end result is an amazing bowl of comfort food.
Per serving: 481 Calories; 29g Fat; 9g Carbs; 29g Protein; 5.2g Sugars
Ingredients
4 pork chops
2 tablespoons grapeseed oil
1/2 teaspoon sea salt
1/4 teaspoon ground black pepper
1/2 teaspoon paprika
1/2 teaspoon garlic powder
1 teaspoon shallot powder
1 teaspoon dried parsley flakes
1 cup water
1 cup winter squash, diced
1 head Iceberg lettuce
1 cucumber, sliced
3 ounces feta cheese, crumbled
Directions
Press the "Sauté" button to heat up the Instant Pot. Heat 1 tablespoon of the grapeseed oil and brown pork chops for 2 minutes per side.
Add the salt, black pepper, paprika, garlic powder, shallot powder, parsley flakes, and water.
Secure the lid. Choose the "Manual" setting and cook for 8 minutes under High pressure. Once cooking is complete, use a quick pressure release; carefully remove the lid.
Meanwhile, preheat your oven to 390 degrees F. Toss winter squash with remaining 1 tablespoon oil; now, bake for 18 minutes on a lightly greased cookie sheet. Allow it to cool completely.
Add cooked squash to a salad bowl; toss with Iceberg lettuce and cucumber.
Mound the salad onto each serving plate. Scatter crumbled feta cheese over the top. Top with pork chops and enjoy.

69. Pork Loin with Goat-Cheese Sauce

(Ready in about 20 minutes | Servings 6)
Pork loin in a creamy sauce with two kinds of cheese! This pork dish will be gone as soon as it hits the table!
Per serving: 449 Calories; 27.5g Fat; 4.5g Carbs; 43.8g Protein; 2.3g Sugars
Ingredients
1 tablespoon grapeseed oil
2 pounds pork loin, sliced
2 garlic cloves, pressed
1 red onion, chopped
1 bell pepper, chopped
1 jalapeño pepper, finely chopped
1/2 cup vegetable stock
1/2 cup double cream
2 ounces Ricotta cheese
1/2 cup goat cheese
1/2 teaspoon dried basil
1/2 teaspoon dried marjoram
1/2 teaspoon celery seeds
1/3 teaspoon pepper
Sea salt, to your liking
Directions
Press the "Sauté" button to heat up the Instant Pot. Heat the oil until sizzling. Now, sear the pork loin until slightly browned on both sides, approximately 3 minutes.
Add the garlic, onion, pepper, and vegetable stock to the Instant Pot.
Secure the lid. Choose the "Manual" setting and cook for 12 minutes under High pressure. Once cooking is complete, use a natural pressure release; carefully remove the lid.
Next, add the remaining ingredients and let it cook in the residual heat or until cheese is melted.
Add pork chops back to the cheese sauce and serve. Bon appétit!

70. Tender Pork Cutlets in Mustard Sauce

(Ready in about 20 minutes | Servings 6)
Mmm, smells good! Pork cutlets are seasoned with aromatics and seared in hot olive oil. Then, they are pressure cooked to perfection. Afterwards, these pork cutlets are dipped into a fantastic cheesy mustard sauce.

Per serving: 497 Calories; 34.3g Fat; 1.6g Carbs; 43.6g Protein; 1.1g Sugars
Ingredients
6 pork cutlets
1/2 teaspoon dried marjoram
1/2 teaspoon dried rosemary
1/4 teaspoon cayenne pepper
1/4 teaspoon paprika
Kosher salt and ground black pepper, to taste
2 tablespoons olive oil
1/2 cup vegetable broth
1/2 cup water
1 tablespoon butter
1 tablespoon yellow mustard
1 cup heavy cream
1/2 cup cheddar cheese, shredded
Directions
Sprinkle pork cutlets with marjoram, rosemary, cayenne pepper, paprika, salt, and black pepper.
Press the "Sauté" button to heat up the Instant Pot. Heat the olive oil until sizzling. Now, sear pork loin until slightly browned on both sides, approximately 3 minutes.
Add vegetable broth and water; secure the lid. Choose the "Manual" setting and cook for 8 minutes under High pressure.
Once cooking is complete, use a quick pressure release; carefully remove the lid and reserve pork cutlets.
Press the "Sauté" button again. Melt the butter and add the mustard, heavy cream, and cheese; cook for a couple of minutes more or until everything is cooked through.
Add the reserved pork cutlets to the sauce and serve. Bon appétit!

71. Easy Curried Pork Steak
(Ready in about 15 minutes | Servings 6)
This pork curry can be on the table in less than 15 minutes. The recipe works well with pork cutlets or tenderloin too.
Per serving: 362 Calories; 25.2g Fat; 2.2g Carbs; 29.6g Protein; 0.9g Sugars
Ingredients
1/2 teaspoon mustard seeds
1 teaspoon fennel seeds
1 teaspoon cumin seeds
2 chili peppers, seeded and minced
1/2 teaspoon ground bay leaf
1 teaspoon mixed peppercorns
1 tablespoon sesame oil
1 ½ pounds pork steak, sliced
1 cup chicken broth
2 tablespoons scallions, chopped
2 cloves garlic, finely minced
1 teaspoon fresh ginger, grated
1 teaspoon curry powder
2 tablespoons balsamic vinegar
3 tablespoons coconut cream
1/4 teaspoon ground black pepper
1/4 teaspoon red pepper flakes, crushed
Sea salt, to taste
Directions
Heat a cast-iron skillet over medium-high heat. Once hot, roast mustard seeds, fennel seeds, cumin, peppers, ground bay leaf and peppercorns until aromatic.
Press the "Sauté" button to heat up the Instant Pot. Heat the sesame oil until sizzling. Then, sear pork steak until delicately browned.
Add the remaining ingredients, including roasted seasonings; stir well.
Add vegetable broth and secure the lid. Choose the "Manual" setting and cook for 8 minutes under High pressure.
Once cooking is complete, use a quick pressure release; carefully remove the lid. Ladle into individual serving bowls and enjoy!

72. Blade Pork Steaks with Sausages and Sauerkraut
(Ready in about 35 minutes | Servings 6)
This is the perfect blend of savory flavors that will delight your taste buds. You can substitute sausages for bacon or you can just skip it according to your personal preferences.
Per serving: 471 Calories; 27.3g Fat; 8.4g Carbs; 47.7g Protein; 2g Sugars
Ingredients
2 pounds blade pork steaks
Sea salt and ground black pepper, to taste
1/2 teaspoon cayenne pepper
1/2 teaspoon dried parsley flakes
1 tablespoon lard
1 ½ cups water
2 cloves garlic, thinly sliced
2 pork sausages, casing removed and sliced
4 cups sauerkraut
Directions
Season the blade pork steaks with salt, black pepper, cayenne pepper, and dried parsley.
Press the "Sauté" button to heat up the Instant Pot. Melt the lard and sear blade pork steaks until delicately browned on all sides.
Wipe down the Instant Pot with a damp cloth; add water and metal rack to the bottom of your Instant Pot.
Place your blade pork steaks on the rack. Make small slits over entire pork with a tip of sharp knife. Now, insert garlic pieces into each slit.
Secure the lid. Choose the "Soup/Broth" setting and cook for 30 minutes under High pressure. Once cooking is complete, use a natural pressure release; carefully remove the lid.
Then, add the sausage and sauerkraut. Press the "Sauté" button and cook for a couple of minutes more or until heated through. Enjoy!

73. Beer Braised Boston-Style Butt
(Ready in about 55 minutes | Servings 4)

Boston-style butt is the queen of low-carb foods. Serve with a selection of low-carb seasonal vegetables.
Per serving: 330 Calories; 13.1g Fat; 2.1g Carbs; 48.4g Protein; 0.4g Sugars
Ingredients
1 tablespoon lard
1 pound Boston-style butt
1/2 cup leeks, chopped
1/4 cup water
1/4 cup beer
1/2 cup chicken stock
1/4 teaspoon ground black pepper
Sea salt, to taste
A pinch of grated nutmeg
Directions
Press the "Sauté" button to heat up the Instant Pot. Once hot, melt the lard.
Cook Boston-style butt for 2 to 3 minutes on each side; reserve.
Now, sauté the leeks until fragrant; add a splash of chicken stock to deglaze the pan. Add the other ingredients and stir to combine.
Secure the lid. Choose the "Manual" setting and cook for 50 minutes under High pressure. Once cooking is complete, use a natural pressure release; carefully remove the lid.
Serve immediately. Enjoy!

74. Elegant Pork Shank with Cauliflower

(Ready in about 55 minutes | Servings 6)
Pressure cooked cauliflower is a classical low-carb side dish. With the addition of a delicious pork shank, it becomes a complete meal!
Per serving: 342 Calories; 20.1g Fat; 6.6g Carbs; 32.7g Protein; 1.9g Sugars
Ingredients
2 pounds pork shank, cubed
Sea salt, to taste
2 teaspoons coconut oil
1 cup chicken stock
1 leek, sliced
4 cloves garlic, sliced
1/2 teaspoon cumin powder
1/2 teaspoon porcini powder
1/2 teaspoon oregano
1/2 teaspoon basil
4 cups cauliflower, broken into small florets
1/2 teaspoon salt
1/4 teaspoon ground black pepper
1/4 teaspoon red pepper flakes, crushed
Directions
Generously season the pork shank with sea salt. Press the "Sauté" button to heat up the Instant Pot. Now, melt the coconut oil. Once hot, cook pork shank until delicately browned on all sides.
Add chicken stock, leeks, garlic, cumin powder, porcini powder, oregano, and basil to the Instant Pot. Secure the lid. Choose the "Meat/Stew" setting and cook for 50 minutes under High pressure. Once cooking is complete, use a natural pressure release; carefully remove the lid. Reserve the cooked meat.
Add the remaining ingredients to the Instant Pot. Secure the lid. Choose the "Manual" setting and cook for 3 minutes under Low pressure. Once cooking is complete, use a natural pressure release; carefully remove the lid.
Serve the cooked cauliflower with reserved pork shank. Bon appétit!

75. Japanese-Style Sirloin Pork Roast

(Ready in about 2 hours 35 minutes | Servings 4)
Japanese foods taste so unique and delicious thanks to amazing seasonings and condiments that might be found in traditional Japanese dishes. If you don't have Ryorishu and Mirin on hand, feel free to use a regular dry wine.
Per serving: 364 Calories; 13.8g Fat; 4g Carbs; 53.1g Protein; 1.2g Sugars
Ingredients
1 ½ pounds sirloin pork roast
Salt and ground black pepper, to taste
1/2 cup leeks, sliced
2 garlic cloves, minced
1 tablespoon Shoyu sauce
2 tablespoons Ryorishu
1 tablespoon Mirin
2 teaspoons sesame oil
6 drops Stevia liquid concentrate
1 teaspoon cayenne pepper
1 cup water
2 tablespoons black sesame seeds
2 tablespoons fresh chives, chopped
Directions
Generously season the sirloin pork roast with sea salt and ground black pepper.
In a mixing bowl, thoroughly combine the leeks, garlic, Shoyu sauce, Ryorishu, mirin, sesame oil, Stevia, cayenne pepper, and water.
Place the pork in a mixing bowl and let it marinate for 2 hours in your refrigerator. Place the pork and 1 cup of marinade in the Instant Pot.
Secure the lid. Choose the "Meat/Stew" setting and cook for 30 minutes at High pressure. Once cooking is complete, use a natural pressure release; carefully remove the lid.
Take the pork out of the Instant Pot. Then, press the "Sauté" button; add the remaining marinade.
Let the cooking liquid cook until it has reduced and thickened. Slice the sirloin pork roast and place on individual serving plates.
Spoon the sauce over the meat; garnish with sesame seeds and fresh chives. Bon appétit!

76. Old-Fashioned Pork Chili

(Ready in about 10 minutes | Servings 6)
You really can't go wrong with this combination of ground pork, breakfast sausages, and shredded yellow

cheese. You can always rely on credible and tested recipes.
Per serving: 532 Calories; 37.6g Fat; 4.4g Carbs; 41.6g Protein; 1.8g Sugars
Ingredients
2 tablespoons lard
1/2 cup leeks, chopped
1 celery stick, cubed
2 breakfast pork sausages, casing removed and sliced
1 jalapeño pepper, seeded and minced
2 pounds ground pork
2 cloves garlic, minced
1 cup tomatoes, puréed
1 cup broth, preferably homemade
1 teaspoon coconut aminos
1 teaspoon mustard seeds
1 teaspoon ground coriander seed
Seasoned salt and ground black pepper, to taste
2 tablespoons fresh cilantro leaves, roughly chopped
1/2 cup Cheddar cheese, shredded
Directions
Press the "Sauté" button to heat up the Instant Pot. Now, melt the lard. Once hot, cook the leeks and celery until softened.
Add the sausage, jalapeño pepper, pork, and garlic; cook an additional 2 minutes, stirring constantly.
Now, add puréed tomatoes, broth, coconut aminos, mustard seeds, coriander seeds, salt, and black pepper. Stir to combine and secure the lid.
Choose the "Manual" setting and cook for 5 minutes at High pressure. Once cooking is complete, use a natural pressure release; carefully remove the lid.
Serve your chili topped with fresh cilantro leaves and Cheddar cheese. Bon appétit!

77. Pork and Bacon Chowder
(Ready in about 30 minutes | Servings 4)
Here's a hearty chowder that is not just delicious! It is ketogenic and healthy as well!
Per serving: 361 Calories; 19.6g Fat; 8.2g Carbs; 37.8g Protein; 3.7g Sugars
Ingredients
1/2 pound bacon
1/2 pound pork stew meat
2 tablespoons butter
1/2 cup yellow onions, chopped
1 celery with leaves, chopped
2 garlic cloves, minced
1 cup white mushrooms, sliced
1/2 teaspoon dried rosemary
1/2 teaspoon dried thyme
Sea salt, to taste
1/2 teaspoon ground black pepper
1/2 teaspoon cayenne pepper
A pinch of hot paprika
A pinch of grated nutmeg
3 ½ cups beef stock
6 ounces Ricotta cheese
1/2 cup double cream
1/3 cup parsley, roughly chopped

Directions
Press the "Sauté" button to heat up the Instant Pot. Once hot, cook the bacon until crisp; crumble with a fork and set aside.
Now, brown the pork stew meat for 2 to 4 minutes, stirring frequently; set aside.
Melt the butter; cook the onion and celery until softened. After that, add the garlic and sliced mushrooms; sauté until fragrant.
Add all seasonings and beef stock. Return the reserved pork to the Instant Pot.
Secure the lid. Choose the "Manual" setting and cook for 8 minutes at High pressure. Once cooking is complete, use a quick pressure release; carefully remove the lid.
Afterwards, add Ricotta cheese, cream and parsley. Cover with the lid and allow it to sit for 15 minutes. Top with reserved bacon and enjoy!

78. Pork Carnitas Burrito Bowl
(Ready in about 20 minutes | Servings 8)
A combo of pork carnitas and salsa sounds like a burrito, right? Actually, this is an Instant Pot burrito bowl, cooked with aromatics and served with freshly sliced avocado. Yummy!
Per serving: 434 Calories; 23.8g Fat; 8g Carbs; 45.2g Protein; 3.2g Sugars
Ingredients
2 teaspoons grapeseed oil
3 pounds pork tenderloin, cut into slices
1/2 teaspoon dried thyme
1/2 teaspoon dried marjoram
1 teaspoon ground cumin
1 teaspoon paprika
Sea salt and ground black pepper, to taste
1 teaspoon granulated garlic
1 cup water
1 avocado, pitted, peeled and sliced
Salsa Sauce:
1 cup pureed tomatoes
2 bell peppers, deveined and chopped
1 teaspoon granulated garlic
1 minced jalapeño, chopped
1 cup onion, chopped
2 tablespoons fresh cilantro, minced
3 teaspoons lime juice
Directions
Press the "Sauté" button to heat up the Instant Pot. Once hot, add the oil; sear the pork until delicately browned on all sides.
Add the seasonings, garlic, and water to the Instant Pot.
Secure the lid. Choose the "Manual" setting and cook for 12 minutes at High pressure. Once cooking is complete, use a natural pressure release; carefully remove the lid.
Shred the pork with two forks and reserve.
In a mixing bowl, thoroughly combine all salsa ingredients. Spoon the salsa mixture over the

prepared pork. Garnish with avocado slices and serve. Bon appétit!

79. Peperonata with Pork Sausages
(Ready in about 15 minutes | Servings 4)
Try this Italian style sausage with lots of onion, peppers and Italian seasonings. If your family expect the same grilled sausages, surprise them and serve Instant Pot sausages tossed with veggies.
Per serving: 582 Calories; 49.3g Fat; 9.1g Carbs; 24.5g Protein; 2.4g Sugars
Ingredients
1 teaspoon olive oil
8 pork sausages, casing removed
1 green bell pepper, seeded and sliced
1 red bell pepper, seeded and sliced
1 jalapeño pepper, seeded and sliced
1 red onion, chopped
2 garlic cloves, minced
2 Roma tomatoes, puréed
1 cup roasted vegetable broth
1 tablespoon Italian seasoning
2 tablespoons fresh Italian parsley
2 tablespoons ripe olives, pitted and sliced
Directions
Press the "Sauté" button to heat up the Instant Pot. Once hot, add the oil; sear your sausages until no longer pink in center.
Add the other ingredients, except for the olives and parsley; stir to combine well.
Secure the lid. Choose the "Manual" setting and cook for 8 minutes at High pressure. Once cooking is complete, use a quick pressure release; carefully remove the lid.
Serve garnished with fresh parsley and olives. Bon appétit!

80. Traditional Greek Youvarlakia
(Ready in about 30 minutes | Servings 4)
Youvarlakia is a traditional Greek meatball soup that was originally made with Greek orzo; in this recipe, it is adapted for a low-carb diet. Avgolemono sauce that is made of eggs and freshly squeezed lemon juice is very popular in Greece.
Per serving: 525 Calories; 37.5g Fat; 3.9g Carbs; 40g Protein; 1.8g Sugars
Ingredients
1 pound ground pork
1/2 cup green onions, chopped
1 teaspoon garlic paste
2 tablespoons parsley, finely chopped
1 tablespoon cilantro, finely chopped
1 teaspoon basil
1 teaspoon dill
1 egg white
Sea salt, to taste
1/2 teaspoon ground black pepper
1/2 teaspoon cayenne pepper
1 tablespoon olive oil
4 cups beef bone broth
1 tablespoon butter
1/2 cup feta cheese, sliced
Avgolemono Sauce:
2 eggs
3 tablespoons freshly squeezed lemon juice
Directions
In a mixing bowl, thoroughly combine ground pork, green onions, garlic paste, parsley, cilantro, basil, dill, egg white, salt, black pepper, and cayenne pepper. Roll the mixture into meatballs.
Press the "Sauté" button to heat up the Instant Pot. Once hot, add the oil; sear your meatballs until no longer pink in center.
Add broth and butter. Secure the lid. Choose the "Soup/Broth" setting and cook for 20 minutes at High pressure. Once cooking is complete, use a quick pressure release; carefully remove the lid.
In a small mixing dish, whisk two eggs with lemon juice. Add Avgolemono sauce to the hot soup. Press the "Sauté" button and let it simmer for a couple of minutes more or until heated through.
Serve garnished with feta cheese. Enjoy!

81. Noodle-less Classic Lasagna
(Ready in about 20 minutes | Servings 6)
Lasagna without traditional noodles is a totally innovative, attractive and delicious family dish. This lasagna will satisfy your cravings for an Italian comfort food.
Per serving: 539 Calories; 41.1g Fat; 5g Carbs; 36.2g Protein; 2.6g Sugars
Ingredients
1 tablespoon olive oil
1 1/3 pounds ground pork
1 teaspoon garlic, finely minced
2 tablespoons scallions, finely chopped
1 teaspoon dried oregano
1 teaspoon dried basil
1/2 teaspoon dried rosemary
20 ounces pasta sauce, sugar-free
1 cup cream cheese
1 cup Romano cheese
2 eggs
6 ounces Swiss cheese, sliced
Directions
Press the "Sauté" button to heat up the Instant Pot. Heat the olive oil and cook the ground meat with the garlic and scallions for 2 to 4 minutes, stirring continuously.
Add oregano, basil, rosemary, and pasta sauce. Now, add 1/2 of this meat sauce to a lightly greased baking dish.
Then, in a mixing bowl, thoroughly combine the cream cheese, Romano cheese, and eggs. Place this cheese mixture over the meat layer.
Add the remaining 1/2 of the meat mixture. Top with Swiss cheese. Cover with a sheet of aluminum foil and make a foil sling if needed.
Add 1 ½ cups of water and metal rack to the Instant Pot. Lower the baking dish onto the metal rack.

Secure the lid. Choose the "Manual" setting and cook for 9 minutes at High pressure. Once cooking is complete, use a quick pressure release; carefully remove the lid. Bon appétit!

82. Quick and Easy Albóndigas Sinaloenses

(Ready in about 15 minutes | Servings 6)
This classic Mexican recipe is perfect for the next ketogenic lunch! If you used to serve hot cooked rice on the side, just swap it for a cauliflower rice. You will be thrilled!

Per serving: 408 Calories; 31.1g Fat; 4.7g Carbs; 26.5g Protein; 2.4g Sugars

Ingredients
1 pound ground pork
1/2 pound Italian sausage, crumbled
2 tablespoons yellow onion, finely chopped
2 garlic cloves, finely minced
1/4 teaspoon fresh ginger, grated
1/2 teaspoon dried oregano
1 sprig fresh mint, finely minced
1/2 teaspoon ground cumin
Seasoned salt and ground black pepper, to taste
1 tablespoon olive oil
1/2 cup yellow onions, finely chopped
2 chipotle chilies in adobo
2 tomatoes, pureed
2 tablespoons tomato passata
1 cup broth, preferably homemade

Directions
In a mixing bowl, thoroughly combine the pork, sausage, 2 tablespoons yellow onion, garlic, ginger, oregano, mint, cumin, salt, and black pepper.
Roll the mixture into meatballs and reserve.
Press the "Sauté" button to heat up the Instant Pot. Heat the olive oil and cook the meatballs for 3 to 4 minutes, stirring continuously.
Stir in 1/2 cup of yellow onions chilies in adobo, tomatoes, passata and broth; afterwards, add reserved meatballs.
Secure the lid. Choose the "Manual" setting and cook for 6 minutes at High pressure. Once cooking is complete, use a quick pressure release; carefully remove the lid. Bon appétit!

83. Pork Tenderloin "Rosa di Parma"

(Ready in about 1 hour 20 minutes | Servings 4)
Your search for the perfect pork tenderloins is over. Pressure cooked tenderloins are buttery tender and sinfully delicious.

Per serving: 333 Calories; 17.6g Fat; 4.1g Carbs; 38g Protein; 0.5g Sugars

Ingredients
4 pork tenderloins, butterflied
1/2 teaspoon ground black pepper
1/2 teaspoon cayenne pepper
Sea salt, to taste
1/2 cup leeks, sliced
1 cup vegetable broth
1 tablespoon olive oil
1 tablespoon rice wine
2 tablespoons coconut aminos
1 teaspoon fresh sage, chopped
4 slices Italian Parma ham
1/2 cup Parmigiano-Reggiano cheese, freshly grated
2 tablespoons butter, divided

Directions
Season the pork tenderloins with black pepper, cayenne pepper, and sea salt.
In a mixing bowl, thoroughly combine the leeks, broth, olive oil, wine, coconut aminos, and sage. Add pork tenderloin and let it marinate at least 1 hour.
Now, place the ham slices on the tenderloins. Divide Parmigiano-Reggiano cheese among pork tenderloins. Then, tightly roll up each tenderloin. Secure with the toothpicks.
Press the "Sauté" button to heat up the Instant Pot. Melt the butter and sear tenderloins until delicately browned on both sides.
Add the marinade and secure the lid. Choose the "Manual" setting and cook for 12 minutes at High pressure.
Once cooking is complete, use a quick pressure release; carefully remove the lid. Bon appétit!

84. Tender Pork Steaks with Pico de Gallo

(Ready in about 15 minutes | Servings 6)
It's so easy to stay on a ketogenic diet thanks to the Instant Pot electric pressure cooker. It is programmable, convenient, 3rd generation multicooker that will make your life so much easier.

Per serving: 448 Calories; 29.2g Fat; 4.1g Carbs; 39.4g Protein; 1.8g Sugars

Ingredients
1 tablespoon lard
2 pounds pork steaks
1 bell pepper, seeded and sliced
1/2 cup shallots, chopped
2 garlic cloves, minced
1 cup chicken bone broth, preferably homemade
1/4 cup water
1/4 cup dry red wine
Salt, to taste
1/4 teaspoon freshly ground black pepper, or more to taste
Pico de Gallo:
1 tomato, chopped
1 chili pepper, seeded and minced
1/2 cup red onion, chopped
2 garlic cloves, minced
1 tablespoon fresh cilantro, finely chopped
Sea salt, to taste

Directions
Press the "Sauté" button to heat up the Instant Pot. Melt the lard and sear the pork steaks about 4 minutes or until delicately browned on both sides.
Add bell pepper, shallot, garlic, chicken bone broth, water, wine, salt, and black pepper to the Instant Pot.

Secure the lid. Choose the "Manual" setting and cook for 8 minutes at High pressure. Once cooking is complete, use a quick pressure release; carefully remove the lid.

Meanwhile, make your Pico de Gallo by mixing all of the above ingredients. Refrigerate until ready to serve.

Serve warm pork steaks with well-chilled Pico de Gallo on the side. Bon appétit!

85. Cheesy Salsa Meatloaf

(Ready in about 35 minutes | Servings 6)
This is another super-easy pork recipe, bursting with incredible flavor. This cheesy, gooey meatloaf will blow your mind!
Per serving: 468 Calories; 35.7g Fat; 1.6g Carbs; 33.6g Protein; 1.2g Sugars
Ingredients
1 ½ pounds ground pork
1/2 pound ground chuck
1/2 teaspoon sea salt
1/2 teaspoon ground black pepper
1 teaspoon red pepper flakes, crushed
1/2 teaspoon ground bay leaf
1 teaspoon brown mustard
2 eggs, whisked
2/3 cup cream cheese
6 thin slices bacon
1/3 cup tomatillo salsa
Directions
Prepare your Instant Pot by adding 1 ½ cups of water and metal rack to the bottom of the inner pot. In a mixing dish, thoroughly combine ground meat, salt, black pepper, red pepper flakes, ground bay leaf, brown mustard, eggs, and cream cheese.

Shape the mixture into the meatloaf. Place the meatloaf in a baking pan.

Now, arrange bacon slices, crosswise over meatloaf, overlapping them slightly. Top with tomatillo salsa. Secure the lid. Choose the "Manual" setting and cook for 30 minutes at High pressure. Once cooking is complete, use a quick pressure release; carefully remove the lid. Enjoy!

86. Summer Barbecue Baby Back Ribs

(Ready in about 25 minutes | Servings 4)
When it comes to the perfect weeknight dinners, family meals are so much better with a barbecue! This no-fuss, one-pot dish is easy to prepare and fun to eat.
Per serving: 404 Calories; 27.7g Fat; 4.5g Carbs; 34.7g Protein; 1.8g Sugars
Ingredients
2 tomatoes, puréed
2 tablespoons rice vinegar
1 tablespoon stone ground mustard
1 cup water
1/2 teaspoon porcini powder
1 teaspoon celery seeds
1 teaspoon coriander seeds
1/2 teaspoon granulated garlic
1/2 teaspoon shallot powder
1/3 teaspoon ground black pepper
1 teaspoon hot paprika
Sea salt, to taste
1 ½ pounds baby back ribs
Directions
Thoroughly combine all of the above ingredients in your Instant Pot.

Secure the lid. Choose the "Meat/Stew" setting and cook for 20 minutes at High pressure. Once cooking is complete, use a natural pressure release; carefully remove the lid.

Serve warm garnished with a fresh salad of choice. Enjoy!

87. Tamarind Pork Spare Ribs

(Ready in about 25 minutes | Servings 4)
Nothing beats fall off the bone pork ribs on a winter's night! Spare ribs are delicious, but only when they are cooked the right way. Luckily, you have your Instant Pot to make tender and juicy ribs like never before.
Per serving: 266 Calories; 9.7g Fat; 6.2g Carbs; 36.7g Protein; 2.9g Sugars
Ingredients
1 ½ pounds spare ribs
1 thin sliced fresh ginger, peeled
4 garlic cloves, halved
1 jalapeño pepper, thinly sliced
1 bay leaf
1/2 teaspoon black peppercorns
1 tablespoon tamarind paste
1 teaspoon shrimp paste
Sea salt and ground black pepper, to taste
1/2 cup marinara sauce
Directions
Arrange spare ribs on the bottom of your Instant Pot. Add fresh ginger, garlic, jalapeño pepper, bay leaf, and peppercorns.

Next, mix the tamarind paste, shrimp paste, salt, black pepper, marinara sauce, and water. Pour this tamarind sauce over the ribs in the Instant Pot. Add enough water to cover the spare ribs.

Secure the lid. Choose the "Manual" setting and cook for 20 minutes at High pressure. Once cooking is complete, use a quick pressure release; carefully remove the lid.

Serve warm and enjoy!

88. Delicious Provolone-Stuffed Meatballs

(Ready in about 15 minutes | Servings 5)
Juicy and gooey meatballs with amazing flavors that are just out-of-this-world! Serve them on a bed of vegetable noodles.
Per serving: 440 Calories; 31.9g Fat; 2.1g Carbs; 34.7g Protein; 0.8g Sugars
Ingredients
1 pound ground pork
1/4 cup double cream

2 eggs, beaten
2 cloves garlic, minced
2 tablespoons green onions, minced
1 tablespoon fresh parsley, minced
1/4 teaspoon dried thyme
1/2 teaspoon dried marjoram
1/2 teaspoon ground black pepper
1 teaspoon kosher salt
10 (1-inch) cubes of provolone cheese
Directions
Prepare your Instant Pot by adding 1 ½ cups of water and a steamer basket to the bottom of the inner pot.
Thoroughly combine all ingredients, except the cubes of provolone cheese, in a mixing bowl.
Shape the mixture into 10 patties by using oiled hands. Now, place a cube of provolone cheese in the center of each patty, wrap the meat around the cheese, and roll into a ball.
Now, arrange the meatballs in the steamer basket. Secure the lid. Choose the "Manual" setting and cook for 6 minutes at High pressure. Once cooking is complete, use a quick pressure release; carefully remove the lid.
Serve immediately, garnished with low-carb salsa. Bon appétit!

89. Hunter's Pork Roast
(Ready in about 40 minutes | Servings 6)
Here is a pork dish that is chock-full of gourmet pork meat, fresh mushrooms, great aromatics, and amazing white wine sauce. The perfect recipe for any connoisseur!
Per serving: 310 Calories; 14.4g Fat; 2.1g Carbs; 43.5g Protein; 0.7g Sugars
Ingredients
2 tablespoons unsalted butter
2 pounds sirloin pork roast, cubed
8 ounces Cremini mushrooms, thinly sliced
2 garlic cloves, minced
1 heaping tablespoon fresh parsley, chopped
1/2 cup roasted vegetable broth
2/3 cup water
2 tablespoons dry white wine
1/2 teaspoon dried sage
1/2 teaspoon dried basil
1 teaspoon dried oregano
Sea salt and ground black pepper, to taste
1 teaspoon cayenne pepper
1/3 cup Castelvetrano olives, pitted and halved
Directions
Press the "Sauté" button to heat up the Instant Pot. Melt the butter and sear the pork about 3 minutes or until delicately browned on all sides; reserve.
In pan drippings, cook the mushrooms and garlic until tender and fragrant.
Add parsley, broth, water, wine, sage, basil, oregano, salt, black pepper, and cayenne pepper; gently stir to combine.

Secure the lid. Choose the "Meat/Stew" setting and cook for 35 minutes at High pressure.
Once cooking is complete, use a natural pressure release; carefully remove the lid. Serve garnished with Castelvetrano olives. Bon appétit!

90. Easy Pork Tortilla Soup
(Ready in about 15 minutes | Servings 5)
If you are looking for something really special for the next family gathering, this Mexican-inspired soup will fit the bill. A good substitute for regular tortilla chips would be oven-roasted kale chips.
Per serving: 425 Calories; 31.1g Fat; 6.6g Carbs; 30.2g Protein; 3.7g Sugars
Ingredients
1 ½ tablespoons olive oil
1 pound pork stew meat, cubed
1/2 cup double cream
1/2 cup canned fire-roasted tomatoes, diced
Sea salt and ground black pepper, to taste
1/2 teaspoon red pepper flakes, crushed
4 cups water
2 tablespoons vegetable bouillon granules
2 tablespoons enchilada sauce
10 ounces Cotija cheese, crumbled
1 cup kale chips
2 tablespoons fresh cilantro, chopped
4 lime wedges, for serving
Directions
Press the "Sauté" button to heat up the Instant Pot. Heat the olive oil and sear the pork about 3 minutes or until delicately browned on all sides.
Stir in double cream, fire-roasted tomatoes, salt, ground black pepper, red pepper flakes, water, vegetable bouillon granules, and enchilada sauce. Secure the lid. Choose the "Manual" setting and cook for 8 minutes at High pressure. Once cooking is complete, use a quick pressure release; carefully remove the lid.
Now, add Cotija cheese and press the "Sauté" button again; let it simmer until cheese is melted.
Ladle into soup bowls; top each serving with kale chips and fresh cilantro.
Serve garnished with lemon wedges and enjoy!

91. Pork Shoulder with Herb Dijon Sauce
(Ready in about 1 hour | Servings 4)
Pork shoulder is one of the favorite main dishes that cook perfectly in the Instant Pot. Pork and Dijon sauce combine very well so feel free to double the recipe!
Per serving: 341 Calories; 23.4g Fat; 1.3g Carbs; 29g Protein; 0.6g Sugars
Ingredients
1 pound pork shoulder
Sea salt and ground black pepper, to taste
1 teaspoon cayenne pepper
1 tablespoon lard, at room temperature
1 cup beef bone broth
Herb Dijon Sauce:

1/2 teaspoon dried thyme
1/2 teaspoon dried rosemary
1/2 teaspoon dried sage
1/3 cup double cream
1 teaspoon balsamic vinegar
2 teaspoons Dijon mustard
Directions
Generously season the pork shoulder with salt, pepper, and cayenne pepper.
Press the "Sauté" button to heat up the Instant Pot. Melt the lard and sear the pork for 5 minutes, turning occasionally.
Use the broth to deglaze the pan.
Secure the lid. Choose the "Manual" setting and cook for 50 minutes at High pressure. Once cooking is complete, use a natural pressure release; carefully remove the lid. Reserve the pork shoulder.
Press the "Sauté" button again. Now, add thyme, rosemary, sage, cream and vinegar. Let it simmer for a couple of minutes.
Afterwards, stir in Dijon mustard and add the reserved pork shoulder back to the Instant Pot. Now, cook an additional minute or so, until heated through. Bon appétit!

92. Ground Pork Taco Bowl
(Ready in about 15 minutes | Servings 6)
The title says it all. Warm, hearty bowl with yummy ground pork, accompanied by zingy tomato sauce and topped with a rustic and mellow Cheddar cheese.
Per serving: 271 Calories; 11.2g Fat; 7g Carbs; 36.1g Protein; 4.2g Sugars
Ingredients
1 teaspoon olive oil
2 pounds lean ground pork
1 cup chicken bone stock
3 ounces dried guajillo chilies, seeded, roasted and minced
1/2 cup yellow onions, chopped
2 cloves garlic, chopped
1 teaspoon dried Mexican oregano
1/2 teaspoon ground coriander
Sea salt and ground black pepper, to taste
1 teaspoon cayenne pepper
1/2 teaspoon sweet paprika
1 cup cherry tomatoes, halved
1 tablespoon fresh lime juice
1/2 cup Cheddar cheese, shredded
Directions
Press the "Sauté" button to heat up the Instant Pot. Heat the olive oil and brown the pork, crumbling with a spatula.
Use the chicken bone stock to deglaze the pan. Now, add dried guajillo chilies, yellow onions, garlic, Mexican oregano, ground coriander, salt, black pepper, cayenne pepper, sweet paprika, and tomatoes.
Secure the lid. Choose the "Manual" setting and cook for 5 minutes at High pressure. Once cooking is complete, use a natural pressure release; carefully remove the lid.
Ladle into soup bowls; drizzle with some fresh lime juice and top with shredded cheese. Bon appétit!

93. Country-Style Pork Loin Ribs
(Ready in about 25 minutes | Servings 6)
Such a perfect dinner recipe! If you don't have champagne on hand, use any type of crisp white wine.
Per serving: 335 Calories; 20.1g Fat; 4.7g Carbs; 29.9g Protein; 2g Sugars
Ingredients
2 pounds country-style pork loin ribs, bone-in
Coarse salt and ground black pepper, to taste
1 tablespoon lard, at room temperature
1 teaspoon chili powder
1 teaspoon porcini powder
1/3 cup champagne
1 cup water
1 celery with leaves, diced
1 parsnip, quartered
1 brown onion, chopped
2 garlic cloves, crushed
1 teaspoon liquid smoke
1 tablespoon coconut aminos
Directions
Generously season the pork ribs with the salt and black pepper.
Press the "Sauté" button to heat up the Instant Pot. Melt the lard and sear the pork ribs for 2 to 3 minutes on each side.
Add the remaining ingredients. Secure the lid. Choose the "Meat/Stew" setting and cook for 20 minutes at High pressure.
Once cooking is complete, use a natural pressure release; carefully remove the lid. Serve with favorite keto sides. Enjoy!

94. Indian Pork Vindaloo
(Ready in about 20 minutes | Servings 6)
Here is a completely new way to cook a pork loin! Indian spices provide a depth of herbal flavor, while fresh cilantro completes the meal with its extraordinary, bright aroma.
Per serving: 354 Calories; 19.3g Fat; 3.3g Carbs; 39.8g Protein; 1.1g Sugars
Ingredients
1 tablespoon olive oil
2 pounds pork loin, sliced into strips
Sea salt, to taste
2 garlic cloves, minced
2 tablespoons coconut aminos
1 teaspoon oyster sauce
1 head cauliflower, broken into florets
1 teaspoon ground cardamom
3 cloves, whole
1/2 teaspoon mixed peppercorns
1 teaspoon brown mustard seeds
1 teaspoon cayenne pepper
1 cup water

2 tablespoons fresh cilantro, roughly chopped
Directions
Press the "Sauté" button to heat up the Instant Pot. Heat the oil and sear the pork loin for 3 to 4 minutes, stirring periodically.
Add the remaining ingredients, except for fresh cilantro.
Secure the lid. Choose the "Meat/Stew" setting and cook for 12 minutes at High pressure.
Once cooking is complete, use a natural pressure release; carefully remove the lid. Serve topped with fresh cilantro. Bon appétit!

95. Thai Shredded Pork Salad
(Ready in about 35 minutes | Servings 4)
Test the pork loin roast for doneness using an instant-read thermometer. Cook the pork loin until internal temperature reaches 145 degrees F.
Per serving: 279 Calories; 12.7g Fat; 8.5g Carbs; 32.5g Protein; 3.9g Sugars
Ingredients
1 pound pork loin roast
1/2 cup broth, preferably homemade
1/2 cup water
1/2 head cabbage, shredded
2 celery with leaves, chopped
4 spring onions, chopped
1 cup baby spinach
1 cup arugula
1 red chili, deseeded and finely chopped
2 teaspoons each sesame oil
1 teaspoon Thai fish sauce
2 teaspoons tamari sauce
Fresh juice of 1 lemon
Directions
Add pork loin roast, broth and water to the Instant Pot that is previously greased with a nonstick cooking spray.
Secure the lid. Choose the "Meat/Stew" setting and cook for 30 minutes at High pressure. Once cooking is complete, use a natural pressure release; carefully remove the lid.
Allow the pork loin roast to cool completely. Shred the meat and transfer to a salad bowl.
Add the cabbage, celery, green onions, spinach, arugula, and chili.
Now, make the dressing by mixing sesame oil with Thai fish sauce, tamari sauce, and lemon juice. Whisk to combine well and dress your salad. Serve well-chilled. Bon appétit!

96. Smoky Marinated Pork Ribs
(Ready in about 4 hours 35 minutes | Servings 6)
American-style pork ribs are marinated for 4 hours, and then, seared in hot olive oil. Finally, they are cooked under high pressure. It results in melt-in-the-mouth, richly flavored ribs.
Per serving: 368 Calories; 22.9g Fat; 6.1g Carbs; 32.1g Protein; 2.6g Sugars
Ingredients
1/4 cup fresh lime juice
1/3 cup sesame oil
1 tablespoon champagne vinegar
3/4 cup tomato sauce
1 long red chili, finely chopped
1/2 teaspoon coarse sea salt
2 teaspoons smoked paprika
2 garlic cloves, crushed
2 pounds American-style pork ribs
1 tablespoon olive oil
Directions
In a large ceramic dish, combine the lime juice, sesame oil, champagne vinegar, tomato sauce, red chili, sea salt, paprika, and garlic.
Add American-style pork ribs and let them marinate at least 4 hours in the refrigerator.
Remove the ribs from the marinade. Heat the olive oil and brown the ribs for 3 to 4 minutes. Add 1/2 of the marinade.
Secure the lid. Choose the "Meat/Stew" setting and cook for 20 minutes at High pressure. Once cooking is complete, use a natural pressure release; carefully remove the lid.
Then, strain remaining marinade into a small skillet and bring it to a boil over moderately high heat.
Then, immediately reduce heat to medium; allow it to simmer for 4 to 6 minutes or until reduced. Pour this sauce over your ribs and serve warm. Bon appétit!

97. Ground Pork Taco Casserole
(Ready in about 35 minutes | Servings 6)
Home chefs like budget-friendly meals! A casserole is one of the best options when you want to please your family and stay on budget.
Per serving: 409 Calories; 31.6g Fat; 4.7g Carbs; 25.7g Protein; 2.7g Sugars
Ingredients
3 ounces Cottage cheese, at room temperature
1/4 cup double cream
2 eggs
1 teaspoon taco seasoning
6 ounces Cotija cheese, crumbled
3/4 pound ground pork
1 tablespoon taco seasoning
1/2 cup tomatoes, puréed
3 ounces chopped green chilies
6 ounces Queso Manchego cheese, shredded
Directions
Prepare your Instant Pot by adding 1 ½ cups of water and a metal rack to the bottom of the inner pot.
In a mixing bowl, thoroughly combine Cottage cheese, double cream, eggs, and taco seasoning.
Lightly grease a casserole dish; spread the Cotija cheese over the bottom. Pour in the Cottage/ egg mixture as evenly as possible.
Lower the casserole dish onto the rack.
Secure the lid. Choose "Manual" mode and High pressure; cook for 20 minutes. Once cooking is complete, use a quick pressure release; carefully remove the lid.

In the meantime, heat a cast-iron skillet over a moderately high heat. Now, brown ground pork, crumbling it with a fork.

Add taco seasoning, tomato purée and green chilies. Spread this mixture over the prepared cheese crust. Top with shredded Queso Manchego.

Secure the lid. Choose "Manual" mode and High pressure; cook for 10 minutes. Once cooking is complete, use a quick pressure release; carefully remove the lid. Serve and enjoy!

98. Ruby Port-Braised Pork with Mustard Greens

(Ready in about 20 minutes | Servings 4)

If you tend to spend your afternoon surrounded by the amazing aromas of the kitchen, grab your Instant Pot and prepare this juicy, tender pork with fresh and bright greens.

Per serving: 320 Calories; 10g Fat; 3.4g Carbs; 46.9g Protein; 0.9g Sugars

Ingredients
1 tablespoon grapeseed oil
1 ½ pounds pork tenderloins
Sea salt and ground pepper, to your liking
1 teaspoon roasted garlic paste
1/2 cup ruby port
1 cup vegetable stock
1/2 cup scallions, chopped
1/4 teaspoon dried dill weed
1/2 teaspoon dried basil
1/4 teaspoon dried oregano
2 cups mustard greens

Directions
Press the "Sauté" button to heat up the Instant Pot. Heat the grapeseed oil until sizzling. Once hot, cook the pork until delicately browned on both sides.

Season with the salt and black pepper; add garlic paste, ruby port, vegetable stock, scallions, dill, basil, and oregano.

Secure the lid. Choose "Manual" mode and High pressure; cook for 12 minutes. Once cooking is complete, use a quick pressure release; carefully remove the lid.

Lastly, add mustard greens; cover your Instant Pot and let it sit until your greens are wilted. Taste, adjust the seasonings, and serve warm. Bon appétit!

99. Buffalo Thick Pork Soup

(Ready in about 20 minutes | Servings 4)

Your Instant Pot, a modern-day pressure cooker, cooks a creamy and rich pork soup perfectly. Go ahead and take advantage of this revolutionary technology to dramatically improve your life!

Per serving: 443 Calories; 32.7g Fat; 3.7g Carbs; 32.6g Protein; 1.9g Sugars

Ingredients
2 tablespoons butter
1 pound pork loin, boneless and cubed
1/2 cup celery, diced
1 tablespoon hot sauce
1/3 cup blue cheese powder
Seasoned salt and ground black pepper, to taste
1/2 teaspoon onion powder
1/2 teaspoon garlic powder
1 teaspoon paprika
1/4 teaspoon dried dill weed
4 cups beef bone stock
1 cup heavy cream

Directions
Press the "Sauté" button to heat up the Instant Pot. Now, melt the butter and cook pork loin for 2 to 4 minutes, stirring frequently.

Add the celery, hot sauce, blue cheese powder, salt, pepper, onion powder, garlic powder, paprika, dill, and beef bone stock.

Secure the lid. Choose "Manual" mode and High pressure; cook for 12 minutes. Once cooking is complete, use a quick pressure release; carefully remove the lid.

Add heavy cream and press the "Sauté" button one more time. Let the soup simmer until thickened. Serve hot and enjoy!

100. Mediterranean Pork Cutlets

(Ready in about 3 hours 15 minutes | Servings 6)

This recipe calls for white rum, which contains zero carbs per serving. Actually, a low-carb alcohol list includes tequila, whiskey, vodka, gin, and brandy.

Per serving: 417 Calories; 25.7g Fat; 4.6g Carbs; 40.4g Protein; 1.5g Sugars

Ingredients
3 tablespoons olive oil
1 lemon, juiced
2 garlic cloves, finely minced
1 bunch of fresh cilantro leaves, chopped
1 tablespoons stone ground mustard
2 sprigs fresh rosemary, chopped
1 sprig lemon thyme, chopped
2 pounds pork cutlets, bone-in
Coarse sea salt and ground black pepper, to taste
1/4 cup white rum
1 cup chicken stock
1/2 cup black olives, pitted and sliced

Directions
Add 2 tablespoons of olive oil, lemon juice, garlic, cilantro, mustard, rosemary, and lemon thyme to a ceramic dish.

Add bone-in pork cutlets and let them marinate at least 3 hours or overnight.

Press the "Sauté" button to heat up the Instant Pot. Now, heat the remaining tablespoon of olive oil and brown the pork for 2 to 4 minutes or until delicately browned on each side.

Season with salt and pepper to taste.

Deglaze the bottom of the inner pot with the white rum until it has almost all evaporated. Pour in the stock.

Secure the lid. Choose "Manual" mode and High pressure; cook for 8 minutes. Once cooking is complete, use a quick pressure release; carefully remove the lid.

Serve warm garnished with black olives. Bon appétit!

BEEF

101. Beef Stew with a Twist

(Ready in about 25 minutes | Servings 6)

Here is a comfort food you will cook again and again! A fresh spinach will add brightness and amazing aromas to your stew.

Per serving: 317 Calories; 15.3g Fat; 5.7g Carbs; 40g Protein; 2.1g Sugars

Ingredients
1 tablespoon tallow, room temperature
1 ½ pounds beef stew meat, cubed
2 slices bacon, chopped
1 parsnip, chopped
1 carrot, chopped
1 celery with leaves, chopped
1/2 cup leeks, chopped
2 cloves garlic, chopped
1 sprig thyme, chopped
1 sprig rosemary, chopped
2 bay leaves
3 cups water
1 teaspoon cayenne pepper
1/2 teaspoon Hungarian paprika
Salt and ground black pepper, to taste
2 cups spinach, torn into pieces

Directions
Press the "Sauté" button to heat up the Instant Pot. Now, melt the tallow until hot; cook the beef for 2 to 3 minutes, stirring frequently.

Add the remaining ingredients, except for spinach, and stir to combine well.

Secure the lid. Choose "Meat/Stew" mode and High pressure; cook for 20 minutes. Once cooking is complete, use a natural pressure release; carefully remove the lid.

Add spinach to the Instant Pot; cover it with the lid and let the spinach wilt. Ladle hot stew into individual bowls and serve with a fresh salad of choice. Bon appétit!

102. Blade Roast with Béarnaise Sauce

(Ready in about 45 minutes | Servings 6)

This juicy and well-marbled beef cut provides a unique menu opportunity for you and your family! Béarnaise sauce makes a great addition to blade chuck roast.

Per serving: 408 Calories; 29.6g Fat; 1.9g Carbs; 33.7g Protein; 0.1g Sugars

Ingredients
1 tablespoon lard, room temperature
2 pounds blade chuck roast
Coarse sea salt, to taste
1/3 teaspoon ground black pepper
1/2 teaspoon cayenne pepper
1/2 teaspoon ground bay leaf
1/2 teaspoon celery seeds
1 teaspoon granulated garlic
1/2 cup radishes, sliced
Béarnaise sauce:
1/4 cup champagne vinegar
1 teaspoon onion powder
1 tablespoon fresh chervil, finely chopped
3 large egg yolks, beaten
1 stick butter
Sea salt, to taste

Directions
Press the "Sauté" button to heat up the Instant Pot. Now, melt the lard until hot. Cook the beef for 3 minutes per side.

Sprinkle with salt, black pepper, cayenne pepper, ground bay leaf, celery seeds, and granulated garlic. Add enough water to cover the beef.

Secure the lid. Choose "Meat/Stew" mode and High pressure; cook for 40 minutes. Once cooking is complete, use a natural pressure release; carefully remove the lid.

Meanwhile, in a small-sized mixing bowl, combine the vinegar, onion powder, and chervil. Whisk in the egg yolks and mix until smooth.

Now, melt the butter in a pan. Add the lukewarm butter into the yolk mixture, whisking constantly. Whisk until the sauce is thickened; salt to taste.

Serve the prepared blade chuck roast with Béarnaise sauce and freshly sliced radishes on the side. Bon appétit!

103. Mexican-Style Beef Brisket

(Ready in about 1 hour 15 minutes | Servings 6)

Beef brisket in an economical and boldly flavored beef cut that can be done so easily in the Instant Pot. Cooking beef to perfection has never been easier!

Per serving: 371 Calories; 24.5g Fat; 6.4g Carbs; 24.2g Protein; 3.1g Sugars

Ingredients
1 tablespoon ghee, at room temperature
2 pounds beef brisket
1 yellow onion, sliced
1/2 teaspoon black peppercorns
1/2 teaspoon salt
1/2 cup roasted tomato salsa
1 cup chicken bone broth
1 teaspoon dried sage, crushed
1 teaspoon dried rosemary
1 teaspoon chili powder
1/2 teaspoon dried Mexican oregano
1 teaspoon fish sauce
1/4 cup vodka

Directions
Press the "Sauté" button to heat up the Instant Pot. Then, melt the ghee until hot. Cook the beef brisket for 3 minutes per side; reserve.

Add yellow onion and cook until tender and aromatic. Now, add the remaining ingredients, except for vodka, to your Instant Pot. Return the beef back to the Instant Pot.

Secure the lid. Choose "Manual" mode and High pressure; cook for 60 minutes. Once cooking is complete, use a natural pressure release; carefully remove the lid.

Now, remove brisket from the Instant Pot; allow it to sit for 10 minutes before slicing. Skim the fat from the top of the cooking liquid.

Press the Sauté" button. Now, add vodka and let it simmer until the cooking liquid is reduced.

Lastly, slice the brisket across the grain. Spoon the vodka sauce over beef brisket and serve. Enjoy!

104. Thick Flank Steak Chili

(Ready in about 20 minutes | Servings 6)
If you've never tried a flank steak chili in the Instant Pot, you're missing out! A beef chili with a good quality flank steak is the perfect winter dish!
Per serving: 268 Calories; 10.2g Fat; 8g Carbs; 34.1g Protein; 4.3g Sugars

Ingredients
1 tablespoon grapeseed oil
2 pounds beef flank steak, cubed
1 jalapeño pepper, seeded and diced
2 shallots, diced
1 celery stalk, diced
2 Romano tomatoes, puréed
Coarse sea salt and ground black pepper, to your liking
2 tablespoons fresh coriander, coarsely chopped
1 tablespoon coconut aminos
1 tablespoon Kashmiri chili powder
1/2 teaspoon smoked cayenne pepper
1/2 teaspoon red pepper flakes, crushed
1/3 cup fresh chives, chopped

Directions
Press the "Sauté" button to heat up the Instant Pot. Now, heat the oil. Once hot, cook the beef for 3 minutes per side or until it is delicately browned. Add the other ingredients, except for fresh chives. Add 1 cup of water and stir.

Secure the lid. Choose "Manual" mode and High pressure; cook for 15 minutes. Once cooking is complete, use a natural pressure release; carefully remove the lid.

Serve in individual bowls garnished with fresh chives. Bon appétit!

105. Beer-Braised Shredded Beef

(Ready in about 45 minutes | Servings 6)
Whether you're an Instant Pot newbie or you are an old hand at pressure cooking, this recipe will amaze you!
Per serving: 244 Calories; 11.5g Fat; 2.1g Carbs; 31.8g Protein; 0.7g Sugars

Ingredients
1 tablespoon olive oil
2 pounds pot roast, boneless
1/2 cup ale beer
1/2 cup beef broth
1 tablespoon coconut aminos
1 tablespoon soy sauce
1 teaspoon dried marjoram
1 teaspoon mustard seeds
2 garlic cloves, pressed

Directions
Press the "Sauté" button to heat up the Instant Pot. Now, heat the olive oil. Once hot, cook the beef pot roast for 3 minutes on each side.

In a mixing bowl, thoroughly combine the other ingredients. Add this mixture to the Instant Pot.

Secure the lid. Choose "Meat/Stew" mode and High pressure; cook for 40 minutes. Once cooking is complete, use a natural pressure release; carefully remove the lid. Bon appétit!

106. Beef Medley with Sausage

(Ready in about 30 minutes | Servings 8)
Beef, sausage, and vegetables are cooked with savory herbs in this rich, hearty, and delicious medley.
Per serving: 319 Calories; 14g Fat; 6.3g Carbs; 42.8g Protein; 1.8g Sugars

Ingredients
1 teaspoon tallow
2 beef sausages, casing removed and sliced
2 pounds beef steak, cubed
1 yellow onion, sliced
2 cloves garlic, minced
1 red bell pepper, chopped
1 jalapeño pepper, chopped
Sea salt and ground black pepper, to taste
1/2 teaspoon paprika
1 teaspoon old bay seasoning
1 sprig rosemary
2 bay leaves
1 sprig thyme
2 fresh ripe tomatoes, puréed
1 ½ cups roasted vegetable broth

Directions
Press the "Sauté" button to heat up the Instant Pot. Then, melt the tallow and cook the sausage and steak for 3 to 4 minutes, stirring periodically; reserve. Now, add the onion; sauté the onion until softened and translucent. Add the remaining ingredients, including reserved beef and sausage.

Secure the lid. Choose "Manual" mode and High pressure; cook for 20 minutes. Once cooking is complete, use a quick pressure release; carefully remove the lid.

Serve immediately over hot cauli rice. Bon appétit!

107. Silky Beef al Sangiovese

(Ready in about 25 minutes | Servings 6)
Are you looking for a surprisingly sensational beef recipe to amaze your family or guests? Get all the ingredients you need and make this amazing ketogenic dish today!
Per serving: 324 Calories; 14.1g Fat; 4.3g Carbs; 43.1g Protein; 2.1g Sugars

Ingredients
1 tablespoon olive oil

2 pounds Osso buco
2 tablespoons champagne vinegar
Sea salt and ground black pepper, to taste
1/3 cup Sangiovese wine
1/4 cup scallions, chopped
2 tablespoons parsley, chopped
2 cloves garlic, minced
1 cup tomato purée
2 bell peppers, sliced
1 chili pepper, finely minced
1/2 teaspoon cumin powder
1/3 teaspoon hot paprika
1/2 tablespoon Mexican oregano

Directions
Press the "Sauté" button to heat up the Instant Pot. Then, heat the olive oil and cook the meat approximately 2 minutes per side.
Add the remaining ingredients and stir to combine well.
Secure the lid. Choose "Meat/Stew" mode and High pressure; cook for 20 minutes. Once cooking is complete, use a natural pressure release; carefully remove the lid.
Remove the meat from the Instant Pot. Shred Osso buco and return it to the Instant Pot. Serve warm and enjoy!

108. Aromatic Beef Curry
(Ready in about 30 minutes | Servings 6)
This curry is loaded with a meltingly tender beef, full-fat coconut milk, and natural yogurt. The secret ingredient is a fragrant, oriental cinnamon stick.
Per serving: 446 Calories; 21.5g Fat; 5g Carbs; 60g Protein; 2.1g Sugars

Ingredients
1 teaspoon coconut oil
2 pounds beef braising steak, cut into bite-sized pieces
1/2 cup banana shallots, chopped
1 ½ tablespoons curry powder
1 cinnamon stick
2 cloves garlic, crushed
1 teaspoon fresh ginger, peeled and grated
1 cup full-fat coconut milk
Sea salt and freshly ground black pepper, to taste
1 teaspoon chili powder
1/2 teaspoon paprika
1/2 teaspoon ground cumin
8 ounces natural yogurt
2 teaspoons garam masala
1 handful fresh coriander, chopped

Directions
Press the "Sauté" button to heat up the Instant Pot. Then, warm the coconut oil and cook the beef approximately 3 minutes, stirring occasionally.
Add shallots and cook for 2 minutes longer or until they're softened.
Add the curry powder, cinnamon, garlic, ginger, milk, salt, black pepper, chili powder, paprika, and cumin; stir to combine well.

Secure the lid. Choose "Meat/Stew" mode and High pressure; cook for 20 minutes. Once cooking is complete, use a quick pressure release; carefully remove the lid.
Afterwards, add natural yogurt and garam masala; cover and let it stand until heated through. Bon appétit!

109. Juicy Beef Shoulder Roast
(Ready in about 50 minutes | Servings 6)
Here's an all-time favorite! A beef shoulder roast goes perfectly with purple onions and peanut oil for searing. Serve with a glass of good red wine.
Per serving: 313 Calories; 16.1g Fat; 6.5g Carbs; 33.5g Protein; 3.1g Sugars

Ingredients
2 tablespoons peanut oil
2 pounds shoulder roast
1/4 cup dark soy sauce
1 cup beef broth
2 cloves garlic, minced
2 tablespoons champagne vinegar
1/2 teaspoon hot sauce
1 teaspoon porcini powder
1 teaspoon garlic powder
1 teaspoon celery seeds
1 cup purple onions, cut into wedges
1 tablespoon flaxseed meal, plus 2 tablespoons water

Directions
Press the "Sauté" button to heat up the Instant Pot. Then, heat the peanut oil and cook the beef shoulder roast for 2 to 3 minutes on each side.
In a mixing dish, thoroughly combine dark soy sauce, broth, garlic, vinegar, hot sauce, porcini powder, garlic powder, and celery seeds.
Pour the broth mixture into the Instant Pot. Add the onions to the top.
Secure the lid. Choose "Meat/Stew" mode and High pressure; cook for 40 minutes. Once cooking is complete, use a natural pressure release; carefully remove the lid.
Now, make the slurry by mixing flaxseed meal with 2 tablespoons of water. Add the slurry to the Instant Pot.
Press the "Sauté" button and allow it to cook until the cooking liquid is reduced and thickened slightly.
Serve warm. Bon appétit!

110. Beef Shawarma Bowls
(Ready in about 20 minutes | Servings 4)
Loaded with a juicy and tender beef, fresh veggies, and extraordinary spices, a traditional beef shawarma is sure to please. Try this low-carb version and enjoy!
Per serving: 367 Calories; 19.1g Fat; 8.4g Carbs; 39.5g Protein; 5g Sugars

Ingredients
2 teaspoons olive oil
1 ½ pounds beef flank steak, thinly sliced
Sea salt and freshly ground black pepper, to taste
1 teaspoon cayenne pepper

1/2 teaspoon ground bay leaf
1/2 teaspoon ground allspice
1/2 teaspoon cumin, divided
1/2 cup Greek yogurt
2 tablespoons sesame oil
1 tablespoon fresh lime juice
1 red onion, thinly sliced
2 English cucumbers, chopped
1 cup cherry tomatoes, halved
1/2 head romaine lettuce, chopped

Directions
Press the "Sauté" button to heat up the Instant Pot. Then, heat the olive oil and cook the beef for about 4 minutes.
Add all seasonings, 1 ½ cups of water, and secure the lid.
Choose "Manual" mode and High pressure; cook for 15 minutes. Once cooking is complete, use a natural pressure release; carefully remove the lid.
Allow the beef to cool completely.
To make the dressing, whisk Greek yogurt, sesame oil, and lime juice in a mixing bowl.
Then, divide red onion, cucumbers, tomatoes and romaine lettuce among four serving bowls. Dress the salad and top with the reserved beef flank steak. Bon appétit!

111. Beef Salad with a Twist

(Ready in about 1 hour 35 minutes | Servings 6)
This light beef salad is both dinner-worthy and healthy lunch option. You will love this recipe, especially on summer days.
Per serving: 346 Calories; 24.8g Fat; 5.7g Carbs; 24.2g Protein; 4.1g Sugars
Ingredients
1 tablespoon champagne vinegar
1/3 cup dry white wine
2 tablespoons Shoyu sauce
1 cup broth, preferably homemade
1 teaspoon finely grated fresh ginger
1 tablespoon stone-ground mustard
1 teaspoon celery seeds
1 ½ pounds beef rump steak
1 cup green onions, chopped
1 cup cherry tomatoes, halved
2 cucumbers, thinly sliced
1 bunch fresh coriander, leaves picked
1 bunch fresh mint, leaves picked
2 tablespoons fresh chives, chopped
2 tablespoons fresh lemon juice
2 tablespoons extra-virgin olive oil

Directions
In a mixing dish, thoroughly combine the vinegar, white wine, Shoyu sauce, broth, fresh ginger, mustard, and celery seeds.
Add the beef steak and allow it to marinate for 40 minutes to 1 hour in your refrigerator.
Add beef steak, along with its marinade to the Instant Pot. Add enough water to cover the beef.
Secure the lid. Choose "Meat/Stew" mode and High pressure; cook for 35 minutes. Once cooking is complete, use a natural pressure release; carefully remove the lid.
Allow the beef to cool completely. Now, slice it into strips and transfer to a nice salad bowl.
Now, add the vegetables, coriander, mint, and fresh chives; toss to combine. Afterwards, drizzle the salad with lemon juice and olive oil. Toss to combine and serve well-chilled. Bon appétit!

112. Winter Beef Soup

(Ready in about 20 minutes | Servings 6)
If you like to simplify things, an Instant Pot old-fashioned beef soup will be your next favorite. Add a tablespoon of two of tomato sauce if desired.
Per serving: 239 Calories; 14.2g Fat; 4.5g Carbs; 24g Protein; 1.6g Sugars
Ingredients
2 tablespoons butter, at room temperature
1 ½ pounds beef short ribs
6 cups water
2 cloves garlic, smashed
1 cup scallions, chopped
1 carrot, chopped
1 celery, chopped
3 beef stock cubes
Kosher salt and ground black pepper, to taste
1 cup Swiss chard, torn into pieces
Directions
Press the "Sauté" button to heat up the Instant Pot. Then, melt the butter; once hot, cook the ribs for 2 to 4 minutes on each side.
Add the water, garlic, scallions, carrot, celery, beef stock cube, salt, and black pepper to the Instant Pot. Choose "Manual" mode and High pressure; cook for 15 minutes. Once cooking is complete, use a natural pressure release; carefully remove the lid.
Add Swiss chard, cover with the lid and allow the greens to wilt completely.
Ladle into individual bowls, serve and enjoy!

113. Ground Beef Chili with Kale

(Ready in about 15 minutes | Servings 6)
Sautéed ground chuck, cooked with peppers and fresh tomatoes, makes a comforting, warming and economical chili for the whole family. Kale is added later to keep it from turning mushy. Enjoy!
Per serving: 238 Calories; 13.6g Fat; 6g Carbs; 23.8g Protein; 2.8g Sugars
Ingredients
2 tablespoons olive oil
1 ½ pounds ground chuck
1 green bell pepper, chopped
1 red bell pepper, chopped
2 red chilies, minced
1 red onion
2 garlic cloves, smashed
1 teaspoon cumin
1 teaspoon Mexican oregano

1 teaspoon cayenne pepper
1 teaspoon smoked paprika
Salt and freshly ground black pepper, to taste
1 ½ cups puréed tomatoes
4 cups kale, fresh
Directions
Press the "Sauté" button to heat up the Instant Pot. Then, heat the oil; once hot, cook the ground chuck for 2 minutes, crumbling it with a fork or a wide spatula.
Add the pepper, onions, and garlic; cook an additional 2 minutes or until fragrant. Stir in the remaining ingredients, minus kale leaves.
Choose the "Manual" setting and cook for 6 minutes at High pressure. Once cooking is complete, use a natural pressure release; carefully remove the lid.
Add kale, cover with the lid and allow the kale leaves to wilt completely. Bon appétit!

114. Father's Day Beef Cheeseburgers
(Ready in about 15 minutes | Servings 6)
For the very first time, make the recipe as written; later, you can experiment with seasonings according to your taste.
Per serving: 284 Calories; 17.8g Fat; 1.6g Carbs; 29.2g Protein; 0.3g Sugars
Ingredients
1 ½ pounds ground chuck
1/2 teaspoon ground bay leaf
1/2 teaspoon dried basil
1/2 teaspoon dried rosemary
1/2 teaspoon dried oregano
1 teaspoon granulated garlic
Sea salt and freshly ground black pepper, to taste
6 slices Colby cheese
1 tomato, sliced
2 cucumbers, sliced
1 red onion, sliced
2 tablespoons Dijon mustard
Directions
Prepare your Instant Pot by adding 1 ½ cups of water and a steamer basket to the bottom of the inner pot.
In a mixing dish, thoroughly combine the ground beef and seasoning.
Then, shape this beef mixture into six patties. Arrange the patties in the steamer basket.
Choose the "Manual" setting and cook for 6 minutes at High pressure. Once cooking is complete, use a natural pressure release; carefully remove the lid.
Add the slice of cheese to each burger; cover and let it sit until cheese melts. Serve on plates with tomato, cucumbers, red onion, and Dijon mustard. Enjoy!

115. Hearty Swiss Meatball Casserole
(Ready in about 30 minutes | Servings 6)
A gooey, hearty casserole dish loaded with cheese, meat, and pasta sauce. A pinch of grated nutmeg for a casserole topping is the top secret from grandma's kitchen.
Per serving: 436 Calories; 32.8g Fat; 9g Carbs; 25.9g Protein; 5.3g Sugars
Ingredients
1 tablespoon olive oil
For the Meatballs:
1/2 pound ground beef
1/4 pound beef sausage, chopped
1/4 pound pork rinds, crushed
1/4 cup Romano cheese, grated
2 garlic cloves, minced
2 tablespoons scallions, chopped
1 egg
Sea salt and ground black pepper, to taste
1/2 teaspoon cayenne pepper
For the Casserole:
2 cups pasta sauce, sugar-free
1/2 cup clotted cream
1/2 cup full-fat milk
A pinch of grated nutmeg
1 cup Swiss cheese, shredded
Directions
Mix all ingredients for the meatballs until everything is well incorporated. Shape the mixture into meatballs.
Press the "Sauté" button to heat up the Instant Pot. Then, heat the oil and brown your meatballs for 3 to 4 minutes, turning them occasionally.
To assemble your casserole, arrange the meatballs in a baking dish that is previously greased with a nonstick cooking spray.
Pour 1/2 of pasta sauce over the meatballs. Mix the cream, milk and nutmeg until well combined; add this cream mixture to the baking dish.
Add the second half of the pasta sauce to the top. Top with shredded Swiss cheese.
Prepare your Instant Pot by adding 1 ½ cups of water and a metal rack to the bottom of the inner pot. Lower the casserole dish onto the metal rack.
Secure the lid. Choose "Manual" mode and High pressure; cook for 20 minutes. Once cooking is complete, use a quick pressure release; carefully remove the lid.

116. Italian-Style Beef and Cauliflower
(Ready in about 30 minutes | Servings 4)
Cauliflower is a powerhouse of vitamin C and vitamin K, riboflavin, niacin, fiber, thiamin, plant-based protein, and magnesium. It has been cooked briefly in the Instant Pot to retain valuable nutrients.
Per serving: 414 Calories; 16.6g Fat; 8.4g Carbs; 55g Protein; 4.1g Sugars
Ingredients
1 tablespoon tallow, room temperature
1 ½ pounds round steak, cubed
2 garlic cloves, pressed
2 bell peppers, sliced
1 cup marinara sauce

1 cup beef bone broth
1 teaspoon Italian seasoning
2 cups cauliflower florets
Directions
Press the "Sauté" button to heat up the Instant Pot. Then, melt the tallow and sear the round steak for 2 to 3 minutes on each side.
Now, add the garlic, bell peppers, marinara sauce, beef bone broth, and Italian seasoning to the Instant Pot.
Secure the lid. Choose "Manual" mode and High pressure; cook for 20 minutes. Once cooking is complete, use a quick pressure release; carefully remove the lid.
Add cauliflower florets and cook an additional 3 minutes on "Manual" mode under High pressure. Serve warm and enjoy!

117. Spring Spicy Meatloaf
(Ready in about 45 minutes | Servings 4)
A meatloaf is always a good idea for a family dinner. Serve this meatloaf with your favorite low-carb sides and enjoy!
Per serving: 353 Calories; 20g Fat; 4.7g Carbs; 35.9g Protein; 2.8g Sugars
Ingredients
1 pound ground sirloin
1/2 cup pork rinds, crushed
2 eggs, beaten
1/4 cup milk
1/2 cup green onions
1 tablespoon green garlic
1 bell pepper, chopped
Sea salt freshly ground black pepper, to taste
1 teaspoon dried basil
1/2 teaspoon dried rosemary
1 cup tomato purée
1/2 teaspoon mustard seeds
1 teaspoon dried ancho chili pepper, minced
1 ½ cups water
Directions
Mix the ground meat, pork rinds, eggs, milk, green onions, green garlic, bell pepper, salt, pepper, basil, and rosemary.
Press the mixture into a loaf pan. Mix the tomato purée with mustard seeds and dried ancho chili pepper. Top the meatloaf with this tomato mixture.
Add the water and a metal rack to the Instant Pot. Now, cover the meatloaf with a sheet of aluminum foil and make a foil sling.
Secure the lid. Choose "Meat/Stew" mode and High pressure; cook for 35 minutes. Once cooking is complete, use a quick pressure release; carefully remove the lid.
Allow the meatloaf to sit for 5 to 10 minutes before slicing and serving. Bon appétit!

118. Zucchini Keto Lasagna
(Ready in about 45 minutes | Servings 6)
An Instant Pot keto lasagna is one of the best ways to comfort yourself and your family. We will use zucchini noodles, but everything else remains the same. Slice your zucchini with a mandolin slicer for the best results.
Per serving: 533 Calories; 42.2g Fat; 6.1g Carbs; 32.6g Protein; 2.6g Sugars
Ingredients
1 ½ pounds ground chuck
1/3 pound bacon, chopped
2 tablespoons yellow onion, chopped
2 cloves garlic, minced
4 eggs
8 ounces puréed tomatoes
1/2 cup double cream
1/2 cup ricotta cheese
Sea salt and ground pepper, to your liking
1 teaspoon cayenne pepper
1/2 teaspoon celery seeds
1 teaspoon dried parsley flakes
10 ounces Monterey-Jack cheese, shredded
1 large zucchini, thinly sliced
Directions
Press the "Sauté" button to heat up the Instant Pot. Then, brown the meat and sausage for 2 to 3 minutes, crumbling it with a fork.
Add the onion and garlic; continue sautéing for 2 minutes more or until they are fragrant.
In a mixing bowl, thoroughly combine the eggs, puréed tomatoes, heavy cream, ricotta, salt, black pepper, cayenne pepper, celery seeds, and dried parsley.
Fold in 5 ounces of Monterey-Jack cheese and gently stir to combine.
In a casserole dish, place a layer of the ground meat. Then, create 2 layers of the zucchini crisscrossing. Add a layer of the egg/cream mixture. Top with remaining 5 ounces of shredded Monterey-Jack cheese.
Secure the lid. Choose "Meat/Stew" mode and High pressure; cook for 35 minutes. Once cooking is complete, use a quick pressure release; carefully remove the lid.
Let your lasagna stand for 10 minutes before slicing and serving. Bon appétit!

119. Steak with Cheese and Porcini Mushroom Sauce
(Ready in about 35 minutes | Servings 6)
This combination of beef blade steak, mushrooms, sour cream and goat cheese is marvelous! Serve with a fresh salad of choice.
Per serving: 311 Calories; 19.7g Fat; 3.1g Carbs; 30.6g Protein; 0.9g Sugars
Ingredients
1 tablespoon olive oil
1 ½ pounds beef blade steak
1 cup stock, preferably homemade
2 garlic cloves, minced
Sea salt and ground black pepper, to taste

1/2 teaspoon cayenne pepper
1 tablespoon coconut aminos
For the Sauce:
1 tablespoon butter, softened
2 cups Porcini mushrooms sliced
1/2 cup onions, thinly sliced
1/2 cup sour cream
4 ounces goat cheese, crumbled
Directions
Press the "Sauté" button to heat up the Instant Pot. Then, heat the olive oil until sizzling. Once hot, cook the blade steak approximately 3 minutes or until delicately browned.
Add the stock, garlic, salt, black pepper, cayenne pepper, and coconut aminos.
Secure the lid. Choose "Manual" mode and High pressure; cook for 20 minutes. Once cooking is complete, use a quick pressure release; carefully remove the lid.
Take the meat out of the Instant Pot. Allow it to cool slightly and then, slice it into strips.
Press the "Sauté" button again and add the butter, mushrooms and onions to the Instant Pot. Let it cook for 5 minutes longer or until the mushrooms are fragrant and the onions are softened.
Add sour cream and goat cheese; continue to simmer for a couple of minutes more or until everything is thoroughly heated.
Return the meat to the Instant Pot and serve. Bon appétit!

120. Quick and Easy Korean Beef Bowl
(Ready in about 15 minutes | Servings 4)
A perfect mix of flavor and textures in this classic Korean dish will amaze your family. Do not be shy about seasonings and enjoy experimenting with them.
Per serving: 307 Calories; 17.2g Fat; 4.1g Carbs; 34.2g Protein; 2g Sugars
Ingredients
1 tablespoon sesame oil
1 ½ pounds ground sirloin
1 teaspoon dried basil
1/2 teaspoon oregano
Sea salt and ground black pepper, to taste
1/2 cup onion, diced
1 teaspoon garlic, minced
1/4 teaspoon ground ginger
1 teaspoon red pepper flakes
1/4 teaspoon allspice
1 tablespoon soy sauce
1/2 cup fresh cilantro leaves, roughly chopped
Directions
Press the "Sauté" button to heat up the Instant Pot. Then, heat the sesame oil until sizzling.
Add ground sirloin and cook for a few minutes or until browned. Add the remaining ingredients, except for cilantro.
Secure the lid. Choose "Manual" mode and High pressure; cook for 5 minutes. Once cooking is complete, use a natural pressure release; carefully remove the lid.
Divide among individual bowls and serve garnished with fresh cilantro. Bon appétit!

121. Family Beef and Cabbage Stew
(Ready in about 20 minutes | Servings 4)
This hearty beef stew can be served on any occasion. You can add a teaspoon of freshly minced jalapeño for some extra oomph!
Per serving: 320 Calories; 15.7g Fat; 7g Carbs; 39.1g Protein; 3.7g Sugars
Ingredients
2 tablespoons butter, at room temperature
1 onion, chopped
2 garlic cloves, minced
1 ½ pounds beef stew meat, cubed
2 ½ cups beef stock
8 ounces tomato sauce, sugar-free
2 cups red cabbage, shredded
1 tablespoon coconut aminos
2 bay leaves
1 teaspoon dried parsley flakes
1/2 teaspoon red pepper flakes, crushed
Sea salt and ground black pepper, to taste
Directions
Press the "Sauté" button to heat up the Instant Pot. Then, melt the butter. Cook the onion and garlic until softened.
Add beef stew meat and cook an additional 3 minutes or until browned. Stir the remaining ingredients into the Instant Pot.
Secure the lid. Choose "Manual" mode and High pressure; cook for 15 minutes. Once cooking is complete, use a quick pressure release; carefully remove the lid.
Discard bay leaves and ladle into individual bowls. Enjoy!

122. Favorite Beef Paprikash
(Ready in about 25 minutes | Servings 6)
Here is a classic comfort food with a little spicy kick! It tends to become the only recipe for a beef paprikash you'll ever need.
Per serving: 271 Calories; 11.3g Fat; 5.1g Carbs; 35.1g Protein; 2.8g Sugars
Ingredients
2 teaspoons grapeseed oil
2 pounds beef steak cubes
Salt and ground black pepper, to your liking
1 tablespoon sweet paprika
1/2 tablespoon hot paprika
1 tablespoon fish sauce
2 cloves garlic, minced
1/2 cup leeks, chopped
1 bell pepper, seeded and sliced
2 carrots, sliced
1 celery with leaves, diced
2 cups chicken stock
1/2 cup water

2 tomatoes, puréed
1 tablespoon flaxseed meal plus 1 ½ tablespoons water
Directions
Press the "Sauté" button to heat up the Instant Pot. Heat the oil and cook the beef until no longer pink. Season with salt and pepper to taste.
Add paprika, fish sauce, garlic, leeks, bell pepper, carrots and celery to the Instant Pot. Pour in the chicken stock, water, and puréed tomatoes.
Secure the lid. Choose "Manual" mode and High pressure; cook for 20 minutes. Once cooking is complete, use a natural pressure release; carefully remove the lid.
Then, mix the flaxseed meal with water to make the slurry. Add the slurry to the cooking liquid, stir well and cover with the lid. Bon appétit!

123. Cheesy Beef and Cauliflower Soup
(Ready in about 25 minutes | Servings 4)
This nutritious and healthy soup is not only easy to cook in the Instant Pot but it has a rich, wonderful taste thanks to the carefully selected ingredients.
Per serving: 587 Calories; 43.5g Fat; 8.1g Carbs; 40.1g Protein; 3.1g Sugars
Ingredients
1 ½ tablespoons olive oil
1 pound beef chuck, cubed
Sea salt, to taste
2 garlic cloves, minced
1 medium-sized leek, chopped
1 cup cauliflower, chopped
1 cup celery, chopped
4 cups beef stock
1/2 teaspoon dried rosemary
1/2 teaspoon red pepper flakes, crushed
Freshly ground black pepper, to taste
6 ounces Cottage cheese, room temperature
1 ½ cups Colby cheese, grated
2 slices bacon, cooked and crumbled
1 small handful fresh parsley, chopped
Directions
Press the "Sauté" button to heat up the Instant Pot. Heat the olive oil and cook the beef until no longer pink. Salt to taste; reserve.
Add the garlic and leek; continue to sauté for a few minute more or until they are fragrant.
Add the cauliflower, celery, beef stock, rosemary, red pepper flakes, and black pepper. Stir to combine.
Secure the lid. Choose "Manual" mode and High pressure; cook for 20 minutes. Once cooking is complete, use a natural pressure release; carefully remove the lid.
Use an immersion blender to puree your soup.
Press the "Sauté" button and stir in cheese; stir until the cheese is completely melted and thoroughly heated.
Serve hot, topped with crumbled bacon and fresh parsley. Bon appétit!

124. Chili Hot Dog Bake
(Ready in about 55 minutes | Servings 6)
Say cheese and enjoy this chili bake loaded with meat, cheese, and hot dogs! You can use a hot tomato pasta sauce to add extra warmth to this appetizing dish.
Per serving: 452 Calories; 30.5g Fat; 7.1g Carbs; 35.6g Protein; 2.9g Sugars
Ingredients
1 tablespoon olive oil
1 ½ pounds beef chuck, ground for chili
Salt and ground black pepper, to taste
2 ripe tomatoes, chopped
1 onion, chopped
2 ounces tomato sauce
2 garlic cloves, pressed
1 chili pepper, minced
1 teaspoon smoked paprika
1/2 cup lager-style beer
1/2 cup water
6 beef hot dogs, sliced lengthwise
1 ½ cups Mexican cheese blend, shredded
Directions
Press the "Sauté" button to heat up the Instant Pot. Heat the olive oil and cook the beef until no longer pink. Season with salt and black pepper to taste.
Transfer the beef to a mixing dish. Then, add tomatoes, onion, tomato sauce, garlic, chili pepper, and smoked paprika to the mixing dish.
Lay hot dogs flat on the bottom of a lightly greased baking dish. Cover with the chili mixture. Pour in the beer and water.
Wipe down the Instant Pot with a damp cloth. Add 1 ½ cups of water and a metal rack to the Instant Pot. Lower the baking dish onto the metal rack.
Secure the lid. Choose "Meat/Stew" mode and High pressure; cook for 35 minutes. Once cooking is complete, use a quick pressure release; carefully remove the lid.
Top with the shredded cheese and seal the lid. Let it sit for 5 minutes or until the cheese is completely melted.
Let the chili hot dog bake sit for 10 minutes before slicing and serving. Bon appétit!

125. Rich Pepperoni Pizza Bake
(Ready in about 40 minutes | Servings 6)
You can make this rich and satisfying pizza bake at the end of the summer, when we have plenty of fresh ripe tomatoes. Otherwise, just use good canned tomatoes.
Per serving: 421 Calories; 26.7g Fat; 8.1g Carbs; 37.1g Protein; 4.2g Sugars
Ingredients
1 pound ground sirloin
1/2 pound ground chuck
Salt and pepper, to taste
1 red bell pepper, sliced
1 green bell pepper, sliced
1 onion, sliced
1 cup mushrooms, sliced
1/2 cup Kalamata olives, pitted and halved

1 teaspoon basil
1 teaspoon oregano
1/2 teaspoon rosemary
8 ounces tomatoes, diced
1 cup pizza sauce
1 cup cheddar cheese, shredded
1 cup mozzarella cheese, shredded
1 cup pepperoni, sliced
Directions
Press the "Sauté" button to heat up the Instant Pot. Once hot, cook the beef until nicely browned. Season with salt and pepper to taste.
Wipe down the Instant Pot with a damp cloth. Add 1 ½ cups of water and a metal rack to the Instant Pot. Pour the prepared ground meat into a casserole dish that is previously greased with a nonstick cooking spray. Add the bell pepper, onion, mushrooms, and olives.
Sprinkle with basil, oregano, and rosemary. Top with tomatoes and pizza sauce. Sprinkle evenly with cheddar and mozzarella cheese.
Top with pepperoni slices. Lower the casserole dish onto the rack. Secure the lid. Choose "Meat/Stew" mode and High pressure; cook for 35 minutes. Once cooking is complete, use a quick pressure release; carefully remove the lid. Bon appétit!

126. Cozy Peasant Chowder

(Ready in about 25 minutes | Servings 4)
Stunning cooking aromas are coming from your kitchen, just as of old. A pressure cooker will bring a spirit of good old times into your home!
Per serving: 530 Calories; 34.7g Fat; 8.1g Carbs; 44.7g Protein; 4.5g Sugars
Ingredients
1 tablespoon grapeseed oil
1 pound beef tenderloin, thinly sliced across the grain
Salt and ground black pepper, to taste
1/2 cup leeks, chopped
1 celery, chopped
4 cups beef bone broth
1 whole egg
1 cup cream cheese, grated
1 tablespoon fresh lime juice
1 teaspoon Sriracha
Directions
Press the "Sauté" button to heat up the Instant Pot; heat the oil. Once hot, cook the beef until nicely browned. Season with salt and pepper to taste.
Add the leeks, celery, and broth to the Instant Pot. Secure the lid. Choose "Soup/Broth" mode and High pressure; cook for 20 minutes. Once cooking is complete, use a quick pressure release; carefully remove the lid.
Add the egg and cream cheese. Cover the Instant Pot and allow the chowder to sit until the cheese melts. Ladle into individual bowls and drizzle fresh lime juice and Sriracha over each serving. Bon appétit!

127. Spaghetti Squash with Meat Sauce

(Ready in about 50 minutes | Servings 6)
This is an easy and appetizing family-friendly recipe! Spaghetti squash is a great source of vitamins C and A as well as calcium, fiber, and antioxidants.
Per serving: 332 Calories; 19.3g Fat; 9.1g Carbs; 30.2g Protein; 4.5g Sugars
Ingredients
2 ½ pounds spaghetti squash
2 tablespoons olive oil
1/2 teaspoon sea salt
1 ½ pounds ground chuck
2 sausages, casing removed and sliced
1 onion, chopped
2 garlic cloves, minced
1 bell pepper, seeded and sliced
1 chili pepper, seeded and minced
1 cup chicken stock
1/4 cup dry white wine
8 ounces ripe tomatoes, puréed
1/2 teaspoon oregano
1/2 teaspoon basil
1/2 teaspoon thyme
1/2 teaspoon cayenne pepper
Sea salt and ground black pepper, to taste
Directions
Preheat your oven to 380 degrees F. Place squash halves, cut-side down on a lightly greased baking pan. Drizzle 1 tablespoon of the olive oil over them and sprinkle with sea salt.
Roast for 40 minutes. Afterwards, scrape the flesh to create "spaghetti".
Press the "Sauté" button to heat up the Instant Pot; heat the remaining 1 tablespoon of the olive oil. Once hot, cook ground chuck and sausages until delicately browned.
Add the other ingredients and stir to combine. Secure the lid. Choose "Manual" mode and High pressure; cook for 5 minutes. Once cooking is complete, use a quick pressure release; carefully remove the lid.
Serve the meat sauce over spaghetti squash and enjoy!

128. Polska Kielbasa with Winter Squash

(Ready in about 15 minutes | Servings 4)
This wonderful dish is quick enough to cook on a weeknight. Garnish with green onions and avocado if desired.
Per serving: 440 Calories; 36.9g Fat; 8.5g Carbs; 18.3g Protein; 4.5g Sugars
Ingredients
1 teaspoon olive oil
1 pound beef Polska Kielbasa, casing removed, sliced
1 pound summer squash, peeled and diced
1 red onion, chopped
1 celery, chopped

1 cup beef stock
1 cup tomato purée
1 tablespoon coconut aminos
1 teaspoon red pepper flakes, crushed
Coarse sea salt and ground black pepper, to taste
1 cup Cremini mushrooms, sliced
1/2 cup chunky salsa
Directions
Press the "Sauté" button to heat up the Instant Pot; heat the olive oil. Once hot, cook kielbasa until no longer pink.
Add the squash, onion, celery, stock, tomato puréed, coconut aminos, red pepper flakes, salt, black pepper, and mushrooms to the Instant Pot.
Secure the lid. Choose "Manual" mode and High pressure; cook for 5 minutes. Once cooking is complete, use a quick pressure release; carefully remove the lid.
Serve with a chunky salsa. Bon appétit!

129. Beef, Bacon and Spinach Chili
(Ready in about 15 minutes | Servings 6)
Ready to cook a gourmet meal in less than 15 minutes? Serve with Dijon mustard on the side.
Per serving: 392 Calories; 25.4g Fat; 5.8g Carbs; 33.6g Protein; 1.8g Sugars
Ingredients
1 ½ pounds ground beef
4 slices bacon, chopped
8 ounces tomato puréed
1 onion, chopped
2 garlic cloves, minced
2 cups chicken stock, preferably homemade
1/2 teaspoon ground cumin
1 teaspoon smoked paprika
1/2 teaspoon dried basil
1/2 teaspoon dried oregano
Sea salt and ground black pepper, to taste
1 teaspoon red pepper flakes, crushed
2 bay leaves
1/4 teaspoon ground allspice
2 cups spinach, fresh or frozen
Directions
Press the "Sauté" button to heat up the Instant Pot. Once hot, cook ground beef and bacon for 2 to 3 minutes, crumbling them with a fork.
Add the remaining ingredients, except for spinach. Secure the lid. Choose "Manual" mode and High pressure; cook for 6 minutes. Once cooking is complete, use a quick pressure release; carefully remove the lid.
Add spinach and cover with the lid. Let it sit until the spinach wilts. Ladle into individual bowls and serve warm. Bon appétit!

130. Beef Steak with Rainbow Noodles
(Ready in about 45 minutes | Servings 6)
Beef steak is the most versatile ingredient ever! In this recipe, we will serve it with innovative, colorful and delicious low-carb veggie noodles.
Per serving: 259 Calories; 12.2g Fat; 3g Carbs; 32.4g Protein; 1.2g Sugars
Ingredients
1 zucchini
1 carrot
1 yellow onion
2 tablespoons ghee
Sea salt, to taste
2 pounds beef steak
2 large cloves garlic
1/3 teaspoon ground black pepper
Directions
Slice the zucchini, carrot, and yellow onion using a mandolin.
Preheat an oven to 390 degrees F. Grease a baking sheet with the ghee; toss the vegetables with salt and bake for 18 to 22 minutes, tossing once or twice.
Meanwhile, add the beef, garlic, and black pepper to your Instant Pot.
Secure the lid. Choose "Manual" mode and High pressure; cook for 20 minutes. Once cooking is complete, use a quick pressure release; carefully remove the lid. Salt the beef to taste.
Serve the prepared beef steak over roasted vegetable noodles and enjoy!

131. Zettuccini with Pepperoni and Cheese Sauce
(Ready in about 10 minutes | Servings 4)
Try different veggie noodles every day. You can use sweet bell peppers, onions, carrots, and so on.
Per serving: 437 Calories; 38.3g Fat; 2.6g Carbs; 19.5g Protein; 1.7g Sugars
Ingredients
2 zucchini
1/2 pound pepperoni, sliced
1/2 cup cream cheese
Sea salt and ground black pepper, to taste
1/2 teaspoon red pepper flakes, crushed
1 teaspoon cayenne pepper
1/2 cup Romano cheese, grated
Directions
Slice the zucchini with a mandolin; add your zettuccini to the Instant Pot.
Now, stir in the pepperoni, cream cheese, salt, black pepper, red pepper, and cayenne pepper.
Secure the lid. Choose "Manual" mode and High pressure; cook for 5 minutes. Once cooking is complete, use a quick pressure release; carefully remove the lid.
Afterwards, stir in Romano cheese, cover and let it melt for a couple of minutes. Bon appétit!

132. Sinfully Delicious Cheeseburger Soup
(Ready in about 20 minutes | Servings 4)

Make this all-star cheeseburger soup using only one revolutionary kitchen gadget – Instant Pot electric pressure cooker! Serve with fresh Iceberg lettuce and mustard.
Per serving: 571 Calories; 39g Fat; 3.6g Carbs; 48.4g Protein; 1.6g Sugars
Ingredients
2 slices bacon, chopped
1 pound ground chuck
1 teaspoon ghee, room temperature
Salt and ground black pepper, to taste
4 cups vegetable stock, preferably homemade
2 garlic cloves, minced
1/2 cup scallions, chopped
1 teaspoon mustard seeds
1 teaspoon paprika
1 teaspoon chili powder
1/2 cup tomato puree
1 bay leaf
1 ½ cups Monterey-Jack cheese, shredded
2 ounces sour cream
1 small handful fresh parsley, roughly chopped
Directions
Press the "Sauté" button to heat up the Instant Pot. Once hot, cook the bacon and ground beef for 2 to 3 minutes, crumbling them with a fork.
Add the ghee, salt, black pepper, vegetable stock, garlic, scallions, mustard seeds, paprika, chili powder, tomato puree, and bay leaf.
Secure the lid. Choose "Manual" mode and High pressure; cook for 8 minutes. Once cooking is complete, use a natural pressure release; carefully remove the lid.
After that, add Monterey-Jack cheese and sour cream; seal the lid and let it stand for at least 5 minutes. Serve warm in individual bowls garnished with fresh parsley. Bon appétit!

133. Hamburgers with Kale and Cheese
(Ready in about 15 minutes | Servings 6)
Here's a great combo of ground meat, sausage, kale, and cheese. It's no shocker that burger is one of the most popular dishes in the world!
Per serving: 323 Calories; 20.3g Fat; 5.8g Carbs; 29.9g Protein; 0.6g Sugars
Ingredients
1 pound ground beef
1/2 pound beef sausage, crumbled
1 ½ cups kale, chopped
1/4 cup scallions, chopped
2 garlic cloves, minced
1/2 Romano cheese, grated
1/3 cup blue cheese, crumbled
Salt and ground black pepper, to taste
1 teaspoon crushed dried sage
1/2 teaspoon oregano
1/2 teaspoon dried basil
1 tablespoon olive oil
Directions
Place 1 ½ cups of water and a steamer basket in your Instant Pot.
Mix all ingredients until everything is well incorporated.
Shape the mixture into 6 equal sized patties. Place the burgers on the steamer basket.
Secure the lid. Choose "Manual" mode and High pressure; cook for 6 minutes. Once cooking is complete, use a quick pressure release; carefully remove the lid. Bon appétit!

134. Beef Stroganoff with a Twist
(Ready in about 20 minutes | Servings 6)
An Instant Pot transforms the beef and regular vegetables into a magical satisfying stew in record time. This appetizing stew showcases mushrooms at its finest.
Per serving: 347 Calories; 20.7g Fat; 7.9g Carbs; 33.5g Protein; 2.2g Sugars
Ingredients
1 tablespoon lard
1 ½ pounds beef stew meat, cubed
1 yellow onion, chopped
2 garlic cloves, chopped
1 red bell pepper, chopped
Kosher salt and freshly ground black pepper, to taste
1/2 teaspoon dried rosemary
1/2 teaspoon dried thyme
2 cups mushrooms, chopped
2 ½ cups broth, preferably homemade
1 (10-ounce) box frozen chopped spinach, thawed and squeezed dry
1 cup sour cream
4 slices Muenster cheese
Directions
Press the "Sauté" button to heat up the Instant Pot. Now, melt the lard; once hot, cook the beef for 3 to 4 minutes.
Add the onion, garlic, bell pepper, salt, black pepper, rosemary, thyme, mushrooms, and broth.
Secure the lid. Choose "Manual" mode and High pressure; cook for 10 minutes. Once cooking is complete, use a quick pressure release; carefully remove the lid.
Lastly, stir in the spinach, sour cream and cheese. Let it stand in the residual heat until everything is well incorporated. Ladle into soup bowls and serve warm. Bon appétit!

135. Spicy Broccoli, Leek and Beef Soup
(Ready in about 20 minutes | Servings 6)
Dump all ingredients into your Instant Pot, turn on the cooker and enjoy a real feast!
Per serving: 373 Calories; 29.2g Fat; 5.7g Carbs; 21.2g Protein; 2.4g Sugars
Ingredients
1 tablespoon olive oil
1 ½ pounds beef stew meat
1/2 cup leeks

1 cup broccoli, chopped into florets
1 carrot, chopped
1 celery with leaves, chopped
1 cup tomatoes, puréed
4 ½ cups roasted vegetable stock
1 teaspoon garlic powder
1 teaspoon dried basil
1 (1-inch) piece ginger root, grated
1 teaspoon Sriracha
Directions
Press the "Sauté" button to heat up the Instant Pot. Now, heat the oil; once hot, cook the beef for 3 to 4 minutes; reserve.
Now, sauté the leeks in pan drippings until tender and fragrant. Add the remaining ingredients, including the reserved beef.
Secure the lid. Choose "Manual" mode and High pressure; cook for 15 minutes. Once cooking is complete, use a quick pressure release; carefully remove the lid.
Ladle into individual bowls and garnish with some extra leek leaves if desired. Bon appétit!

136. Red Wine Stew with Smoked Cheddar Cheese

(Ready in about 30 minutes | Servings 6)
Cooking with dry red wine brings a layer of depth and balance to your favorite beef recipes. You can enjoy a glass of red wine while you cook, too. Win-win!
Per serving: 381 Calories; 16.7g Fat; 4.5g Carbs; 49.2g Protein; 1.8g Sugars
Ingredients
1 tablespoon tallow, at room temperature
2 pounds bottom round roast, trimmed and diced
Coarse sea salt and ground black pepper, to taste
1 tablespoon Montreal steak seasoning
1 banana shallot, chopped
1 carrot, chopped
1 celery, chopped
1/2 cup dry red wine
2 cups beef stock
2 bay leaves
1 cup smoked cheddar cheese, grated
Directions
Press the "Sauté" button to heat up the Instant Pot. Now, melt the tallow; once hot, cook the bottom round roast for 3 to 4 minutes. Season with salt and black pepper.
Now, add Montreal steak seasoning, shallot, carrot, celery, wine, beef stock, and bay leaves to your Instant Pot.
Secure the lid. Choose "Meat/Stew" mode and High pressure; cook for 25 minutes. Once cooking is complete, use a quick pressure release; carefully remove the lid.
Divide the stew among 6 serving bowls; top each serving with grated cheese and serve warm. Bon appétit!

137. Bottom Eye Roast in Hoisin Sauce

(Ready in about 45 minutes | Servings 8)
Here is a classic Chinese beef! Do not forget to add a hot sauce to make the recipe outstanding!
Per serving: 313 Calories; 17.3g Fat; 3.8g Carbs; 35.8g Protein; 2.3g Sugars
Ingredients
1 tablespoon tallow
3 pounds bottom eye roast
Sea salt and ground black pepper, to taste
3 garlic cloves, halved
Hoisin Sauce:
3 tablespoons soy sauce
2 tablespoons peanut butter
1 tablespoon black vinegar
2 cloves garlic, minced
2 ½ tablespoons toasted sesame oil
1 teaspoon Chinese chili sauce
1/2 teaspoon Chinese five spice powder
1 tablespoon Splenda
Directions
Press the "Sauté" button to heat up the Instant Pot. Now, melt the tallow; once hot, cook the bottom eye roast for 2 to 3 minutes on each side. Season with salt and black pepper.
Then, make small slits along the surface of the beef cut and place garlic in them.
Secure the lid. Choose "Meat/Stew" mode and High pressure; cook for 40 minutes. Once cooking is complete, use a natural pressure release; carefully remove the lid.
Meanwhile, process all sauce ingredients in your blender; blitz until everything is well mixed.
Add the hoisin sauce to the Instant Pot; stir for a couple of minutes more. Serve immediately and enjoy!

138. Festive Bayrischer Gulasch

(Ready in about 30 minutes | Servings 8)
This German dish is rich, flavorful, and sophisticated. A rump roast pairs well with German red wines like Siegrist Dornfelder, Spätburgunder (Pinot Noir), etc.
Per serving: 334 Calories; 15.3g Fat; 8g Carbs; 38.2g Protein; 3.3g Sugars
Ingredients
1 tablespoon olive oil
3 pounds rump roast, boneless and cubed
Salt and ground black pepper, to taste
1 red onion, chopped
2 cloves garlic, minced
2 tomatoes, puréed
1 habanero pepper, seeded and sliced
1 green bell pepper, seeded and sliced
1 red bell peppers, seeded and sliced
2 cups chicken stock
1/2 cup dry red wine
1/2 teaspoon dried rosemary
1/2 teaspoon dried basil
1/2 teaspoon dried oregano

1/2 teaspoon caraway seed
1 tablespoon coconut aminos
1 cup sour cream, to serve
Directions
Press the "Sauté" button to heat up the Instant Pot. Now, heat the oil; once hot, cook the rump roast for 3 to 4 minutes.
Season with salt and black pepper to taste. Add a splash of wine to scrape up any browned bits from the bottom.
Add the onion, garlic, tomatoes, peppers, chicken stock, remaining wine, rosemary, basil, oregano, caraway seeds, and coconut aminos.
Secure the lid. Choose "Meat/Stew" mode and High pressure; cook for 25 minutes. Once cooking is complete, use a natural pressure release; carefully remove the lid.
Ladle into serving bowls; serve dolloped with sour cream. Bon appétit!

139. Garbure Gersoise Soup
(Ready in about 30 minutes | Servings 6)
The key to the amazing and unique flavor of this French soup is the slab bacon. Be sure to find a meaty bacon and good quality veggies.
Per serving: 324 Calories; 17.9g Fat; 6.8g Carbs; 34.6g Protein; 1.9g Sugars
Ingredients
1 tablespoon grapeseed oil
2 pounds top chuck, trimmed, boneless and cubed
3 slices slab bacon, chopped
1/2 cup yellow onion, chopped
1 celery ribs, sliced
1 parsnip, sliced
4 teaspoons beef base
6 cups water
1/4 cup dry white wine
7 ounces tomato purée
1 head savoy cabbage
Sea salt, to your liking
1 teaspoon dried juniper berries
1/2 teaspoon dried sage, crushed
1/2 teaspoon dried rosemary, leaves picked
1 teaspoon whole mixed peppercorns
2 sprigs parsley, roughly chopped
Directions
Press the "Sauté" button to heat up the Instant Pot. Now, heat the oil; once hot, cook the chuck for 2 to 3 minutes on each side.
Add the remaining ingredients and stir to combine well.
Secure the lid. Choose "Meat/Stew" mode and High pressure; cook for 25 minutes. Once cooking is complete, use a quick pressure release; carefully remove the lid.
Serve in individual bowls garnished with some extra fresh parsley if desired. Bon appétit!

140. Spezzatino di Manzo
(Ready in about 50 minutes | Servings 6)
Italian dishes are one of the most popular dishes in the world thanks to their authenticity and abundance of flavors. Spezzatino di Manzo is an Italian beef stew that is enriched with tons of spices.
Per serving: 324 Calories; 17.9g Fat; 6.8g Carbs; 34.6g Protein; 1.9g Sugars
Ingredients
1 tablespoon bacon grease
2 pounds chuck roast, trimmed and cubed
1 onion, diced
2 cloves garlic, sliced
4 ounces celery, diced
1 cup cabbage, diced
1 cup fennel, diced
1 carrot, sliced
1/2 cup tomato puree
4 cups broth, preferably homemade
2 tablespoons balsamic vinegar
2 bay leaves
1 teaspoon winter savory
1/2 teaspoon black peppercorns, crushed
1 teaspoon dried rosemary
1 teaspoon dried thyme
Sea salt, to taste
2 tablespoons fresh basil, snipped
Directions
Press the "Sauté" button to heat up the Instant Pot. Now, melt the bacon grease; once hot, cook the chuck for 2 to 3 minutes on each side; reserve.
Add the onion and cook an additional 3 minutes or until it is translucent.
Add the vegetables to the Instant Pot. Then, stir in tomato puree, broth, balsamic vinegar, bay leaves, winter savory, black peppercorns, dried rosemary, thyme, and sea salt.
Secure the lid. Choose "Meat/Stew" mode and High pressure; cook for 40 minutes. Once cooking is complete, use a natural pressure release; carefully remove the lid.
Serve garnished with fresh basil. Bon appétit!

141. German Leberkäse with Sauerkraut
(Ready in about 15 minutes | Servings 6)
The original recipe for German sauerkraut calls with an apple cider but we used a sauerkraut juice to make it low-carb and keto-friendly. Such a clever choice!
Per serving: 382 Calories; 27.1g Fat; 9.1g Carbs; 24.5g Protein; 5.7g Sugars
Ingredients
2 pounds Leberkäse
18 ounces sauerkraut plus 1 cup sauerkraut juice
2 garlic cloves, minced
1 yellow onion, sliced
1 teaspoon dried thyme
1/2 cup water
1/2 cup chicken stock
1 bay leaf
Directions

Press the "Sauté" button to heat up the Instant Pot. Once hot, cook your Leberkäse for 2 to 3 minutes, turning periodically.
Place all ingredients in your Instant Pot.
Secure the lid. Choose "Manual" mode and High pressure; cook for 8 minutes. Once cooking is complete, use a quick pressure release; carefully remove the lid.
Discard bay leaf and serve warm. Bon appétit!

142. Christmas Bacon Meatloaf

(Ready in about 40 minutes | Servings 6)
A festive meatloaf with fine cheddar cheese and bacon, flavored with the best aromatics. If you are not in a hurry, sweat the shallot before adding it to your meatloaf.
Per serving: 589 Calories; 44.9g Fat; 6.9g Carbs; 38.6g Protein; 3.9g Sugars
Ingredients
1 ½ pounds ground chuck
1/2 cup heavy whipping cream
1 cup cheddar cheese, shredded
Sea salt and ground black pepper, to taste
1 tablespoon dried parsley
1 shallot, chopped
1 cup mushrooms, diced
2 eggs, whisked
1 teaspoon fresh thyme
1/2 teaspoon dried rosemary
1 teaspoon dried marjoram
1/2 teaspoon caraway seeds
1 teaspoon mustard powder
16 long slices bacon
1/2 cup tomato chili sauce
Directions
Prepare your Instant Pot by adding 1 ½ cups of water and a metal rack to the bottom of the inner pot.
In a mixing bowl, thoroughly combine all ingredients, except for bacon and tomato chili sauce.
Shape the mixture into a loaf. Place the bacon slices on the top. Weave the bacon (under, over...under, over)
Place the meatloaf in a lightly greased baking pan; lower the baking pan onto the rack.
Secure the lid. Choose "Manual" mode and High pressure; cook for 23 minutes. Once cooking is complete, use a quick pressure release; carefully remove the lid.
Spread the tomato chili sauce over the meatloaf. Place the meatloaf under the broiler for 6 to 7 minutes. Allow your meatloaf to sit for 10 minutes before slicing. Bon appétit!

143. Perfect Filet Mignon in Beer Sauce

(Ready in about 20 minutes | Servings 4)
When it comes to the keto salads, filet mignon steaks go perfectly with shallots, tomato, leeks, escarole, and so on.
Per serving: 499 Calories; 38g Fat; 5.6g Carbs; 32.1g Protein; 1.9g Sugars
Ingredients
2 tablespoons sesame oil
4 (8-ounce) filet mignon steaks
1 onion, diced
2 garlic cloves, minced
1/2 teaspoon dried rosemary
1 teaspoon cayenne pepper
Sea salt and ground black pepper, to taste
1/3 cup ale beer
1 cup stock, preferably homemade
Directions
Press the "Sauté" button to heat up the Instant Pot. Heat the sesame oil. Once hot, cook filet mignon steaks for 2 to 3 minutes per side.
Now, add the remaining ingredients and secure the lid.
Secure the lid. Choose "Manual" mode and High pressure; cook for 12 minutes. Once cooking is complete, use a natural pressure release; carefully remove the lid.
Serve with a fresh salad of choice. Bon appétit!

144. Restaurant-Style Oxtail Soup

(Ready in about 55 minutes | Servings 6)
This old-fashioned oxtail soup is both dinner-worthy and healthy lunch option. In addition, the soup is loaded with fresh vegetables and greens that are chock-full of valuable nutrients.
Per serving: 474 Calories; 25.9g Fat; 5.3g Carbs; 51.4g Protein; 2.3g Sugars
Ingredients
2 tablespoons canola oil
2 pounds meaty oxtails
5 cups broth, preferably homemade
1 cup tomato puree
1 onion, chopped
1 carrot, diced
1 celery, diced
1 teaspoon granulated garlic
1/2 teaspoon dried marjoram
1/2 teaspoon dried basil
1/2 teaspoon dried thyme
1/2 teaspoon ground bay leaf
2 cups Swiss chard
Directions
Press the "Sauté" button to heat up the Instant Pot. Heat the canola oil. Once hot, cook oxtails for 7 to 10 minutes.
Stir in the remaining ingredients, except for Swiss chard.
Secure the lid. Choose "Meat/Stew" mode and High pressure; cook for 45 minutes. Once cooking is complete, use a natural pressure release; carefully remove the lid.
Add Swiss chard and seal the lid; let it stand until the green wilts. Taste, adjust the seasonings, and ladle into individual bowls. Bon appétit!

145. Extraordinary Steak Sandwiches

(Ready in about 40 minutes | Servings 4)

Purchase a good beef rump steak and make these rich and satisfying sandwiches for your family. With fresh salad and other keto condiments, these sandwiches are addictive!

Per serving: 486 Calories; 30.2g Fat; 4.9g Carbs; 49.3g Protein; 2.9g Sugars

Ingredients
1 ½ pounds beef rump steak, boneless
Sea salt and ground black pepper, to taste
1 teaspoon garlic powder
1 teaspoon dried oregano
1 teaspoon dried basil
1/2 teaspoon caraway seeds
1/2 teaspoon red pepper flakes, crushed
1 cucumber, sliced
2 plum tomatoes, sliced
1/2 red onion, sliced
8 leaves lettuce
1 tablespoon Dijon mustard
Low Carb Wraps:
4 ounces pork rinds, crushed
1/2 teaspoon baking soda
4 ounces cream cheese, softened
2 eggs, whisked
1/4 teaspoon turmeric powder
1/2 teaspoon shallot powder
1/4 cup water

Directions
Place beef rump steak along with the salt, black pepper, garlic powder, oregano, basil, caraway seeds, and red pepper flakes, in your Instant Pot.
Secure the lid. Choose "Manual" mode and High pressure; cook for 25 minutes. Once cooking is complete, use a natural pressure release; carefully remove the lid.
Slice the beef against the grain.
To make low-carb wraps, blitz the pork rinds in your food processor until they become a fine powder.
Add the other ingredients; process until everything is well mixed. Allow the batter to rest approximately 12 minutes.
Cook four wraps on the preheated pancake griddle over a moderate flame. To assemble your sandwiches, divide the prepared beef steak slices among low-carb wraps.
Add cucumber, tomatoes, onions, lettuce and mustard. Serve and enjoy!

146. Top Blade Roast with Horseradish Sauce

(Ready in about 35 minutes | Servings 6)

An Instant Pot transforms any cut of beef into a satisfying dish in record time. Serve a pressure-cooked roast beef with a horseradish sauce just like your grandma used to make.

Per serving: 406 Calories; 24.6g Fat; 4.8g Carbs; 41.9g Protein; 1.3g Sugars

Ingredients
1 tablespoon sesame oil
2 pounds top blade roast
Sea salt and ground black pepper, to taste
1/2 teaspoon cayenne pepper
1/3 cup port wine
1 cup water
1 bouillon cube
2 tablespoons green onions
3 cloves garlic
1 teaspoon mustard seeds
1 teaspoon fennel seeds
Horseradish Sauce:
1 teaspoon stone-ground mustard
1/4 cup sour cream
2 tablespoons mayonnaise
3 tablespoons prepared horseradish

Directions
Press the "Sauté" button to heat up the Instant Pot. Heat the oil. Once hot, cook the top blade roast for 3 minutes on each side.
Season with salt, black pepper, and cayenne pepper. Now, add the wine, water, bouillon cube, green onions, garlic, mustard seeds, and fennel seeds.
Secure the lid. Choose "Manual" mode and High pressure; cook for 25 minutes. Once cooking is complete, use a natural pressure release; carefully remove the lid.
Meanwhile, mix all of the ingredients for the horseradish sauce. Serve your blade roast with horseradish sauce on the side. Bon appétit!

147. Chipolatas with Spinach and Cheese

(Ready in about 15 minutes | Servings 6)

A chipolata sausage (40 grams) contains only 3 grams of carbohydrates per serving size. It pairs perfectly with dry red wine and yellow onions.

Per serving: 403 Calories; 33g Fat; 5.5g Carbs; 16g Protein; 0.7g Sugars

Ingredients
1 tablespoon lard, at room temperature
2 pounds chipolata sausages
1 yellow onion, chopped
1/2 cup dry red wine
1 cup water
Freshly ground black pepper, to taste

Directions
Press the "Sauté" button to heat up the Instant Pot. Heat the oil. Once hot, cook the sausage for a couple of minutes, moving them around.
Add the remaining ingredients.
Secure the lid. Choose "Manual" mode and High pressure; cook for 8 minutes. Once cooking is complete, use a quick pressure release; carefully remove the lid. Serve warm. Bon appétit!

148. Herbed Mustard Beef Shanks
(Ready in about 35 minutes | Servings 8)
This rich and flavorful beef dish is sure to please because it simply melts in your mouth. With aromatic herbs, these beef dish is a crave-worthy combination.
Per serving: 210 Calories; 6.6g Fat; 4.2g Carbs; 31.1g Protein; 0g Sugars
Ingredients
2 teaspoons lard, room temperature
2 ½ pounds beef shanks, 1 ½-inch wide
1 ½ cups beef broth
1 teaspoon Dijon mustard
1/2 teaspoon cayenne pepper
1/4 teaspoon freshly cracked black pepper
1 teaspoon salt
1 bay leaf
1/2 teaspoon dried marjoram, crushed
1/2 teaspoon caraway seeds
1 teaspoon dried sage, crushed
2 sprigs mint, roughly chopped
Directions
Press the "Sauté" button to heat up the Instant Pot. Melt the lard. Once hot, sear the beef shanks for 2 to 3 minutes per side.
Add the remaining ingredients, except for the mint. Secure the lid. Choose "Meat/Stew" mode and High pressure; cook for 30 minutes. Once cooking is complete, use a quick pressure release; carefully remove the lid.
Serve garnished with fresh mint and enjoy!

149. Beef and Yogurt Curry
(Ready in about 30 minutes | Servings 6)
What's the secret to a great beef curry? Choosing the best cut of beef, of course! You can experiment with this recipe and use frozen low-carb vegetables too.
Per serving: 375 Calories; 17.7g Fat; 7.4g Carbs; 43.9g Protein; 4.9g Sugars
Ingredients
2 tablespoons olive oil
2 ½ pounds beef steaks, cubed
Sea salt and ground black pepper, to taste
1/2 teaspoon red pepper flakes, crushed
1 shallot, chopped
2 garlic cloves, minced
1 habanero pepper, minced
1 ½ teaspoons red curry paste
1/4 teaspoon ground cinnamon
1 ½ tablespoons rice vinegar
1 ½ cups chicken stock, preferably homemade
1 cup canned coconut milk, unsweetened
1/2 cup yogurt
A small handful coriander, chopped
Directions
Press the "Sauté" button to heat up the Instant Pot. Now, heat the olive oil. Once hot, sear the beef steaks for 3 to 4 minutes, stirring periodically; season with salt, black pepper, and red pepper; reserve.
Then, cook the shallot, garlic and habanero pepper in pan drippings until fragrant.
Add red curry paste, cinnamon, vinegar, and chicken stock.
Secure the lid. Choose "Manual" mode and High pressure; cook for 18 minutes. Once cooking is complete, use a quick pressure release; carefully remove the lid.
Then, add coconut milk and yogurt. Stir to combine well and press the "Sauté" button one more time; let it simmer until thoroughly heated.
Serve in individual bowls, garnished with fresh coriander. Bon appétit!

150. Beef Short Ribs with Cilantro Cream
(Ready in about 25 minutes | Servings 8)
Beef short ribs cook perfectly in the Instant Pot and pair wonderfully with a cheesy, creamy cilantro sauce. Enjoy!
Per serving: 346 Calories; 24.1g Fat; 2.1g Carbs; 31g Protein; 1.1g Sugars
Ingredients
1 tablespoon sesame oil
2 ½ pounds beef short ribs
1/2 teaspoon red pepper flakes, crushed
Sea salt and ground black pepper, to taste
Cilantro Cream:
1 cup cream cheese, softened
1/3 cup sour cream
A pinch of celery salt
A pinch of paprika
1 teaspoon garlic powder
1 bunch fresh cilantro, chopped
1 tablespoon fresh lime juice
Directions
Press the "Sauté" button to heat up the Instant Pot. Now, heat the sesame oil. Sear the ribs until nicely browned on all sides.
Season the ribs with red pepper, salt, and black pepper.
Secure the lid. Choose "Manual" mode and High pressure; cook for 20 minutes. Once cooking is complete, use a quick pressure release; carefully remove the lid.
Meanwhile, mix all ingredients for the cilantro cream. Place in the refrigerator until ready to serve. Serve warm ribs with the chilled cilantro cream on the side. Bon appétit!

FISH & SEAFOOD

151. Tilapia Fillets with Arugula
(Ready in about 10 minutes | Servings 4)
Tilapia is chock-full of very important nutrients; this is, actually, a significant protein powerhouse. Serve with dry white wine and enjoy!
Per serving: 145 Calories; 4.9g Fat; 2.4g Carbs; 23.3g Protein; 1.1g Sugars
Ingredients
1 lemon, juiced
1 pound tilapia fillets
2 teaspoons ghee
Sea salt and ground black pepper, to taste
1/2 teaspoon cayenne pepper, or more to taste
1/2 teaspoon dried basil
2 cups arugula
Directions
Add fresh lemon juice and 1 cup of water to the bottom of your Instant Pot. Add a metal steamer insert.
Brush the fish fillets with melted ghee.
Season the fish with salt, black pepper, cayenne pepper; arrange the tilapia fillets in the steamer insert; sprinkle dried basil on top of the fish.
Secure the lid. Choose "Manual" mode and Low pressure; cook for 4 minutes. Once cooking is complete, use a quick pressure release; carefully remove the lid.
Serve with fresh arugula and enjoy!

152. Cod Fillets with Sautéed Vegetables
(Ready in about 50 minutes | Servings 4)
Cod is loaded with protein, selenium, and vitamin B12. It can control your blood pressure and lower the risk of cardiovascular disease, cancer, and leukemia.
Per serving: 159 Calories; 7.3g Fat; 1.8g Carbs; 18.1g Protein; 0.4g Sugars
Ingredients
1/4 cup dry white wine
1 tablespoon lemon juice
1 (1-inch) fresh ginger, grated
2 garlic cloves, minced
1 tablespoon coconut aminos
1 teaspoon Dijon mustard
2 tablespoons olive oil
4 cod fillets
1 shallot, chopped
1 celery stalk, chopped
1 zucchini, sliced
Directions
In a mixing bowl, whisk white wine with lemon juice, ginger, garlic, coconut aminos, mustard, and 1 tablespoon of the olive oil.
Add fish fillets and allow it to marinate for 40 minutes. Reserve the marinade.
Add 1 ½ cups of water and a steamer basket to your Instant Pot. Now, arrange the fish fillets in the steamer basket.
Secure the lid. Choose "Manual" mode and Low pressure; cook for 4 minutes. Once cooking is complete, use a quick pressure release; carefully remove the lid.
Heat a pan over medium-high heat. Heat the remaining tablespoon of olive oil.
Then, sauté the shallots until softened. Add the celery and cook an additional 3 minutes. Afterwards, add zucchini slices and continue to sauté until the vegetables are nice and softened.
Now, pour in the reserved marinade; allow the mixture to boil vigorously until it is thoroughly heated. Spoon the vegetables and sauce over the fish fillets and serve. Bon appétit!

153. The Best Jambalaya Ever
(Ready in about 25 minutes | Servings 6)
This Jambalaya is one of the tastiest things that you can prepare in an Instant Pot. You can use turkey sausage as well as taco seasoning in this recipe.
Per serving: 351 Calories; 12.1g Fat; 8.9g Carbs; 49g Protein; 3.9g Sugars
Ingredients
2 teaspoons olive oil
1 pound chicken breasts, boneless, skinless and cubed
1 cup smoked sausage, chopped
3/4 pound prawns
1 teaspoon Creole seasoning
Sea salt and ground black pepper, to taste
1/2 cup onion, chopped
2 cloves garlic, minced
2 bell peppers, chopped
1 habanero pepper, chopped
1 stalk celery, chopped
2 ripe tomatoes, puréed
2 cups vegetable stock
1 tablespoon freshly squeezed lemon juice
1 tablespoon fresh cilantro, chopped
Directions
Press the "Sauté" button to heat up the Instant Pot. Now, heat the olive oil. Now, cook the chicken and sausage until no longer pink.
Then, add prawns and cook for 2 minutes more; season the meat with Creole seasoning, salt, and black pepper and reserve.
Add the onion, garlic, peppers, celery, tomatoes, and vegetable stock.
Secure the lid. Choose "Manual" mode and High pressure; cook for 9 minutes. Once cooking is complete, use a quick pressure release; carefully remove the lid.
Now, add the reserved chicken, sausage, and prawns. Seal the lid and allow it to sit for 6 to 7 minutes.

Drizzle fresh lemon over each serving and garnish with fresh cilantro. Bon appétit!

154. Classic Mussel Stew with Asiago Cheese

(Ready in about 10 minutes | Servings 6)
This mussel stew is made unbelievably delicious in record time thanks to the magic of pressure cooking.
Per serving: 293 Calories; 13g Fat; 9.1g Carbs; 31.9g Protein; 2.2g Sugars
Ingredients
1 ½ pounds mussels, scrubbed and debearded
2 tablespoons olive oil
2 tablespoons fresh coriander, chopped
2 heaping tablespoons green onions, chopped
1/2 teaspoon dried marjoram
1/2 teaspoon paprika
A pinch ground nutmeg
Sea salt and ground black pepper, to taste
1 cup chicken broth, preferably homemade
1/2 cup dry red wine
1/2 (28-ounce) can San Marzano tomatoes, crushed
2 cloves garlic, crushed
1 cup Asiago cheese, shredded
1 tablespoon fresh dill, chopped
1 lemon, sliced
Directions
Place all ingredients, except for cheese, dill and lemon, in your Instant Pot.
Secure the lid. Choose "Manual" mode and Low pressure; cook for 3 minutes. Once cooking is complete, use a quick pressure release; carefully remove the lid.
Divide the prepared dish among serving bowls and garnish with shredded cheese and fresh dill. Serve with lemon slices. Bon appétit!

155. Creamy Cheesy Shrimp Salad

(Ready in about 10 minutes | Servings 4)
Shrimp cooks up perfectly in an Instant Pot, while condiments and veggies make this a must-cook recipe for a family gathering. The trick is in a good mayo and silky cream cheese.
Per serving: 326 Calories; 15.3g Fat; 4.1g Carbs; 41.9g Protein; 1.9g Sugars
Ingredients
28 ounces shrimp, peeled and deveined
1/2 cup apple cider vinegar
1/2 cup water
1/3 cup mayonnaise
1/4 cup cream cheese
1 celery with leaves, chopped
1 red onion, chopped
1 large-sized cucumber, sliced
1 tablespoon lime juice
2 tablespoons cilantro, roughly chopped
Directions
Toss the shrimp, apple cider vinegar and water in your Instant Pot.
Secure the lid. Choose "Manual" mode and Low pressure; cook for 2 minutes. Once cooking is complete, use a quick pressure release; carefully remove the lid.
Allow your shrimp to cool completely. Toss the shrimp with the remaining ingredients. Serve this salad well-chilled and enjoy!

156. Halászlé Hungarian Fisherman's Soup

(Ready in about 10 minutes | Servings 4)
Hungarian Halászlé or traditional Fisherman's soup is famous for being very, very spicy. Therefore, do not be shy with Hungarian hot paprika.
Per serving: 366 Calories; 17.7g Fat; 8.3g Carbs; 37.1g Protein; 3.6g Sugars
Ingredients
2 tablespoons olive oil
1/2 cup green onions, chopped
1 red bell pepper, thinly sliced
1 green bell pepper, minced
1 celeriac root, chopped
1/2 teaspoon coarse sea salt
1/3 teaspoon freshly ground black pepper
1 bay leaf
1 teaspoon cayenne pepper
2 ripe tomatoes, crushed
1 teaspoon granulated garlic
1 tablespoon Hungarian hot paprika
1/2 cup dry white wine
1 cup chicken broth
2 carp fillets, finger-thick
10 little neck clams
Directions
Press the "Sauté" button to heat up the Instant Pot. Now, heat the olive oil. Now, cook the onions, peppers, and celeriac until softened; season with salt and pepper.
Add the other ingredients and gently stir to combine. Secure the lid. Choose "Manual" mode and High pressure; cook for 6 minutes. Once cooking is complete, use a quick pressure release; carefully remove the lid.
Ladle into individual bowls and serve hot. Bon appétit!

157. Mom's Halibut Stew

(Ready in about 15 minutes | Servings 4)
A thick, rich and flavorful fish stew is super easy to prepare in an Instant Pot. Cottage cheese adds just the right amount of tanginess to this robust family stew.
Per serving: 432 Calories; 29.9g Fat; 5.4g Carbs; 34.6g Protein; 4.3g Sugars
Ingredients
4 slices bacon, chopped
1/2 cup shallots, chopped
1 teaspoon garlic, smashed
1 celery, chopped
1 parsnip, chopped
2 cups fish stock

1 tablespoon coconut oil, softened
1 pound halibut
Sea salt and crushed black peppercorns, to taste
1/4 teaspoon ground allspice
1 cup double cream
1 cup Cottage cheese, at room temperature
Directions
Press the "Sauté" button to heat up the Instant Pot. Now, cook the bacon until it is nice and crispy.
Add the shallots, garlic, celery, and parsnip. Continue to sauté for 2 minutes longer or until vegetables are just tender.
Stir in the stock, coconut oil, halibut, salt, black peppercorns, and allspice.
Secure the lid. Choose "Manual" mode and Low pressure; cook for 7 minutes. Once cooking is complete, use a natural pressure release; carefully remove the lid.
After that, stir in double cream and cheese. Press the "Sauté" button again and let it simmer for a couple of minutes or until everything is heated through. Bon appétit!

158. Creamed Seafood Chowder with Bacon
(Ready in about 15 minutes | Servings 6)
This seafood chowder features halibut and clams cooked with high-quality aromatics and full-bodied rose wine.
Per serving: 425 Calories; 25.8g Fat; 8.1g Carbs; 35.6g Protein; 4.5g Sugars
Ingredients
1/4 pound meaty bacon, chopped
1/2 cup leeks, diced
1 serrano pepper, minced
1 celery with leaves, diced
1 carrot, diced
1 ½ pounds halibut fillets, cut into 2-inch pieces
10 ounces clams, minced, juice reserved
2 garlic cloves, pressed
Sea salt and ground black pepper, to taste
2 sprigs fresh thyme
2 sprigs fresh rosemary
3 cups fish stock
1/2 cup Rose wine
2 cups double cream
2 tablespoons fresh chives, chopped
Directions
Press the "Sauté" button to heat up the Instant Pot. Now, cook the bacon until it is nice and crisp; reserve.
Then, cook the leeks, pepper, celery and carrot in pan drippings. Continue to sauté an additional 3 minutes or until softened.
Next, sir in the fish, clams, garlic, salt, black pepper, thyme, rosemary, stock, and wine.
Secure the lid. Choose "Manual" mode and Low pressure; cook for 7 minutes. Once cooking is complete, use a quick pressure release; carefully remove the lid.
After that, stir in double cream. Press the "Sauté" button again and let it simmer until heated through. Ladle into soup bowls; top with the reserved bacon and fresh chopped chives, and serve immediately. Enjoy!

159. Herbed Cod Steaks
(Ready in about 10 minutes | Servings 4)
Steamed fish steaks are especially loved by those on weight loss. As a matter of fact, cod is one of the best types of fish for weight loss. You should eat three to five servings of cod per week in order to see the results. Be inspired and use a different combo of herbs every time.
Per serving: 190 Calories; 7.7g Fat; 2.6g Carbs; 26.2g Protein; 1.1g Sugars
Ingredients
4 cod steaks, 1 ½-inch thick
2 tablespoons garlic-infused oil
Sea salt, to taste
1/2 teaspoon mixed peppercorns, crushed
1 sprig rosemary
2 sprigs thyme
1 yellow onion, sliced
Directions
Prepare your Instant Pot by adding 1 ½ cups of water and a metal rack to the inner pot.
Then, massage the garlic-infused oil into the cod steaks; sprinkle them with salt and crushed peppercorns.
Lower the cod steaks onto the rack skin side down; place rosemary, thyme, and onion on the top.
Secure the lid. Choose "Manual" mode and High pressure; cook for 4 minutes. Once cooking is complete, use a quick pressure release; carefully remove the lid.
Serve immediately with a fresh salad of choice. Bon appétit!

160. Zingy Shrimp Salad
(Ready in about 10 minutes + chilling time | Servings 4)
This refreshing, zingy, and delicious salad can be served as a delicious everyday dinner or an elegant Sunday brunch.
Per serving: 243 Calories; 14.2g Fat; 6.6g Carbs; 24.6g Protein; 0.8g Sugars
Ingredients
1 pound shrimp, peeled and deveined
Juice of 1 fresh lemon
1 celery stalk, thinly sliced
2 cloves garlic, minced
Sea salt, to taste
1/4 teaspoon freshly ground black pepper
1/2 teaspoon cayenne pepper
1 cucumber, sliced
1 avocado, pitted and diced
2 cups baby spinach
1 tablespoon Dijon mustard
4 tablespoons extra-virgin olive oil

Directions
Toss the shrimp and fresh lemon juice in your Instant Pot. Add enough water to cover the shrimp. Secure the lid. Choose "Manual" mode and Low pressure; cook for 2 minutes. Once cooking is complete, use a quick pressure release; carefully remove the lid.

Allow the shrimp to cool completely. Toss the shrimp with the remaining ingredients and transfer to a salad bowl. Bon appétit!

161. Warm Tuna Salad
(Ready in about 10 minutes | Servings 4)
This good-for-you tuna salad is loaded with vegetables, olives and simple seasonings. Moreover, tuna steaks are a cinch to make in the Instant Pot.
Per serving: 163 Calories; 4.7g Fat; 7.4g Carbs; 23.5g Protein; 4.1g Sugars
Ingredients
1 pound tuna steaks
2 Roma tomatoes, sliced
1 red bell pepper, sliced
1 green bell pepper, sliced
1 head lettuce
2 tablespoons Kalamata olives, pitted and halved
1 red onion, chopped
2 tablespoons balsamic vinegar
2 tablespoons extra-virgin olive oil
Sea salt, to taste
1/2 teaspoon chili flakes
Directions
Prepare your Instant Pot by adding 1 ½ cups of water and steamer basket to the inner pot.
Place the tuna steaks in your steamer basket. Place the tomato slices and bell peppers on top of the fish. Secure the lid. Choose "Manual" mode and High pressure; cook for 4 minutes. Once cooking is complete, use a quick pressure release; carefully remove the lid. Flake the fish with a fork.
Divide lettuce leaves among serving plates to make a bad for your salad. Now, add olives and onions. Drizzle balsamic vinegar and olive oil over the salad. Sprinkle salt and chili flakes over your salad. Top with the prepared fish, tomatoes, and bell peppers. Enjoy!

162. Chinese-Style Snapper Soup
(Ready in about 10 minutes | Servings 4)
Cooking the snapper under the intense pressure keeps it moist and full of nutrients. Chinese cabbage is the perfect accompaniment to the snapper in this amazing soup with an Asian flair.
Per serving: 218 Calories; 6.9g Fat; 6.2g Carbs; 31.2g Protein; 2.4g Sugars
Ingredients
1 teaspoon toasted sesame seeds
1/2 cup scallions, chopped
2 cloves garlic, minced
1 pound snapper
1/2 teaspoon fine sea salt
1/3 teaspoon black peppercorns, freshly ground
1/2 teaspoon dried grated lemon peel
1/3 teaspoon dried marjoram
1/3 cup dry white wine
1 tablespoon dark soy sauce
1 ½ cups Chinese cabbage, shredded
2 tablespoons fresh coriander, chopped
1 carrot, diced
1 celery, diced
4 cups roasted vegetable broth
1 jalapeño pepper, minced
1 teaspoon Chinese five-spice powder
Directions
Press the "Sauté" button to heat up the Instant Pot. Now, heat the oil and sauté the scallions until tender and fragrant.
Add the remaining ingredients. Secure the lid. Choose "Manual" mode and High pressure; cook for 6 minutes. Once cooking is complete, use a quick pressure release; carefully remove the lid.
Ladle into individual serving bowls and serve garnished with fresh chives, if desired. Bon appétit!

163. Trout Casserole with Pepper-Jack Cheese
(Ready in about 15 minutes | Servings 3)
Fresh-from-the-sea trout fillets are a great family dish for any occasion. Trout is an excellent source of omega-3 fatty acids, protein, and vitamin B complex.
Per serving: 408 Calories; 24.2g Fat; 3.6g Carbs; 42.3g Protein; 1.8g Sugars
Ingredients
1 ½ tablespoons olive oil
3 plum tomatoes, sliced
1 teaspoon dried basil
1/2 teaspoon dried oregano
3 trout fillets
1/2 teaspoon cayenne pepper, or more to taste
1/3 teaspoon black pepper
Salt, to taste
1 bay leaf
1 cup Pepper-Jack cheese, shredded
Directions
Prepare your Instant Pot by adding 1 ½ cups of water and a metal rack to the bottom of the inner pot.
Now, grease a baking dish with olive oil. Place the slices of tomatoes on the bottom of the baking dish. Sprinkle the basil and oregano over them.
Now, add fish fillets; season with cayenne pepper, black pepper, and salt. Add bay leaf. Lower the baking dish onto the rack.
Secure the lid. Choose "Manual" mode and High pressure; cook for 10 minutes. Once cooking is complete, use a quick pressure release; carefully remove the lid.
Lastly, top with Pepper-Jack cheese, seal the lid and allow the cheese to melt. Serve warm. Bon appétit!

164. Prawn Salad in Portobello "Buns"

(Ready in about 20 minutes | Servings 4)

These Portobello "buns" are simply adorable. They will forever change the way you think about sandwiches. This recipe might look complicated but, actually, it is so simple and quick to prepare.

Per serving: 436 Calories; 29.2g Fat; 7.5g Carbs; 37.1g Protein; 4.1g Sugars

Ingredients

1 ½ pounds prawns, peeled and deveined
Juice of one lemon, freshly squeezed
2/3 cup water
1/2 teaspoon sea salt
1/4 teaspoon chili flakes
1 red onion, chopped
1 celery stalk with leaves, chopped
1 bell pepper, chopped
1 ½ tablespoons balsamic vinegar
1 cup mayonnaise
1 teaspoon yellow mustard
2 heaping tablespoons fresh cilantro, chopped
8 large Portobello mushroom caps, stems removed
1 tablespoon olive oil

Directions

Toss the prawns, lemon juice, and water into your Instant Pot.

Secure the lid. Choose "Manual" mode and Low pressure; cook for 2 minutes. Once cooking is complete, use a quick pressure release; carefully remove the lid.

Allow your prawns to cool completely.

Then, toss the prawns with sea salt, chili flakes, onion, celery, bell pepper, vinegar, mayonnaise, and mustard. Gently stir to combine and set aside.

Now, drizzle 1 tablespoon of olive oil over Portobello mushroom caps and roast them for 10 to 13 minutes at 450 degrees F.

To assemble your sandwiches, divide the prepared shrimp salad among roasted Portobello mushroom caps. Garnish with fresh cilantro and serve right now.

165. Buttery and Lemony Tuna Fillets

(Ready in about 10 minutes | Servings 4)

This elegant dish may become your favorite weeknight staple. The fish is buttery tender and a little chewy, perfect for an everyday family meal as well as for festive dinner.

Per serving: 175 Calories; 6.9g Fat; 1.9g Carbs; 25.2g Protein; 0.3g Sugars

Ingredients

1 cup water
1/3 cup lemon juice
2 sprigs fresh rosemary
2 sprigs fresh thyme
2 sprigs fresh parsley
1 pound tuna fillets
4 cloves garlic, pressed
Sea salt, to taste
1/4 teaspoon black pepper, or more to taste
2 tablespoons butter, melted
1 lemon, sliced

Directions

Prepare your Instant Pot by adding 1 cup of water, lemon juice, rosemary, thyme, and parsley to the bottom. Add a steamer basket too.

Now, place tuna fillets in the steamer basket. Place the garlic on the top of fish fillets; sprinkle with salt and black pepper.

Drizzle the melted butter over the fish fillets and top with the sliced lemon.

Secure the lid. Choose "Manual" mode and Low pressure; cook for 3 minutes. Once cooking is complete, use a quick pressure release; carefully remove the lid. Serve warm and enjoy!

166. Greek-Style Fish and Vegetable Bake

(Ready in about 15 minutes | Servings 4)

This Instant Pot bake is so simple and quick to make and contains great flavors of succulent tilapia, tender-crisp cauliflower, and authentic Greek feta cheese.

Per serving: 272 Calories; 14.6g Fat; 6.2g Carbs; 29.6g Protein; 3.1g Sugars

Ingredients

Nonstick cooking oil
2 ripe tomatoes, sliced
1 teaspoon dried basil
1 teaspoon dried oregano
1/2 teaspoon dried rosemary
2 cloves garlic, minced
1 head cauliflower, cut into florets
1 red onion, sliced
1 pound tilapia fillets, sliced
Sea salt, to taste
1 tablespoon olive oil
1 cup feta cheese, crumbled
1/3 cup Kalamata olives, pitted and halved

Directions

Prepare your Instant Pot by adding 1 ½ cups of water and a metal rack to the bottom of the inner pot.

Now, generously grease a casserole dish with a nonstick cooking spray. Place the slices of tomatoes on the bottom of the baking dish. Sprinkle the basil, oregano, rosemary, and garlic over them.

Now, add the cauliflower and onion; then, place a layer of sliced fish; season with the salt and drizzle with olive oil.

Afterwards, top with feta cheese and Kalamata olives. Lower the baking dish onto the rack.

Secure the lid. Choose "Manual" mode and High pressure; cook for 5 minutes. Once cooking is complete, use a quick pressure release; carefully remove the lid.

Allow the dish to stand for 5 minutes before serving. Bon appétit!

167. Easy Scallops with Parsley and Wine

(Ready in about 10 minutes | Servings 3)

Pressure cooking is one of the best ways to cook scallops since the shorter cooking time retains the vitamins and maximizes their nutritional value.

Per serving: 165 Calories; 7.6g Fat; 5.7g Carbs; 17.6g Protein; 0.3g Sugars

Ingredients

1 tablespoon sesame oil
3/4 pound scallops
2 garlic cloves, crushed
Sea salt, to taste
1/3 teaspoon ground black pepper
1/2 teaspoon paprika
1 cup broth, preferably homemade
1/4 cup dry white wine
2 tablespoons fresh parsley, chopped
1 tablespoon fresh lemon juice

Directions

Press the "Sauté" button to heat up the Instant Pot. Now, heat the oil and sauté the scallops for 1 to 2 minutes.

Add the garlic and continue to sauté for 30 seconds longer. Add the salt, black pepper, paprika, broth, and wine.

Secure the lid. Choose "Manual" mode and Low pressure; cook for 2 minutes. Once cooking is complete, use a quick pressure release; carefully remove the lid.

Toss the scallops with fresh parsley and lemon juice. Bon appétit!

168. Oysters with Chive-Mayo Sauce

(Ready in about 10 minutes | Servings 6)

Oysters are elegant but deceptively easy to make in an Instant Pot. Simply cook them with port wine and aromatics and you will see the difference.

Per serving: 202 Calories; 13.4g Fat; 7.7g Carbs; 12g Protein; 0.6g Sugars

Ingredients

2 teaspoons toasted sesame oil
2 pounds fresh oysters, shucked
1/3 cup port wine
1 cup roasted vegetable broth
Sea salt and ground black pepper, to your liking
1/2 teaspoon hot paprika
1 teaspoon celery seeds
1/2 teaspoon mustard seeds
1/2 teaspoon dried basil
2 garlic cloves, minced
1 teaspoon fish sauce
Mayo Sauce:
1/2 cup full-fat mayonnaise
1/2 teaspoon granulated garlic
2 tablespoons fresh chives, roughly chopped

Directions

Press the "Sauté" button to heat up the Instant Pot. Now, heat the oil and sauté the oysters for 1 minute. Add wine, broth, salt, black pepper, paprika, celery seeds, mustard seeds, basil, garlic, and fish sauce. Secure the lid. Choose "Manual" mode and Low pressure; cook for 6 minutes. Once cooking is complete, use a quick pressure release; carefully remove the lid.

Meanwhile, make the sauce by mixing mayonnaise, granulated garlic, and chives. Serve the oysters with the chive-mayo sauce on the side. Bon appétit!

169. Aromatic Mahi-Mahi Filets with Peppers

(Ready in about 10 minutes | Servings 3)

The mahi-mahi, also known as dolphinfish, is a great source of Vitamin B-complex, protein and selenium. It is a lean fish with a mild taste, so it goes well with pungent Mediterranean herbs.

Per serving: 205 Calories; 9.8g Fat; 5.4g Carbs; 24.1g Protein; 2.8g Sugars

Ingredients

1 cup water
2 sprigs fresh rosemary
1 sprig fresh thyme
2 sprigs dill, tarragon
1 lemon, sliced
3 mahi-mahi filets
2 tablespoons coconut oil, melted
Sea salt and ground black pepper, to taste
1 red bell pepper, sliced
1 green bell pepper, sliced
1 serrano pepper, seeded and sliced

Directions

Add water, herbs, and lemon slices to the Instant Pot; add a steamer basket.

Place mahi-mahi filets in the steamer basket. Drizzle mahi-mahi with melted coconut oil; sprinkle with salt and black pepper.

Secure the lid. Choose "Manual" mode and Low pressure; cook for 3 minutes. Once cooking is complete, use a natural pressure release; carefully remove the lid.

Arrange the peppers on the top of fish fillets. Press the "Sauté" button and let it cook for just 1 minute or so. Serve immediately.

170. Chunky Fish Paprikash

(Ready in about 15 minutes | Servings 4)

This classic paprikash usually takes an hour to prepare using a traditional stovetop method, but in the Instant Pot, it's ready in a fraction of the time.

Per serving: 179 Calories; 6.6g Fat; 5.7g Carbs; 23.9g Protein; 3.2g Sugars

Ingredients

2 teaspoons olive oil
1 yellow onion, chopped
1 carrot, sliced
1 celery, diced
1 bell pepper, sliced

2 garlic cloves, minced
2 ripe tomatoes, crushed
3 cups fish stock
3/4 pound haddock fillets
1 cup shrimp
1/2 teaspoon caraway seeds
1 tablespoon sweet Hungarian paprika
1 teaspoon hot Hungarian paprika
Directions
Press the "Sauté" button to heat up the Instant Pot. Now, heat the oil and sauté the onions until softened and fragrant.
Add the carrot, celery, pepper, and garlic; continue sautéing until softened.
Add the remaining ingredients. Secure the lid. Choose "Manual" mode and High pressure; cook for 5 minutes. Once cooking is complete, use a quick pressure release; carefully remove the lid.
Ladle into individual soup bowls and serve hot. Bon appétit!

171. Simple Garlicky Halibut Steak
(Ready in about 10 minutes | Servings 3)
So simple, so delicious! Garlic is definitely one of the best flavor-enhancing ingredients you can ever use!
Per serving: 287 Calories; 20.9g Fat; 1.3g Carbs; 21.9g Protein; 0g Sugars
Ingredients
3 halibut steaks
4 garlic cloves, crushed
Coarse sea salt, to taste
1/4 teaspoon ground black pepper, to taste
Directions
Prepare your Instant Pot by adding 1 ½ cups of water and steamer basket to the inner pot.
Place the halibut steaks in the steamer basket; season them with salt and black pepper.
Secure the lid. Choose "Manual" mode and High pressure; cook for 5 minutes. Once cooking is complete, use a quick pressure release; carefully remove the lid.
Serve with favorite keto sides. Bon appétit!

172. Malabar Fish Curry
(Ready in about 15 minutes | Servings 4)
You can have amazing tastes of fish curry that used to take about an hour in the oven, but you can pressure cook it in less than 15 minutes. In addition to saving you time, you get a healthier meal.
Per serving: 235 Calories; 13.8g Fat; 9g Carbs; 19.5g Protein; 3.8g Sugars
Ingredients
1 tablespoon canola oil
1/2 cup Cheriya ulli, finely sliced
1 red bell pepper, chopped
1 serrano pepper, chopped
1 teaspoon garlic, pressed
1 (1-inch) piece fresh ginger root, grated
4-5 curry leaves
1 pound Ocean perch, cut into bite-size pieces
1 teaspoon tamarind paste
2 tablespoons curry paste
2 ripe tomatoes, chopped
1/2 cup unsweetened coconut milk
1 ½ cup broth, preferably homemade
Salt and ground black pepper, to taste
Directions
Press the "Sauté" button to heat up the Instant Pot. Now, heat the oil and sauté Cheriya ulli and peppers until softened and fragrant.
Then, stir in the garlic, ginger, and curry leaves. Continue to sauté an additional minute or until they are fragrant.
Deglaze the bottom with the broth and add the remaining ingredients.
Secure the lid. Choose "Manual" mode and Low pressure; cook for 6 minutes. Once cooking is complete, use a quick pressure release; carefully remove the lid.
Taste, adjust the seasonings, and serve right now. Bon appétit!

173. Faster-than-Fast-Food Salmon Burgers
(Ready in about 10 minutes | Servings 4)
Fish burgers are very versatile dish so you can just combine the ingredients and spices you have on hand. You could also try adding some chili peppers to give your burgers an extra kick.
Per serving: 307 Calories; 18.4g Fat; 2.1g Carbs; 31.9g Protein; 0.9g Sugars
Ingredients
1 pound salmon, boneless and skinless
2 tablespoons scallions, chopped
1 teaspoon garlic, finely minced
Sea salt and ground black pepper, to taste
1 teaspoon cayenne pepper
1 teaspoon stone-ground mustard
1 cup Romano cheese, grated
1 tablespoon fresh coriander, chopped
1/2 teaspoon dried dill
Directions
Mix all of the above ingredients in your food processor until everything is well incorporated.
Now, shape the mixture into 4 patties and set aside.
Prepare your Instant Pot by adding 1 ½ cups of water and steamer basket to the inner pot.
Place fish burgers in the steamer basket.
Secure the lid. Choose "Manual" mode and Low pressure; cook for 3 minutes. Once cooking is complete, use a quick pressure release; carefully remove the lid.
Serve with mayo, lettuce, tomato, and keto buns. Enjoy!

174. Snapper in Aromatic Tomato Sauce
(Ready in about 10 minutes | Servings 6)

This recipe calls for fire-roasted tomatoes; they will add a rich and char flavor to your dish. However, you can use any kind of canned tomatoes you have on hand.
Per serving: 175 Calories; 5.2g Fat; 5.8g Carbs; 25.5g Protein; 3.2g Sugars
Ingredients
2 teaspoons coconut oil, melted
1/2 teaspoon cumin seeds
1 teaspoon celery seeds
1/2 teaspoon fresh ginger, grated
1 yellow onion, chopped
2 cloves garlic, minced
1 ½ pounds snapper fillets
3/4 cup vegetable broth
1 (14-ounce) can fire-roasted diced tomatoes
1 bell pepper, sliced
1 jalapeño pepper, minced
Sea salt and ground black pepper, to taste
1/4 teaspoon chili flakes
1/2 teaspoon turmeric powder
Directions
Press the "Sauté" button to heat up your Instant Pot. Now, heat the oil and cook the cumin seeds, celery seeds, and fresh ginger.
Then, add the onion and sauté until it is softened and fragrant.
Add minced garlic and continue to sauté an additional 30 seconds. Stir in the remaining ingredients.
Secure the lid. Choose "Manual" mode and Low pressure; cook for 3 minutes. Once cooking is complete, use a quick pressure release; carefully remove the lid. Serve warm.

175. Basil Wine Scallops

(Ready in about 10 minutes | Servings 5)
Scallops pair wonderfully with port wine, fresh, ripe tomatoes and garlic. Serve this gourmet seafood dish with a top-notch cream cheese to make it tastes even more special.
Per serving: 209 Calories; 10.5g Fat; 8.8g Carbs; 19.2g Protein; 2.6g Sugars
Ingredients
1 tablespoon olive oil
1 brown onion, chopped
2 garlic cloves, minced
1/2 cup port wine
1 ½ pounds scallops, peeled and deveined
1/2 cup fish stock
1 ripe tomato, crushed
Sea salt and ground black pepper, to taste
1 teaspoon smoked paprika
2 tablespoons fresh lemon juice
1/2 cup cream cheese, at room temperature
2 tablespoons fresh basil, chopped
Directions
Press the "Sauté" button to heat up your Instant Pot. Now, heat the oil and cook the onion and garlic until fragrant.
Add the wine to deglaze the bottom. Add the scallops, fish stock, tomato, salt, black pepper, and paprika.
Secure the lid. Choose "Manual" mode and Low pressure; cook for 1 minute. Once cooking is complete, use a quick pressure release; carefully remove the lid.
Drizzle fresh lemon juice over the scallops and top them with cream cheese. Cover and let it sit in the residual heat for 3 to 5 minutes. Serve warm garnished with fresh basil leaves, and enjoy!

176. Poached Salmon with Bok Choy

(Ready in about 15 minutes | Servings 4)
Salmon fillets are one of the easiest things that you can cook in an Instant Pot. It is flavorful and delish enough for a holiday dinner.
Per serving: 220 Calories; 12.1g Fat; 1.9g Carbs; 24.6g Protein; 2.6g Sugars
Ingredients
2 tablespoons unsalted butter
4 (1-inch thick) salmon fillets
Sea salt and freshly ground pepper, to taste
1/2 teaspoon cayenne pepper
3 cloves garlic, minced
2 cups Bok choy, sliced
1 cup broth, preferably homemade
1 teaspoon grated lemon zest
1/2 teaspoon dried dill weed
Directions
Start by adding 1 ½ cups of water and a metal rack to the bottom of your Instant Pot.
Brush the salmon with melted butter; sprinkle the fish with salt, black pepper, and cayenne pepper on all sides.
Secure the lid. Choose "Manual" mode and Low pressure; cook for 3 minutes. Once cooking is complete, use a quick pressure release; carefully remove the lid. Reserve your salmon.
Now, add the remaining ingredients.
Secure the lid. Choose "High" mode and High pressure; cook for 5 minutes. Once cooking is complete, use a quick pressure release; carefully remove the lid.
Serve the poached salmon with the vegetables on the side.

177. Foil-Packet Haddock with Veggies

(Ready in about 15 minutes | Servings 4)
There is more than one way to cook haddock fillets. Nevertheless, when you want to please your family, pressure-cooked flaky and buttery fish fillets in packets are a must!
Per serving: 180 Calories; 3.9g Fat; 2.4g Carbs; 32g Protein; 1.2g Sugars
Ingredients
1 ½ cups of water
1 lemon, sliced
1 brown onion, sliced into rings

2 bell peppers, sliced
2 sprigs rosemary
4 sprigs parsley
2 sprigs thyme
4 haddock fillets
Sea salt, to taste
1/3 teaspoon ground black pepper, or more to taste
2 tablespoons extra-virgin olive oil
Directions
Start by adding water and lemon to your Instant Pot. Now, add a steamer basket.
Assemble the packets with large sheets of heavy-duty foil.
Mound onions rings, peppers, rosemary, parsley, and thyme in the center of each foil. Place the fish fillet on the top of the vegetables.
Season with salt and black pepper, and drizzle with olive oil. Place the packets in the steamer basket.
Secure the lid. Choose "Manual" mode and Low pressure; cook for 10 minutes. Once cooking is complete, use a quick pressure release; carefully remove the lid. Serve warm.

178. Hot Oyster Stew with Sour Cream

(Ready in about 15 minutes | Servings 4)
Are you ready for a light and nutritious protein lunch? Oysters are a powerhouse of proteins, vitamins, and minerals. Serve with an oven-roasted cabbage on the side.
Per serving: 421 Calories; 25.6g Fat; 7.2g Carbs; 39.1g Protein; 2.3g Sugars
Ingredients
1 tablespoon ghee
1 medium-sized leek, chopped
2 cloves garlic, pressed
1 ½ cups double cream
1 ½ cups fish stock
2 tablespoons sherry
1 parsnip, trimmed and sliced
1 celery with leaves, diced
1 ½ pounds oysters, shucked
Sea salt and ground black pepper, to taste
1 tablespoon paprika
1 or 2 dashes Tabasco
1/2 cup sour cream
Directions
Press the "Sauté" button to heat up your Instant Pot. Now, melt the ghee and cook the leek and garlic until aromatic.
Add coconut milk, fish stock, sherry, parsnip, celery, oysters, salt, pepper, paprika, and Tabasco.
Secure the lid. Choose "Manual" mode and Low pressure; cook for 6 minutes. Once cooking is complete, use a quick pressure release; carefully remove the lid.
Serve dolloped with chilled sour cream. Bon appétit!

179. Favorite Monkfish Stew

(Ready in about 40 minutes | Servings 6)
Monkfish can help you lower the cholesterol level, protect and grow muscle tissues, and boost your immune system.
Per serving: 163 Calories; 7.6g Fat; 3.4g Carbs; 19.8g Protein; 1.6g Sugars
Ingredients
Juice of 1 lemon
1 tablespoon fresh parsley
1 tablespoon fresh basil
1 teaspoon garlic, minced
1 tablespoon olive oil
1 ½ pounds monkfish
1 tablespoon butter
1 onion, sliced
1 bell pepper, chopped
1/4 teaspoon ground cumin
1/4 teaspoon turmeric powder
1/2 teaspoon cayenne pepper
Sea salt and ground black pepper, to taste
2 cups fish stock
1/2 cup water
1/4 cup dry white wine
1 ripe tomato, crushed
2 bay leaves
1/2 teaspoon mixed peppercorns
Directions
In a ceramic dish, whisk the lemon juice, parsley, basil, garlic, and olive oil; add monkfish and let it marinate for 30 minutes.
Press the "Sauté" button to heat up your Instant Pot. Now, melt the butter and cook the onion and bell peppers until fragrant.
Add the remaining ingredients and gently stir to combine.
Secure the lid. Choose "Manual" mode and High pressure; cook for 6 minutes. Once cooking is complete, use a quick pressure release; carefully remove the lid.
Afterwards, discard bay leaves and ladle your stew into serving bowls. Serve hot.

180. Carp Steaks with Homemade Aioli

(Ready in about 10 minutes | Servings 4)
Pressure cooking is one of the best ways to cook fish since the shorter cooking time retains the vitamins and maximizes the nutritional value of your ingredients.
Per serving: 315 Calories; 24.8g Fat; 0.6g Carbs; 21.1g Protein; 0.1g Sugars
Ingredients
1 pound carp steaks
2 tablespoons ghee
1 teaspoon granulated garlic
1 teaspoon onion powder
1/2 teaspoon dried dill
Salt, to taste
1/4 teaspoon freshly ground black pepper
1/2 teaspoon cayenne pepper
For Aioli:
1 egg yolk

1 teaspoon garlic, minced
1 tablespoon fresh lemon juice
1/2 cup extra-virgin olive oil
1/3 teaspoon Dijon mustard
Directions
Start by adding 1 ½ cups water and a steamer basket to the Instant Pot. Now, place the fish in the steamer basket.
Drizzle the fish with melted ghee; sprinkle granulated garlic, onion powder, dill, salt, black pepper, and cayenne pepper over the fish.
Secure the lid. Choose "Manual" mode and High pressure; cook for 4 minutes. Once cooking is complete, use a quick pressure release; carefully remove the lid.
Then, make your homemade aioli by mixing the egg yolk, garlic, and lemon juice. Add olive oil and mix with an immersion blender; add mustard and mix again.
Serve the prepared carp steaks with the homemade aioli on the side. Bon appétit!

181. Creole Lobster with Lime Cream Sauce

(Ready in about 15 minutes | Servings 4)
What could be better than delectable lobster tails dipped in a zingy, creamy sauce? This recipe is both easy and sophisticated, so keep it in your back pocket.
Per serving: 322 Calories; 26.5g Fat; 1.8g Carbs; 19.3g Protein; 0.7g Sugars
Ingredients
1 pound lobster tails
1 tablespoon Creole seasoning blend
Lime Cream Sauce:
1 stick butter
2 tablespoons shallots, finely chopped
1/4 teaspoon salt
1/4 teaspoon black pepper
1/4 teaspoon cayenne pepper
2 tablespoons lime juice
1/4 cup heavy cream
Directions
Prepare the Instant Pot by adding 1 ½ cups of water and a steamer basket to the bottom of the inner pot. Place lobster tails in the steamer basket. Sprinkle with Creole seasoning blend.
Secure the lid. Choose "Manual" mode and Low pressure; cook for 3 minutes. Once cooking is complete, use a quick pressure release; carefully remove the lid.
Wipe down the Instant Pot with a damp cloth. Now, press the "Sauté" button and melt the butter.
Now, add the shallots, salt, black pepper, and cayenne pepper; cook for 1 minute and add lime juice and heavy cream. Cook until the sauce has reduced. Spoon the sauce over the fish and serve right now. Bon appétit!

182. Ahi Tuna Salad To-Go

(Ready in about 10 minutes + chilling time | Servings 4)
This tuna salad is perfect as an appetizer or complete dinner. The key to success is to use ahi tuna, also sold as yellowfin tuna.
Per serving: 252 Calories; 12.8g Fat; 5.8g Carbs; 27.8g Protein; 3g Sugars
Ingredients
1 cup water
2 sprigs parsley
2 sprigs thyme
2 sprigs rosemary
1 lemon, sliced
1 pound ahi tuna
1/3 teaspoon ground black pepper
1 cup cherry tomatoes, halved
1 head lettuce
1 red bell pepper julienned
1 carrot julienned
Sea salt, to taste
2 tablespoons extra-virgin olive oil
1 teaspoon Dijon mustard
Directions
Pour 1 cup of water into the Instant Pot; add the parsley, thyme, rosemary, and lemon; place a metal trivet inside.
Lower the fish onto the trivet; sprinkle with ground black pepper.
Secure the lid. Choose "Manual" mode and High pressure; cook for 4 minutes. Once cooking is complete, use a quick pressure release; carefully remove the lid.
Place the other ingredients in a salad bowl; toss to combine. Add flaked tuna and toss again. Serve well-chilled.

183. Beer-Poached Alaskan Cod

(Ready in about 10 minutes | Servings 4)
Are you ready for a light and nutritious protein dinner? Try this simple but endlessly delicious cod dish!
Per serving: 310 Calories; 23.5g Fat; 2.7g Carbs; 17.9g Protein; 0g Sugars
Ingredients
1 pound Alaskan cod fillets
1/2 cup butter
1 cup white ale beer
1 tablespoon fresh basil, chopped
1 teaspoon fresh tarragon, chopped
2 garlic cloves, minced
1 teaspoon whole black peppercorns
1/2 teaspoon coarse sea salt
Directions
Add all of the above ingredients to your Instant Pot. Secure the lid. Choose "Manual" mode and Low pressure; cook for 3 minutes. Once cooking is complete, use a quick pressure release; carefully remove the lid.
Serve right away. Bon appétit!

184. The Best Fish Chili

(Ready in about 10 minutes | Servings 4)
This fish chili turned out amazing in the Instant Pot. The recipe calls for snapper but you can use any type of firm white fish.
Per serving: 213 Calories; 12.7g Fat; 8g Carbs; 17.1g Protein; 4.1g Sugars

Ingredients
2 tablespoons olive oil
1 red onion, coarsely chopped
1 teaspoon ginger-garlic paste
1 celery stalk, diced
1 carrot, sliced
1 bell pepper, deveined and thinly sliced
1 jalapeño pepper, deveined and minced
2 ripe Roma tomatoes, crushed
1/2 pound snapper, sliced
1/2 cup water
1/2 cup broth, preferably homemade
2 tablespoons fresh coriander, minced
Sea salt and ground black pepper, to taste
1/2 teaspoon cayenne pepper
1 bay leaf
1/4 teaspoon dried dill
1/2 cup Cheddar cheese, grated

Directions
Press the "Sauté" button to heat up your Instant Pot. Now, heat the olive oil and cook the onion until translucent and tender.
Now, add the remaining ingredients, except for the grated Cheddar cheese.
Secure the lid. Choose "Manual" mode and High pressure; cook for 6 minutes. Once cooking is complete, use a quick pressure release; carefully remove the lid.
Ladle into individual bowl and serve garnished with grated Cheddar cheese. Bon appétit!

185. Haddock and Cheese Stuffed Peppers

(Ready in about 15 minutes | Servings 3)
Add some nutrition to your stuffed peppers while still achieving amazing results! With less fat and a large amount of nutrients, these peppers are sure to please everyone!
Per serving: 352 Calories; 20.1g Fat; 7.6g Carbs; 35.3g Protein; 3.6g Sugars

Ingredients
3 bell peppers, stems and seeds removed, halved
3/4 pound haddock fillets. Flaked
1 cup Romano cheese, grated
4 tablespoons scallion, chopped
2 garlic cloves, minced
4 tablespoons fresh coriander, chopped
1 tablespoon ketchup
Sea salt and ground black pepper, to taste
1 teaspoon cayenne pepper
1/2 cup tomato sauce
1 cup water
2 ounces Pepper-Jack cheese, shredded

Directions
In a mixing bowl, thoroughly combine the fish, Romano cheese, scallions, garlic, coriander, ketchup, salt, black pepper, and cayenne pepper; mix to combine well.
Now, divide this mixture among pepper halves. Add 1 cup of water and a metal rack to your Instant Pot. Arrange the peppers on the rack. Top each pepper with tomato sauce.
Secure the lid. Choose "Manual" mode and High pressure; cook for 10 minutes. Once cooking is complete, use a natural pressure release; carefully remove the lid.
Lastly, top with Pepper-Jack cheese, cover and allow the cheese to melt. Serve warm and enjoy!

186. Swai with Port Wine Sauce

(Ready in about 15 minutes | Servings 4)
Swai fish is moist fish with a mild flavor and delicate texture so you should cook it under low pressure. Swai fish is a good choice for a heart-healthy diet.
Per serving: 109 Calories; 3.3g Fat; 1.2g Carbs; 17.6g Protein; 0.5g Sugars

Ingredients
1 tablespoon butter, melted
2 garlic cloves, minced
2 tablespoon green onions, chopped
1 teaspoon fresh ginger, grated
1 pound swai fish fillets
1/2 cup port wine
1/2 tablespoon lemon juice
1 teaspoon parsley flakes
1/2 teaspoon chili flakes
Coarse sea salt and ground black pepper, to taste
1/2 teaspoon cayenne pepper
1/4 teaspoon ground bay leaf
1/2 teaspoon fennel seeds

Directions
Press the "Sauté" button to heat up your Instant Pot. Now, melt the butter and cook the garlic, green onions and ginger until softened and aromatic.
Add the remaining ingredients and gently stir to combine well.
Secure the lid. Choose "Manual" mode and Low pressure; cook for 6 minutes. Once cooking is complete, use a quick pressure release; carefully remove the lid.
Serve warm over cauli rice. Bon appétit!

187. Authentic Garam Masala Fish

(Ready in about 15 minutes | Servings 4)
If you prefer spicy food, add a certain amount of chili peppers to the Instant Pot. One tablespoon of light soy sauce works well with this dish, too.
Per serving: 159 Calories; 7.4g Fat; 4.7g Carbs; 18.1g Protein; 2.2g Sugars

Ingredients
2 tablespoons sesame oil
1/2 teaspoon cumin seeds
1/2 cup leeks, chopped

1 teaspoon ginger-garlic paste
1 pound cod fillets, boneless and sliced
2 ripe tomatoes, chopped
1/2 teaspoon turmeric powder
1/2 teaspoon garam masala
1 ½ tablespoons fresh lemon juice
1 tablespoon fresh parsley leaves, chopped
1 tablespoon fresh dill leaves, chopped
1 tablespoon fresh curry leaves, chopped
Coarse sea salt, to taste
1/4 teaspoon ground black pepper, or more to taste
1/2 teaspoon smoked cayenne pepper
Directions
Press the "Sauté" button to heat up the Instant Pot. Now, heat the sesame oil. Once hot, sauté the cumin seeds for 30 seconds.
Add the leeks and cook an additional 2 minutes or until translucent. After that, add the ginger-garlic paste and cook for 40 seconds more.
Add the other ingredients and stir to combine. Secure the lid. Choose "Manual" mode and Low pressure; cook for 6 minutes. Once cooking is complete, use a quick pressure release; carefully remove the lid. Bon appétit!

188. Easy Party Seafood Dip
(Ready in about 10 minutes | Servings 8)
With fresh shallots, superb seafood, and creamy Ricotta, this appetizer recipe is flavorful and extremely comforting. Mediterranean herbs are the best flavor-enhancing ingredients for this recipe!
Per serving: 151 Calories; 8.3g Fat; 2.6g Carbs; 15.6g Protein; 0.7g Sugars
Ingredients
1/2 pound shrimp
1/2 pound crab
1/2 cup apple cider vinegar
1/2 cup water
1/4 cup heavy cream
1/2 tablespoon lime juice
2 tablespoons shallots, chopped
1 teaspoon garlic, minced
Kosher salt and white pepper, to taste
1/2 teaspoon dried rosemary
1/2 teaspoon dried oregano
1/2 teaspoon cayenne pepper
10 ounces Ricotta cheese
Directions
Place the shrimp, crab, vinegar and water in your Instant Pot.
Secure the lid. Choose "Manual" mode and Low pressure; cook for 3 minutes. Once cooking is complete, use a quick pressure release; carefully remove the lid.
Then, process all of the remaining ingredients in your blender. Add the cooked shrimp and crab. Continue blending until your desired consistency is achieved.
Spoon the dip into a nice serving bowl. Serve with vegetable dippers and enjoy!

189. Red Curry Perch Fillets
(Ready in about 10 minutes | Servings 4)
Perch is an excellent source of protein, calcium and omega fatty acids. Red curry, also known as "spicy curry", is an ingredient that is commonly used in Thai cooking.
Per serving: 135 Calories; 4.1g Fat; 1.3g Carbs; 22.3g Protein; 0.6g Sugars
Ingredients
1 cup water
1 large-sized lemon, sliced
2 sprigs rosemary
1 pound perch fillets
Sea salt and ground black pepper, to taste
1 teaspoon cayenne pepper
1 tablespoon red curry paste
1 tablespoons butter
Directions
Pour 1 cup of water into the Instant Pot; add the lemon slices and rosemary; place a metal trivet inside.
Now, sprinkle the perch fillets with salt, black pepper, and cayenne pepper. Spread red curry paste and butter over the fillets.
Lower the fish onto the trivet.
Secure the lid. Choose "Manual" mode and Low pressure; cook for 6 minutes. Once cooking is complete, use a quick pressure release; carefully remove the lid.
Serve with your favorite keto sides. Bon appétit!

190. Milky Mackerel Chowder
(Ready in about 10 minutes | Servings 4)
Comforting, warming and economical chowder loaded with milk, double cream, and fish. This chowder is always a good idea for a family lunch.
Per serving: 332 Calories; 20.3g Fat; 7g Carbs; 29.1g Protein; 6g Sugars
Ingredients
1 tablespoon olive oil
1 yellow onion, chopped
2 garlic cloves, minced
1 teaspoon grated ginger
1 pound mackerel fillets, sliced
1 ½ cups milk
2 cups chicken stock
1/2 cup double cream
1 tablespoon butter
Directions
Press the "Sauté" button to heat up the Instant Pot. Now, heat the olive oil. Once hot, sauté the onion until softened.
Then, sauté the garlic and ginger for 30 to 40 seconds more.
Add the remaining ingredients and stir to combine. Secure the lid. Choose "Manual" mode and High pressure; cook for 6 minutes. Once cooking is complete, use a quick pressure release; carefully remove the lid. Bon appétit!

191. Bluefish in Tarragon-Vermouth Sauce

(Ready in about 10 minutes | Servings 4)

Vermouth enlivens the herbed sauce in this elegant and delicious bluefish dish. This fragrant sauce goes perfectly with a flaky, pressure-cooked bluefish.

Per serving: 204 Calories; 7.9g Fat; 4.4g Carbs; 23.5g Protein; 2.3g Sugars

Ingredients
2 teaspoons butter
1/2 yellow onion, chopped
1 garlic clove, minced
1 pound bluefish fillets
Sea salt and ground black pepper, to taste
1/4 cup vermouth
1 tablespoon rice vinegar
2 teaspoons tamari
1 teaspoon fresh tarragon leaves, chopped

Directions
Press the "Sauté" button to heat up the Instant Pot. Now, melt the butter. Once hot, sauté the onion until softened.

Add garlic and sauté for a further minute or until aromatic. Stir in the remaining ingredients.

Secure the lid. Choose "Manual" mode and Low pressure; cook for 3 minutes. Once cooking is complete, use a quick pressure release; carefully remove the lid. Bon appétit!

192. Grouper with Mushrooms and Smoked Sausage

(Ready in about 15 minutes | Servings 4)

This dish smells like a summer day at the beach! Any type of smoked meaty sausage can be substituted for turkey sausage in this recipe.

Per serving: 431 Calories; 13.7g Fat; 7.9g Carbs; 62.4g Protein; 4.3g Sugars

Ingredients
2 tablespoons butter
1/2 pound smoked turkey sausage, casing removed
1 pound Cremini mushrooms, sliced
2 garlic cloves, minced
4 grouper fillets
Sea salt, to taste
1/2 teaspoon black peppercorns, freshly cracked
1/2 cup dry white wine
1 tablespoon fresh lime juice
2 tablespoons fresh cilantro, chopped

Directions
Press the "Sauté" button to heat up the Instant Pot. Now, melt the butter. Once hot, cook the sausage until nice and browned on all sides; reserve.

Then, cook Cremini mushrooms in pan drippings for about 3 minutes or until fragrant.

Add the garlic and continue to sauté an additional 30 seconds. Now, add the fish, salt, black peppercorns, and wine. Return the sausage back to the Instant Pot.

Secure the lid. Choose "Manual" mode and Low pressure; cook for 3 minutes. Once cooking is complete, use a quick pressure release; carefully remove the lid. Bon appétit!

Afterwards, divide your dish among serving plates and drizzle fresh lime juice over each serving. Serve garnished with fresh cilantro. Bon appétit!

193. King Crab with Baby Bellas

(Ready in about 10 minutes | Servings 6)

Baby bella mushrooms, also known as crimini mushrooms, are white mushrooms with rich and earthy flavor. Sautéing is the best method to prepare baby bellas.

Per serving: 176 Calories; 8.5g Fat; 2.4g Carbs; 22.3g Protein; 1.1g Sugars

Ingredients
1 ½ pounds king crab legs, halved
1/2 stick butter, softened
10 ounces baby Bella mushrooms
2 garlic cloves, minced
1 lemon, sliced

Directions
Start by adding 1 cup water and a steamer basket to your Instant Pot.

Now, add the king crab legs to the steamer basket. Secure the lid. Choose "Manual" mode and Low pressure; cook for 3 minutes. Once cooking is complete, use a quick pressure release; carefully remove the lid.

Wipe down the Instant Pot with a damp cloth; then, warm the butter. Once hot, cook baby Bella mushrooms with minced garlic for 2 to 3 minutes. Spoon the mushrooms sauce over prepared king crab legs and serve with lemon. Bon appétit!

194. Rainbow Trout with Buttery Mixed Greens

(Ready in about 20 minutes | Servings 4)

This ketogenic lunch is both, light and fulfilling. We opted for salt and pepper but you can toss in whatever spices you have on hand!

Per serving: 341 Calories; 17.7g Fat; 6.4g Carbs; 38.3g Protein; 1.2g Sugars

Ingredients
1 ½ pounds rainbow trout fillets
4 tablespoons butter
Sea salt and ground black pepper, to taste
1 bunch of scallions
1 pound mixed greens, trimmed and torn into pieces
1/2 cup chicken broth
1 tablespoon apple cider vinegar
1 teaspoon cayenne pepper

Directions
Start by adding 1 cup water and a steamer basket to your Instant Pot.

Now, add the fish to the steamer basket. Drizzle 1 tablespoon of the melted butter over them and sprinkle with salt and black pepper.

Secure the lid. Choose "Manual" mode and Low pressure; cook for 12 minutes. Once cooking is

complete, use a quick pressure release; carefully remove the lid.
Wipe down the Instant Pot with a damp cloth; then, warm the remaining 3 tablespoons of butter. Once hot, cook the scallions, greens, broth, vinegar and cayenne pepper until the greens start to wilt.
Serve the prepared trout fillets with the sautéed greens on the side. Bon appétit!

195. Simply Creole Sea Scallops

(Ready in about 10 minutes | Servings 4)
With their subtle flavors, scallops are perfect for any occasion. One of the best ways to prepare scallops is to cook them briefly in the Instant Pot.
Per serving: 163 Calories; 4.7g Fat; 6.1g Carbs; 22.6g Protein; 0g Sugars
Ingredients
2 teaspoon butter, melted
1 ½ pounds sea scallops
2 garlic cloves, finely chopped
1 (1-inch) piece fresh ginger root, grated
1/3 cup dry white wine
2/3 cup fish stock
Coarse sea salt and ground black pepper, to taste
1 teaspoon Creole seasoning blend
2 tablespoons fresh parsley, chopped
Directions
Press the "Sauté" button to heat up the Instant Pot. Now, melt the butter. Once hot, cook the sea scallops until nice and browned on all sides.
Now, stir in the garlic and ginger; continue sautéing for 1 minute more or until fragrant. Dump the remaining ingredients, except for the fresh parsley, into your Instant Pot.
Secure the lid. Choose "Manual" mode and High pressure; cook for 1 minutes. Once cooking is complete, use a quick pressure release; carefully remove the lid.
Serve garnished with fresh parsley and enjoy!

196. Tuna and Parmesan Stuffed Zucchini

(Ready in about 15 minutes | Servings 4)
Try this delicious and budget-friendly stuffed zucchini! This is an innovative and lighter version of classic meat-stuffed vegetables. Enjoy!
Per serving: 203 Calories; 9.5g Fat; 6.1g Carbs; 22.5g Protein; 2.8g Sugars
Ingredients
1 tablespoon olive oil
1 yellow onion, finely chopped
1 garlic clove, smashed
3/4 pound tuna fillets, chopped
1/4 cup Parmesan cheese, grated
2 tablespoons fresh cilantro, chopped
Salt and ground black pepper, to taste
1/2 teaspoon mustard seeds
2 large-sized zucchini cut the ends off, halved
2 ripe tomatoes, puréed
1/2 cup water

Directions
Press the "Sauté" button to heat up the Instant Pot. Now, heat the olive oil and sauté the onions and garlic until tender and fragrant.
Transfer the sautéed onion and garlic to a mixing bowl. Add the fish, cheese, cilantro, salt, black pepper, and mustard seeds.
Core out your zucchini with a spoon to make little "boats". Stuff these zucchini boats with the tuna mixture.
Mix the puréed tomatoes with water; now, pour this mixture over the stuffed zucchini.
Secure the lid. Choose "Manual" mode and High pressure; cook for 5 minutes.
Once cooking is complete, use a quick pressure release; carefully remove the lid. Serve garnished with some additional cheese, if desired. Bon appétit!

197. Salmon Steaks with Garlic Yogurt

(Ready in about 10 minutes | Servings 4)
Prepare to become totally addicted to this amazing salmon dish. Bear in mind that cooking salmon too long in an Instant Pot can dry it out so it can lose its natural texture and flavors.
Per serving: 364 Calories; 21.2g Fat; 4.2g Carbs; 37.2g Protein; 3.3g Sugars
Ingredients
2 tablespoons olive oil
4 salmon steaks
Coarse sea salt and ground black pepper, to taste
Garlic Yogurt:
1 (8-ounce) container full-fat Greek yogurt
2 tablespoons mayonnaise
1/3 teaspoon Dijon mustard
2 cloves garlic, minced
Directions
Start by adding 1 cup of water and a steamer rack to the Instant Pot.
Now, massage olive oil into the fish; generously season with salt and black pepper on all sides. Place the fish on the steamer rack.
Secure the lid. Choose "Manual" mode and High pressure; cook for 4 minutes. Once cooking is complete, use a quick pressure release; carefully remove the lid.
Then, make the garlic yogurt by whisking Greek yogurt, mayonnaise, Dijon mustard, and garlic.
Serve salmon steaks with the garlic yogurt on the side. Bon appétit!

198. Spicy Chanterelles and Scampi Boil

(Ready in about 10 minutes | Servings 4)
Just a touch of Sriracha hot sauce gives this recipe a different twist on the usual scampi boil. Meaty and chewy chanterelles go wonderfully with this appetizing, pressure-cooked scampi.
Per serving: 281 Calories; 13.6g Fat; 9.1g Carbs; 23.6g Protein; 0.9g Sugars

Ingredients
12 ounces lager beer
1 tablespoon Creole seasoning
1/2 teaspoon paprika
1/3 teaspoon dried dill weed
Sea salt and ground black pepper, to taste
1 shallot, chopped
2 cloves garlic, crushed
1/2 teaspoon Sriracha
1/2 pound chanterelles, sliced
1 pound scampi, deveined

Directions
Simply throw all of the above ingredients into your Instant Pot.
Secure the lid. Choose "Manual" mode and Low pressure; cook for 2 minutes. Once cooking is complete, use a quick pressure release; carefully remove the lid.
Serve with fresh cucumbers and radishes on the side.

199. Hangover Seafood Bowl

(Ready in about 15 minutes | Servings 6)
Ay Dios Mio! Hangover! A bowl full of seafood, tomato, olives, and chilies will help cure your hangover.
Per serving: 280 Calories; 14g Fat; 9g Carbs; 32g Protein; 2.8g Sugars

Ingredients
1 ½ pounds shrimp, peeled and deveined
1/2 pound calamari, cleaned
1/2 pound lobster
2 bay leaves
2 rosemary sprigs
2 thyme sprigs
4 garlic cloves, halved
1/2 cup fresh lemon juice
Sea salt and ground black pepper, to taste
3 ripe tomatoes, puréed
1/2 cup olives, pitted and halved
2 tablespoons fresh coriander, chopped
2 tablespoons fresh parsley, chopped
3 tablespoons extra-virgin olive oil
3 chili peppers, deveined and minced
1/2 cup red onion, chopped
1 avocado, pitted and sliced

Directions
Add shrimp, calamari, lobster, bay leaves, rosemary, thyme, and garlic to your Instant Pot. Pour in 1 cup of water.
Secure the lid. Choose "Manual" mode and Low pressure; cook for 3 minutes. Once cooking is complete, use a quick pressure release; carefully remove the lid.
Drain the seafood and transfer to a serving bowl.
In a mixing bowl, thoroughly combine lemon juice, salt, black pepper, tomatoes, olives, coriander, parsley, olive oil, chili peppers, and red onion.
Transfer this mixture to the serving bowl with the seafood. Stir to combine well; serve well-chilled, garnished with avocado. Bon appétit!

200. Tiger Prawns with Herbed Butter Sauce

(Ready in about 10 minutes | Servings 6)
Try these saucy, buttery, melt-in-your-mouth tiger prawns! Crisp dry sherry will add just the right amount of tanginess to this sensational butter sauce.
Per serving: 246 Calories; 16.1g Fat; 1.8g Carbs; 23.3g Protein; 0.6g Sugars

Ingredients
1 ½ pounds raw tiger prawns, peeled and deveined
1/4 cup rice wine vinegar
1 stick butter
1 teaspoon cumin seeds
1/2 teaspoon fennel seeds
1/2 teaspoon mustard seeds
1 teaspoon dried rosemary
1 teaspoon garlic paste
1 teaspoon red pepper flakes, crushed
Salt and ground black pepper, to taste
2 tablespoons dry sherry
2 tablespoons fresh parsley, chopped
2 tablespoons fresh cilantro, chopped
2 tablespoons fresh lemon juice

Directions
Toss the prawns and rice wine vinegar into your Instant Pot. Pour in 1 cup of water.
Secure the lid. Choose "Manual" mode and Low pressure; cook for 2 minutes. Once cooking is complete, use a quick pressure release; carefully remove the lid. Drain tiger prawns and reserve.
Then, wipe down the Instant Pot with a damp cloth. Press the "Sauté" button to heat up the Instant Pot; then, warm the butter.
Now, sauté cumin seeds, fennel seeds, mustard seeds, rosemary, and garlic paste for 40 seconds, stirring continuously.
Now, add the reserved prawns, along with red pepper, salt, black pepper, dry sherry, parsley, cilantro, and lemon juice. Serve immediately and enjoy!

VEGETABLES & SIDE DISHES

201. Easy Cheesy Artichokes
(Ready in about 10 minutes | Servings 3)
Artichokes and shredded Monterey-Jack cheese combine very well in this recipe! Serve as a side dish or a complete vegetarian meal.
Per serving: 173 Calories; 12.5g Fat; 9g Carbs; 8.1g Protein; 0.9g Sugars
Ingredients
3 medium-sized artichokes, cleaned and trimmed
3 cloves garlic, smashed
3 tablespoons butter, melted
Sea salt, to taste
1/2 teaspoon cayenne pepper
1/4 teaspoon ground black pepper, or more to taste
1 lemon, freshly squeezed
1 cup Monterey-Jack cheese, shredded
1 tablespoon fresh parsley, roughly chopped
Directions
Start by adding 1 cup of water and a steamer basket to the Instant Pot. Place the artichokes in the steamer basket; add garlic and butter.
Secure the lid. Choose "Manual" mode and High pressure; cook for 8 minutes. Once cooking is complete, use a quick pressure release; carefully remove the lid.
Season your artichokes with salt, cayenne pepper, and black pepper. Now, drizzle them with lemon juice.
Top with cheese and parsley and serve immediately. Bon appétit!

202. Chinese Bok Choy
(Ready in about 10 minutes | Servings 4)
Bok choy, also sold as Chinese cabbage, is a nutritional powerhouse! In this recipe, it is flavored with butter, garlic, Five-spice powder, and soy sauce. Yummy!
Per serving: 83 Calories; 6.1g Fat; 5.7g Carbs; 3.2g Protein; 2.4g Sugars
Ingredients
2 tablespoons butter, melted
2 cloves garlic, minced
1 (1/2-inch) slice fresh ginger root, grated
1 ½ pounds Bok choy, trimmed
1 cup vegetable stock
Celery salt and ground black pepper to taste
1 teaspoon Five-spice powder
2 tablespoons soy sauce
Directions
Press the "Sauté" button to heat up the Instant Pot. Now, warm the butter and sauté the garlic until tender and fragrant.
Now, add grated ginger and cook for a further 40 seconds.
Add Bok choy, stock, salt, black pepper, and Five-spice powder.
Secure the lid. Choose "Manual" mode and High pressure; cook for 6 minutes. Once cooking is complete, use a quick pressure release; carefully remove the lid.
Drizzle soy sauce over your Bok choy and serve immediately. Bon appétit!

203. Green Cabbage with Bacon
(Ready in about 10 minutes | Servings 4)
There are many recipes for a classic cabbage side dish out there. However, this Southern-style cabbage is one of the tastiest cabbage dishes you will ever try.
Per serving: 166 Calories; 13g Fat; 7.1g Carbs; 6.8g Protein; 2.7g Sugars
Ingredients
2 teaspoons olive oil
4 slices bacon, chopped
1 head green cabbage, cored and cut into wedges
1 cups vegetable stock
Sea salt, to taste
1/2 teaspoon whole black peppercorns
1 teaspoon cayenne pepper
1 bay leaf
Directions
Press the "Sauté" button to heat up the Instant Pot. Then, heat olive oil and cook the bacon until it is nice and delicately browned.
Then, add the remaining ingredients; gently stir to combine.
Secure the lid. Choose "Manual" mode and High pressure; cook for 3 minutes. Once cooking is complete, use a quick pressure release; carefully remove the lid.
Serve warm and enjoy!

204. Warm Broccoli Salad Bowl
(Ready in about 10 minutes | Servings 4)
Prepare a crunchy, make-ahead broccoli salad that is sure to please the whole family! Broccoli is a great source of vitamins C, K, and E as well as dietary fiber and minerals.
Per serving: 95 Calories; 3.1g Fat; 8.1g Carbs; 9.9g Protein; 3.8g Sugars
Ingredients
1 pound broccoli, broken into florets
2 tablespoons balsamic vinegar
2 garlic cloves, minced
1 teaspoon mustard seeds
1 teaspoon cumin seeds
Salt and pepper, to taste
1 cup Cottage cheese, crumbled
Directions
Place 1 cup of water and a steamer basket in your Instant Pot.
Place the broccoli in the steamer basket.
Secure the lid. Choose "Manual" mode and High pressure; cook for 5 minutes. Once cooking is complete, use a quick pressure release; carefully remove the lid.

Then, toss your broccoli with the other ingredients. Serve and enjoy!

205. Creamed Spinach with Cheese
(Ready in about 10 minutes | Servings 4)
This dish is simply irresistible. Simply toss fresh spinach leaves with a cheese, spices and garlic to achieve your keto requirements.
Per serving: 283 Calories; 23.9g Fat; 9g Carbs; 10.7g Protein; 3.2g Sugars
Ingredients
2 tablespoons butter, melted
1/2 cup scallions, chopped
2 cloves garlic, smashed
1 ½ pounds fresh spinach
1 cup vegetable broth, preferably homemade
1 cup cream cheese, cubed
Seasoned salt and ground black pepper, to taste
1/2 teaspoon dried dill weed
Directions
Press the "Sauté" button to heat up the Instant Pot. Then, melt the butter; cook the scallions and garlic until tender and aromatic.
Add the remaining ingredients and stir to combine well.
Secure the lid. Choose "Manual" mode and High pressure; cook for 2 minutes. Once cooking is complete, use a quick pressure release; carefully remove the lid.
Ladle into individual bowls and serve warm. Bon appétit!

206. Turnip Greens with Sausage
(Ready in about 10 minutes | Servings 4)
Turnip greens are a good source of vitamin A, vitamin B2, vitamin B6, vitamin C, vitamin K, copper, calcium, manganese, iron, and dietary fiber.
Per serving: 149 Calories; 7.2g Fat; 9g Carbs; 14.2g Protein; 2.2g Sugars
Ingredients
2 teaspoons sesame oil
2 pork sausages, casing removed sliced
2 garlic cloves, minced
1 medium-sized leek, chopped
1 pound turnip greens
1 cup turkey bone stock
Sea salt, to taste
1/4 teaspoon ground black pepper, or more to taste
1 bay leaf
1 tablespoon black sesame seeds
Directions
Press the "Sauté" button to heat up the Instant Pot. Then, heat the sesame oil; cook the sausage until nice and delicately browned; set aside.
Add the garlic and leeks; continue to cook in pan drippings for a minute or two.
Add the greens, stock, salt, black pepper, and bay leaf.
Secure the lid. Choose "Manual" mode and Low pressure; cook for 3 minutes. Once cooking is complete, use a quick pressure release; carefully remove the lid.
Serve garnished with black sesame seeds and enjoy!

207. Asparagus with Colby Cheese
(Ready in about 10 minutes | Servings 4)
Here's a completely new way to eat your asparagus! Asparagus is funny and delicious!
Per serving: 164 Calories; 12.2g Fat; 8.1g Carbs; 7.8g Protein; 3.3g Sugars
Ingredients
1 ½ pounds fresh asparagus
2 tablespoons olive oil
4 garlic cloves, minced
Sea salt, to taste
1/4 teaspoon ground black pepper
1/2 cup Colby cheese, shredded
Directions
Add 1 cup of water and a steamer basket to your Instant Pot.
Now, place the asparagus on the steamer basket; drizzle your asparagus with olive oil. Scatter garlic over the top of the asparagus.
Season with salt and black pepper.
Secure the lid. Choose "Manual" mode and High pressure; cook for 1 minute. Once cooking is complete, use a quick pressure release; carefully remove the lid.
Transfer the prepared asparagus to a nice serving platter and scatter shredded cheese over the top. Enjoy!

208. Mediterranean Aromatic Zucchini
(Ready in about 10 minutes | Servings 4)
Zucchini, garlic and puréed tomatoes are tossed with Mediterranean spices for a quick vegan dinner or an elegant appetizer.
Per serving: 85 Calories; 7.1g Fat; 4.7g Carbs; 1.6g Protein; 3.3g Sugars
Ingredients
2 tablespoons olive oil
2 garlic cloves, chopped
1 pound zucchini, sliced
1/2 cup tomato purée
1/2 cup water
1 teaspoon dried thyme
1/2 teaspoon dried oregano
1/2 teaspoon dried rosemary
Directions
Press the "Sauté" button to heat up the Instant Pot. Then, heat the olive oil; sauté the garlic until aromatic.
Add the remaining ingredients.
Secure the lid. Choose "Manual" mode and Low pressure; cook for 3 minutes. Once cooking is complete, use a quick pressure release; carefully remove the lid. Bon appétit!

209. Chanterelles with Cheddar Cheese

(Ready in about 10 minutes | Servings 4)
Chanterelle mushrooms pair wonderfully with tomatoes and Cheddar Cheese. So good, right?
Per serving: 218 Calories; 15.1g Fat; 9.5g Carbs; 9.9g Protein; 2.3g Sugars

Ingredients
1 tablespoon olive oil
2 cloves garlic, minced
1 (1-inch) ginger root, grated
1/2 teaspoon dried dill weed
1 teaspoon dried basil
1/2 teaspoon dried thyme
16 ounces Chanterelle mushrooms, brushed clean and sliced
1/2 cup water
1/2 cup tomato purée
2 tablespoons dry white wine
1/3 teaspoon freshly ground black pepper
Kosher salt, to taste
1 cup Cheddar cheese

Directions
Press the "Sauté" button to heat up the Instant Pot. Then, heat the olive oil; sauté the garlic and grated ginger for 1 minute or until aromatic.
Add dried dill, basil, thyme, Chanterelles, water, tomato purée, dry white wine, black pepper, and salt.
Secure the lid. Choose "Manual" mode and Low pressure; cook for 5 minutes. Once cooking is complete, use a quick pressure release; carefully remove the lid.
Top with shredded cheese and serve immediately. Bon appétit!

210. Family Cauliflower Soup

(Ready in about 10 minutes | Servings 4)
Is there anything better than a thick vegetable soup during winter weekdays? In addition, you will have a meal on the table in no time.
Per serving: 167 Calories; 13.7g Fat; 8.7g Carbs; 3.8g Protein; 5.1g Sugars

Ingredients
4 tablespoons butter, softened
1/2 cup leeks, thinly sliced
2 cloves garlic, minced
3/4 pound cauliflower, broken into florets
1 cup water
2 cups chicken stock
1 cup full-fat milk
Kosher salt, to taste
1/3 teaspoon ground black pepper

Directions
Press the "Sauté" button to heat up your Instant Pot. Then, melt the butter; sauté the leeks until softened.
Then, sauté the garlic until fragrant, about 30 seconds. Add the remaining ingredients and gently stir to combine.
Secure the lid. Choose "Manual" mode and Low pressure; cook for 5 minutes. Once cooking is complete, use a quick pressure release; carefully remove the lid.
Ladle into individual bowls and serve warm. Bon appétit!

211. Cauliflower and Kohlrabi Mash

(Ready in about 15 minutes | Servings 4)
This is a great way to get kids to eat veggies! This flavorful mashed vegetables fitting for light dinner or a party appetizer. Be inspired and try sprinkling in a pinch of chili powder.
Per serving: 89 Calories; 4.7g Fat; 9.6g Carbs; 3.6g Protein; 2.6g Sugars

Ingredients
1/2 pound cauliflower, cut into florets
1/2 pound kohlrabi, peeled and diced
1 cup water
3/4 cup sour cream
1 garlic clove, minced
Sea salt, to taste
1/3 teaspoon ground black pepper
1/2 teaspoon cayenne pepper

Directions
Add 1 cup of water and a steamer basket to the bottom of your Instant Pot.
Then, arrange cauliflower and kohlrabi in the steamer basket.
Secure the lid. Choose "Manual" mode and Low pressure; cook for 3 minutes. Once cooking is complete, use a quick pressure release; carefully remove the lid.
Now, puree the cauliflower and kohlrabi with a potato masher. Add the remaining ingredients and stir well. Bon appétit!

212. Old-Fashioned Stuffed Peppers

(Ready in about 20 minutes | Servings 3)
Here's one of the best keto dishes to make for an easy, no-stress family dinner. We opted for Mediterranean spices but you can toss in whatever spices and herbs you have on hand.
Per serving: 488 Calories; 38.2g Fat; 7.1g Carbs; 29.1g Protein; 4.1g Sugars

Ingredients
2 tablespoons olive oil
1 yellow onion, chopped
2 garlic cloves, smashed
2 tablespoons coriander, chopped
1/3 pound ground beef
1/2 pound ground pork
Sea salt, to taste
1/4 teaspoon black peppercorns, freshly crushed
3 bell peppers, deveined, tops removed
2 ripe tomatoes, puréed
1 teaspoon dried basil
1/2 teaspoon dried oregano
1/2 teaspoon dried rosemary
1/2 cup Romano cheese, freshly grated

Directions

Press the "Sauté" button to heat up the Instant Pot; heat the oil.
Once hot, sweat the onions for 2 minutes. Add garlic and coriander cook an additional 30 seconds. Then, stir in ground meat and cook until no longer pink. Season with salt and black peppercorns.
Stuff the peppers with this meat mixture; do not pack the peppers too tightly.
In a mixing bowl, thoroughly combine pureed tomatoes, basil, oregano, and rosemary. Pour this mixture over the peppers.
Wipe down the Instant Pot with a damp cloth; add 1 ½ cups of water and a metal trivet to the Instant Pot. Place the peppers on the trivet and secure the lid. Choose "Poultry" mode and High pressure; cook for 15 minutes. Once cooking is complete, use a quick pressure release; carefully remove the lid.
Top with grated Romano cheese, cover, and let it sit in the residual heat. Serve warm and enjoy!

213. Aromatic Tomato Soup
(Ready in about 10 minutes | Servings 2)
A tangy and refreshing tomato soup is always a good idea! Prepare this amazing, nutritious soup and make the most of the fall season!
Per serving: 339 Calories; 29.5g Fat; 9.1g Carbs; 10.8g Protein; 5.6g Sugars
Ingredients
1 tablespoon avocado oil
2 cloves garlic, minced
2 ripe tomatoes, puréed
1/2 cup double cream
1/3 cup water
1/2 teaspoon basil
1 teaspoon dried sage
Salt, to taste
1/4 teaspoon ground black pepper
1/2 teaspoon cayenne pepper
1/2 cup Colby cheese, shredded
Directions
Press the "Sauté" button to heat up the Instant Pot; heat the oil. Once hot, cook the garlic until aromatic.
Add the remaining ingredients and stir to combine.
Secure the lid. Choose "Manual" mode and Low pressure; cook for 3 minutes. Once cooking is complete, use a quick pressure release; carefully remove the lid.
Ladle into individual bowls and serve immediately. Bon appétit!

214. Bok Choy with Tofu
(Ready in about 8 minutes | Servings 4)
This is a recipe you will be making again and again. It is best served at room temperature.
Per serving: 133 Calories; 8.6g Fat; 5.1g Carbs; 11.1g Protein; 2g Sugars
Ingredients
1 tablespoon olive oil
12 ounces extra-firm tofu, pressed and cubed
1 ½ teaspoons ginger-garlic paste
1 ½ pounds Bok choy
1 cup water
2 tablespoons coconut aminos
1/4 cup rice wine vinegar
1 teaspoon smoked paprika
Himalayan pink salt, to taste
1/4 teaspoon ground black pepper
Directions
Press the "Sauté" button to heat up the Instant Pot; heat the oil. Once hot, cook the tofu until delicately browned.
Add the ginger-garlic paste and Bok choy; sauté 1 minute more. Add the remaining ingredients. Secure the lid. Choose "Manual" mode and Low pressure; cook for 4 minutes. Once cooking is complete, use a quick pressure release; carefully remove the lid.
Serve immediately. Bon appétit!

215. Braised Garlicky Endive
(Ready in about 6 minutes | Servings 3)
Belgians call their endive "white gold". It is a solid source of vitamin B-complex, vitamin A, and manganese. It is an endlessly versatile ingredient for your keto diet.
Per serving: 91 Calories; 5.3g Fat; 9.1g Carbs; 3.6g Protein; 1.8g Sugars
Ingredients
1 tablespoon extra-virgin olive oil
2 garlic cloves, minced
2 large-sized Belgian endive, halved lengthwise
1/2 cup apple cider vinegar
1/2 cup broth, preferably homemade
Sea salt and freshly ground black pepper, to taste
1 teaspoon cayenne pepper
Directions
Press the "Sauté" button to heat up the Instant Pot; heat the oil. Once hot, cook the garlic for 30 seconds or until aromatic and browned.
Add Belgian endive, vinegar, broth, salt, black pepper, and cayenne pepper.
Secure the lid. Choose "Manual" mode and Low pressure; cook for 2 minutes or until tender when pierced with the tip of a knife.
Once cooking is complete, use a quick pressure release; carefully remove the lid. Bon appétit!

216. Italian Pancetta and Cabbage Soup
(Ready in about 10 minutes | Servings 4)
Mama mia! You won't be able to resist this hearty soup that is loaded with fresh vegetables, pancetta and Italian seasonings!
Per serving: 196 Calories; 17.8g Fat; 8.4g Carbs; 2.2g Protein; 2.5g Sugars
Ingredients
1 tablespoon olive oil
2 ounces pancetta, finely diced
1/2 cup shallots, chopped
1 red bell pepper, deveined and sliced

1 green bell pepper, deveined and sliced
1 carrot, sliced
2 celery stalks with leaves, diced
2 cloves garlic
2 ripe Roma tomatoes, puréed
3/4 pound green cabbage, cut into wedges
4 cups water
2 bouillon cubes
1 tablespoon Italian seasoning blend
1 cup baby spinach
Directions
Press the "Sauté" button to heat up your Instant Pot; heat the olive oil. Once hot, cook pancetta until crisp, about 3 minutes; reserve.
Now, cook the shallots, peppers, carrot, celery, and garlic until tender.
Add tomatoes, cabbage, water, bouillon cubes, Italian seasoning blend; stir to combine.
Secure the lid. Choose "Manual" mode and Low pressure; cook for 3 minutes. Once cooking is complete, use a quick pressure release; carefully remove the lid.
Lastly, add baby spinach, cover, and let it sit in the residual heat until it wilts. Ladle into four soup bowls and top with the reserved pancetta. Enjoy!

217. Buttery and Garlicky Fennel

(Ready in about 6 minutes | Servings 6)
With its bright, anise-like flavor, fennel is one of the favorite ingredients on a ketogenic diet. Not only are the bulbs edible, but so are the leaves and seeds.
Per serving: 111 Calories; 7.8g Fat; 8.7g Carbs; 2.1g Protein; 4.7g Sugars
Ingredients
1/2 stick butter
2 garlic cloves, sliced
1/2 teaspoon sea salt
1 ½ pounds fennel bulbs, cut into wedges
1/4 teaspoon ground black pepper, or more to taste
1/2 teaspoon cayenne pepper
1/4 teaspoon dried dill weed
1/3 cup dry white wine
2/3 cup chicken stock
Directions
Press the "Sauté" button to heat up your Instant Pot; now, melt the butter. Cook garlic for 30 seconds, stirring periodically.
Add the remaining ingredients.
Secure the lid. Choose "Manual" mode and Low pressure; cook for 3 minutes. Once cooking is complete, use a quick pressure release; carefully remove the lid. Bon appétit!

218. Vegetables à la Grecque

(Ready in about 10 minutes | Servings 4)
This authentic Greek dish can be adapted according to your personal preferences. Feel free to top your vegetables with Pepper-Jack or Swiss cheese. Enjoy!
Per serving: 326 Calories; 25.1g Fat; 8.4g Carbs; 15.7g Protein; 4.3g Sugars
Ingredients
2 tablespoons olive oil
2 garlic cloves, minced
1 red onion, chopped
10 ounces button mushrooms, thinly sliced
1 (1-pound) eggplant, sliced
1/2 teaspoon dried basil
1 teaspoon dried oregano
1 thyme sprig, leaves picked
2 rosemary sprigs, leaves picked
1/2 cup tomato sauce
1/4 cup dry Greek wine
1/4 cup water
8 ounces Halloumi cheese, cubed
4 tablespoons Kalamata olives, pitted and halved
Directions
Press the "Sauté" button to heat up your Instant Pot; now, heat the olive oil. Cook the garlic and red onions for 1 to 2 minutes, stirring periodically.
Stir in the mushrooms and continue to sauté an additional 2 to 3 minutes.
Add the eggplant, basil, oregano, thyme, rosemary, tomato sauce, Greek wine, and water.
Secure the lid. Choose "Manual" mode and Low pressure; cook for 3 minutes. Once cooking is complete, use a quick pressure release; carefully remove the lid.
Top with cheese and olives. Bon appétit!

219. Caramelized Endive with Goat Cheese

(Ready in about 10 minutes | Servings 4)
A fresh endive with its mellow and sharp sweetness and goat cheese with its creaminess and deliciousness make an elegant first course that everyone will love!
Per serving: 221 Calories; 18.5g Fat; 6.6g Carbs; 8.7g Protein; 0.8g Sugars
Ingredients
1/2 stick butter
1 ½ pounds endive, cut into bite-sized chunks
Sea salt, to taste
1/3 teaspoon cayenne pepper
1/3 teaspoon ground black pepper
1/4 cup dry white wine
1/2 cup chicken broth
1/4 cup water
2 tablespoons fresh parsley, roughly chopped
2 ounces goat cheese, crumbled
Directions
Press the "Sauté" button to heat up your Instant Pot; now, melt the butter. Cook endive for 1 to 2 minutes or until it is caramelized.
Season with salt, cayenne pepper, and black pepper. Next, pour in wine, broth, and water.
Secure the lid. Choose "Manual" mode and Low pressure; cook for 2 minutes. Once cooking is complete, use a quick pressure release; carefully remove the lid.
Serve topped with goat cheese. Bon appétit!

220. Loaded Tuscan Rapini Soup

(Ready in about 8 minutes | Servings 4)

Broccoli rabe, also known as rapini, is commonly used in Italian cuisine. It is a cruciferous, leafy vegetable that is related to the turnip.

Per serving: 95 Calories; 6.7g Fat; 5.2g Carbs; 4.2g Protein; 1.4g Sugars

Ingredients
2 tablespoons butter, melted
1/2 cup leeks, sliced
2 garlic cloves, minced
4 cups broccoli rabe, broken into pieces
2 cups water
2 cups broth, preferably homemade
1 zucchini, shredded
1 carrot, trimmed and grated
Sea salt, to taste
1/4 teaspoon ground black pepper

Directions
Press the "Sauté" button to heat up your Instant Pot; now, melt the butter. Cook the leeks for about 2 minutes or until softened.
Add minced garlic and cook an additional 40 seconds.
Add the remaining ingredients. Secure the lid. Choose "Manual" mode and Low pressure; cook for 3 minutes. Once cooking is complete, use a quick pressure release; carefully remove the lid. Bon appétit!

221. Nopales with Sour Cream

(Ready in about 8 minutes | Servings 4)

Nopales are actually cactus leaves that are commonly used in Mexican cuisine. Nopales are so easy to cook in an Instant Pot.

Per serving: 109 Calories; 7.3g Fat; 8.8g Carbs; 3.5g Protein; 3.7g Sugars

Ingredients
1 pound nopales, cleaned and diced
1 white onion, chopped
2 garlic cloves, smashed
2 tablespoons fresh parsley, chopped
2 dried chiles negros
1 cup ripe tomatoes, chopped
1/2 teaspoon mustard seeds
1/2 teaspoon Mexican oregano
2 tablespoons olive oil
Sea salt and ground black pepper, to taste
1 cup chicken broth
1/2 cup sour cream

Directions
Place all ingredients, except for sour cream, in your Instant Pot.
Secure the lid. Choose "Manual" mode and High pressure; cook for 5 minutes. Once cooking is complete, use a quick pressure release; carefully remove the lid.
Spoon into serving bowls and serve dolloped with sour cream. Bon appétit!

222. Swiss Chard with Ham Hock

(Ready in about 45 minutes | Servings 4)

Are you looking for creative ways to cook with Swiss chard? This dish is both healthy and gourmet. Enjoy!

Per serving: 268 Calories; 12.3g Fat; 8.1g Carbs; 30.9g Protein; 2.2g Sugars

Ingredients
2 tablespoons olive oil
1 cup leeks, chopped
2 garlic cloves, minced
Sea salt and ground black pepper, to taste
1/2 teaspoon cayenne pepper
3 cups beef bone broth
1 (1-pound) ham hock
1 pound Swiss chard, torn into pieces

Directions
Press the "Sauté" button to heat up your Instant Pot; now, heat the olive oil. Cook the leeks for about 2 minutes or until softened.
Stir in the garlic and cook an additional 40 seconds or until aromatic.
Add the salt, black pepper, cayenne pepper, broth, and ham hock.
Secure the lid. Choose "Meat/Stew" mode and High pressure; cook for 35 minutes. Once cooking is complete, use a natural pressure release; carefully remove the lid.
Then, add Swiss chard and choose "Manual" mode; cook for 5 minutes. Once cooking is complete, use a quick pressure release; carefully remove the lid. Bon appétit!

223. Green Beans with Canadian Bacon

(Ready in about 10 minutes | Servings 6)

Need more ideas for what to make with green beans on your ketogenic diet? You'll be eating this dish all day long – for breakfast, lunch, and dinner.

Per serving: 133 Calories; 2.9g Fat; 8.1g Carbs; 19.1g Protein; 2.6g Sugars

Ingredients
2 (6-ounce) packages Canadian bacon, chopped
1/2 cup scallions, chopped
2 cloves garlic, minced
1 pound green beans, trimmed
Kosher salt and ground black pepper, to taste
1/2 teaspoon paprika
1/2 teaspoon dried dill weed
1/2 teaspoon red pepper flakes
2 tablespoons apple cider vinegar
1 cup water

Directions
Press the "Sauté" button to heat up your Instant Pot. Once hot, cook Canadian bacon until crisp, about 4 minutes; reserve.
Add the scallions and garlic. Cook an additional 1 minute or until aromatic.
Add the other ingredients; stir to combine
Secure the lid. Choose "Manual" mode and Low pressure; cook for 3 minutes. Once cooking is

complete, use a quick pressure release; carefully remove the lid.
Serve warm, garnished with the reserved bacon. Bon appétit!

224. Cauliflower Soup with Blue Cheese

(Ready in about 10 minutes | Servings 4)
If you do not have dried chile negro, use a pickled jalapeño to enhance the flavor of your soup.
Per serving: 221 Calories; 15.7g Fat; 8.9g Carbs; 11.4g Protein; 3.9g Sugars
Ingredients
2 tablespoons ghee, melted
1 medium-sized shallot, chopped
2 garlic cloves, minced
1 cup cauliflower, chopped into small florets
1 celery stalk, chopped
1 cup half-and-half
2 ½ cups vegetable broth
A pinch of grated nutmeg
1 dried chile negro
1/4 teaspoon ground black pepper
1/3 teaspoon sea salt
4 ounces blue cheese, crumbled
Directions
Press the "Sauté" button to heat up your Instant Pot. Once hot, melt the ghee. Sauté the shallot and garlic until aromatic or approximately 2 minutes.
Now, add the cauliflower, celery stalk, half-and-half, vegetable broth, nutmeg, chile, pepper, and salt.
Secure the lid. Choose "Manual" mode and Low pressure; cook for 3 minutes. Once cooking is complete, use a quick pressure release; carefully remove the lid.
Ladle into soup bowls, top with blue cheese, and serve warm. Bon appétit!

225. Balkan Autumn Satarash

(Ready in about 15 minutes | Servings 4)
Satarash is a traditional dish with autumn vegetables such as peppers, ripe tomatoes and spices. Serve over cauli rice, if desired.
Per serving: 151 Calories; 11.5g Fat; 8.8g Carbs; 4.2g Protein; 4.1g Sugars
Ingredients
2 tablespoons olive oil
1 white onion, chopped
2 cloves garlic
1 red bell pepper, seeded and sliced
1 green bell pepper, seeded and sliced
2 ripe tomatoes, puréed
1/2 teaspoon turmeric
1 teaspoon paprika
1/2 teaspoon dried oregano
Kosher salt and ground black pepper, to taste
1 cup water
4 large eggs, lightly whisked
Directions
Press the "Sauté" button to heat up your Instant Pot. Heat the oil and sauté the onion and garlic until aromatic, about 2 minutes.
Add the peppers, tomatoes, turmeric, paprika, oregano, salt, black pepper, and water.
Secure the lid. Choose "Manual" mode and High pressure; cook for 3 minutes. Once cooking is complete, use a quick pressure release; carefully remove the lid.
Fold in the eggs and stir to combine. Cover with the lid and let it sit in the residual heat for 5 minutes. Serve warm.

226. Vegetable Medley with Pork Sausage

(Ready in about 15 minutes | Servings 4)
If you're looking for a way to mix your favorite veggies and cook them together, this is your ticket! An easy, healthy, and delicious dinner in an Instant Pot is ready in 15 minutes.
Per serving: 248 Calories; 20.5g Fat; 8.5g Carbs; 9.1g Protein; 2.9g Sugars
Ingredients
2 tablespoons olive oil
2 garlic cloves, minced
1/2 cup scallions
2 pork sausages, casing removed, sliced
2 cups cauliflower, chopped into small florets
1/2 pound button mushrooms, sliced
2 bell peppers, chopped
1 red chili pepper, chopped
2 cups turnip greens
Sea salt and freshly ground black pepper, to taste
1 teaspoon cayenne pepper
2 bay leaves
1 cup water
Directions
Press the "Sauté" button to heat up your Instant Pot. Heat the oil and sauté the garlic and scallions until aromatic, about 2 minutes.
Add sausage and cook an additional 3 minutes or until it is no longer pink. Now, stir in the remaining ingredients.
Secure the lid. Choose "Manual" mode and High pressure; cook for 5 minutes. Once cooking is complete, use a quick pressure release; carefully remove the lid. Bon appétit!

227. Southern-Style Sausage Gumbo

(Ready in about 10 minutes | Servings 6)
To keep it simple, use easy-to-find ingredients: tomatoes, sausage, okra, and seasonings. It needs only 10 minutes to cook.
Per serving: 303 Calories; 17.8g Fat; 9g Carbs; 27g Protein; 2.4g Sugars
Ingredients
2 tablespoons olive oil
2 pounds Gyulai sausage links, sliced
1/2 cup leeks, chopped

3 cloves garlic, minced
1 celery, diced
1/2 cup tomato purée
1 ½ cups water
1 ½ cups beef bone broth
1 tablespoon coconut aminos
Kosher salt, to taste
1/2 teaspoon black peppercorns, crushed
1/2 teaspoon caraway seeds
1 bay leaf
2 cups frozen okra, chopped
Directions
Press the "Sauté" button to heat up your Instant Pot. Heat the oil and cook the sausage until no longer pink; reserve.
Then, sauté the leeks until translucent, about 2 minutes. Now, add the garlic and cook an additional 30 seconds.
Add the celery, tomato, water, broth, coconut aminos, salt, pepper, caraway seeds, bay leaf, and okra. Stir to combine.
Secure the lid. Choose "Manual" mode and Low pressure; cook for 3 minutes. Once cooking is complete, use a quick pressure release; carefully remove the lid.
Ladle into individual bowls and serve warm. Bon appétit!

228. Braised Sauerkraut with Bacon

(Ready in about 15 minutes | Servings 6)
Sauerkraut is a healthy, flavorful and easy to cook ingredient. This versatile food can be served for lunch or as a side dish for dinner.
Per serving: 184 Calories; 13.5g Fat; 7.1g Carbs; 7.1g Protein; 3.2g Sugars
Ingredients
6 ounces meaty bacon, roughly chopped
1 yellow onion, chopped
2 garlic cloves, minced
1/4 cup dry white wine
1 carrot, grated
1 bell pepper, chopped
2 anchos, minced
3 cups sauerkraut, rinsed and drained
1 teaspoon cayenne pepper
1 bay leaf
1 teaspoon mixed peppercorns
4 cups beef bone broth
Directions
Press the "Sauté" button to heat up your Instant Pot. Once hot, cook the bacon until crisp; reserve.
Now, cook the onion and garlic in pan drippings. Add a splash of wine to deglaze the bottom of the Instant Pot.
Then, stir in the remaining ingredients.
Secure the lid. Choose "Manual" mode and High pressure; cook for 10 minutes. Once cooking is complete, use a natural pressure release; carefully remove the lid.

Divide your sauerkraut among serving bowls and top with the reserved bacon. Bon appétit!

229. Aromatic Okra with Pancetta

(Ready in about 10 minutes | Servings 4)
There are so many reasons to add okra to your keto meal plan. Okra can improve your digestion and skin health, lower blood pressure and boost the immune system.
Per serving: 202 Calories; 17.1g Fat; 8.4g Carbs; 4.9g Protein; 3.2g Sugars
Ingredients
2 tablespoons olive oil
1 red onion, chopped
1/2 pound okra
1 teaspoon ginger-garlic paste
4 slices pancetta, chopped
1 teaspoon celery seeds
1/2 teaspoon caraway seeds
1/2 teaspoon cayenne pepper
1/2 teaspoon turmeric powder
1 cup water
1 cup tomato purée
Directions
Press the "Sauté" button to heat up your Instant Pot. Once hot, heat the olive oil; sauté the onion until softened.
Add okra, ginger-garlic paste, and pancetta; sauté for 1 minute more or until fragrant. Add the remaining ingredients and stir to combine.
Secure the lid. Choose "Manual" mode and High pressure; cook for 3 minutes. Once cooking is complete, use a natural pressure release; carefully remove the lid. Bon appétit!

230. Hearty Root Vegetable Soup

(Ready in about 15 minutes | Servings 4)
The array of different low-carb vegetables adds tons of flavors to this rich and delicious soup that can be served for lunch or dinner.
Per serving: 190 Calories; 15.6g Fat; 7.1g Carbs; 6.7g Protein; 2.6g Sugars
Ingredients
4 tablespoons olive oil
4 cups chicken stock
2 cups cauliflower, cut into small florets
1 celery, diced
1 carrot, sliced
1 parsnip, sliced
1 garlic clove, minced
1 bay leaf
1 tablespoon fresh parsley, roughly chopped
1 teaspoon fresh sage
Kosher salt and freshly ground black pepper, to taste
Directions
Simply drop all of the above ingredients into your Instant Pot.
Secure the lid. Choose "Manual" mode and High pressure; cook for 10 minutes. Once cooking is

complete, use a natural pressure release; carefully remove the lid.
Taste, adjust the seasonings and serve immediately. Bon appétit!

231. Paprika Kohlrabi with Asiago
(Ready in about 20 minutes | Servings 4)
If you have not tried kohlrabi yet, here is a great opportunity! It is good to know that it tastes like jicama, broccoli stems or collard greens. It has a little bit of natural sweetness and mild, pleasant taste.
Per serving: 269 Calories; 19.9g Fat; 9.4g Carbs; 14.7g Protein; 3.7g Sugars
Ingredients
2 tablespoons olive oil
1 red onion, chopped
2 garlic cloves, pressed
1 (1-inch) piece ginger root, peeled and grated
3/4 pound Kohlrabi root, peeled, and slices into bite-sized chunks
2 cups chicken stock
1/3 cup dry white wine
Kosher salt, to taste
1/3 teaspoon ground black pepper
1 tablespoon paprika
1/4 teaspoon ground bay leaf
1 cup Asiago cheese, grated
Directions
Press the "Sauté" button to heat up your Instant Pot. Once hot, heat the olive oil; sauté the onion until softened.
Stir in the garlic and ginger; sauté until just tender and aromatic, about 30 seconds. Next, add kohlrabi and cook for a further 4 minutes.
After that, add chicken stock, wine, salt, black pepper, paprika, and ground bay leaf.
Secure the lid. Choose "Manual" mode and High pressure; cook for 10 minutes. Once cooking is complete, use a natural pressure release; carefully remove the lid.
Top with freshly grated Asiago cheese; cover, let it sit in the residual heat for 4 to 5 minutes or until the cheese is melted; serve immediately.

232. French-Style Cauliflower with Bacon
(Ready in about 15 minutes | Servings 4)
Here's one of the easiest low-carb casseroles to make for an elegant Sunday lunch. We opted for Comté cheese **and** *Crottin de Chavignol but you can toss in whatever French cheese you have on hand!*
Per serving: 372 Calories; 24.4g Fat; 9.4g Carbs; 29g Protein; 2.9g Sugars
Ingredients
4 slices bacon
1 pound cauliflower, broken into florets
3 eggs, beaten
4 ounces Comté cheese
1/4 cup full-fat yogurt
1 cup Crottin de Chavignol cheese, grated
1/4 cup green onions, chopped
1/2 teaspoon granulated garlic
1/2 teaspoon cayenne pepper
1/4 teaspoon ground black pepper
1/8 teaspoon grated nutmeg
Directions
Press the "Sauté" button to heat up your Instant Pot. Once hot, cook the bacon until nice and crisp; crumble it with a fork and set aside.
Wipe down the Instant Pot with a damp cloth. Add 1 cup of water and a metal trivet to the bottom of your Instant Pot.
Combine the remaining ingredients in a baking dish that is previously greased with a nonstick cooking spray. Lower the baking dish onto the trivet and secure the lid.
Choose "Manual" mode and High pressure; cook for 10 minutes. Once cooking is complete, use a natural pressure release; carefully remove the lid. Top with the reserved bacon and serve. Bon appétit!

233. Lazy Sunday Bok Choy Soup
(Ready in about 15 minutes | Servings 4)
Chicken thighs, Bok choy, and beef bone broth are tossed with spices and herbs for a quick and elegant Sunday lunch.
Per serving: 479 Calories; 33.7g Fat; 3.5g Carbs; 38.5g Protein; 1.2g Sugars
Ingredients
4 chicken thighs
4 cups beef bone broth
1 pound Bok choy
Sea salt and ground black pepper, to taste
1/4 teaspoon dried dill weed
1 teaspoon bay leaf
Directions
Add chicken thighs and 1 cup of broth to your Instant Pot.
Choose "Poultry" mode and High pressure; cook for 8 minutes. Once cooking is complete, use a natural pressure release; carefully remove the lid.
Then, add the remaining ingredients. Secure the lid. Choose "Manual" mode and High pressure; cook for 5 minutes. Once cooking is complete, use a quick pressure release; carefully remove the lid. Bon appétit!

234. Savoy Cabbage Soup with Cabécou Cheese
(Ready in about 20 minutes | Servings 4)
If you are new to the ketogenic diet, you might be wondering what type of soups you could eat. This recipe offers an answer, so give it a try!
Per serving: 173 Calories; 10.3g Fat; 9.1g Carbs; 11.3g Protein; 4g Sugars
Ingredients
1 tablespoon lard, melted
1 leek, sliced
1 celery stalk, diced

1 carrot, sliced
4 cups beef bone broth
3 cups Savoy cabbage, shredded
Salt and ground black pepper, to taste
1/4 teaspoon garlic powder
1/4 teaspoon dried dill
1/2 cup full-fat milk
1/2 cup Cabécou cheese, crumbled
Directions
Press the "Sauté" button to heat up your Instant Pot. Once hot, melt the lard; then, sweat the leek until just tender.
Add the celery, carrot, broth, Savoy cabbage, salt, black pepper, garlic, dill, and milk. Secure the lid. Choose "Poultry" mode and High pressure; cook for 15 minutes. Once cooking is complete, use a quick pressure release; carefully remove the lid.
Afterwards, fold in Cabécou cheese; cover and let it sit in the residual heat until everything is completely incorporated. Bon appétit!

235. Spicy Crimini Mushroom and Asparagus Soup

(Ready in about 10 minutes | Servings 4)
Here's a great lunch idea for all those who are on a low-carb diet! Moreover, for everyone else! Crimini mushrooms are a powerhouse of vitamin B-complex, selenium, copper, manganese, and potassium.
Per serving: 104 Calories; 7g Fat; 8.1g Carbs; 3.9g Protein; 4.5g Sugars
Ingredients
2 tablespoons butter, softened
1 shallot, diced
2 cloves garlic, diced
2 cups Crimini mushrooms
4 cups water
2 chicken bouillon cubes
1/2 cup soy milk
1 cup celery, diced
1/2 pound asparagus, diced
1 tablespoon coconut aminos
Sea salt and black pepper, to taste
1 teaspoon Taco seasoning
1/4 teaspoon freshly ground black pepper
1 bay leaf
Directions
Press the "Sauté" button to heat up your Instant Pot. Once hot, melt the butter; then, sweat the shallot until softened.
Stir in garlic; cook an additional 40 seconds, stirring frequently.
Add the remaining ingredients.
Secure the lid. Choose "Manual" mode and High pressure; cook for 7 minutes. Once cooking is complete, use a quick pressure release; carefully remove the lid.
Ladle into individual bowls and serve warm. Bon appétit!

236. Broccoli Medley with Bacon and Colby Cheese

(Ready in about 15 minutes | Servings 4)
Try this perfect blend of savory flavors that will delight your taste buds: broccoli, cream, Colby cheese, bacon, and spices. Enjoy!
Per serving: 303 Calories; 27.2g Fat; 5.8g Carbs; 9.8g Protein; 3.6g Sugars
Ingredients
4 slices bacon, chopped
1 teaspoon ginger-garlic paste
1 cup broccoli, broken into florets
1 celery with leaves, chopped
2 cups water
2 beef bouillon cubes
Salt and ground black pepper, to your liking
1/2 teaspoon red pepper flakes, crushed
1 cup double cream
1/2 cup Colby cheese, shredded
2 tablespoons fresh chives, sliced
Directions
Press the "Sauté" button to heat up your Instant Pot. Once hot, cook the bacon until nice and crisp; set aside.
Add ginger-garlic paste and cook an additional 30 seconds. Add the broccoli, celery, water, beef bouillon cubes, salt, black pepper, red pepper, and double cream.
Secure the lid. Choose "Manual" mode and High pressure; cook for 6 minutes. Once cooking is complete, use a natural pressure release; carefully remove the lid.
Top with Colby cheese and press the "Sauté" button. Let it simmer an additional 4 minutes or until the cheese is melted.
Garnish with fresh chives and the reserved bacon; serve immediately and enjoy!

237. Cabbage and Turkey Delight

(Ready in about 10 minutes | Servings 4)
This simple but endlessly crave-worthy casserole is both sophisticated and rustic. Just like grandma used to make.
Per serving: 247 Calories; 12.5g Fat; 9.1g Carbs; 25.3g Protein; 4.7g Sugars
Ingredients
1 tablespoon lard, at room temperature
1/2 cup onion, chopped
1 pound ground turkey
10 ounces puréed tomatoes
Sea salt and ground black pepper, to taste
1 teaspoon cayenne pepper
1/4 teaspoon caraway seeds
1/4 teaspoon mustard seeds
1/2 pound cabbage, cut into wedges
4 garlic cloves, minced
1 cup chicken broth
2 bay leaves
Directions

Press the "Sauté" button to heat up your Instant Pot. Then, melt the lard. Cook the onion until translucent and tender.
Add ground turkey and cook until it is no longer pink; reserve the turkey/onion mixture.
Mix puréed tomatoes with salt, black pepper, cayenne pepper, caraway seeds, and mustard seeds.
Spritz the bottom and sides of the Instant Pot with a nonstick cooking spray. Then, place 1/2 of cabbage wedges on the bottom of your Instant Pot.
Spread the meat mixture over the top of the cabbage. Add minced garlic. Add the remaining cabbage.
Now, pour in the tomato mixture and chicken broth; lastly, add bay leaves.
Secure the lid. Choose "Manual" mode and High pressure; cook for 5 minutes. Once cooking is complete, use a natural pressure release; carefully remove the lid. Bon appétit!

238. Warm Eggplant and Chicken Bowl

(Ready in about 10 minutes | Servings 4)
Eggplant is full of vitamins C and K, vitamin B-complex, phosphorus, niacin, magnesium, and so forth. It goes perfectly with tender chicken breasts and ripe tomatoes.
Per serving: 317 Calories; 20.9g Fat; 9g Carbs; 22.9g Protein; 5.3g Sugars
Ingredients
1 tablespoon olive oil
1 leek, chopped
2 chicken breasts, diced
1 pound eggplant, peeled and sliced
1 teaspoon garlic paste
1/2 teaspoon turmeric powder
1 teaspoon red pepper flakes
1 cup broth, preferably homemade
1 cup tomatoes, puréed
Kosher salt and ground black pepper, to taste

Directions
Press the "Sauté" button to heat up your Instant Pot. Then, heat the oil. Cook the leeks until softened.
Now, add the chicken breasts; cook for 3 to 4 minute or until they are no longer pink. Then, add the remaining ingredients; stir to combine well.
Secure the lid. Choose "Poultry" mode and High pressure; cook for 5 minutes. Once cooking is complete, use a natural pressure release; carefully remove the lid.
Divide your dish among serving bowls and serve warm. Bon appétit!

239. Celery Soup with Salsiccia

(Ready in about 30 minutes | Servings 4)
Get ready for this fabulous combination of ingredients: fresh celery, Italian sausage, and coconut oil. Salsiccia is actually a pork sausage with herbs that can be eaten raw or cooked.
Per serving: 150 Calories; 5.9g Fat; 7.9g Carbs; 16.4g Protein; 4.7g Sugars
Ingredients
3 cups celery, chopped
1 carrot, chopped
1/2 cup brown onion, chopped
1 garlic clove, pressed
1/2 pound with Salsiccia links, casing removed and sliced
1/2 cup full-fat milk
3 cups roasted vegetable broth
Kosher salt, to taste
1/2 teaspoon ground black pepper
1/2 teaspoon dried chili flakes
2 teaspoon coconut oil
Directions
Simply throw all of the above ingredients into your Instant Pot; gently stir to combine.
Secure the lid. Choose "Soup/Broth" mode and High pressure; cook for 25 minutes. Once cooking is complete, use a quick pressure release; carefully remove the lid.
Ladle into four soup bowls and serve hot. Enjoy!

240. Chinese-Style Warm Pe-Tsai Salad

(Ready in about 10 minutes | Servings 4)
Chinese Pe-Tsai warm salad is flavorful, healthy, and inspirational. Serve as a side dish or a complete vegetarian meal.
Per serving: 116 Calories; 7.7g Fat; 8.2g Carbs; 2.1g Protein; 3.9g Sugars
Ingredients
2 tablespoons sesame oil
1 yellow onion, chopped
1 teaspoon garlic, finely minced
1 pound pe-tsai cabbage, shredded
1/4 cup rice wine vinegar
1/4 teaspoon Szechuan pepper
1/2 teaspoon salt
1 tablespoon soy sauce
Directions
Press the "Sauté" button to heat up your Instant Pot. Then, heat the sesame oil. Cook the onion until softened.
Add the remaining ingredients.
Secure the lid. Choose "Manual" mode and High pressure; cook for 3 minutes. Once cooking is complete, use a quick pressure release; carefully remove the lid.
Transfer the cabbage mixture to a nice salad bowl and serve immediately. Enjoy!

241. Asparagus alla Fontina

(Ready in about 10 minutes | Servings 2)
This amazing asparagus dish makes eating healthy way easier. Asparagus is chock-full of vitamins, minerals and fiber.
Per serving: 223 Calories; 17.5g Fat; 7.1g Carbs; 11.4g Protein; 2.9g Sugars

Ingredients
1 tablespoon avocado oil
1/2 pound asparagus, trimmed
1/2 teaspoon celery salt
1/2 teaspoon cayenne pepper
1/4 teaspoon freshly ground black pepper
2 cloves garlic, crushed
1 (1-inch) piece ginger, grated
1 tablespoon coconut aminos
1 teaspoon dried basil
1/2 teaspoon dried oregano
1/2 cup Fontina cheese, grated
2 tablespoons fresh Italian parsley, roughly chopped

Directions
Add all ingredients, except for cheese and parsley, to your Instant Pot.
Secure the lid. Choose "Manual" mode and High pressure; cook for 2 minutes. Once cooking is complete, use a quick pressure release; carefully remove the lid.
After that, top your asparagus with cheese and press the "Sauté" button. Allow it to simmer for 3 to 4 minutes or until cheese is melted.
Serve garnished with fresh parsley. Enjoy!

242. Chunky Cabbage and Capocollo Soup

(Ready in about 10 minutes | Servings 4)
Transform an ordinary vegetable such as cabbage into a completely new ketogenic dish with this appetizing recipe. Toss it with Capocollo sausage and enjoy a delicious weeknight meal.
Per serving: 258 Calories; 20.4g Fat; 9.1g Carbs; 9.9g Protein; 4.2g Sugars

Ingredients
1/2 pound Capocollo, chopped
Coarse sea salt and ground black pepper, to your liking
1/2 teaspoon cayenne pepper
1 onion, chopped
1 celery stalk, chopped
1 parsnip, chopped
1 pound cabbage, cut into wedges
2 cups broth, preferably homemade
1 cup tomatoes, puréed
1 cup water
1 bay leaf

Directions
Add all of the above ingredients to your Instant Pot.
Secure the lid. Choose "Manual" mode and High pressure; cook for 3 minutes. Once cooking is complete, use a quick pressure release; carefully remove the lid.
Ladle into four soup bowls and serve hot. Bon appétit!

243. Rich and Easy Portobello Mushroom Casserole

(Ready in about 15 minutes | Servings 4)
It's going to be the best casserole ever! The secret lies in the simple approach – fresh Portobello mushrooms, homemade broth and seasonings.
Per serving: 229 Calories; 10.6g Fat; 5.7g Carbs; 28.2g Protein; 2.6g Sugars

Ingredients
2 tablespoons olive oil
2 chicken breasts, boneless, skinless and cut into slices
Sea salt, to taste
1/4 teaspoon ground black pepper
1/2 teaspoon cayenne pepper
1 teaspoon fresh rosemary, finely minced
1 pound Portobello mushrooms, sliced
1/2 cup scallions, chopped
2 garlic cloves, minced
1 teaspoon yellow mustard
1 cup vegetable broth
1 tablespoon Piri-Piri sauce

Directions
Press the "Sauté" button to heat up your Instant Pot. Then, heat the oil. Cook the chicken until delicately browned on all sides.
Season with salt, black pepper, cayenne pepper, and rosemary; reserve.
Spritz the bottom and sides of your Instant Pot with a nonstick cooking spray. Add 1/2 of the mushrooms to the bottom.
Add a layer of chopped scallions and minced garlic. Add the chicken mixture. Top with the remaining mushrooms.
In a mixing bowl, thoroughly combine vegetable broth and Piri-Piri sauce. Pour this sauce into the Instant Pot.
Secure the lid. Choose "Manual" mode and High pressure; cook for 5 minutes. Once cooking is complete, use a quick pressure release; carefully remove the lid. Serve warm and enjoy!

244. Zucchini with Green Peppercorn Sauce

(Ready in about 10 minutes | Servings 4)
Carrots are full of nutrients and flavors. They go perfectly with creamy, peppery sauce like this one with cognac and cream.
Per serving: 251 Calories; 15.3g Fat; 3.2g Carbs; 20.2g Protein; 1.5g Sugars

Ingredients
1 cup water
2 zucchini, sliced
Sea salt, to taste
Green Peppercorn Sauce:
2 tablespoons butter
1/2 cup green onions, minced
2 tablespoons Cognac
1 ½ cups chicken broth
1 cup whipping cream
1 ½ tablespoons green peppercorns in brine, drained and crushed slightly

Directions

Add water and a steamer basket to the Instant Pot. Arrange your zucchini on the steamer basket. Secure the lid. Choose "Manual" mode and Low pressure; cook for 3 minutes. Once cooking is complete, use a quick pressure release; carefully remove the lid.

Season zucchini with salt and set aside.

Wipe down the Instant Pot with a damp cloth. Press the "Sauté" button to heat up your Instant Pot. Melt the butter and then, sauté green onions until tender. Add Cognac and cook for 2 minutes longer. Then, pour in chicken broth and let it boil another 4 minutes.

Lastly, stir in the cream and peppercorns. Continue to simmer until the sauce is thickened and thoroughly warmed.

Serve your zucchini with the sauce on the side. Bon appétit!

245. Spicy Collards with Caciocavallo

(Ready in about 15 minutes | Servings 4)

Fresh collard greens, flavorful Caciocavallo cheese and crispy pancetta combine very well! Serve as a side dish or a complete vegetarian meal.

Per serving: 219 Calories; 10.4g Fat; 8.8g Carbs; 24.9g Protein; 2.2g Sugars

Ingredients

4 slices pancetta
18 ounces collard greens, chopped
1 cup beef bone broth
2 tablespoons Port wine
1 teaspoon Sriracha
Sea salt and ground black pepper, to taste
1/2 teaspoon cayenne pepper
1 teaspoon dried basil
1/2 teaspoon dried oregano
1/2 teaspoon dried thyme
1/2 cup Caciocavallo cheese, grated

Directions

Press the "Sauté" button to heat up your Instant Pot. Once hot, cook pancetta until crisp; crumble pancetta with a fork and reserve.

Add the remaining ingredients, except for the cheese. Secure the lid. Choose "Manual" mode and Low pressure; cook for 4 minutes. Once cooking is complete, use a quick pressure release; carefully remove the lid.

Afterwards, top your collards with cheese, cover with the lid and let it sit for a further 5 minutes. Top each serving with pancetta and serve warm.

246. Traditional Caramelized Onion Soup

(Ready in about 15 minutes | Servings 4)

Stay warm with a great combination of a chicken stock base, caramelized onions, and freshly grated Swiss cheese.

Per serving: 228 Calories; 18g Fat; 7.3g Carbs; 10.5g Protein; 4.5g Sugars

Ingredients

1/2 stick butter, softened
3/4 pound yellow onions, sliced
4 cups chicken stock
1/2 teaspoon dried basil
Kosher salt and ground black pepper, to taste
1/2 cup Swiss cheese, freshly grated

Directions

Press the "Sauté" button to heat up your Instant Pot. Once hot, melt the butter and sauté the onions until caramelized and tender.

Add chicken stock, basil, salt, and black pepper. Secure the lid. Choose "Manual" mode and High pressure; cook for 10 minutes. Once cooking is complete, use a quick pressure release; carefully remove the lid.

Ladle the soup into individual bowls and top with grated cheese. Enjoy!

247. The Best Mushroom Ragoût

(Ready in about 10 minutes | Servings 4)

Serve this French-style stew on its own, as the base for a cauliflower risotto, a filling for pasta, as a side dish, and so on. The possibilities are literally endless!

Per serving: 279 Calories; 22.3g Fat; 8.3g Carbs; 8.7g Protein; 4.2g Sugars

Ingredients

3 tablespoons butter, at room temperature
1/2 cup white onions, peeled and sliced
1 cup chicken sausage, casing removed, sliced
1 pound Chanterelle mushrooms, sliced
2 stalks spring garlic, diced
Kosher salt and ground black pepper, to taste
1/2 teaspoon red pepper flakes
2 tablespoons tomato paste
1/2 cup good Pinot Noir
1 cup chicken stock
1/2 cup double cream
2 tablespoons fresh chives, chopped

Directions

Press the "Sauté" button to heat up your Instant Pot. Once hot, melt the butter and sauté the onions until tender and translucent.

Add the sausage and mushrooms; continue to sauté until the sausage is no longer pink and the mushrooms are fragrant.

Then, stir in garlic and cook it for 30 to 40 seconds more or until aromatic. Now, add the salt, black pepper, red pepper, tomato paste, Pinot Noir, and chicken stock.

Secure the lid. Choose "Manual" mode and High pressure; cook for 5 minutes. Once cooking is complete, use a quick pressure release; carefully remove the lid.

After that, add double cream and press the "Sauté" button. Continue to simmer until everything is heated through and slightly thickened.

Lastly, divide your stew among individual bowls; top with fresh chopped chives and serve warm.

248. Cheesy Leek and Chorizo Soup

(Ready in about 10 minutes | Servings 4)

There are many recipes for a classic leek soup, but this richly colored soup is one of the tastiest that you have ever tried. Chorizo is a spiced pork sausage that is widely used in Mexican cuisine.

Per serving: 428 Calories; 36g Fat; 7.1g Carbs; 18.9g Protein; 2.1g Sugars

Ingredients
1 tablespoon sesame oil
1 cup leeks, chopped
1/2 pound chorizo, sliced
2 cloves garlic, minced
1 green chili, deseeded and finely chopped
4 cups water
1/2 cup tomato purée
1/2 cup heavy cream
2 chicken bouillon cubes
1 bay leaf
1/2 cup Monterey-Jack cheese, shredded

Directions
Press the "Sauté" button to heat up your Instant Pot. Once hot, heat the oil and sauté the leeks until tender.
Now, stir in chorizo, garlic, and green chili; continue to cook until aromatic. Then, add water, tomato puree, heavy cream, bouillon cubes, and bay leaf.
Secure the lid. Choose "Manual" mode and High pressure; cook for 6 minutes. Once cooking is complete, use a natural pressure release; carefully remove the lid.
Then, press the "Sauté" button and add the cheese; let it simmer until the cheese is melted and heated through.

249. The Best Italian Zuppa Ever

(Ready in about 10 minutes | Servings 4)

Cotechino di Modena is a fresh pork sausage that will add a rich and rustic flavor to your pressure-cooked soup. In this recipe, you can use a homemade marinara sauce, too.

Per serving: 340 Calories; 27.9g Fat; 8g Carbs; 14.1g Protein; 3.6g Sugars

Ingredients
2 tablespoons olive oil
1 onion, chopped
16 ounces Cotechino di Modena, sliced
2 cups tomatoes, purée
3 cups roasted vegetable broth
1 cup water
Sea salt and ground black pepper, to taste
1/2 teaspoon crushed chili
1 tablespoon Italian seasonings
1/2 cup Parmigiano-Reggiano cheese, shaved

Directions
Press the "Sauté" button to heat up your Instant Pot. Once hot, heat the oil and sauté the onions until tender and translucent.
Now, add the sausage and cook an additional 3 minutes,
Stir in tomatoes, broth, water, sea salt, black pepper, crushed chili, and Italian seasonings.
Secure the lid. Choose "Manual" mode and High pressure; cook for 5 minutes. Once cooking is complete, use a quick pressure release; carefully remove the lid.
Top with shaved Parmigiano-Reggiano cheese and serve warm.

250. Simple Steamed Tomato Salad

(Ready in about 10 minutes | Servings 4)

Vegetables are an extremely important part of every healthy diet and the same goes for a ketogenic diet. There are a few important health benefits of eating cooked tomatoes. Cooking tomatoes increases their trans-lycopene and antioxidant content.

Per serving: 168 Calories; 12.4g Fat; 9.6g Carbs; 6.2g Protein; 6.5g Sugars

Ingredients
1 cup water
8 tomatoes, sliced
2 tablespoons extra-virgin olive oil
1/2 cup Halloumi cheese, crumbled
2 garlic cloves, smashed
2 tablespoons fresh basil, snipped

Directions
Add 1 cup of water and a steamer rack to the Instant Pot.
Place the tomatoes on the steamer rack.
Secure the lid. Choose "Manual" mode and High pressure; cook for 3 minutes. Once cooking is complete, use a quick pressure release; carefully remove the lid.
Toss the tomatoes with the remaining ingredients and serve. Enjoy!

FAST SNACKS & APPETIZERS

251. Easy Buttery Brussels Sprouts
(Ready in about 10 minutes | Servings 4)
You will love this buttery and sophisticated Brussels sprout appetizer. Brussels sprouts are a good source of vitamin B1, vitamin B6, vitamin C, vitamin K, manganese, copper, omega-3 fatty acids, and dietary fiber.
Per serving: 68 Calories; 3.3g Fat; 7.8g Carbs; 3.5g Protein; 1.9g Sugars
Ingredients
1 tablespoon butter
1/2 cup shallots, chopped
3/4 pound whole Brussels sprouts
Sea salt, to taste
1/4 teaspoon ground black pepper
1/2 cup water
1/2 cup chicken stock
Directions
Press the "Sauté" button to heat up your Instant Pot. Once hot, melt the butter and sauté the shallots until tender and translucent.
Add the remaining ingredients to the Instant Pot. Secure the lid. Choose "Manual" mode and High pressure; cook for 4 minutes. Once cooking is complete, use a quick pressure release; carefully remove the lid.
Transfer Brussels sprouts to a serving platter. Serve with cocktail sticks and enjoy!

252. Easy Spinach Dip
(Ready in about 5 minutes | Servings 10)
This dipping sauce is so creamy and tasty but light and diet-friendly at the same time. Serve with your favorite ketogenic dippers and enjoy!
Per serving: 43 Calories; 1.7g Fat; 3.5g Carbs; 4.1g Protein; 1.3g Sugars
Ingredients
1 pound spinach
4 ounces Cottage cheese, at room temperature
4 ounces Cheddar cheese, grated
1 teaspoon garlic powder
1/2 teaspoon shallot powder
1/2 teaspoon celery seeds
1/2 teaspoon fennel seeds
1/2 teaspoon cayenne pepper
Salt and black pepper, to taste
Directions
Add all of the above ingredients to your Instant Pot. Secure the lid. Choose "Manual" mode and High pressure; cook for 1 minute. Once cooking is complete, use a quick pressure release; carefully remove the lid.
Serve warm or at room temperature. Bon appétit!

253. Asparagus with Chervil Dip
(Ready in about 5 minutes | Servings 6)
This snack is so easy to make at home! It is low carb, healthy and oh so delicious!
Per serving: 116 Calories; 8.5g Fat; 6.9g Carbs; 4.5g Protein; 2.4g Sugars
Ingredients
1 ½ pounds asparagus spears, trimmed
1/2 cup sour cream
1/2 cup mayonnaise
2 tablespoons fresh chervil
2 tablespoons scallions, chopped
1 teaspoon garlic, minced
Salt, to taste
Directions
Add 1 cup of water and a steamer basket to you Instant Pot.
Secure the lid. Choose "Manual" mode and High pressure; cook for 1 minute. Once cooking is complete, use a quick pressure release; carefully remove the lid.
Then, thoroughly combine the remaining ingredients to make your dipping sauce. Serve your asparagus with the dipping sauce on the side. Bon appétit!

254. Cheesy Mustard Greens Dip
(Ready in about 10 minutes | Servings 10)
This is a rich and flavorful keto dip worth trying as soon as possible! You can toss in any type of greens that you have on hand.
Per serving: 153 Calories; 10.6g Fat; 7g Carbs; 8.7g Protein; 3.6g Sugars
Ingredients
2 tablespoons butter, melted
20 ounces mustard greens
2 bell peppers, chopped
1 white onion, chopped
1 teaspoon garlic, minced
Sea salt and ground black pepper, to taste
1 cup chicken stock
8 ounces Neufchâtel cheese, crumbled
1/2 teaspoon dried thyme
1/2 teaspoon dried dill
1/2 teaspoon turmeric powder
3/4 cup Romano cheese, preferably freshly grated
Directions
Add the butter, mustard greens, bell peppers, onion, and garlic to the Instant Pot.
Secure the lid. Choose "Manual" mode and High pressure; cook for 3 minutes. Once cooking is complete, use a quick pressure release; carefully remove the lid.
Then, add the remaining ingredients and press the "Sauté" button. Let it simmer until the cheese is melted; then, gently stir this mixture until everything is well incorporated.
Serve with your favorite low-carb dippers.

255. Asian-Style Cocktail Sausage
(Ready in about 10 minutes | Servings 8)

These saucy mini sausages can be served on any occasion. You can add a pinch of Sichuan peppercorn for some extra oomph!
Per serving: 330 Calories; 24.8g Fat; 2.7g Carbs; 22.7g Protein; 1.2g Sugars
Ingredients
1 teaspoon sesame oil
20 mini cocktail sausages
1/2 cup tomato puree
1/2 cup chicken stock
1 tablespoon dark soy sauce
1/3 teaspoon ground black pepper
1/2 teaspoon paprika
Himalayan salt, to taste
1/2 teaspoon mustard seeds
1/2 teaspoon fennel seeds
1/4 teaspoon fresh ginger root, peeled and grated
1 teaspoon garlic paste
Directions
Simply throw all ingredients into your Instant Pot. Secure the lid. Choose "Manual" mode and High pressure; cook for 4 minutes. Once cooking is complete, use a quick pressure release; carefully remove the lid.
Serve with cocktail sticks and enjoy!

256. Colorful Stuffed Mushrooms
(Ready in about 10 minutes | Servings 5)
Button mushrooms stuffed with sautéed shallots, cheese, peppers, and herbs! These easy, colorful and flavorful stuffed mushrooms will be your next favorite Instant Pot meal!
Per serving: 151 Calories; 9.2g Fat; 6g Carbs; 11.9g Protein; 3.6g Sugars
Ingredients
1 tablespoon butter, softened
1 shallot, chopped
2 cloves garlic, minced
1 ½ cups Cottage cheese, at room temperature
1/2 cup Romano cheese, grated
1 red bell pepper, chopped
1 green bell pepper, chopped
1 jalapeno pepper, minced
1/2 teaspoon dried basil
1/2 teaspoon dried oregano
1/2 teaspoon dried rosemary
10 medium-sized button mushrooms, stems removed
Directions
Press the "Sauté" button to heat up your Instant Pot. Once hot, melt the butter and sauté the shallots until tender and translucent.
Stir in the garlic and cook an additional 30 seconds or until aromatic. Now, add the remaining ingredients, except for the mushroom caps, and stir to combine well.
Then, fill the mushroom caps with this mixture.
Add 1 cup of water and a steamer basket to you Instant Pot. Arrange the stuffed mushrooms in the steamer basket.
Secure the lid. Choose "Manual" mode and High pressure; cook for 5 minutes. Once cooking is complete, use a quick pressure release; carefully remove the lid.
Arrange the stuffed mushroom on a serving platter and serve. Enjoy!

257. Dad's Cocktail Meatballs
(Ready in about 15 minutes | Servings 6)
Fun, easy and delicious, meatballs are perfect for any party! In addition, these balls look spectacular on a serving platter.
Per serving: 384 Calories; 22.2g Fat; 6.1g Carbs; 38.4g Protein; 3.6g Sugars
Ingredients
1/2 pound ground pork
1 pound ground beef
1/2 cup Romano cheese, grated
1/2 cup pork rinds, crushed
1 egg, beaten
Coarse sea salt and ground black pepper, to taste
1 teaspoon granulated garlic
1/2 teaspoon cayenne pepper
1/2 teaspoon dried basil
1/4 cup milk, lukewarm
1 ½ cups BBQ sauce
Directions
Thoroughly combine ground meat, cheese, pork rinds, egg, salt, black pepper, garlic, cayenne pepper, basil, and milk in the mixing bowl.
Then, roll the mixture into 20 meatballs.
Pour BBQ sauce into your Instant Pot. Now, add the meatballs and secure the lid.
Choose "Manual" mode and High pressure; cook for 8 minutes. Once cooking is complete, use a quick pressure release; carefully remove the lid. Bon appétit!

258. Herbed and Caramelized Mushrooms
(Ready in about 10 minutes | Servings 4)
These herby mushrooms bring the flavors of summer days to your home. Serve with a garlic mayo for a full low-carb experience!
Per serving: 91 Calories; 6.4g Fat; 5.5g Carbs; 5.2g Protein; 2.8g Sugars
Ingredients
2 tablespoons butter, melted
20 ounces button mushrooms, brushed clean
2 cloves garlic, minced
1 teaspoon dried basil
1 teaspoon dried rosemary
1 teaspoon dried sage
1 bay leaf
Sea salt, to taste
1/2 teaspoon freshly ground black pepper
1/2 cup water
1/2 cup broth, preferably homemade
1 tablespoon soy sauce
1 tablespoon fresh parsley leaves, roughly chopped

Directions
Press the "Sauté" button to heat up your Instant Pot. Once hot, melt the butter and sauté the mushrooms and garlic until aromatic.
Add seasonings, water, and broth. Add garlic, oregano, mushrooms, thyme, basil, bay leaves, veggie broth, and salt and pepper to your instant pot.
Secure the lid. Choose "Manual" mode and High pressure; cook for 5 minutes. Once cooking is complete, use a quick pressure release; carefully remove the lid.
Arrange your mushrooms on a serving platter and serve with cocktail sticks. Bon appétit!

259. Colby Cheese Dip with Peppers
(Ready in about 10 minutes | Servings 8)
It's not a party without a spicy and peppery dip. This is an utterly addicting snack so consider preparing a double batch.
Per serving: 237 Calories; 20.6g Fat; 3.1g Carbs; 10.2g Protein; 1.8g Sugars
Ingredients
1 tablespoon butter
2 red bell peppers, sliced
1 teaspoon red Aleppo pepper flakes
1 cup cream cheese, room temperature
2 cups Colby cheese, shredded
1 teaspoon sumac
2 garlic cloves, minced
1 cup chicken broth
Salt and ground black pepper, to taste
Directions
Press the "Sauté" button to heat up your Instant Pot. Once hot, melt the butter. Sauté the peppers until just tender.
Add the remaining ingredients; gently stir to combine.
Secure the lid. Choose "Manual" mode and High pressure; cook for 3 minutes. Once cooking is complete, use a quick pressure release; carefully remove the lid.
Serve with your favorite keto dippers. Bon appétit!

260. Party Chicken Drumettes
(Ready in about 15 minutes | Servings 8)
These chicken drumettes can truly be a lifesaver on a low-carb diet. They're shockingly tasty and easy to make in the Instant Pot!
Per serving: 237 Calories; 20.6g Fat; 3.1g Carbs; 10.2g Protein; 1.8g Sugars
Ingredients
2 pounds chicken drumettes
1 stick butter
1 tablespoon coconut aminos
Sea salt and ground black pepper, to taste
1/2 teaspoon dried dill weed
1/2 teaspoon dried basil
1 teaspoon hot sauce
1 tablespoon fish sauce
1/2 cup tomato sauce
1/2 cup water
Directions
Add all ingredients to your Instant Pot.
Secure the lid. Choose "Poultry" mode and High pressure; cook for 10 minutes. Once cooking is complete, use a natural pressure release; carefully remove the lid.
Serve at room temperature and enjoy!

261. Cheesy Cauliflower Balls
(Ready in about 25 minutes | Servings 8)
Bring these delicate cauliflower balls to the next potluck and you're sure to get invited back! They will literally melt in your mouth!
Per serving: 157 Calories; 12.1g Fat; 3.6g Carbs; 8.9g Protein; 1.2g Sugars
Ingredients
1 head of cauliflower, broken into florets
2 tablespoons butter
Coarse sea salt and white pepper, to taste
1/2 teaspoon cayenne pepper
1 garlic clove, minced
1/2 cup Parmesan cheese, grated
1 cup Asiago cheese, shredded
2 tablespoons fresh chopped chives, minced
2 eggs, beaten
Directions
Add 1 cup of water and a steamer basket to the Instant Pot. Now, add cauliflower to the steamer basket.
Secure the lid. Choose "Manual" mode and High pressure; cook for 3 minutes. Once cooking is complete, use a quick pressure release; carefully remove the lid.
Transfer the cauliflower to a food processor. Add the remaining ingredients; process until everything is well incorporated.
Shape the mixture into balls. Bake in the preheated oven at 400 degrees F for 18 minutes. Bon appétit!

262. Crave-Worthy Balsamic Baby Carrots
(Ready in about 10 minutes | Servings 8)
An amazingly quick appetizer that features baby carrots and balsamic vinegar. You can add another combo of spices, if desired.
Per serving: 94 Calories; 6.1g Fat; 8.9g Carbs; 1.4g Protein; 4.1g Sugars
Ingredients
28 ounces baby carrots
1 cup chicken broth
1/2 cup water
1/2 stick butter
2 tablespoons balsamic vinegar
Coarse sea salt, to taste
1/2 teaspoon red pepper flakes, crushed
1/2 teaspoon dried dill weed
Directions

Simply add all of the above ingredients to your Instant Pot.
Secure the lid. Choose "Manual" mode and High pressure; cook for 3 minutes. Once cooking is complete, use a quick pressure release; carefully remove the lid.
Transfer to a nice serving bowl and serve. Enjoy!

263. Super Bowl Pizza Dip
(Ready in about 10 minutes | Servings 10)
This ooey-gooey, cheesy dip will deliver the wow factor and incredible taste! Prepare this dip for your next, memorable party!
Per serving: 280 Calories; 20.4g Fat; 3.7g Carbs; 20.6g Protein; 2.5g Sugars
Ingredients
10 ounces cream cheese
10 ounces Pepper-Jack cheese
1 pound tomatoes, pureed
10 ounces pancetta, chopped
1 cup green olives, pitted and halved
1/2 teaspoon garlic powder
1 teaspoon dried oregano
1 cup chicken broth
4 ounces Mozzarella cheese, thinly sliced
Directions
Combine cream cheese, Pepper-Jack cheese, tomatoes, pancetta, olives, garlic, powder, and oregano in your Instant Pot.
Secure the lid. Choose "Manual" mode and High pressure; cook for 4 minutes. Once cooking is complete, use a quick pressure release; carefully remove the lid.
Top with Mozzarella cheese; cover and let it sit in the residual heat. Serve warm or at room temperature. Bon appétit!

264. Minty Party Meatballs
(Ready in about 15 minutes | Servings 6)
Use lean turkey with pork so you can stuff these meatballs with cheese. It's all about the balance.
Per serving: 280 Calories; 20.4g Fat; 3.7g Carbs; 20.6g Protein; 2.5g Sugars
Ingredients
1/2 pound ground pork
1/2 pound ground turkey
2 eggs
1/3 cup almond flour
Sea salt and ground black pepper, to taste
2 garlic cloves, minced
1 cup Romano cheese, grated
1 teaspoon dried basil
1/2 teaspoon dried thyme
1/4 cup minced fresh mint, plus more for garnish
1/2 cup beef bone broth
1/2 cup tomatoes, puréed
 2 tablespoons scallions
Directions
Thoroughly combine all ingredients, except for broth, tomatoes, and scallions in a mixing bowl.
Shape the mixture into 2-inch meatballs and reserve. Add beef bone broth, tomatoes, and scallions to your Instant Pot. Place the meatballs in this sauce.
Secure the lid. Choose "Manual" mode and High pressure; cook for 8 minutes. Once cooking is complete, use a quick pressure release; carefully remove the lid. Bon appétit!

265. Chicken Wings Italiano
(Ready in about 20 minutes | Servings 12)
When you need to get fancy with classic chicken wings, this Italian-style recipe is here to help. You can use Romano or Asiago cheese as well.
Per serving: 443 Calories; 30.8g Fat; 6.2g Carbs; 33.2g Protein; 3.5g Sugars
Ingredients
4 pounds chicken wings cut into sections
1/2 cup butter, melted
1 tablespoon Italian seasoning mix
1/2 teaspoon onion powder
1/2 teaspoon garlic powder
1 teaspoon paprika
1/2 teaspoon coarse sea salt
1/2 teaspoon ground black pepper
1 cup Parmigiano-Reggiano cheese, shaved
2 eggs, lightly whisked
Directions
Add chicken wings, butter, Italian seasoning mix, onion powder, garlic powder, paprika, salt, and black pepper to your Instant Pot.
Secure the lid. Choose "Poultry" mode and High pressure. Cook the chicken wings for 10 minutes. Once cooking is complete, use a natural pressure release; carefully remove the lid.
Mix Parmigiano-Reggiano cheese with eggs. Spoon this mixture over the wings.
Secure the lid. Choose "Manual" mode and High pressure; cook for 4 minutes longer. Once cooking is complete, use a quick pressure release; carefully remove the lid. Bon appétit!

266. Amazing Cauliflower Tots
(Ready in about 25 minutes | Servings 6)
These cauliflower tots are perfect for the best Saturday night plans ever. This recipe uses sneaky sharp cheese instead of breadcrumbs for a keto version. So clever!
Per serving: 132 Calories; 8.7g Fat; 4.5g Carbs; 9.2g Protein; 1.3g Sugars
Ingredients
1 head of cauliflower, broken into florets
2 eggs, beaten
1 shallot, peeled and chopped
1/2 cup Swiss cheese, grated
1/2 cup Parmesan cheese, grated
2 tablespoons fresh coriander, chopped
Sea salt and ground black pepper, to taste
Directions
Start by adding 1 cup of water and a steamer basket to your Instant Pot.
Arrange the cauliflower florets in the steamer basket.

Secure the lid. Choose "Manual" mode and High pressure; cook for 3 minutes. Once cooking is complete, use a quick pressure release; carefully remove the lid.

Mash the cauliflower and add the remaining ingredients. Form the mixture into a tater-tot shape with oiled hands.

Place cauliflower tots on a lightly greased baking sheet. Bake in the preheated oven at 390 degrees F approximately 20 minutes; make sure to flip them halfway through the cooking time.

Serve at room temperature. Bon appétit!

267. Mexican-Style Broccoli Balls Ole

(Ready in about 25 minutes | Servings 8)
Fun, easy and spicy, cheese balls are perfect for a cocktail party! In addition, they look spectacular on a serving platter.
Per serving: 137 Calories; 9.5g Fat; 4.8g Carbs; 8.9g Protein; 1.5g Sugars
Ingredients
1 head broccoli, broken into florets
1/2 cup Añejo cheese, shredded
1 ½ cups Cotija cheese, crumbled
3 ounces Ricotta cheese, cut into small chunks
1 teaspoon chili pepper flakes
Directions
Add 1 cup of water and a steamer basket to the Instant Pot.
Place broccoli florets in the steamer basket.
Secure the lid. Choose "Manual" mode and Low pressure; cook for 5 minutes. Once cooking is complete, use a quick pressure release; carefully remove the lid.
Add the broccoli florets along with the remaining ingredients to your food processor. Process until everything is well incorporated.
Shape the mixture into balls and place your balls on a parchment-lined baking sheet. Bake in the preheated oven at 390 degrees F for 15 minutes. Bon appétit!

268. Gruyère, Rutabaga and Bacon Bites

(Ready in about 10 minutes | Servings 8)
Looking for creative ways to eat rutabaga on a keto diet? These flavorful bites are both healthy and gourmet.
Per serving: 187 Calories; 14.2g Fat; 5.2g Carbs; 9.4g Protein; 3.4g Sugars
Ingredients
1/2 pound rutabaga, grated
4 slices meaty bacon, chopped
7 ounces Gruyère cheese, shredded
3 eggs, beaten
3 tablespoons almond flour
1 teaspoon granulated garlic
1 teaspoon shallot powder
Sea salt and ground black pepper, to taste
Directions
Add 1 cup of water and a metal trivet to the Instant Pot.
Mix all of the above ingredients until everything is well incorporated.
Put the mixture into a silicone pod tray that is previously greased with a nonstick cooking spray. Cover the tray with a sheet of aluminum foil and lower it onto the trivet.
Secure the lid. Choose "Manual" mode and Low pressure; cook for 5 minutes. Once cooking is complete, use a quick pressure release; carefully remove the lid. Bon appétit!

269. Shrimp Cocktail Salad on a Stick

(Ready in about 10 minutes | Servings 6)
Try your favorite seafood salad on a stick! Your guests will be amazed!
Per serving: 187 Calories; 9.3g Fat; 6.3g Carbs; 19.9g Protein; 3.9g Sugars
Ingredients
1 pound shrimp, peeled and deveined
1/4 cup rice wine vinegar
3/4 cup water
1 celery stalk, diced
2 bell peppers, sliced
4 ounces blue cheese, cubed
1/2 cup olives, pitted
1 cup cherry tomatoes
1 tablespoon olive oil
Sea salt and ground black pepper, to taste
1/2 teaspoon cayenne pepper
1/2 teaspoon paprika
Directions
Place shrimp, rice wine vinegar, and water in your Instant Pot.
Secure the lid. Choose "Manual" mode and High pressure; cook for 1 minute. Once cooking is complete, use a quick pressure release; carefully remove the lid.
Thread shrimp, celery, peppers, blue cheese, olives and cherry tomatoes onto cocktail sticks.
Drizzle olive oil over them; sprinkle with salt, black pepper, cayenne pepper, and paprika. Arrange these skewers on a serving platter and serve. Bon appétit!

270. Spring Deviled Eggs

(Ready in about 25 minutes | Servings 8)
Can you imagine a cocktail party without charming deviled eggs? They are elegant, appetizing and easy to make in the Instant Pot.
Per serving: 158 Calories; 12.1g Fat; 2.1g Carbs; 9.5g Protein; 1.2g Sugars
Ingredients
8 eggs
Salt and white pepper, to taste
1/4 cup mayonnaise
1/2 can tuna in spring water, drained
2 tablespoons spring onions, finely chopped
1 teaspoon smoked cayenne pepper

1/3 teaspoon fresh or dried dill weed
1 teaspoon Dijon mustard
1 pickled jalapeño, minced
Directions
Place 1 cup of water and a steamer basket in your Instant Pot. Now, arrange the eggs on the steamer basket.
Secure the lid. Choose "Manual" mode and Low pressure; cook for 5 minutes. Once cooking is complete, use a quick pressure release; carefully remove the lid.
Allow the eggs to cool for 15 minutes.
Peel the eggs and slice them into halves. Smash the egg yolks with a fork and add the remaining ingredients. Stir to combine well.
Afterwards, stuff the egg whites with tuna mixture. Serve well-chilled and enjoy!

271. Easy Cheesy Taco Dip
(Ready in about 10 minutes | Servings 12)
This dipping sauce brings the flavors of Mexico to your kitchen. Serve with fresh celery sticks for a full keto experience!
Per serving: 275 Calories; 23.7g Fat; 2.6g Carbs; 12.4g Protein; 1.2g Sugars
Ingredients
2 teaspoons sesame oil
1/2 cup yellow onion, chopped
1 pound ground turkey
1 teaspoon roasted garlic paste
1 teaspoon ancho chili powder
1/2 teaspoon dried basil
1/2 teaspoon dried Mexican oregano
1/4 teaspoon freshly ground black pepper, or more to taste
Sea salt, to taste
10 ounces Ricotta cheese, at room temperature
1 cup Mexican cheese, shredded
1 cup broth, preferably homemade
2 ripe tomatoes, chopped
1/3 cup salsa verde
Directions
Press the "Sauté" button to heat up your Instant Pot. Once hot, heat the sesame oil; now, sauté the onion until translucent.
Stir in ground turkey and continue to sauté until it is no longer pink. Add the remaining ingredients and stir until everything is combined well.
Secure the lid. Choose "Manual" mode and High pressure; cook for 6 minutes. Once cooking is complete, use a natural pressure release; carefully remove the lid. Bon appétit!

272. Cheese-Stuffed Cocktail Meatballs
(Ready in about 15 minutes | Servings 8)
Here is a keto twist on an old party favorite! Colby cheese tucked inside each meatball creates a burst of flavor.
Per serving: 277 Calories; 17.4g Fat; 3.1g Carbs; 25.8g Protein; 0.9g Sugars
Ingredients
1 pound ground beef
1/2 cup pork chicharron, crushed
1/2 cup Parmesan cheese, grated
2 eggs, beaten
2 tablespoons fresh scallions, chopped
2 tablespoons fresh cilantro, chopped
1 teaspoon garlic, minced
Sea salt, to your liking
1/2 teaspoon ground black pepper
1/2 teaspoon cayenne pepper
1 cup Colby cheese, cubed
2 teaspoons olive oil
1/2 cup chicken broth
1/2 cup BBQ sauce
Directions
In a mixing dish, thoroughly combine ground beef, pork chicharron, Parmesan cheese, eggs, scallions, cilantro, garlic, salt, black pepper, and cayenne pepper; mix until everything is well incorporated.
Now, shape the mixture into balls. Press one cheese cube into center of each meatball, sealing it inside. Press the "Sauté" button and heat the olive oil. Sear the meatballs for a couple of minutes or until browned on all sides. Pour in chicken broth and BBQ sauce.
Secure the lid. Choose the "Manual" setting and cook for 8 minutes under High pressure. Once cooking is complete, use a quick pressure release; carefully remove the lid.
Serve your meatballs with the sauce. Bon appétit!

273. Chorizo and Halloumi Fat Bombs
(Ready in about 10 minutes | Servings 8)
These low-carb fat bombs made even heartier with halloumi and chorizo! Fresh plum tomato gives the right amount of tanginess to these bites.
Per serving: 307 Calories; 26.8g Fat; 5.1g Carbs; 10.9g Protein; 2.9g Sugars
Ingredients
1 tablespoon tallow, melted
1 yellow onion, chopped
1 pound Chorizo sausage
1 garlic clove, minced
1 red bell pepper, chopped
1 cup chicken broth
1/2 teaspoon deli mustard
1 plum tomato, puréed
10 ounces Halloumi cheese, crumbled
1/3 cup mayonnaise
Directions
Press the "Sauté" button and melt the tallow. Once hot, cook the onion until tender and translucent. Add Chorizo and garlic to your Instant Pot; cook until the sausage is no longer pink; crumble the sausage with a fork.
Now, stir in bell pepper, broth, mustard, and tomato.

Secure the lid. Choose "Manual" mode and High pressure; cook for 4 minutes. Once cooking is complete, use a quick pressure release; carefully remove the lid.

Add the cheese and mayo. Shape the mixture into 2-inch balls and serve. Bon appétit!

274. Bacon Wrapped Cocktail Wieners

(Ready in about 10 minutes | Servings 10)
Here's your foolproof, basic party recipe you'll never want to be without. The next-level cocktail wieners your party guests will love!
Per serving: 257 Calories; 22.7g Fat; 1.4g Carbs; 10.8g Protein; 0.2g Sugars
Ingredients
1 pound cocktail wieners
1/2 pound sliced bacon, cold cut into slices
1/2 cup chicken broth
1/2 cup water
1/4 cup low-carb ketchup
2 tablespoons apple cider vinegar
1 tablespoon onion powder
1 tablespoon ground mustard
Salt and pepper to taste
Directions
Wrap each cocktail wiener with a slice of bacon; secure with a toothpick.

Then, place one layer of bacon wrapped cocktail wieners in the bottom of the Instant Pot. Repeat layering until you run out of the cocktail wieners. In a mixing bowl, thoroughly combine the remaining ingredients. Pour this mixture over the bacon wrapped cocktail wieners.

Secure the lid. Choose "Manual" mode and Low pressure; cook for 3 minutes. Once cooking is complete, use a natural pressure release; carefully remove the lid. Enjoy!

275. Brussels Sprouts with Aioli

(Ready in about 10 minutes | Servings 4)
You will love this super-easy appetizer. It features a few basic ingredients and takes under 10 minutes to make.
Per serving: 161 Calories; 13.4g Fat; 9g Carbs; 3.1g Protein; 2.5g Sugars
Ingredients
1 tablespoon butter
1/2 cup scallions, chopped
3/4 pound Brussels sprouts
Aioli Sauce:
1/4 cup mayonnaise
1 garlic clove, minced
1 tablespoon fresh lemon juice
1/2 teaspoon Dijon mustard
Directions
Press the "Sauté" button and melt the butter. Once hot, cook the scallions until softened. Now, add Brussels sprouts and sauté them for 1 minute more.

Secure the lid. Choose "Manual" mode and High pressure; cook for 4 minutes. Once cooking is complete, use a quick pressure release; carefully remove the lid.
Meanwhile, mix mayonnaise, garlic, lemon juice, Dijon mustard. Serve Brussels sprouts with Aioli sauce on the side. Bon appétit!

276. Creole Egg and Pancetta Balls

(Ready in about 25 minutes | Servings 6)
You can make your own Creole seasonings by mixing salt, paprika, garlic powder, oregano, thyme, black pepper, cayenne pepper, and onion powder. You can use bacon bits in this recipe.
Per serving: 236 Calories; 18.6g Fat; 3.1g Carbs; 13.4g Protein; 1.7g Sugars
Ingredients
6 eggs
1 teaspoon Creole seasonings
1/4 cup mayonnaise
1/4 cup cream cheese
1/3 cup Cheddar cheese, grated
Sea salt and ground black pepper, to taste
4 slices pancetta, chopped
Directions
Place 1 cup of water and a steamer basket in your Instant Pot. Now, arrange the eggs on the steamer basket.

Secure the lid. Choose "Manual" mode and Low pressure; cook for 5 minutes. Once cooking is complete, use a quick pressure release; carefully remove the lid.

Allow the eggs to cool for 15 minutes; then, chop the eggs and add the remaining ingredients; mix to combine well.

Shape the mixture into balls. Serve well-chilled. Keep in the refrigerator up to 4 days.

277. Umami Party Chicken Wings

(Ready in about 15 minutes | Servings 6)
Here's one of the favorite party appetizers. Just omit a miso paste to make your wings keto-friendly.
Per serving: 200 Calories; 5.5g Fat; 9g Carbs; 25.6g Protein; 8g Sugars
Ingredients
2 teaspoons butter, melted
1 ½ pounds chicken wings
1/2 cup chicken broth
1/2 cup barbecue sauce
1 tablespoon fish sauce
1/4 cup rice vinegar
1 teaspoon grated fresh ginger
Sea salt ground black pepper, to your liking
1/2 teaspoon cumin
1/2 teaspoon caraway seeds
1/2 teaspoon celery seeds
1/2 teaspoon garlic powder
1/2 teaspoon red pepper, crushed
2 tablespoons Thai basil
Directions

Add butter, chicken wings, broth, barbecue sauce, fish sauce, vinegar, ginger, and spices to your Instant Pot.
Secure the lid. Choose "Poultry" mode and High pressure. Cook the chicken wings for 10 minutes. Once cooking is complete, use a natural pressure release; carefully remove the lid.
Serve garnished with Thai basil. Bon appétit!

278. Chicken Salad Skewers

(Ready in about 10 minutes | Servings 4)
Refreshing and colorful, these chicken skewers are perfect for the next party! These skewers carry some of the flavors of Mexican cuisine, so you can omit Sriracha chili sauce to make them kid-friendly if necessary.
Per serving: 287 Calories; 18.2g Fat; 5.6g Carbs; 24.6g Protein; 2.8g Sugars
Ingredients
1 pound chicken breast halves, boneless and skinless
Celery salt and ground black pepper, to taste
1/2 teaspoon Sriracha
1 red onion, cut into wedges
1 cup cherry tomatoes, halved
1 zucchini, cut into thick slices
1/4 cup olives, pitted
2 tablespoons olive oil
1 tablespoon lemon juice, freshly squeezed
Directions
Add 1 cup of water and a metal trivet to the Instant Pot.
Arrange the chicken on the metal trivet.
Secure the lid. Choose "Poultry" mode and High pressure. Cook the chicken for 5 minutes. Once cooking is complete, use a natural pressure release; carefully remove the lid.
Slice the chicken into cubes. Sprinkle chicken cubes with salt, pepper, and Sriracha.
Thread chicken cubes, onion, cherry tomatoes, zucchini, and olives onto bamboo skewers. Drizzle olive oil and lemon juice over skewers and serve.

279. Zucchini Loaded Meatballs

(Ready in about 15 minutes | Servings 8)
Here's your foolproof, basic party recipe! Veggie loaded meatballs will surprise and amaze your guests.
Per serving: 161 Calories; 9.2g Fat; 4.2g Carbs; 14.7g Protein; 2.1g Sugars
Ingredients
1 pound ground turkey
1/2 cup Romano cheese, grated
1 teaspoon dried basil
1/2 teaspoon dried oregano
1/2 teaspoon dried dill
1 teaspoon dried chives
2 tablespoons shallots, chopped
1 garlic clove, minced
1 egg, beaten
1 cup zucchini, grated
1 tablespoon olive oil
1/2 cup chili sauce
1/2 cup broth, preferably homemade
Directions
In a mixing bowl, thoroughly combine ground turkey, grated cheese, basil, oregano, dill, chives, shallots, garlic, egg, and zucchini.
Shape the mixture into meatballs.
Press the "Sauté" button and heat the oil. Once hot, brown your meatballs for 2 to 3 minutes, turning them occasionally.
Add chili sauce and broth to your Instant Pot. Place the meatballs in the liquid.
Secure the lid. Choose "Manual" mode and High pressure; cook for 8 minutes. Once cooking is complete, use a quick pressure release; carefully remove the lid.
Serve with toothpicks. Bon appétit!

280. Queso Fundido Dip

(Ready in about 15 minutes | Servings 10)
This elegant, Mexican-inspired dipping sauce makes a delicious appetizer that suits almost any diet. Serve with celery sticks or pickled onions.
Per serving: 232 Calories; 19.1g Fat; 2.9g Carbs; 12.1g Protein; 1.5g Sugars
Ingredients
1 pound chorizo sausage, chopped
1/2 cup water
1/2 cup tomato salsa
1 cup cream cheese
1 red onion, chopped
1/4 teaspoon ground black pepper
1/2 teaspoon cayenne pepper
1 teaspoon Mexican oregano
1 teaspoon coriander
1 cup Cotija cheese
Directions
Stir sausage, water, tomato salsa, cream cheese, red onion, black pepper, cayenne pepper, oregano, and coriander into your Instant Pot.
Secure the lid. Choose "Manual" mode and High pressure; cook for 6 minutes. Once cooking is complete, use a natural pressure release; carefully remove the lid.
Add Cotija cheese and press the "Sauté" button. Stir until everything is heated through. Enjoy!

281. Asian-Style Appetizer Ribs

(Ready in about 25 minutes | Servings 6)
It's not a holiday party without sticky and saucy spare ribs. This is an utterly addicting appetizer so consider preparing a double batch.
Per serving: 331 Calories; 15.8g Fat; 3.1g Carbs; 42.1g Protein; 1.8g Sugars
Ingredients
2 tablespoons sesame oil
1 ½ pounds spare ribs
Salt and ground black pepper, to taste
1/2 cup green onions, chopped
1 teaspoon ginger-garlic paste

1/2 teaspoon red pepper flakes, crushed
1/2 teaspoon dries parsley
2 tomatoes, crushed
1/2 cup chicken stock
1 tablespoon tamari sauce
2 tablespoons sherry
2 tablespoons sesame seeds
Directions
Season spare ribs with salt and black pepper. Press the "Sauté" button and heat the oil. Once hot, brown your spare ribs approximately 3 minutes per side.
Add the remaining ingredients, except for sesame seeds, and secure the lid.
Choose "Meat/Stew" mode and High pressure; cook for 18 minutes. Once cooking is complete, use a natural pressure release; carefully remove the lid. Sprinkle sesame seed over the top of your ribs and serve immediately. Bon appétit!

282. Two-Cheese Artichoke Dip

(Ready in about 15 minutes | Servings 10)
A crunchy texture of artichokes and its mild flavor, when prepared in this manner, pair so well with cheese, mayo, and herbs.
Per serving: 204 Calories; 15.4g Fat; 5.6g Carbs; 11.5g Protein; 1.3g Sugars
Ingredients
2 medium-sized artichokes, trimmed and cleaned
1 cup Ricotta cheese, softened
2 cups Monterey-jack cheese, shredded
1/2 cup mayonnaise
1/2 cup Greek yogurt
1 garlic clove, minced
2 tablespoons coriander
1/4 cup scallions
1/4 teaspoon ground black pepper, or more to taste
1 teaspoon dried rosemary
Directions
Start by adding 1 cup of water and a steamer basket to the Instant Pot. Place the artichokes in the steamer basket.
Secure the lid. Choose "Manual" mode and High pressure; cook for 8 minutes. Once cooking is complete, use a quick pressure release; carefully remove the lid.
Coarsely chop your artichokes and add the remaining ingredients.
Press the "Sauté" button and let it simmer until everything is heated through. Bon appétit!

283. Easy Party Mushrooms

(Ready in about 10 minutes | Servings 6)
Button mushrooms are a good source of plant-based protein copper, selenium, and potassium. Moreover, even those who don't like keto food may have a change of heart when they try this party appetizer!
Per serving: 73 Calories; 7g Fat; 2g Carbs; 1.7g Protein; 1.1g Sugars
Ingredients
3 tablespoons sesame oil
3/4 pound small button mushrooms
1 teaspoon garlic, minced
1/2 teaspoon cayenne pepper
1/2 teaspoon smoked paprika
Salt and ground black pepper, to taste
Directions
Press the "Sauté" button and heat the oil. Once hot, cook your mushrooms for 4 to 5 minutes.
Add the other ingredients.
Secure the lid. Choose "Manual" mode and High pressure; cook for 5 minutes. Once cooking is complete, use a quick pressure release; carefully remove the lid.
Serve with toothpicks and enjoy!

284. Herbed Party Shrimp

(Ready in about 10 minutes | Servings 4)
Serve this shrimp recipe as an appetizer on Christmas Eve and your guests will go wild over it!
Per serving: 142 Calories; 7.5g Fat; 0.2g Carbs; 18.3g Protein; 0g Sugars
Ingredients
2 tablespoons olive oil
3/4 pound shrimp, peeled and deveined
1 teaspoon paprika
1/2 teaspoon dried oregano
1/2 teaspoon dried thyme
1/2 teaspoon dried rosemary
1/2 teaspoon dried basil
1/4 teaspoon red pepper flakes
1 teaspoon dried parsley flakes
1 teaspoon onion powder
1 teaspoon garlic powder
Coarse sea salt and ground black pepper, to taste
1 cup chicken broth, preferably homemade
Directions
Press the "Sauté" button and heat the olive oil. Once hot, cook your shrimp for 2 to 3 minutes.
Sprinkle all seasoning over your shrimp, pour the chicken broth into your Instant Pot, and secure the lid.
Choose "Manual" mode and Low pressure; cook for 2 minutes. Once cooking is complete, use a quick pressure release; carefully remove the lid.
Arrange shrimp on a serving platter and serve with toothpicks. Bon appétit!

285. Crispy and Yummy Beef Bites

(Ready in about 25 minutes | Servings 6)
Wow your party guests with these crispy, succulent meat bites. To serve, use your favorite sauce like blue-cheese sauce, keto ranch dip, etc.
Per serving: 169 Calories; 9.9g Fat; 1.1g Carbs; 17.9g Protein; 0.5g Sugars
Ingredients
2 tablespoons olive oil
1 pound beef steak, cut into cubes
Sea salt and ground black pepper, to taste
1 teaspoon cayenne pepper
1/2 teaspoon dried marjoram

1 cup beef bone broth
1/4 cup dry white wine
Directions
Press the "Sauté" button and heat the olive oil. Once hot, cook the beef for 2 to 3 minutes, stirring periodically.
Add the remaining ingredients to the Instant Pot. Secure the lid. Choose "Manual" mode and High pressure; cook for 20 minutes. Once cooking is complete, use a natural pressure release; carefully remove the lid.
Arrange beef cubes on a nice serving platter and serve with sticks. Bon appétit!

286. Asparagus with Greek Aioli
(Ready in about 10 minutes | Servings 6)
You can use a pasteurized egg yolk in this recipe. Keep this aioli for 5 days in your refrigerator.
Per serving: 194 Calories; 19.2g Fat; 4.5g Carbs; 2.6g Protein; 2.4g Sugars
Ingredients
1 pound asparagus spears
Sea salt and ground black pepper, to taste
Homemade Aioli Sauce:
1 teaspoon garlic, minced
1 egg yolk
1/2 cup olive oil
Sea salt and ground black pepper, to your liking
1/4 cup Greek yogurt
2 teaspoons freshly squeezed lemon juice
Directions
Start by adding 1 cup of water and a steamer basket to the Instant Pot. Place the asparagus in the steamer basket.
Secure the lid. Choose "Manual" mode and High pressure; cook for 1 minute. Once cooking is complete, use a quick pressure release; carefully remove the lid.
Season your asparagus with salt and pepper; reserve.
In a blender or a food processor, mix garlic, egg yolk, and oil until well incorporated.
Now, add the salt, ground black pepper, and Greek yogurt. Afterwards, add the lemon juice and mix until your aioli is thickened and emulsified.
Serve the reserved asparagus spears with this homemade aioli on the side. Enjoy!

287. Carrot Sticks with Blue-Cheese Sauce
(Ready in about 10 minutes | Servings 8)
Here's a great way to avoid unhealthy proceed food for an afternoon snack! This delicious snack is low in cholesterol and high in dietary fiber, potassium and Vitamin A.
Per serving: 202 Calories; 16.8g Fat; 7.1g Carbs; 6.1g Protein; 3.9g Sugars
Ingredients
1 pound carrots, cut into sticks
Himalayan salt and white pepper, to taste
1/4 teaspoon red pepper flakes, crushed
1 cup water
Blue-Cheese Sauce:
6 ounces blue cheese
1/2 cup full-fat yogurt
1/2 cup mayonnaise
1 teaspoon deli mustard
1 tablespoon fresh chives, chopped
3 tablespoons water
Directions
Simply add carrots, salt, white pepper, red pepper and 1 cup of water to your Instant Pot.
Secure the lid. Choose "Manual" mode and High pressure; cook for 2 minutes. Once cooking is complete, use a quick pressure release; carefully remove the lid.
Meanwhile, thoroughly combine the remaining ingredients in a mixing bowl. Serve the prepared carrot sticks with the sauce on the side. Bon appétit!

288. Zingy Zucchini Bites
(Ready in about 10 minutes | Servings 6)
Your Instant Pot transforms regular zucchini into a zingy and healthy fast snack with the outstanding flavor of olive oil and coriander. Ta-da!
Per serving: 70 Calories; 5.1g Fat; 4.4g Carbs; 3.2g Protein; 0.9g Sugars
Ingredients
2 tablespoons olive oil
1 red chili pepper, chopped
1 pound zucchini, cut into thick slices
1 teaspoon garlic powder
1 cup chicken broth
Coarse sea salt and ground black pepper, to taste
1/2 teaspoon paprika
1/2 teaspoon ground coriander
Directions
Press the "Sauté" button and heat the olive oil. Once hot, cook chili pepper for 1 minute.
Add the remaining ingredients.
Secure the lid. Choose "Manual" mode and Low pressure; cook for 3 minutes. Once cooking is complete, use a quick pressure release; carefully remove the lid. Bon appétit!

289. Kohlrabi Sticks with Hungarian Mayo
(Ready in about 10 minutes | Servings 6)
Kohlrabi contains 2.6 grams of carbohydrates per 100 grams of product. Adjust the sauce to suit your taste by increasing or decreasing the seasonings.
Per serving: 148 Calories; 13.8g Fat; 5.4g Carbs; 1.5g Protein; 2.6g Sugars
Ingredients
1 pound kohlrabi, cut into sticks
1 cup water
Salt and pepper, to taste
1/2 cup mayonnaise
1 teaspoon whole-grain mustard
1/2 teaspoon Hungarian paprika
1 teaspoon shallot powder

1/4 teaspoon porcini powder
1 teaspoon granulated garlic
Directions
Add kohlrabi sticks and water to your Instant Pot. Now, season with salt and pepper.
Secure the lid. Choose "Manual" mode and Low pressure; cook for 3 minutes. Once cooking is complete, use a quick pressure release; carefully remove the lid.
In the meantime, mix the remaining ingredients until everything is well incorporated. Serve with the prepared kohlrabi sticks. Bon appétit!

290. Bok Choy Boats with Shrimp Salad
(Ready in about 10 minutes | Servings 8)
A flavorful appetizer with a Mediterranean flair. This appetizer is a powerhouse of many minerals and vitamin so you can snack without guilt.
Per serving: 124 Calories; 10.6g Fat; 3.1g Carbs; 4.7g Protein; 1.8g Sugars
Ingredients
26 shrimp, cleaned and deveined
2 tablespoons fresh lemon juice
1 cup of water
Sea salt and ground black pepper, to taste
2 tomatoes, diced
4 ounces feta cheese, crumbled
1/3 cup olives, pitted and sliced
4 tablespoons olive oil
2 tablespoons apple cider vinegar
8 Bok choy leaves
2 tablespoons fresh basil leaves, snipped
2 tablespoons fresh mint leaves, chopped
Directions
Toss the shrimp and fresh lemon juice in your Instant Pot. Add 1 cup of water.
Secure the lid. Choose "Manual" mode and Low pressure; cook for 2 minutes. Once cooking is complete, use a quick pressure release; carefully remove the lid.
Season the shrimp with sea salt and ground black pepper, and allow them to cool completely. Toss the shrimp with tomatoes, feta cheese, olives, olive oil, and vinegar.
Mound the salad onto each Bok choy leaf and arrange them on a serving platter. Top with basil and mint leaves. Bon appétit!

291. Game Day Sausage Dip
(Ready in about 45 minutes | Servings 12)
This sumptuous dipping sauce is easy to make in the Instant Pot so that it could become a part of your weekly routine. It will make your game days ad movie nights even better!
Per serving: 251 Calories; 18.3g Fat; 7.2g Carbs; 14.5g Protein; 5.3g Sugars
Ingredients
1 tablespoon ghee
3/4 pound spicy breakfast sausage, casings removed and crumbled
16 ounces Velveeta cheese
8 ounces Cotija cheese shredded
2 (10-ounce) cans diced tomatoes with green chilies
1 cup chicken broth
1 package taco seasoning
Directions
Press the "Sauté" button and melt the ghee. Once hot, cook the sausage until it is no longer pink.
Add the remaining ingredients.
Secure the lid. Choose "Slow Cook" mode and Low pressure; cook for 40 minutes. Once cooking is complete, use a quick pressure release; carefully remove the lid.
Serve with your favorite keto dippers. Bon appétit!

292. Stuffed Baby Bell Peppers
(Ready in about 10 minutes | Servings 5)
These mini peppers can be served as a side dish or a vegetarian main course; however, this is the meal that your family will love for sure!
Per serving: 224 Calories; 17.5g Fat; 9g Carbs; 8.7g Protein; 5.5g Sugars
Ingredients
10 baby bell peppers, seeded and sliced lengthwise
1 tablespoon olive oil
4 ounces cream cheese
4 ounces Monterey-Jack cheese, shredded
1 teaspoon garlic, minced
2 tablespoons scallions, chopped
1/4 teaspoon ground black pepper, or more to taste
1/2 teaspoon cayenne pepper
Directions
Start by adding 1 cup of water and a steamer basket to the Instant Pot.
In a mixing bowl, thoroughly combine all ingredients, except for bell peppers. Then, stuff the peppers with cheese mixture.
Place the stuffed peppers in the steamer basket.
Secure the lid. Choose "Manual" mode and High pressure; cook for 5 minutes. Once cooking is complete, use a quick pressure release; carefully remove the lid.
Serve at room temperature and enjoy!

293. Party Garlic Prawns
(Ready in about 10 minutes | Servings 6)
Inspired by seafood, you can come up with this appetizer recipe that is just scrumptious! Prawns are incredibly easy to make in an Instant Pot.
Per serving: 122 Calories; 5.8g Fat; 2.7g Carbs; 14.2g Protein; 0.5g Sugars
Ingredients
2 tablespoons olive oil
1 pound prawns, cleaned and deveined
2 garlic cloves, minced
Sea salt and ground black pepper, to taste
1 teaspoon cayenne pepper
1/2 teaspoon dried dill

2 tablespoons fresh lime juice
1 cup roasted vegetable broth, preferably homemade
Directions
Press the "Sauté" button and heat the olive oil. Once hot, cook your prawns for 2 to 3 minutes.
Add garlic and cook an additional 40 seconds.
Stir in the remaining ingredients.
Secure the lid. Choose "Manual" mode and Low pressure; cook for 2 minutes. Once cooking is complete, use a quick pressure release; carefully remove the lid.
Arrange prawns on a serving platter and serve with toothpicks. Bon appétit!

294. Barbecue Lil Smokies
(Ready in about 10 minutes | Servings 8)
These cocktail wieners are very easy to make in an Instant Pot and they have a rich taste thanks to the spices and ale beer. This stunning appetizer recipe showcases cocktail wieners at their finest.
Per serving: 120 Calories; 4.9g Fat; 1.2g Carbs; 17.5g Protein; 0.6g Sugars
Ingredients
1 ½ pounds beef cocktail wieners
1 cup water
1/4 cup apple cider vinegar
1/2 tablespoon onion powder
1/2 teaspoon ground black pepper
1 teaspoon ground mustard
2 ounces ale
Directions
Simply throw all ingredients into your Instant Pot.
Secure the lid. Choose "Manual" mode and High pressure; cook for 2 minutes. Once cooking is complete, use a natural pressure release; carefully remove the lid.
Serve with cocktail sticks and enjoy!

295. Two-Cheese and Caramelized Onion Dip
(Ready in about 15 minutes | Servings 12)
With two types of cheese, butter, sautéed onions and homemade broth, this dipping sauce is flavorful and extremely comforting. If you could use a roasted vegetable broth, it will be even better!
Per serving: 148 Calories; 10g Fat; 7.2g Carbs; 7.5g Protein; 4.1g Sugars
Ingredients
3 tablespoons butter
2 pounds white onions, chopped
Sea salt and freshly ground black pepper, to taste
1/4 teaspoon dill
1 tablespoon coconut aminos
1 cup broth, preferably homemade
10 ounces Ricotta cheese
6 ounces Swiss cheese
Directions
Press the "Sauté" button and melt the butter. Once hot, cook the onions until they are caramelized.
Add the salt, pepper, dill, coconut aminos, and broth.
Secure the lid. Choose "Manual" mode and High pressure; cook for 10 minutes. Once cooking is complete, use a natural pressure release; carefully remove the lid.
Fold in the cheese and stir until everything is well combined. Serve with your favorite dippers. Bon appétit!

296. Hot Lager Chicken Wings
(Ready in about 15 minutes | Servings 6)
Are you looking for a surprisingly sensational chicken recipe to amaze your guests? Here is a great opportunity to use this versatile food and make something fabulous!
Per serving: 216 Calories; 16.4g Fat; 2.2g Carbs; 12.9g Protein; 0.5g Sugars
Ingredients
2 tablespoons butter, melted
1 pound chicken thighs
Coarse sea salt and ground black pepper, to taste
1 teaspoon cayenne pepper
1 teaspoon shallot powder
1 teaspoon garlic powder
1 teaspoon hot sauce
1/2 cup lager
1/2 cup water
Directions
Press the "Sauté" button and melt the butter. Once hot, brown the chicken thighs for 2 minutes per side.
Add the remaining ingredients to your Instant Pot.
Secure the lid. Choose "Poultry" mode and High pressure; cook for 6 minutes. Once cooking is complete, use a quick pressure release; carefully remove the lid.
Serve at room temperature and enjoy!

297. Braised Spring Kale Appetizer
(Ready in about 10 minutes | Servings 6)
Besides being delicious, this recipe is easy to make. If you do not have spring onions on hand, simply use regular scallions or shallots.
Per serving: 103 Calories; 6.1g Fat; 8.1g Carbs; 6.1g Protein; 2.1g Sugars
Ingredients
3 teaspoons butter, melted
1 cup spring onions, chopped
1 pound kale, torn into pieces
Himalayan salt and ground black pepper, to taste
1/2 teaspoon cayenne pepper
1 cup water
1/2 cup Colby cheese, shredded
Directions
Press the "Sauté" button and melt butter. Add spring onions to your Instant Pot and cook for 1 minute or until wilted.
Stir in kale leaves, salt, black pepper, cayenne pepper, and water.
Secure the lid. Choose "Manual" mode and High pressure; cook for 1 minute. Once cooking is

complete, use a quick pressure release; carefully remove the lid.
Transfer to a serving bowl and top with grated cheese. Bon appétit!

298. Wax Beans with Pancetta
(Ready in about 10 minutes | Servings 6)
This easy and healthy appetizer can be assembled ahead of time. You will love its fresh and rich taste. Add a few sprinkles of Hungarian paprika just before serving!
Per serving: 194 Calories; 8.7g Fat; 5.8g Carbs; 24.3g Protein; 2.9g Sugars
Ingredients
1 tablespoon peanut oil
1/2 cup shallots, chopped
4 slices pancetta, diced
1 teaspoon roasted garlic paste
1 pound yellow wax beans, cut in half
Kosher salt and ground black pepper, to your liking
1 cup water
Directions
Press the "Sauté" button to heat up your Instant Pot. Now, heat the peanut oil and sauté the shallot until softened.
Now, add pancetta and continue to cook for a further 3 to 4 minutes; reserve.
Add the other ingredients; stir to combine
Secure the lid. Choose "Manual" mode and Low pressure; cook for 3 minutes. Once cooking is complete, use a quick pressure release; carefully remove the lid.
Serve warm, garnished with the reserved shallots and pancetta. Bon appétit!

299. Middle-Eastern Eggplant Dip
(Ready in about 10 minutes | Servings 10)
Peppers are very versatile ingredients. In this recipe, we use a fabulous eggplant-peppers-spices-oil combination to make an easy and crowd-pleasing dipping sauce.
Per serving: 81 Calories; 6.6g Fat; 5g Carbs; 1.4g Protein; 2.7g Sugars
Ingredients
1/4 cup sesame oil
2 bell peppers, seeded and sliced
1 serrano pepper, seeded and sliced
1 eggplant, peeled and sliced
3 cloves garlic, minced
1 cup broth, preferably homemade
Kosher salt and ground black pepper, to taste
1/2 teaspoon cayenne pepper
1/2 teaspoon chili flakes
A few drops of liquid smoke
2 tablespoons coriander, chopped
2 teaspoons extra-virgin olive oil
Directions
Press the "Sauté" button to heat up your Instant Pot. Now, heat the oil and sauté the peppers and eggplant until softened.
Add the garlic, broth, salt, black pepper, cayenne pepper, chili flakes, liquid smoke, and coriander. Secure the lid. Choose "Manual" mode and Low pressure; cook for 3 minutes. Once cooking is complete, use a quick pressure release; carefully remove the lid.
Transfer the mixture to a serving bowl; drizzle olive oil over the top and serve well-chilled. Enjoy!

300. Cheesy Cauliflower Bites
(Ready in about 10 minutes | Servings 6)
The Instant Pot transforms "dull" veggies into a stunning and super healthy appetizer. You can substitute Cheddar cheesy with Pepper-Jack or Swiss cheese.
Per serving: 130 Calories; 9.6g Fat; 5.1g Carbs; 6.9g Protein; 2g Sugars
Ingredients
1 pound cauliflower, broken into florets
Sea salt and ground black pepper, to taste
2 tablespoons lemon juice
2 tablespoons extra-virgin olive oil
1 cup Cheddar cheese, preferably freshly grated
Directions
Add 1 cup of water and a steamer basket to your Instant Pot.
Now, arrange cauliflower florets on the steamer basket.
Secure the lid. Choose "Manual" mode and Low pressure; cook for 3 minutes. Once cooking is complete, use a quick pressure release; carefully remove the lid.
Sprinkle salt and pepper over your cauliflower; drizzle with lemon juice and olive oil. Scatter grated cheese over the cauliflower florets.
Press the "Sauté" button to heat up your Instant Pot. Let it cook until the cheese is melted or about 5 minutes. Bon appétit!

EGGS & DAIRY

301. Kale and Tomato Frittata
(Ready in about 10 minutes | Servings 3)
You will love this super-easy breakfast recipe. It features basic ingredients and takes under 10 minutes to make.
Per serving: 140 Calories; 7.3g Fat; 8.1g Carbs; 11.2g Protein; 2.8g Sugars
Ingredients
5 eggs, whisked
1 cup fresh kale leaves, torn into pieces
1 green bell pepper, seeded and chopped
1 jalapeño pepper, seeded and minced
1 fresh ripe tomato, chopped
Sea salt and ground black pepper, to taste
1/2 teaspoon cayenne pepper
2 tablespoons scallions, chopped
1 garlic clove, minced
Directions
Spritz a baking pan that fits inside your Instant Pot with a nonstick cooking spray.
Thoroughly combine all ingredients and spoon the mixture into the prepared baking pan. Cover with a sheet of foil.
Add 1 cup of water and a metal trivet to the Instant Pot. Lower the baking pan onto the trivet.
Secure the lid. Choose "Manual" mode and Low pressure; cook for 6 minutes. Once cooking is complete, use a natural pressure release; carefully remove the lid.
Serve warm. Bon appétit!

302. Tyrolese Egg Salad
(Ready in about 30 minutes | Servings 4)
Hard-boiled eggs, bright green beans, and mellow, crumbled Gorgonzola cheese! Enjoy this fresh egg salad inspired by western Austrian cuisine.
Per serving: 342 Calories; 29.2g Fat; 7.2g Carbs; 12.7g Protein; 3.6g Sugars
Ingredients
6 eggs
1/2 pound green beans, trimmed
1 cup of water
3 slices prosciutto, chopped
1/2 cup green onions, chopped
1 carrot, shredded
1/2 cup mayonnaise
1 tablespoon apple cider vinegar
1 teaspoon yellow mustard
4 tablespoons Gorgonzola cheese, crumbled
Directions
Pour the water into the Instant Pot; add a steamer basket to the bottom. Arrange the eggs in a steamer basket.
Secure the lid. Choose "Manual" mode and High pressure; cook for 5 minutes. Once cooking is complete, use a natural pressure release; carefully remove the lid.
Allow the eggs to cool for 15 minutes. Peel the eggs and cut them into slices.
Then, add green beans and 1 cup of water to your Instant Pot.
Secure the lid. Choose "Manual" mode and Low pressure; cook for 5 minutes. Once cooking is complete, use a quick pressure release; carefully remove the lid.
Transfer green beans to a salad bowl. Add prosciutto, green onions, carrot, mayonnaise, vinegar, and mustard. Top with Gorgonzola cheese and sliced eggs. Enjoy!

303. Mom's Cheesy Soup
(Ready in about 25 minutes | Servings 4)
Cheddar cheese soup is an ultimate comfort food and it is sure to satisfy the whole family. Make this top-rated classic in your Instant Pot and you will see the difference!
Per serving: 530 Calories; 37.6g Fat; 4.2g Carbs; 43.1g Protein; 1.9g Sugars
Ingredients
2 tablespoons butter, melted
1/2 cup leeks, chopped
2 chicken breasts, trimmed and cut into bite-sized chunks
1 carrot, chopped
1 celery stalk, chopped
1/2 teaspoon granulated garlic
1 teaspoon basil
1/2 teaspoon oregano
1/2 teaspoon dill weed
4 ½ cups vegetable stock
3 ounces heavy cream
3/4 cup Cheddar cheese, shredded
1 heaping tablespoon fresh parsley, roughly chopped
Directions
Press the "Sauté" button to heat up your Instant Pot. Now, melt the butter and cook the leeks until tender and fragrant.
Add the chicken, carrot, celery, garlic, basil, oregano, dill, and stock.
Secure the lid. Choose "Manual" mode and High pressure; cook for 17 minutes. Once cooking is complete, use a natural pressure release; carefully remove the lid.
Add cream and cheese, stir, and press the "Sauté" button one more time. Now, cook the soup for a couple of minutes longer or until thoroughly heated.
Serve in individual bowls, garnished with fresh parsley. Bon appétit!

304. Asian-Style Savory Egg Custard
(Ready in about 15 minutes | Servings 3)
Steamed eggs go wonderfully with homemade sauce and freshly grated Comté cheese. Best of all, you only need 15 minutes to get your breakfast ready!

Per serving: 234 Calories; 16.8g Fat; 3.6g Carbs; 16.4g Protein; 1.8g Sugars
Ingredients
3 eggs, well beaten
1 cup broth, preferably homemade
Kosher salt and white pepper, to taste
1 tablespoon tamari sauce
1/2 tablespoon oyster sauce
1/2 cup Comté cheese, grated
Directions
Place the beaten eggs in a mixing bowl. Slowly and gradually, add broth, whisking constantly as you go. Season with salt and paper. Then, pour this mixture through a strainer. Add tamari sauce and oyster sauce.
Pour the mixture into three ramekins. Now, cover the ramekins with a piece of foil. Place the ramekins on the metal trivet.
Secure the lid. Choose "Manual" mode and Low pressure; cook for 7 minutes. Once cooking is complete, use a natural pressure release; carefully remove the lid.
Top with cheese and serve immediately. Bon appétit!

305. Fluffy Scrambled Eggs

(Ready in about 10 minutes | Servings 2)
Here is a perfect breakfast packed with protein. This recipe is so easy and handy, keep it in your back pocket.
Per serving: 322 Calories; 25.6g Fat; 3.1g Carbs; 18.4g Protein; 1.3g Sugars
Ingredients
4 eggs, beaten
2 tablespoons full cream milk
1 tablespoon ghee, melted
Salt, to taste
1/4 teaspoon ground black pepper, or more to taste
1/2 teaspoon smoked paprika
Directions
Begin by adding 1 cup of water and a metal rack to the Instant Pot.
Spritz a heatproof bowl with a nonstick cooking spray. Mix all ingredients until well combined.
Spoon the mixture into the prepared bowl; lower the bowl onto the rack.
Secure the lid. Choose "Manual" mode and Low pressure; cook for 6 minutes. Once cooking is complete, use a natural pressure release; carefully remove the lid.
Serve with a dollop of sour cream and tomatoes if desired. Bon appétit!

306. Golden Cheddar Muffins with Chard

(Ready in about 10 minutes | Servings 4)
These golden muffins will blow your mind! They make a great accompaniment to your keto dishes, too.
Per serving: 207 Calories; 14.8g Fat; 4.9g Carbs; 13.4g Protein; 2.7g Sugars
Ingredients
6 eggs
4 tablespoons double cream
Sea salt and ground black pepper, to taste
1 cup Swiss chard, chopped
1 red bell pepper, chopped
1/2 cup white onion, chopped
1/2 cup Cheddar cheese, grated
Directions
Begin by adding 1 cup of water and a metal rack to the Instant Pot.
Mix all of the above ingredients. Then, fill silicone muffin cups about 2/3 full.
Then, place muffin cups on the rack.
Secure the lid. Choose "Manual" mode and High pressure; cook for 7 minutes. Once cooking is complete, use a natural pressure release; carefully remove the lid. Enjoy!

307. Broccoli with Asiago Cheese

(Ready in about 12 minutes | Servings 4)
This easy but effective dish is a delightful combination of bright, crispy broccoli and smooth, mellow Asiago cheese. Enjoy!
Per serving: 160 Calories; 11.7g Fat; 5.3g Carbs; 10.1g Protein; 0.9g Sugars
Ingredients
1 tablespoon olive oil
2 tablespoons green onion, chopped
4 cloves garlic, pressed
1 pound broccoli, broken into florets
1 cup water
2 chicken bouillon cubes
Sea salt and ground black pepper, to taste
3/4 cup Asiago cheese, shredded
Directions
Press the "Sauté" button to heat up your Instant Pot. Now, heat the oil and sweat green onions for 2 minutes.
Stir in the garlic and continue to sauté an additional 30 seconds. Add broccoli, water, bouillon cubes, salt, and black pepper.
Secure the lid. Choose "Manual" mode and High pressure; cook for 7 minutes. Once cooking is complete, use a natural pressure release; carefully remove the lid.
Top with shredded cheese and serve immediately. Bon appétit!

308. The Best Homemade Cheese Ever

(Ready in about 1 hour | Servings 14)
Is there anything better than a homemade, fresh cheese? No additives, no preservatives, no artificial colors. It's just perfect!
Per serving: 134 Calories; 6.9g Fat; 9.1g Carbs; 6.8g Protein; 10.9g Sugars
Ingredients
3 quarts milk
1/2 cup distilled vinegar
1/2 cup heavy cream
1 teaspoon kosher salt

Directions

Add milk to your Instant Pot and secure the lid. Choose "Yogurt" mode; now, press the "Adjust" button until you see the word "Boil". Whisk a few times during the cooking time.

Use a food thermometer to read temperature; 180 degrees is fine. Gradually whisk in the vinegar. Turn off the Instant Pot.

Cover with the lid; now, allow it to sit for 40 minutes. Stir in the cream and salt.

Pour the cheese into a colander lined with a tea towel; allow it to sit and drain for 15 minutes.

Afterwards, squeeze it as dry as possible and transfer to your refrigerator. Enjoy!

309. Scamorza Open Tart

(Ready in about 30 minutes | Servings 4)

Comforting and irresistible, this open tart is loaded with protein. Eggs, speck and Scamorza cheese are definitely a match made in heaven!

Per serving: 350 Calories; 25.1g Fat; 4.8g Carbs; 25.9g Protein; 2.9g Sugars

Ingredients
5 eggs, beaten
1/3 cup double cream
Salt and ground black pepper, to taste
1 teaspoon cayenne pepper
5 ounces speck, chopped
1/4 cup scallions, chopped
1/2 cup Scamorza cheese, crumbled
1 bunch of Rucola, to serve

Directions

Begin by adding 1 cup of water and a metal rack to your Instant Pot. Then, spritz a heatproof bowl and set aside.

In a mixing dish, thoroughly combine the eggs, cream, salt, black pepper, and cayenne pepper. Add chopped speck, scallions, and cheese.

Spoon the mixture into the prepared heatproof bowl; cover with a piece of aluminum foil, making a foil sling.

Secure the lid. Choose "Manual" mode and High pressure; cook for 25 minutes. Once cooking is complete, use a quick pressure release; carefully remove the lid.

Garnish with Rucola and serve. Bon appétit!

310. Bacon and Pepper Casserole with Goat Cheese

(Ready in about 30 minutes | Servings 4)

Cascabella chili pepper, also known as the rattle chili, has slightly smoky taste, which makes it perfect for this rich, peppery casserole.

Per serving: 494 Calories; 41.3g Fat; 7.8g Carbs; 25.5g Protein; 3.5g Sugars

Ingredients
6 ounces bacon, chopped
1 green bell pepper, seeded and chopped
1 orange bell pepper, seeded and chopped
1 Cascabella chili pepper, seeded and minced
5 eggs
3/4 cup heavy cream
6 ounces goat cheese, crumbled
Sea salt and ground black pepper, to your liking

Directions

Add 1 cup of water and a metal trivet to the Instant Pot. Lower the baking pan onto the trivet.

Spritz a baking dish that fits inside your Instant Pot with a nonstick cooking spray.

Place the bacon on the bottom of the dish. Add the peppers on the top.

In a mixing bowl, thoroughly combine the eggs, heavy cream, goat cheese, salt, and black pepper. Spoon this mixture over the top.

Secure the lid. Choose "Manual" mode and High pressure; cook for 15 minutes. Once cooking is complete, use a natural pressure release; carefully remove the lid.

Allow your frittata to cool for 10 minutes before slicing and serving. Bon appétit!

311. Savory Muffins with Canadian Bacon

(Ready in about 10 minutes | Servings 4)

This recipe is so versatile so you can try a different low-carb breakfast every morning! Combine the eggs with a ham, speck, chicken sausage, or prosciutto.

Per serving: 301 Calories; 41.3g Fat; 7.8g Carbs; 25.5g Protein; 3.5g Sugars

Ingredients
5 ounces Canadian bacon, sliced
1/2 cup Asiago cheese, shredded
4 eggs, beaten
2 tablespoons butter
2 tablespoons double cream
Salt and black pepper, to taste
1/2 teaspoon red pepper flakes, crushed
1/2 teaspoon granulated garlic
1/4 cup shallots, minced
2 tablespoons coriander, chopped

Directions

Line muffin cups with bacon slices. Then, add a layer of cheese.

In a mixing dish, whisk the eggs, butter, double cream, salt, black pepper, red pepper, and garlic. Pour the egg mixture over cheese. Sprinkle with minced shallots and coriander.

Add 1 cup of water and a metal trivet to the Instant Pot. Now, place the muffin cups on the trivet.

Secure the lid. Choose "Manual" mode and High pressure; cook for 6 minutes. Once cooking is complete, use a natural pressure release; carefully remove the lid.

Allow the muffins to stand for a few minutes before removing from the cups. Bon appétit!

312. Swiss Cheese and Celery Soup

(Ready in about 15 minutes | Servings 4)

Here's a hearty soup that is not just delicious! It's low-carb, high- protein and healthy dish as well!

Per serving: 165 Calories; 10.7g Fat; 4.2g Carbs; 13.2g Protein; 1.8g Sugars

Ingredients
1 cup celery, diced
3 cups vegetable stock
Salt and black pepper, to taste
1/2 teaspoon hot paprika
1 shallot, chopped
1 cup Swiss cheese, shredded

Directions
Add celery, stock, salt, black pepper, paprika, and shallot to your Instant Pot.
Secure the lid. Choose "Manual" mode and High pressure; cook for 8 minutes. Once cooking is complete, use a quick pressure release; carefully remove the lid.
Press the "Sauté" button to heat up your Instant Pot. Fold in cheese; stir until everything is heated through. Enjoy!

313. Peppery and Cheesy Deviled Eggs

(Ready in about 25 minutes | Servings 4)

Serve these devilishly tasty bites as part of Christmas feast. Red peppers go wonderfully with Colby cheese and mayo.

Per serving: 264 Calories; 21.1g Fat; 6g Carbs; 11.7g Protein; 3.8g Sugars

Ingredients
6 eggs
1 teaspoon canola oil
1 onion, chopped
2 bell peppers, drained and chopped
Seasoned salt and freshly ground black pepper, to taste
1/4 cup mayonnaise
1 teaspoon mustard
1 tablespoon fresh lemon juice
4 tablespoons Colby cheese, grated
1 teaspoon smoked Hungarian paprika

Directions
Pour the water into the Instant Pot; add a steamer basket to the bottom.
Arrange the eggs in a steamer basket if you have one.
Secure the lid. Choose "Manual" mode and High pressure; cook for 5 minutes. Once cooking is complete, use a natural pressure release; carefully remove the lid.
Allow the eggs to cool for 15 minutes. Peel the eggs and separate egg whites from yolks.
Press the "Sauté" button to heat up your Instant Pot; heat the oil. Now, sauté the onion along with peppers until softened. Season with salt and pepper.
Add the reserved egg yolks to the pepper mixture. Stir in mayo, mustard, and lemon juice. Now, stuff the egg whites with this mixture.
Top with grated Colby cheese and arrange the stuffed eggs on a serving platter. Afterwards, sprinkle Hungarian paprika over eggs and serve.

314. Spicy Stuffed Avocado Boats

(Ready in about 10 minutes | Servings 2)

Hot and spicy avocado boats with eggs and cheese! Load up basic ingredients into avocado halves for a quick and easy breakfast.

Per serving: 281 Calories; 23.6g Fat; 8g Carbs; 10.1g Protein; 0.8g Sugars

Ingredients
2 avocados, pitted and cut into halves
4 eggs
Salt and pepper, to taste
4 tablespoons Cheddar cheese, freshly grated
1 teaspoon Sriracha sauce

Directions
Start by adding 1 cup of water and a steamer basket to your Instant Pot.
Line the steamer basket with a piece of aluminum foil. Now, spoon out some of the avocado flesh and set it aside for another use (for example, you can make guacamole). Arrange avocado halves on your steamer basket.
Add an egg to each avocado cavity. Sprinkle with salt and pepper. Top with cheese and drizzle Sriracha sauce over them.
Secure the lid. Choose "Manual" mode and High pressure; cook for 3 minutes. Once cooking is complete, use a natural pressure release; carefully remove the lid. Serve warm and enjoy!

315. Three-Cheese and Beer Dip

(Ready in about 10 minutes | Servings 10)

You don't have to make a rock-solid plan to stay on your keto diet during the holidays. Make this cheesy dip and you'll be just fine.

Per serving: 220 Calories; 14.9g Fat; 2.9g Carbs; 18.1g Protein; 1.7g Sugars

Ingredients
16 ounces Cottage cheese, softened
5 ounces goat cheese, softened
1/2 teaspoon garlic powder
1 teaspoon stone-ground mustard
1/2 cup chicken stock, preferably homemade
1/2 cup lager beer
6 ounces pancetta, chopped
1 cup Monterey-Jack cheese, shredded
2 tablespoons fresh chives, roughly chopped

Directions
Add Cottage cheese, goat cheese, garlic powder, mustard, chicken stock, beer, and pancetta to the Instant Pot.
Secure the lid. Choose "Manual" mode and High pressure; cook for 4 minutes. Once cooking is complete, use a quick pressure release; carefully remove the lid.
Press the "Sauté" button to heat up your Instant Pot. Add Monterey-Jack cheese and stir until everything is thoroughly warmed.
Sprinkle with fresh chopped chives and serve. Bon appétit!

316. Breakfast Lettuce Wraps

(Ready in about 10 minutes | Servings 4)

If you're craving something simple but delicious, look no further. Try this recipe today!

Per serving: 202 Calories; 13.7g Fat; 4.7g Carbs; 15.4g Protein; 2.6g Sugars

Ingredients

4 eggs, whisked
1/3 cup double cream
2 ounces Mozzarella cheese, crumbled
1/3 teaspoon red pepper flakes, crushed
Salt, to taste
8 leaves of Looseleaf lettuce

Directions

Begin by adding 1 cup of water and a metal rack to your Instant Pot. Spritz a baking dish with a nonstick cooking spray.

Then, thoroughly combine the eggs, double cream, cheese, red pepper, and salt. Spoon this combination into the baking dish.

Secure the lid. Choose "Manual" mode and High pressure; cook for 3 minutes. Once cooking is complete, use a natural pressure release; carefully remove the lid.

Divide the egg mixture among lettuce leaves, wrap each leaf, and serve immediately. Bon appétit!

317. Indian Egg Muffins

(Ready in about 10 minutes | Servings 5)

These low-carb muffins with an Indian flair are perfect for a grab-and-go breakfast. Feel free to add a pinch of curry powder if desired.

Per serving: 202 Calories; 13.7g Fat; 4.7g Carbs; 15.4g Protein; 2.6g Sugars

Ingredients

5 eggs
Seasoned salt and ground black pepper, to taste
2 green chilies, minced
5 tablespoons feta cheese, crumbled
1/2 tablespoon Chaat masala powder
1 tablespoon fresh cilantro, finely chopped

Directions

Begin by adding 1 cup of water and a steamer basket to your Instant Pot.

Mix all ingredients together; then, spoon the egg/cheese mixture into silicone muffin cups. Next, lower your muffin cups onto the steamer basket.

Secure the lid. Choose "Manual" mode and High pressure; cook for 7 minutes. Once cooking is complete, use a quick pressure release; carefully remove the lid.

Let your muffins sit for a few minutes before removing from the cups; serve warm. Bon appétit!

318. Egg and Bell Pepper "Sandwich"

(Ready in about 10 minutes | Servings 2)

Once you try an Instant Pot, you'll never go back. You will make even scrambled eggs and sandwiches in the Instant Pot.

Per serving: 320 Calories; 25.5g Fat; 7.1g Carbs; 15.7g Protein; 4.3g Sugars

Ingredients

2 teaspoons butter
5 eggs
4 tablespoons whipped cream
Seasoned salt to taste
1/3 teaspoon red pepper flakes, crushed
2 bell peppers
1/2 tomato, sliced
1/2 cucumber, sliced

Directions

Press the "Sauté" button to heat up your Instant Pot. Now, warm the butter.

Thoroughly combine the eggs, cream, salt, and red pepper. Stir with a wooden spoon until the eggs are softly set.

Now, cut the top and bottom off of each pepper; remove seeds and veins. Then, slices each bell pepper in half.

Place the scrambled eggs, tomato, and cucumber between the two pieces. Serve and enjoy!

319. Manchego, Sausage and Vegetable Bake

(Ready in about 25 minutes | Servings 4)

Winter is better with a veggie-sausage bake! You can use a turkey or beef sausage in this recipe; however, do not forget to count carbohydrates.

Per serving: 344 Calories; 27.4g Fat; 3g Carbs; 20.3g Protein; 1.3g Sugars

Ingredients

8 slices pork sausage, chopped
1 ½ cups mushrooms, sliced
1 garlic clove, minced
1 cup kale leaves, torn into pieces
7 eggs
1/3 cup milk
1 cup Manchego cheese, shredded
Sea salt and freshly ground black pepper, to taste

Directions

Press the "Sauté" button to heat up the Instant Pot. Now, cook the sausage until no longer pink.

Then, add mushrooms and garlic; continue to cook until they are fragrant; turn off the Instant Pot; add kale and let it sit for 5 minutes.

Wipe down your Instant Pot with a damp cloth. Add 1 cup of water and a metal rack. Spritz a baking dish that fits into your Instant Pot.

In a mixing bowl, thoroughly combine the eggs, milk, cheese, salt and black pepper; add the sausage/vegetable mixture to the mixing bowl.

Spoon the mixture into the baking dish. Lower the baking dish onto the rack.

Secure the lid. Choose "Manual" mode and High pressure; cook for 15 minutes. Once cooking is

complete, use a quick pressure release; carefully remove the lid. Enjoy!

320. Goat Cheese, Avocado and Egg Muffins

(Ready in about 15 minutes | Servings 6)
This is another super-easy muffin recipe, bursting with incredible flavor. Make these no-flour muffins and amaze your family.
Per serving: 227 Calories; 17.5g Fat; 4.3g Carbs; 13.6g Protein; 1.3g Sugars
Ingredients
6 whole eggs
Seasoned salt and freshly ground black pepper
1/2 teaspoon cayenne pepper
1/2 teaspoon dried dill weed
2 tablespoons fresh parsley, chopped
1 large-sized avocado, peeled, pitted and chopped
1/2 cup tomatoes, chopped
5 ounces goat cheese, crumbled
Directions
Begin by adding 1 cup of water and a steamer basket to your Instant Pot.
Mix all ingredients together; then, spoon the mixture into silicone muffin cups.
Next, lower your muffin cups onto the steamer basket.
Secure the lid. Choose "Manual" mode and High pressure; cook for 7 minutes. Once cooking is complete, use a quick pressure release; carefully remove the lid.
Allow these muffins to rest for 5 to 7 minutes before removing from the cups; serve warm. Bon appétit!

321. Ooey Gooey, Cheesy Pizza

(Ready in about 20 minutes | Servings 6)
Who needs a pizza crust when you can have no-flour pizza loaded with cheese, eggs, pepperoni, and vegetables?
Per serving: 334 Calories; 25.1g Fat; 5.9g Carbs; 20.5g Protein; 2.8g Sugars
Ingredients
1 tablespoon olive oil
1 large-sized tomato, chopped
6 ounces pepperoni
1 yellow onion, chopped
2 bell peppers, chopped
1 cup mozzarella cheese, sliced
1/2 cup provolone cheese, sliced
3 eggs, whisked
1/2 teaspoon dried basil
1/2 teaspoon dried oregano
1/2 teaspoon dried rosemary
1/2 cup Kalamata olives, pitted and halved
Directions
Grease the bottom and sides of your Instant Pot with olive oil. Place 1/2 of chopped tomato on the bottom. Then, layer 3 ounces of pepperoni, 1/2 of yellow onion, 1 bell pepper, 1/2 cup of mozzarella cheese and 1/4 cup of provolone cheese.
Continue layering until you run out of ingredients. Pour in the whisked eggs. Afterwards, sprinkle seasonings and olives over the top.
Secure the lid. Choose "Manual" mode and High pressure; cook for 15 minutes. Once cooking is complete, use a natural pressure release; carefully remove the lid. Serve warm.

322. Zingy Habanero Eggs

(Ready in about 25 minutes | Servings 4)
If you like even fatter and richer eggs, simply add in prosciutto crumbles. Refrigerate up to 3 days.
Per serving: 338 Calories; 25.7g Fat; 5.8g Carbs; 19.8g Protein; 2.8g Sugars
Ingredients
8 eggs
2 teaspoons habanero chili pepper, minced
1 teaspoon cumin seeds
1/4 cup sour cream
1/4 cup mayonnaise
1 teaspoon stone-ground mustard
1/2 teaspoon cayenne pepper
Sea salt and freshly ground black pepper, to taste
Directions
Pour 1 cup of water into the Instant Pot; add a steamer basket to the bottom.
Arrange the eggs in the steamer basket.
Secure the lid. Choose "Manual" mode and High pressure; cook for 5 minutes. Once cooking is complete, use a natural pressure release; carefully remove the lid.
Allow the eggs to cool for 15 minutes. Peel the eggs and separate egg whites from yolks.
Press the "Sauté" button to heat up your Instant Pot; heat the oil. Now, sauté habanero chili pepper and cumin seeds until they are fragrant.
Add the reserved egg yolks to the pepper mixture. Stir in sour cream, mayonnaise, mustard, cayenne pepper, salt, and black pepper. Now, stuff the egg whites with this mixture. Bon appétit!

323. Egg Salad with Poppy Seed Dressing

(Ready in about 25 minutes | Servings 4)
Did you know that poppy seeds can make an amazing salad dressing? Simply mix poppy seeds with extra-virgin olive oil, champagne vinegar, and yellow mustard.
Per serving: 340 Calories; 27.5g Fat; 8.1g Carbs; 16.4g Protein; 2.9g Sugars
Ingredients
5 medium-sized eggs
1/2 pound kale leaves, torn into pieces
1/2 cup radishes, sliced
1 white onion, thinly sliced
2 tablespoons champagne vinegar
1/2 tablespoon poppy seeds
Sea salt and white pepper, to taste
1/2 teaspoon cayenne pepper
1 teaspoon yellow mustard

1/4 cup extra-virgin olive oil
3 ounces goat cheese, crumbled
Directions
Pour 1 cup of water into the Instant Pot; add a steamer basket to the bottom.
Arrange the eggs in the steamer basket.
Secure the lid. Choose "Manual" mode and High pressure; cook for 5 minutes. Once cooking is complete, use a natural pressure release; carefully remove the lid.
Allow the eggs to cool for 15 minutes. Then, place them in your refrigerator and reserve.
Then, place kale in the steamer basket.
Secure the lid. Choose "Manual" mode and High pressure; cook for 1 minute. Once cooking is complete, use a quick pressure release; carefully remove the lid.
Now, place radishes and onion in a salad bowl. Add kale and sliced eggs.
In a mixing dish, thoroughly combine vinegar, poppy seeds, salt, white pepper, cayenne pepper, and olive oil.
Pour the dressing over your salad. Top with goat cheese and serve well-chilled. Bon appétit!

324. Fat Bombs with Peppers and Manchego

(Ready in about 25 minutes | Servings 8)
Try these fat balls loaded with eggs, cheese, peppers. There's no better way to surprise your little ones today!
Per serving: 172 Calories; 12.3g Fat; 3.9g Carbs; 11.3g Protein; 1.3g Sugars
Ingredients
6 whole eggs
1 green bell pepper, deveined and chopped
1 red bell pepper, deveined and chopped
1 yellow bell pepper, deveined and chopped
1/2 cup scallion, minced
1 garlic clove, minced
1 cup Manchego cheese, shredded
Salt and black pepper, to taste
Directions
Pour 1 cup of water into the Instant Pot; add a steamer basket to the bottom.
Arrange the eggs in the steamer basket.
Secure the lid. Choose "Manual" mode and High pressure; cook for 5 minutes. Once cooking is complete, use a natural pressure release; carefully remove the lid.
Allow the eggs to cool for 15 minutes; chop the eggs and add them to a mixing bowl.
Add peppers, scallions and garlic to the Instant Pot.
Secure the lid. Choose "Manual" mode and Low pressure; cook for 4 minutes. Once cooking is complete, use a quick pressure release; carefully remove the lid.
Transfer the pepper mixture to the mixing bowl with eggs; add cheese to the warm mixture; season with salt and pepper.

Now, roll the mixture into 2-inch balls and serve. Bon appétit!

325. Egg Curry in a Hurry

(Ready in about 20 minutes | Servings 6)
This recipe is good for brunch or lunch and it takes less than 20 minutes to make in an Instant Pot. Serve with fresh or pickled salad.
Per serving: 253 Calories; 19.7g Fat; 4.9g Carbs; 13.9g Protein; 2.5g Sugars
Ingredients
1 ½ tablespoons butter, melted
1 yellow onion, chopped
1 ½ tablespoons curry paste
2 ripe tomatoes, peeled and chopped
1 cup water
7 eggs, whisked
1/2 cup cheddar cheese, grated
Directions
Press the "Sauté" button to heat up the Instant Pot. Now, warm the butter; once hot, sauté the onion until softened and fragrant.
Add the remaining ingredients and stir to combine.
Secure the lid. Choose "Manual" mode and High pressure; cook for 10 minutes. Once cooking is complete, use a quick pressure release; carefully remove the lid. Enjoy!

326. Italian Sausage and Fontina Bake

(Ready in about 30 minutes | Servings 6)
A winning combination – eggs, sausage and cheese! Don't be shy about seasonings and enjoy experimenting with them.
Per serving: 276 Calories; 21.1g Fat; 6.8g Carbs; 14.6g Protein; 3.4g Sugars
Ingredients
2 tablespoons butter, melted
5 eggs
1 shallot, sliced
1 bell pepper, chopped
1 tablespoon Italian seasoning mix
Sea salt and ground black pepper, to taste
2 garlic cloves, minced
1/3 cup milk
4 ounces Italian pork sausage, crumbled
5 ounces Fontina cheese, crumbled
2 tablespoons fresh coriander, minced
Directions
Add 1 cup of water and a metal rack to the casserole dish. Butter a baking dish.
Mix the eggs, shallot, bell pepper, Italian seasoning mix, salt, black pepper, garlic, milk, and sausage.
Pour the egg/milk mixture into the baking dish.
Secure the lid. Choose "Manual" mode and High pressure; cook for 18 minutes. Once cooking is complete, use a natural pressure release; carefully remove the lid.

Top with Fontina cheese and cover with the lid; let it sit in the residual heat for 5 to 8 minutes. Serve garnished with fresh coriander. Bon appétit!

327. Egg Drop Soup with Gorgonzola

(Ready in about 20 minutes | Servings 4)

This delicious soup, also known as Stracciatella in Italian traditional cuisine, will be a big hit with your family. All flavors blend wonderfully and you can enjoy it throughout the year.

Per serving: 163 Calories; 11.7g Fat; 3.1g Carbs; 10.8g Protein; 1.1g Sugars

Ingredients
1 tablespoon olive oil
1 carrot, chopped
1 clove garlic, minced
3 cups beef bone broth
1/2 cup water
2 eggs, slightly whisked
Sea salt and ground black pepper, to your liking
1 teaspoon celery seeds
1/2 teaspoon paprika
1/2 cup Gorgonzola cheese, crumbled
1 heaping tablespoon fresh chives, minced

Directions
Press the "Sauté" button to heat up the Instant Pot. Now, heat the olive oil and cook the carrot and garlic until fragrant.
Add broth and water.
Secure the lid. Choose "Manual" mode and High pressure; cook for 10 minutes. Once cooking is complete, use a quick pressure release; carefully remove the lid.
Then, mix the eggs, salt, black pepper, celery seeds, paprika, and cheese until well blended.
Stir this mixture into the Instant Pot and press the "Sauté" button. Whisk until heated through.
Serve in individual bowls, garnished with fresh chives. Enjoy!

328. Family Taco Casserole

(Ready in about 25 minutes | Servings 6)

This Mexican-inspired casserole promotes the best of a keto diet – ground beef, eggs and hard, yellow cheese. With a negligible amount of carbs, it is obviously perfect for your diet!

Per serving: 259 Calories; 17.9g Fat; 4.5g Carbs; 19.5g Protein; 2.1g Sugars

Ingredients
1 ½ tablespoons olive oil
1/2 cup leeks, chopped
6 ounces ground beef
6 whole eggs
2 cups Swiss chard, torn into pieces
1 teaspoon garlic paste
1 cup Cotija cheese, grated
1/3 cup milk
1 teaspoon Taco seasoning mix
Seasoned salt and ground black pepper, to taste
1/2 teaspoon cayenne pepper
1 jalapeño pepper, minced

Directions
Press the "Sauté" button to heat up the Instant Pot. Now, heat the olive oil.
Once hot, cook the leeks until softened. Now, add ground beef and cook until it is no longer pink.
Stir in the remaining ingredients.
Wipe down your Instant Pot with a damp cloth. Add 1 cup of water and a metal rack. Spritz a baking dish that fits into your Instant Pot.
Pour the egg/beef mixture into the prepared dish; lower the dish onto the rack.
Secure the lid. Choose "Meat/Stew" mode and High pressure; cook for 20 minutes. Once cooking is complete, use a quick pressure release; carefully remove the lid.
Serve with a homemade keto salsa if desired! Bon appétit!

329. Kid-Friendly Mini Frittatas

(Ready in about 15 minutes | Servings 4)

Everyone will love these fancy mini frittatas, especially your kids. Chorizo sausage makes a lovely addition to these flavorful cups.

Per serving: 314 Calories; 25.6g Fat; 2.9g Carbs; 16.7g Protein; 1.7g Sugars

Ingredients
4 eggs
1/4 cup full-fat milk
Sea salt, to taste
1/4 teaspoon ground black pepper
1/4 teaspoon cayenne pepper, or more to taste
1/2 teaspoon granulated garlic
1/3 teaspoon ground bay leaf
1/2 teaspoon dried dill weed
1 cup Chorizo sausage, chopped
1/2 cup green onions, chopped

Directions
Prepare your Instant Pot by adding 1 cup of water and a metal trivet to the bottom of the inner pot.
Thoroughly combine all ingredients until everything is well mixed. Spoon the mixture into silicone molds. Lower the silicone molds onto the trivet.
Secure the lid. Choose "Manual" mode and High pressure; cook for 7 minutes. Once cooking is complete, use a quick pressure release; carefully remove the lid. Bon appétit!

330. Breakfast Egg Salad Bowl

(Ready in about 25 minutes | Servings 4)

This breakfast will keep you full until lunch. Hard-boiled eggs are so easy to make in an Instant Pot.

Per serving: 276 Calories; 22.6g Fat; 6.7g Carbs; 12.5g Protein; 1.4g Sugars

Ingredients
8 eggs
1 avocado, pitted, peeled and chopped
1/4 mayonnaise
1 tablespoon fresh lime juice

1 tablespoon champagne vinegar
1 teaspoon ground mustard
Sea salt and ground black pepper, to taste
1/2 teaspoon celery seeds
8 black olives, pitted and sliced
1/2 cup basil leaves, loosely packed
Directions
Place 1 cup of water and a steamer basket in your Instant Pot. Now, arrange the eggs on the steamer basket.
Secure the lid. Choose "Manual" mode and Low pressure; cook for 5 minutes. Once cooking is complete, use a quick pressure release; carefully remove the lid.
Allow the eggs to cool for 15 minutes. Peel the eggs and slice them lengthwise.
Place avocado, mayonnaise, lemon juice, vinegar, mustard, salt, black pepper, celery seeds in a serving bowl; stir to combine well.
Top with the reserved eggs, olives and basil. Enjoy!

331. Asparagus and Colby Cheese Frittatas

(Ready in about 25 minutes | Servings 6)
Asparagus is an excellent source of fiber, Vitamins C, A, E, K, and B6, as well as minerals such as iron, calcium, and copper. It combines with eggs and dairy very well!
Per serving: 272 Calories; 21.1g Fat; 4.7g Carbs; 15.5g Protein; 2.3g Sugars
Ingredients
1 tablespoon butter, softened
1/2 cup leeks, chopped
2 garlic cloves, minced
10 asparagus spears, chopped
6 eggs, beaten
4 tablespoons milk
3 tablespoons cream cheese
Kosher salt and white pepper, to taste
1/2 teaspoon thyme, minced
1/2 teaspoon rosemary, minced
1 cup Colby cheese, shredded
Directions
Press the "Sauté" button to heat up the Instant Pot. Now, melt the butter and sauté the leeks until softened.
Add garlic and cook an additional 30 seconds. Turn off your Instant Pot. Add the remaining ingredients and mix to combine.
Spoon the mixture into lightly greased ramekins. Wipe down your Instant Pot with a damp cloth. Place 1 cup of water and a rack in your Instant Pot.
Lower the ramekins onto the rack. Cover them with a piece of foil.
Secure the lid. Choose "Soup/Broth" mode and Low pressure; cook for 20 minutes. Once cooking is complete, use a quick pressure release; carefully remove the lid. Bon appétit!

332. Special Breakfast Eggs

(Ready in about 10 minutes | Servings 3)
A perfect breakfast idea for your busy mornings. Simple, healthy, and nourishing.
Per serving: 259 Calories; 19.2g Fat; 2g Carbs; 17.9g Protein; 1.3g Sugars
Ingredients
6 large eggs
Salt and paprika, to taste
Directions
Add 1 cup of water and a metal trivet to the Instant Pot.
Spritz six silicone cups with a nonstick cooking spray. Crack an egg into each cup.
Then, lower the silicone cups onto the metal trivet.
Secure the lid. Choose "Steam" mode and High pressure; cook for 4 minutes. Once cooking is complete, use a quick pressure release; carefully remove the lid.
Season your eggs with salt and paprika. Bon appétit!

333. Two-Cheese and Mustard Green Dip

(Ready in about 10 minutes | Servings 8)
An Instant Pot makes feeding a crowd a breeze! Serve with lots of vegetable stick (cucumber, carrot, celery, bell pepper) or homemade pickles.
Per serving: 49 Calories; 3.1g Fat; 1.4g Carbs; 3.9g Protein; 0.8g Sugars
Ingredients
1 cup mustard greens, chopped
4 ounces Cottage cheese, at room temperature
1/2 cup goat cheese, at room temperature
Salt and ground black pepper, to taste
1 teaspoon Dijon mustard
Directions
Simply throw all of the above ingredients into your Instant Pot.
Secure the lid. Choose "Manual" mode and Low pressure; cook for 3 minutes. Once cooking is complete, use a quick pressure release; carefully remove the lid.
Serve warm and enjoy!

334. Paneer and Cauliflower Dipping Sauce

(Ready in about 10 minutes | Servings 10)
This Indian-inspired dipping sauce is vegetarian, low-carb, and high-protein dish. Serve with bell pepper sticks if desired.
Per serving: 97 Calories; 8.7g Fat; 1.2g Carbs; 3.9g Protein; 0.5g Sugars
Ingredients
1 cup water
1/2 pound cauliflower, broken into florets
1/2 cup chicken stock, warm
1/2 stick butter
1 cup Paneer cheese, crumbled
2 tablespoons fresh coriander, chopped
1 teaspoon Kala namak
1/4 teaspoon black pepper
Directions

Start by adding water and a steamer basket to your Instant Pot. Now, place cauliflower florets in the steamer basket.
Secure the lid. Choose "Manual" mode and Low pressure; cook for 3 minutes. Once cooking is complete, use a quick pressure release; carefully remove the lid.
Then, purée the cauliflower florets in your food processor.
Add the remaining ingredients; purée until everything is well combined. Bon appétit!

335. Portobello Mushrooms Baked Eggs and Cheese

(Ready in about 10 minutes | Servings 4)
This is incredibly tasty and easy to make for breakfast or brunch! Garnish with some extra herbs such as parsley or watercress.
Per serving: 256 Calories; 18.6g Fat; 5.3g Carbs; 17g Protein; 2.9g Sugars
Ingredients
4 medium-sized Portobello mushrooms, stems removed
4 eggs
1 red bell pepper, deveined and chopped
1 green bell pepper, deveined and chopped
Sea salt and ground black pepper, to your liking
1/2 teaspoon cayenne pepper
1/2 teaspoon dried dill weed
1 cup Pepper-Jack cheese, grated
Directions
Start by adding 1 cup of water and a metal trivet to your Instant Pot. Spritz Portobello mushrooms with a nonstick cooking spray.
Mix the eggs, pepper, salt, black pepper, cayenne pepper, and dill; mix until everything is well combined. Spoon this mixture into the prepared mushrooms caps.
Place the stuffed mushrooms onto the metal trivet. Secure the lid. Choose "Manual" mode and High pressure; cook for 6 minutes. Once cooking is complete, use a quick pressure release; carefully remove the lid.
Top with shredded cheese. Bon appétit!

336. Eggs, Cheese, and Mortadella Roll-Ups

(Ready in about 10 minutes | Servings 4)
You don't need to be an expert chef to make a great low-carb breakfast. Make these roll-ups and you will amaze everyone with your creativity.
Per serving: 298 Calories; 24.2g Fat; 3.6g Carbs; 15.7g Protein; 1.3g Sugars
Ingredients
2 teaspoons butter, at room temperature
4 eggs
Salt and red pepper, to taste
1/2 cup Cheddar cheese, shredded
8 slices mortadella
1/4 cup mayonnaise
1 tablespoon Dijon mustard
8 leaves of Romaine lettuce
Directions
Press the "Sauté" button to heat up your Instant Pot. Now, warm the butter.
Add the eggs and stir them with a wooden spoon until the eggs are softly set. Add the salt, red pepper, and cheese.
Continue to cook an additional 40 seconds or until the cheese is melted. Turn off the Instant Pot.
Now, divide the egg/cheese mixture among mortadella slices; add mayo and mustard. Add one leaf of lettuce to each roll.
Create roll-ups and use toothpicks to secure them. Serve immediately and enjoy!

337. Eggs with Peppers in Tomato Sauce

(Ready in about 10 minutes | Servings 4)
Not sure what to make for dinner? Everyone will love this classic and belly-warming dish. You can add a teaspoon or two of red chili pepper if desired.
Per serving: 171 Calories; 12.2g Fat; 7.6g Carbs; 8.4g Protein; 4.1g Sugars
Ingredients
2 tablespoons olive oil
1 shallot, diced
1 teaspoon garlic paste
2 bell peppers, diced
Salt and freshly ground black pepper, to taste
1 teaspoon cayenne pepper
1 teaspoon dried basil
2 ripe tomatoes, puréed
5 eggs
2 heaping tablespoons chives, chopped
Directions
Press the "Sauté" button to heat up your Instant Pot. Now, heat the olive oil and sauté the shallot until tender and aromatic.
Add the garlic paste, peppers, salt, black pepper, cayenne pepper, basil, and tomatoes.
Then, crack the eggs into the vegetable mixture. Secure the lid. Choose "Manual" mode and Low pressure; cook for 5 minutes. Once cooking is complete, use a quick pressure release; carefully remove the lid.
Serve garnished with chopped chives. Enjoy!

338. Tocino and Egg Cups

(Ready in about 10 minutes | Servings 4)
Spanish bacon, tocino, is made from the pork belly. In Puerto Rico and Cuba, this bacon is made from pork fatback.
Per serving: 331 Calories; 25.1g Fat; 8.6g Carbs; 17.9g Protein; 6.4g Sugars
Ingredients
1 ½ tablespoons butter, at room temperature
5 eggs
2 slices tocino, chopped
1/2 purple onion, chopped

1 green bell pepper, chopped
1 (4-ounce) jar diced pimentos, drained
1 plum tomato, chopped
1 cup goat cheese, shredded
3 tablespoons full-fat milk
Sea salt and ground black pepper, to taste
2-3 green onions, chopped
Directions
Thoroughly combine all of the above ingredients, except for green onions, in a mixing bowl.
Divide the mixture between sterilized jars; cover with the lids but not too tightly.
Prepare your Instant Pot by adding 1 ½ cups of water and a metal trivet to the bottom. Lower the jars onto the trivet.
Secure the lid. Choose "Manual" mode and High pressure; cook for 6 minutes. Once cooking is complete, use a quick pressure release; carefully remove the lid.
Serve immediately, topped with green onions. Bon appétit!

339. Mélange with Spanish Chorizo
(Ready in about 25 minutes | Servings 6)
Need an innovative recipe for Sunday supper? Try this Spanish-inspired dish! You can also use paprika-spiced Chistorra instead of chorizo sausage. Enjoy!
Per serving: 385 Calories; 30.2g Fat; 6.5g Carbs; 21.2g Protein; 3.1g Sugars
Ingredients
8 eggs
2 tablespoons olive oil
1/2 cup leeks, chopped
1 carrot, chopped
1 teaspoon fresh garlic, minced
1/2 cup Spanish chorizo, finely diced
2 ripe Roma tomatoes, puréed
2 sprigs fresh thyme
2 sprigs fresh rosemary
1 bay leaf
Sea salt and ground black pepper, to taste
1/2 teaspoon smoked paprika
1 cup chicken stock
1 cup white cheddar cheese, shredded
Directions
Place 1 cup of water and a steamer basket in your Instant Pot. Now, arrange the eggs on the steamer basket.
Secure the lid. Choose "Manual" mode and Low pressure; cook for 5 minutes. Once cooking is complete, use a quick pressure release; carefully remove the lid.
Allow the eggs to cool and then, chop them roughly. Press the "Sauté" button to heat up your Instant Pot. Now, heat the olive oil until sizzling. Once hot, cook the leeks until they are softened.
Add the carrot, garlic and chorizo; cook an additional minute or until just softened. Add tomatoes, thyme, rosemary, bay leaf, salt, pepper, paprika, and stock.
Add the reserved hard-boiled eggs.

Secure the lid. Choose "Manual" mode and High pressure; cook for 10 minutes. Once cooking is complete, use a quick pressure release; carefully remove the lid.
Top with cheddar cheese, cover with the lid and let it sit until the cheese is completely melted. Bon appétit!

340. Italian Great-Grandmother Eggs
(Ready in about 20 minutes | Servings 6)
Scrambled eggs made in the Instant Pot is the perfect family dinner – easy and delicious! In addition, you only have one pot to clean up.
Per serving: 309 Calories; 25.5g Fat; 3.1g Carbs; 16.5g Protein; 1.5g Sugars
Ingredients
1 tablespoon grapeseed oil
1/2 pound Genoa salami, diced
6 large-sized eggs, whisked
1/2 cup chicken broth
Table salt and black pepper, to taste
1/2 teaspoon cayenne pepper
1/2 teaspoon chili pepper
1 cup grape tomatoes, halved
1 cup Pecorino cheese, preferably freshly grated
Directions
Press the "Sauté" button to heat up your Instant Pot. Now, heat the oil until sizzling.
Then, cook genoa salami until crisp and lightly brown or 2 minutes per side.
Add the eggs, chicken broth, salt, black pepper, cayenne pepper, and chili pepper. Top with grape tomatoes.
Secure the lid. Choose "Manual" mode and High pressure; cook for 6 minutes. Once cooking is complete, use a quick pressure release; carefully remove the lid.
Top with cheese and cover with the lid. Let it sit in the residual heat for 5 to 10 minutes. Bon appétit!

341. Ground Meat and Cheese Dip
(Ready in about 10 minutes | Servings 10)
Party dinners just wouldn't be the party dinners without a rich and delicious cheese and meat sauce. You can substitute ground beef with ground turkey and Mascarpone with Neufchâtel cheese.
Per serving: 254 Calories; 17.9g Fat; 3.9g Carbs; 18.8g Protein; 2.6g Sugars
Ingredients
2 teaspoons olive oil
1 yellow onion, chopped
1/2 pound ground pork
1/2 pound ground beef
1 teaspoon chili powder
Sea salt, to taste
1/3 teaspoon freshly ground black pepper
1 tomato, chopped
1/3 cup salsa verde
1/2 cup chicken stock
7 ounces Mascarpone cheese, room temperature

5 ounces Colby cheese, grated
Directions
Press the "Sauté" button to heat up your Instant Pot. Now, heat the oil and cook the onion until tender. Next, cook the pork and beef until no longer pink, about 4 minutes.
After that, add chili powder, salt, black pepper, tomato, and salsa verde.
Secure the lid. Choose "Manual" mode and High pressure; cook for 5 minutes. Once cooking is complete, use a natural pressure release; carefully remove the lid.
Add cheese and cover with the lid. Let it sit in the residual heat until everything is well combined. Enjoy!

342. Italian-Style Greens with Eggs and Cheese
(Ready in about 10 minutes | Servings 4)
Light, vegetarian and full of nutrition, this dish will fill you up until lunch. You can make this old-fashioned dish with green cabbage, chard or spinach.
Per serving: 291 Calories; 19.8g Fat; 8.8g Carbs; 20.9g Protein; 1.8g Sugars
Ingredients
2 teaspoons butter, melted
6 eggs
2 tablespoons cream cheese
Sea salt and ground black pepper, to taste
1/2 teaspoon paprika
1/2 teaspoon ground bay leaf
1 pound collard greens, torn into pieces
1 cup broth, preferably homemade
1 cup Provolone cheese, crumbled
Directions
Press the "Sauté" button to heat up your Instant Pot. Now, warm the butter.
Whisk the eggs with cream cheese in a mixing dish. Once hot, add the egg/cheese mixture to the Instant Pot.
Now, add the salt, black pepper, ground bay leaf and collard greens.
Secure the lid. Choose "Manual" mode and Low pressure; cook for 3 minutes. Once cooking is complete, use a quick pressure release; carefully remove the lid.
Add Provolone cheese on top and press the "Sauté" button again. Continue to cook until everything is heated through; serve warm. Bon appétit!

343. B.E.L.T – Bacon, Egg, Lettuce Tomato
(Ready in about 10 minutes | Servings 4)
Looking for a right keto sandwich? Look no further, B.E.L.T is a budget-friendly sandwich that is easy to make and fun to eat!
Per serving: 258 Calories; 20.1g Fat; 5.5g Carbs; 14.1g Protein; 3.1g Sugars
Ingredients
4 eggs
Salt and freshly ground black pepper, to taste
4 slices bacon
8 leaves lettuce
1 large-sized tomato, sliced
Directions
Add 1 cup of water and a metal trivet to the Instant Pot.
Spritz four silicone cups with a nonstick cooking spray. Crack an egg into each cup.
Then, lower the silicone cups onto the metal trivet. Secure the lid. Choose "Steam" mode and High pressure; cook for 4 minutes. Once cooking is complete, use a quick pressure release; carefully remove the lid.
Season your eggs with salt and pepper.
Press the "Sauté" button to heat up your Instant Pot. Once hot, cook the bacon until crisp and browned.
Divide lettuce leaves between four serving plates. Add bacon slice on each serving; place a few slices of tomato on each serving.
Top with poached eggs and serve warm. Bon appétit!

344. Mini Meatloaves with Cheese
(Ready in about 20 minutes | Servings 6)
An Instant Pot makes homemade savory muffins easily and effortlessly. Serve with lots of crispy, fresh lettuce.
Per serving: 276 Calories; 17.5g Fat; 3.3g Carbs; 25.6g Protein; 1.7g Sugars
Ingredients
1/2 pound ground pork
1/2 pound ground turkey
1/2 yellow onion, chopped
1/2 cup pork rinds, crushed
1 tablespoon coconut aminos
2 tablespoons fresh cilantro, chopped
3 eggs, whisked
Sea salt and ground black pepper, to taste
1 teaspoon cayenne pepper
1/2 teaspoon dried dill weed
1/2 teaspoon oregano
1 tablespoon mint, chopped
1/2 cup pasta sauce, no sugar
1/2 cup cheddar cheese, grated
Directions
Mix all ingredients, except for pasta sauce and cheddar cheese, until everything is well incorporated.
Now, add 1 cup of water and a metal trivet to the Instant Pot.
Divide the mixture among muffin cups; top with pasta sauce. Lower the muffin cups onto the trivet. Secure the lid. Choose "Manual" mode and High pressure; cook for 6 minutes. Once cooking is complete, use a natural pressure release; carefully remove the lid.
Top with the shredded cheese; cover with the lid and allow your muffins to sit in the residual heat for 4 to 7 minutes.
Allow the muffins to stand for a few minutes before removing from the cups. Bon appétit!

345. Green Beans with Cheese and Eggs

(Ready in about 10 minutes | Servings 4)

Thanks to the Instant Pot, green beans have never tasted better! Fresh or frozen green beans, garlic, eggs and feta is all you need to make this classic dish.

Per serving: 249 Calories; 19.4g Fat; 7.2g Carbs; 12.2g Protein; 2.6g Sugars

Ingredients
2 tablespoons olive oil
2 garlic cloves, pressed
1 pound green beans, sliced
4 eggs, slightly whisked
Salt and freshly ground black pepper, to taste
1 cup stock, preferably homemade
1 cup feta cheese, crumbled

Directions
Press the "Sauté" button to heat up your Instant Pot. Now, heat the olive oil until sizzling.
Once hot, stir in garlic and cook for 40 seconds or until fragrant. Add green beans, eggs, salt, pepper, and stock.
Secure the lid. Choose "Manual" mode and Low pressure; cook for 3 minutes. Once cooking is complete, use a quick pressure release; carefully remove the lid.
Afterwards, add feta cheese and serve immediately.

346. Eggs with Green Cabbage

(Ready in about 10 minutes | Servings 4)

Try this extraordinary vegetable recipe for dinner tonight! It is like eating an elegant and rich-flavored cabbage salad with eggs.

Per serving: 164 Calories; 11.2g Fat; 9.1g Carbs; 7.3g Protein; 4.9g Sugars

Ingredients
2 tablespoons olive oil
1 pound green cabbage, shredded
1 teaspoon garlic, smashed
4 eggs, whisked
1/2 teaspoon celery seeds
1/2 teaspoon mustard seeds
1/2 teaspoon dried parsley flakes
1/2 teaspoon red pepper flakes, crushed
Sea salt and ground black pepper, to your liking
1 tablespoon Worcestershire sauce

Directions
Press the "Sauté" button to heat up your Instant Pot. Now, heat the olive oil until sizzling.
Then, sauté green cabbage for 1 to 2 minutes. Add garlic and cook an additional 30 seconds. Add the remaining ingredients.
Secure the lid. Choose "Manual" mode and Low pressure; cook for 3 minutes. Once cooking is complete, use a quick pressure release; carefully remove the lid.
Divide the mixture between serving plates and serve warm. Bon appétit!

347. Indian Egg Bhurji

(Ready in about 15 minutes | Servings 4)

Egg bhurji is Indian scrambled eggs that are cooked with caramelized onions, scallions, hot chili peppers, tomatoes and a variety of spices.

Per serving: 259 Calories; 20.6g Fat; 4.6g Carbs; 13.4g Protein; 2.6g Sugars

Ingredients
1 ½ tablespoons sesame oil
1/2 yellow onion, chopped
2 garlic cloves, minced
1 (1/2-inch) piece fresh ginger, grated
2 cups Cremini mushrooms, sliced
4 eggs, beaten
4 tablespoons full-fat milk
Table salt and ground black pepper, to taste
1/4 teaspoon turmeric
1 teaspoon garam masala
1/2 cup Pepper-Jack cheese, preferably freshly grated

Directions
Press the "Sauté" button to heat up your Instant Pot. Heat the oil and cook the onion until they are caramelized; add a splash of water if needed.
After that, stir in the garlic, ginger, and mushrooms; continue to cook an additional 1 minute or until fragrant.
Add beaten eggs, milk, salt, pepper, turmeric, and garam masala.
Secure the lid. Choose "Manual" mode and High pressure; cook for 7 minutes. Once cooking is complete, use a quick pressure release; carefully remove the lid.
Add Pepper-Jack cheese and put the lid on the Instant Pot. Let it sit in the residual heat for 3 to 5 minutes. Serve warm and enjoy!

348. Garden Omelet with Colby Cheese

(Ready in about 15 minutes | Servings 4)

The Instant Pot will take your omelet to a whole new level. Colby cheese makes a great addition to your classic comfort food.

Per serving: 284 Calories; 24.2g Fat; 6g Carbs; 10.5g Protein; 2.4g Sugars

Ingredients
2 tablespoons olive oil
1 yellow onion, chopped
1 zucchini, sliced
2 garlic cloves, minced
4 eggs, beaten
4 tablespoons heavy whipped cream
Sea salt and ground black pepper, to taste
1 teaspoon cayenne pepper
1 tablespoon Cajun seasoning
1/2 cup Colby cheese, shredded

Directions
Press the "Sauté" button to heat up your Instant Pot. Heat the oil and sauté the onion until tender and translucent.

Now, add zucchini and garlic and cook for 1 minute more.

Thoroughly combine the eggs, heavy whipped cream, salt, black pepper, cayenne pepper, and Cajun seasoning. Add the egg mixture to the Instant Pot. Secure the lid. Choose "Manual" mode and High pressure; cook for 6 minutes. Once cooking is complete, use a quick pressure release; carefully remove the lid.

Add shredded cheese and put the lid on the Instant Pot. Let it sit in the residual heat for 4 minutes. Serve warm and enjoy!

349. Winter Bacon and Leek Quiche

(Ready in about 35 minutes | Servings 6)
Wow your family with this low-carb quiche, loaded with eggs, bacon and cheese. Making luxuries family quiche is so much easier than it looks.
Per serving: 231 Calories; 15.2g Fat; 6.9g Carbs; 16.5g Protein; 3.1g Sugars

Ingredients
4 slices Canadian bacon, chopped
1 cup leeks, chopped
1 garlic clove, minced
8 eggs
1/2 cup half-and-half
1/2 cup cream cheese, room temperature
Seasoned salt and ground black pepper, to taste
1 tablespoon dried sage, crushed
1/2 teaspoon marjoram
1/2 cup Swiss cheese, freshly grated

Directions
Press the "Sauté" button to heat up your Instant Pot. Once hot, cook the bacon until crisp and browned.
Add the leeks and garlic and cook 1 minute more.
Add the eggs, half-and-half, cream cheese, salt, black pepper, sage and marjoram.
Grease a baking pan with a nonstick cooking spray. Spoon the bacon/egg mixture into the prepared baking pan.
Now, add 1 cup of water and a metal trivet to the Instant Pot; lower the baking pan onto the trivet.
Secure the lid. Choose "Meat/Stew" mode and High pressure; cook for 25 minutes. Once cooking is complete, use a quick pressure release; carefully remove the lid.
Add Swiss cheese and cover with the lid; let it sit in the residual heat for 5 minutes. Serve with Dijon mustard.

350. Weeknight Meat and Egg Muffins

(Ready in about 10 minutes | Servings 4)
Whether you make this recipe for holidays or eat it all year long, savory muffins are a classic dish that everyone loves. Remember to season your muffins with lots of love before serving!
Per serving: 438 Calories; 27.2g Fat; 4.5g Carbs; 42.2g Protein; 1.8g Sugars

Ingredients
2 teaspoons grapeseed oil
1/2 yellow onion, chopped
1 cup brown mushrooms, chopped
2 cloves garlic, smashed
1 teaspoon ground mustard
1 tablespoon coconut aminos
Kosher salt and freshly ground black pepper, to taste
1 pound ground beef
2 eggs
1 cup Romano cheese, grated
1/2 teaspoon dried rosemary
1 teaspoon dried sage
1/2 teaspoon dried thyme
1/2 teaspoon garlic powder
1/2 cup tomato, puréed

Directions
Thoroughly combine all ingredients until everything is well combined.
Then, add 1 cup of water and a metal trivet to the Instant Pot.
Divide the mixture among muffin cups; lower the muffin cups onto the trivet.
Secure the lid. Choose "Manual" mode and High pressure; cook for 6 minutes. Once cooking is complete, use a natural pressure release; carefully remove the lid. Serve warm.

VEGAN

351. Aromatic Garlicky Zucchini
(Ready in about 10 minutes | Servings 4)
Place your garlicky zucchini on a decorative platter with lime wedges. Serve with a favorite salad on the side. Enjoy!
Per serving: 88 Calories; 5.9g Fat; 5.1g Carbs; 5.3g Protein; 0.1g Sugars
Ingredients
1 ½ tablespoons olive oil
2 garlic cloves, minced
1 ½ pounds zucchinis, sliced
1/2 cup vegetable broth
Salt and pepper, to taste
1/2 teaspoon dried rosemary
1 teaspoon dried basil
1/2 teaspoon smoked paprika
Directions
Press the "Sauté" button to heat up your Instant Pot. Now, heat the olive oil and cook garlic until aromatic. Add the remaining ingredients.
Secure the lid. Choose "Manual" mode and Low pressure; cook for 3 minutes. Once cooking is complete, use a quick pressure release; carefully remove the lid. Bon appétit!

352. Thai-Style Tempeh Curry
(Ready in about 10 minutes | Servings 4)
This delicious, one-pot recipe is so easy to make. Once you're done preparing and sautéing the leeks, everything goes fast.
Per serving: 192 Calories; 13.5g Fat; 9.1g Carbs; 11.3g Protein; 1.4g Sugars
Ingredients
1 tablespoon sesame oil
1 medium-sized leek, sliced
1 teaspoon whole coriander seeds
8 ounces tempeh, steamed
1/2 cup water, hot
1/2 cup vegetable broth, hot
1/2 teaspoon curry powder
1/2 teaspoon cumin
2 ounces coconut milk, unsweetened
Celery salt and ground black pepper, to taste
Directions
Press the "Sauté" button to heat up your Instant Pot. Now, heat the sesame oil.
Then, cook the leek and coriander seeds until aromatic, about 40 seconds. Add the remaining ingredients.
Secure the lid. Choose "Manual" mode and Low pressure; cook for 5 minutes. Once cooking is complete, use a quick pressure release; carefully remove the lid.
Press the "Sauté" button and let it simmer until the sauce has thickened. Taste, adjust the seasonings and serve hot!

353. Tangy Green Cabbage Stew
(Ready in about 10 minutes | Servings 4)
This vegetable dish is easy and fun to prepare in the Instant Pot. It can be served as a side dish or light meal.
Per serving: 114 Calories; 8.4g Fat; 8.1g Carbs; 2.8g Protein; 4.3g Sugars
Ingredients
2 tablespoons olive oil
1/2 cup yellow onion, sliced
1 teaspoon garlic, smashed
Sea salt and freshly ground black pepper, to taste
1 teaspoon turmeric powder
1 serrano pepper, chopped
1 pound green cabbage, shredded
1 celery stalk, chopped
2 tablespoons rice wine
1 cup roasted vegetable broth
Directions
Place all of the above ingredients in the Instant Pot. Secure the lid. Choose "Manual" mode and High pressure; cook for 4 minutes. Once cooking is complete, use a quick pressure release; carefully remove the lid.
Divide between individual bowls and serve warm. Bon appétit!

354. Vegan Mushroom Stroganoff
(Ready in about 10 minutes | Servings 4)
Let's explore new ways to prepare mushrooms in an Instant Pot! This classic dish with a new twist will amaze your family!
Per serving: 128 Calories; 9.1g Fat; 7.2g Carbs; 6g Protein; 3.7g Sugars
Ingredients
2 tablespoons olive oil
1/2 teaspoon caraway seeds, crushed
1/2 cup onion, chopped
2 garlic cloves, smashed
1/4 cup vodka
3/4 pound button mushrooms, chopped
1 celery stalk, chopped
1 ripe tomato, puréed
1 teaspoon mustard seeds
Sea salt and freshly ground pepper, to your liking
2 cups vegetable broth
Directions
Press the "Sauté" button to heat up your Instant Pot. Now, heat the oil and sauté caraway seeds until fragrant, about 40 seconds.
Then, add the onion and garlic, and continue sautéing for 1 to 2 minutes more, stirring frequently.
After that, add the remaining ingredients and stir to combine.
Secure the lid. Choose "Manual" mode and High pressure; cook for 5 minutes. Once cooking is complete, use a quick pressure release; carefully remove the lid.

Ladle into individual bowls and serve warm. Bon appétit!

355. Braised Kale with Red Wine

(Ready in about 10 minutes | Servings 4)
Greens are having a renaissance! This vegetable dish pairs perfectly with light-bodied wines.
Per serving: 91 Calories; 5.9g Fat; 7.5g Carbs; 3.7g Protein; 1.1g Sugars

Ingredients
1 pound Collards, torn into pieces
1 ½ tablespoons sesame oil
1 teaspoon ginger-garlic paste
Sea salt and ground black pepper, to taste
1/2 teaspoon mustard seeds
1/2 teaspoon fennel seeds
3/4 cup water
1/4 cup dry red wine

Directions
Simply throw all of the above ingredients into your Instant Pot.
Secure the lid. Choose "Manual" mode and High pressure; cook for 2 minutes. Once cooking is complete, use a quick pressure release; carefully remove the lid.
Ladle into individual bowls and serve warm. Bon appétit!

356. Indian-Style Cauliflower

(Ready in about 10 minutes | Servings 4)
Ajwain, also sold as carom seeds or oomam, can treat asthma, bronchitis, cold, toothache, and arthritis. It is an excellent source of minerals, vitamins, fiber, and antioxidants too. Amazing!
Per serving: 101 Calories; 7.2g Fat; 8.6g Carbs; 2.3g Protein; 3.6g Sugars

Ingredients
2 tablespoons grapeseed oil
1/2 cup scallions, chopped
2 cloves garlic, pressed
1 tablespoon garam masala
1 teaspoon curry powder
1 red chili pepper, minced
1/2 teaspoon ground cumin
Sea salt and ground black pepper, to taste
1 tablespoon fresh coriander, chopped
1 teaspoon ajwain
2 tomatoes, puréed
1 pound cauliflower, broken into florets
1/2 cup water
1/2 cup almond yogurt

Directions
Press the "Sauté" button to heat up your Instant Pot. Now, heat the oil and sauté the scallions for 1 minute. Add garlic and continue to cook an additional 30 seconds or until aromatic.
Add garam masala, curry powder, chili pepper, cumin, salt, black pepper, coriander, ajwain, tomatoes, cauliflower, and water.
Secure the lid. Choose "Manual" mode and High pressure; cook for 3 minutes. Once cooking is complete, use a quick pressure release; carefully remove the lid.
Pour in the almond yogurt, stir well and serve warm. Bon appétit!

357. Saucy King Oysters

(Ready in about 10 minutes | Servings 6)
Instant Pot king oysters are cooked with olive oil, tomato, and seasonings. This is not a typical one-pot dish!
Per serving: 105 Calories; 5.7g Fat; 9g Carbs; 0.9g Protein; 2.7g Sugars

Ingredients
2 tablespoons olive oil
30 ounces king oyster mushrooms, brushed clean and sliced
2 cloves garlic, minced
1 teaspoon dried rosemary
1 teaspoon dried basil
1/2 teaspoon dried thyme
1 bay leaf
1/2 cup vegetable broth
1/4 teaspoon freshly ground black pepper
1/4 teaspoon cayenne pepper
Kosher salt, to taste
1/2 cup tomato sauce
1 ripe tomato, puréed
2 tablespoons fresh watercress leaves, chopped

Directions
Add all ingredients, except for watercress leaves, to your Instant Pot.
Secure the lid. Choose "Manual" mode and High pressure; cook for 5 minutes. Once cooking is complete, use a quick pressure release; carefully remove the lid.
Ladle into individual bowls, garnish with watercress leaves and serve warm. Bon appétit!

358. Sauerkraut and Mushroom Casserole

(Ready in about 15 minutes | Servings 6)
Tangy sauerkraut, sophisticated mushrooms and lots of spices! It's like November in a bowl!
Per serving: 90 Calories; 2.6g Fat; 8.1g Carbs; 2.1g Protein; 3.3g Sugars

Ingredients
1 tablespoon olive oil
1 celery rib, diced
1/2 cup leeks, chopped
2 pounds canned sauerkraut, drained
6 ounces brown mushrooms, sliced
1 teaspoon caraway seeds
1 teaspoon brown mustard
1 bay leaf
1 cup dry white wine

Directions

Press the "Sauté" button to heat up your Instant Pot. Now, heat the oil and cook celery and leeks until softened.
Add the sauerkraut and mushrooms and cook for 2 minutes more.
Add the remaining ingredients and stir to combine well.
Secure the lid. Choose "Manual" mode and High pressure; cook for 10 minutes. Once cooking is complete, use a natural pressure release; carefully remove the lid. Bon appétit!

359. Korean Kimchi and Tofu Stew
(Ready in about 15 minutes | Servings 4)
If you've never had a Korean kimchi in an Instant Pot, then you've been missing out. As a matter of fact, kimchi and tofu cook wonderfully under a high pressure!
Per serving: 115 Calories; 7.7g Fat; 9.1g Carbs; 3.3g Protein; 3.7g Sugars
Ingredients
2 tablespoons olive oil
8 ounces white mushrooms, sliced
2 garlic cloves, minced
1 yellow onion, chopped
1 bell pepper, seeded and chopped
1 cup vegetable stock
3/4 pound kimchi
2 teaspoon coconut aminos
1 tablespoons Korean chili flakes
8 slices tofu
2 bay leaves
1/2 teaspoon whole black peppercorns
Directions
Press the "Sauté" button to heat up your Instant Pot. Now, heat the oil. Once hot, sauté the mushrooms, garlic, onion, and bell pepper until they are softened.
Stir in the remaining ingredients.
Secure the lid. Choose "Manual" mode and High pressure; cook for 10 minutes. Once cooking is complete, use a natural pressure release; carefully remove the lid.
Ladle into four serving bawls, discard bay leaves and serve immediately. Bon appétit!

360. Spinach with Almond Cheese
(Ready in about 10 minutes | Servings 4)
Start by making the recipe as written and then adjust it according to your taste. You can add the peppers, carrot or celery to your spinach as well.
Per serving: 108 Calories; 6.2g Fat; 8.6g Carbs; 7.8g Protein; 1.2g Sugars
Ingredients
1 tablespoon olive oil
A bunch of scallions, chopped
3 cloves garlic, smashed
2 pounds spinach, washed
1 cup vegetable broth
1 tablespoon champagne vinegar
Seasoned salt and ground black pepper, to taste
1/4 teaspoon cayenne pepper
1/2 teaspoon dried dill weed
1/2 cup almonds, soaked overnight
2 tablespoons water
2 teaspoons lemon juice
1 tablespoon extra-virgin olive oil
1 teaspoon garlic powder
1 teaspoon onion powder
2 tablespoons green olives, pitted and halved
Directions
Press the "Sauté" button to heat up your Instant Pot. Now, heat the oil and sauté the scallions and garlic for 1 to 2 minutes.
Add spinach, broth, vinegar, salt, black pepper, cayenne pepper, and dill.
Secure the lid. Choose "Manual" mode and High pressure; cook for 1 minute. Once cooking is complete, use a quick pressure release; carefully remove the lid.
Then, drain the almonds and blend them with water, lemon juice, extra-virgin olive oil, garlic powder, onion powder, and olives; mix until well combined.
Stir the almond cheese into the spinach mixture, and serve. Bon appétit!

361. Porridge with Coconut and Seeds
(Ready in about 10 minutes | Servings 4)
Don't settle for ordinary, boring porridge bowl. Grab your Instant Pot and make one of the best low-carb porridges you've ever eaten!
Per serving: 116 Calories; 10.5g Fat; 4.4g Carbs; 2.7g Protein; 0.8g Sugars
Ingredients
4 tablespoons shredded coconut, unsweetened
2 tablespoons pumpkin seeds
2 tablespoons flaxseed
1/2 cup almonds, chopped
1/2 teaspoon grated nutmeg
1/4 teaspoon ground cloves
1 teaspoon ground cinnamon
Himalayan salt, to taste
1 cup boiling water
Directions
Add all ingredients to the Instant Pot.
Secure the lid. Choose "Manual" mode and High pressure; cook for 5 minutes. Once cooking is complete, use a quick pressure release; carefully remove the lid.
Serve garnished with some extra slivered almonds if desired. Enjoy!

362. Raspberry and Walnut Granola
(Ready in about 2 hours 10 minutes | Servings 4)
Keto granola? Seriously?! This grain-free, keto-friendly, vegan granola is delicious on its own or served with non-dairy milk!
Per serving: 199 Calories; 17.7g Fat; 9g Carbs; 3.1g Protein; 6.8g Sugars
Ingredients

3/4 cup walnuts, soaked overnight and chopped
Himalayan salt, to taste
3/4 cup water
2 tablespoons coconut oil
1 tablespoon sunflower seeds
1/2 cup dried raspberries
1/2 teaspoon vanilla paste
1/4 teaspoon star anise, ground
1/4 teaspoon grated nutmeg
1/2 teaspoon ground cinnamon
Directions
Add all ingredients to your Instant Pot.
Secure the lid. Choose "Slow Cook" mode and High pressure; cook for 2 hours. Once cooking is complete, use a quick pressure release; carefully remove the lid.
Spoon into individual bowls and serve warm. Bon appétit!

363. Zucchini Lasagna with Cashew-Spinach Cream

(Ready in about 1 hour 20 minutes | Servings 4)
Everyone will love this fancy lasagna. Every bite will melt in your mouth thanks to its creaminess and deliciousness.
Per serving: 170 Calories; 14.7g Fat; 8g Carbs; 3.5g Protein; 2.7g Sugars
Ingredients
Herbed Tomato Sauce:
2 teaspoons olive oil
1/2 cup green onions, chopped
1 garlic clove, minced
2 ripe tomatoes, crushed
1/2 cup water
1/2 teaspoon dried rosemary
1/2 teaspoon dried basil
Sea salt and ground black pepper, to taste
1/2 teaspoon cayenne pepper
Cashew-Spinach Sour Cream:
1/2 cup cashews, soaked
1 cup water
1 cup spinach leaves, torn into pieces
2 garlic cloves
Sea salt and ground black pepper, to taste
Zoodles:
4 zucchinis, sliced
1 tablespoon salt
1/2 teaspoon dried dill
2 tablespoons olive oil
Directions
Press the "Sauté" button to heat up your Instant Pot. Now, heat 2 teaspoons of olive oil and sauté the green onions and garlic approximately 2 minutes. Add the tomatoes, water, rosemary, basil, salt, black pepper, and cayenne pepper. Cook until thoroughly heated or approximately 5 minutes.
Mix cashews, water, spinach, garlic, salt, and black pepper until everything is well incorporated; reserve.
Slice zucchinis and add 1 tablespoon of salt. Let it sit for 30 minutes; drain your zucchinis and season them with dried dill. Now, place 1/2 of zucchini slices on the bottom of a lightly greased casserole dish. Drizzle with 1 tablespoon of olive oil.
Add the prepared tomato sauce. Add the remaining 1/2 zucchini slices. Drizzle with 1 tablespoon of olive oil. Top with Cashew-Spinach Sour Cream.
Cover the casserole dish with a piece of foil.
Secure the lid. Choose "Bean/Chili" mode and High pressure; cook for 25 minutes. Once cooking is complete, use a quick pressure release; carefully remove the lid.
Allow this lasagna to cool for 10 to 15 minutes until slicing and serving. Serve warm.

364. The Best Sunday Tacos Ever

(Ready in about 45 minutes | Servings 4)
Whether it's for Taco Sunday or a dinner party, we all need a reliable vegan taco recipe! These tacos are sinfully delicious.
Per serving: 251 Calories; 21.2g Fat; 6.7g Carbs; 12.3g Protein; 3.1g Sugars
Ingredients
1 cup water
1 teaspoon ginger-garlic paste
2 tablespoons tamari sauce
1/4 cup dry white wine
Salt and pepper, to taste
1/2 teaspoon turmeric powder
1 teaspoon hot sauce
14 ounces extra-firm tofu, pressed and cubed
2 tablespoons olive oil
1 cup cherry tomatoes, halved
1 tablespoon Dijon mustard
1 bell pepper, seeded and chopped
1 red chili pepper, seeded and minced
Vegan Keto Tortillas:
2 tablespoons psyllium husks
1 cup almond flour
1/4 teaspoon baking soda
1/4 teaspoon baking powder
Sea salt, to taste
2 tablespoons coconut oil, softened
Hot water, as needed
Directions
In a mixing dish, combine water, ginger-garlic paste, tamari sauce, wine, salt, pepper, turmeric powder, and hot sauce; add tofu and let it marinate for 30 minutes.
Press the "Sauté" button to heat up your Instant Pot. Heat the olive oil and brown tofu for 1 to 2 minutes per side.
Add the marinade. Secure the lid. Choose "Manual" mode and High pressure; cook for 6 minutes. Once cooking is complete, use a quick pressure release; carefully remove the lid.
Thoroughly combine dry ingredients for vegan keto tortillas; add coconut oil and mix again. Now, pour in hot water to form a dough.
Divide dough into 4 balls. Flatten each ball into tortilla shapes.

Afterwards, grill your tortillas at 350 degrees F until slightly browned on each side.
Assemble your tortillas with the prepared tofu, cherry tomatoes, mustard, bell pepper and chili pepper. Enjoy!

365. Creamed Asparagus and Mushroom Soup

(Ready in about 15 minutes | Servings 4)
To serve, add vegan sour cream to the top of the soup. You can also make cream swirls on soup for even better presentation! Further, you can garnish this soup with caramelized onions or roasted chili peppers.
Per serving: 171 Calories; 11.7g Fat; 9.2g Carbs; 9.7g Protein; 3.4g Sugars
Ingredients
2 tablespoons coconut oil
1/2 cup shallots, chopped
2 cloves garlic, minced
1 pound asparagus, washed, trimmed and chopped
4 ounces button mushrooms, sliced
4 cups vegetable broth
2 tablespoons balsamic vinegar
Himalayan salt, to taste
1/4 teaspoon ground black pepper
1/4 teaspoon paprika
1/4 cup vegan sour cream
Directions
Press the "Sauté" button to heat up your Instant Pot. Heat the oil and cook the shallots and garlic for 2 to 3 minutes.
Add the remaining ingredients, except for sour cream, to the Instant Pot.
Secure the lid. Choose "Manual" mode and High pressure; cook for 4 minutes. Once cooking is complete, use a quick pressure release; carefully remove the lid.
Spoon into four soup bowls; add a dollop of sour cream to each serving and serve immediately. Bon appétit!

366. Mushrooms with Barbecue Sauce

(Ready in about 10 minutes | Servings 4)
Enjoy delicious and easy one-pot meals! Grab your ingredients, throw everything into the Instant Pot and set the timer. Sit back and relax.
Per serving: 60 Calories; 0.7g Fat; 8.7g Carbs; 4.6g Protein; 3g Sugars
Ingredients
1 pound brown mushrooms
Barbecue sauce:
10 ounces tomato paste
1 cup water
Sea salt and ground black pepper, to taste
1/2 teaspoon porcini powder
1 teaspoon shallot powder
1 teaspoon garlic powder
1 teaspoon mustard seeds
1/2 teaspoon fennel seeds
2 tablespoons lime juice
1 tablespoon coconut aminos
A few drops liquid Stevia
1 teaspoon liquid smoke
Directions
Clean and slice the mushrooms; set them aside.
Add the remaining ingredients to your Instant Pot and stir to combine; stir in the mushrooms.
Secure the lid. Choose "Manual" mode and High pressure; cook for 4 minutes. Once cooking is complete, use a natural pressure release; carefully remove the lid. Serve warm.

367. Zoodles with Mediterranean Sauce and Avocado

(Ready in about 10 minutes | Servings 2)
Avocado is a powerhouse of vitamins E, K, C and B-6. It can protect your heart and bones, fight cancer and improve digestion.
Per serving: 226 Calories; 21.2g Fat; 9.3g Carbs; 2.4g Protein; 2.8g Sugars
Ingredients
2 tablespoon olive oil
2 tomatoes, chopped
1 teaspoon garlic, smashed
1 tablespoon fresh rosemary, chopped
1/2 cup fresh parsley, roughly chopped
1/2 cup water
3 tablespoons almonds, ground
1 tablespoon apple cider vinegar
2 zucchinis, spiralized
1/2 avocado, pitted and sliced
Salt and ground black pepper, to taste
Directions
Add olive oil, tomatoes, garlic, rosemary, parsley, water, ground almonds, and apple cider vinegar to your Instant Pot.
Secure the lid. Choose "Manual" mode and High pressure; cook for 5 minutes. Once cooking is complete, use a natural pressure release; carefully remove the lid.
Divide zoodles between two serving plates. Spoon the sauce over each serving. Top with avocado slices. Season with salt and black pepper to taste. Bon appétit!

368. Asian-Style Vegan Stew

(Ready in about 20 minutes | Servings 4)
A rich, hearty stew, full of amazing vegetables and Asian spices! With the help of your Instant Pot, this excellent vegan stew could not be easier to bring to the table.
Per serving: 136 Calories; 7.3g Fat; 9.3g Carbs; 2.6g Protein; 3.5g Sugars
Ingredients
2 tablespoons sesame oil
1 red onion, chopped
1 teaspoon ginger-garlic paste
1 celery stalk, sliced
1 carrot, sliced

3 cups brown mushrooms, sliced
2 ripe Roma tomatoes, puréed
1 cup vegetable broth, preferably homemade
1 (12-ounce) bottle amber beer
2 bay leaves
1/2 teaspoon caraway seeds
1/4 teaspoon cumin seeds
1/2 teaspoon fenugreek seeds
Sea salt and ground black pepper, to taste
1 teaspoon Hungarian hot paprika
1 tablespoon soy sauce
Directions
Press the "Sauté" button to heat up your Instant Pot. Heat the sesame oil and cook the onions for 2 to 3 minutes or until tender and translucent.
Now, add ginger-garlic paste, celery, carrot and mushrooms; continue to cook for a further 2 minutes or until fragrant.
Add the remaining ingredients, except for soy sauce.
Secure the lid. Choose "Manual" mode and High pressure; cook for 10 minutes. Once cooking is complete, use a quick pressure release; carefully remove the lid.
Ladle into individual bowls, add a few drizzles of soy sauce and serve warm. Bon appétit!

369. Easy Chunky Autumn Soup
(Ready in about 10 minutes | Servings 4)
Vegetable soup is a big hit during autumn season. Make a delicious meal for your family without having to spend all day in your kitchen.
Per serving: 99 Calories; 5.5g Fat; 9.2g Carbs; 2g Protein; 3.4g Sugars
Ingredients
1 ½ tablespoons olive oil
1 leek, chopped
2 cloves garlic, smashed
1 parsnip, chopped
1 celery stalk, chopped
4 cups water
2 bouillon cubes
1/2 pound green cabbage, shredded
1 zucchini, sliced
2 bay leaves
1/2 teaspoon ground cumin
1/2 teaspoon turmeric powder
1 teaspoon dried basil
Kosher salt and ground black pepper, to taste
6 ounces Swiss chard
Directions
Press the "Sauté" button to heat up your Instant Pot. Heat the olive oil and cook the leek for 2 to 3 minutes or until it is softened.
Add the other ingredients, except for Swiss chard, to the Instant Pot; stir to combine well.
Secure the lid. Choose "Manual" mode and High pressure; cook for 3 minutes. Once cooking is complete, use a quick pressure release; carefully remove the lid.
Add Swiss chard and cover with the lid. Allow it to sit in the residual heat until it is wilted.
Discard bay leaves and ladle into soup bowls. Serve warm and enjoy!

370. Cauliflower Medley with Spinach
(Ready in about 10 minutes | Servings 4)
Looking for a last-minute dish for your vegan guests? This stunning medley recipe will fit the bill! Serve with a dollop of cashew cream.
Per serving: 124 Calories; 9.5g Fat; 8.7g Carbs; 2.9g Protein; 3.4g Sugars
Ingredients
1 pound cauliflower, broken into florets
2 tablespoons olive oil
2 garlic cloves, crushed
1 yellow onion, peeled and chopped
1 celery stalk, chopped
1 red bell pepper, seeded and chopped
Sea salt and ground black pepper, to taste
1 teaspoon Hungarian paprika
1 tablespoon grated lemon zest
2 cups spinach, torn into pieces
Directions
Add cauliflower, olive oil, garlic, onion, celery, bell pepper, salt, pepper, paprika, and lemon zest to the Instant Pot.
Secure the lid. Choose "Manual" mode and High pressure; cook for 3 minutes. Once cooking is complete, use a quick pressure release; carefully remove the lid.
Add spinach and put the lid on the Instant Pot. Let it sit in the residual heat until wilted. Serve warm and enjoy!

371. Rum Coconut Granola
(Ready in about 2 hours 35 minutes | Servings 6)
Treat yourself to a comforting bowl of something warm and satisfying like this fabulous granola. Add a drizzle of liquid stevia if you want a bit more sweetness.
Per serving: 166 Calories; 14.2g Fat; 4.4g Carbs; 4.8g Protein; 0.9g Sugars
Ingredients
1 cup almonds
1 cup walnuts
2 ounces shredded coconut, unsweetened
1/4 cup sunflower seeds
1/4 cup pumpkin seeds
1 teaspoon vanilla paste
1/2 teaspoon ground cinnamon
A pinch of kosher salt
1/4 teaspoon star anise, ground
2 tablespoons dark rum
Directions
Place all ingredients in your Instant Pot.
Secure the lid. Choose "Slow Cook" mode and High pressure; cook for 2 hours 30 minutes. Once cooking is complete, use a quick pressure release; carefully remove the lid.

Spoon into individual bowls and serve warm. Bon appétit!

372. Zucchini "Tagliatelle" with Almond Butter

(Ready in about 10 minutes | Servings 4)

Here's a pure vegetable goodness! While it is cooking, sit back and relax as the entire kitchen fills with the wonderful smells.

Per serving: 145 Calories; 14.8g Fat; 2.9g Carbs; 0.7g Protein; 1.2g Sugars

Ingredients
2 tablespoons coconut oil
1 yellow onion, chopped
2 zucchini, julienned
1 cup Chinese cabbage, shredded
2 garlic cloves, minced
2 tablespoons almond butter
Sea salt and freshly ground black pepper, to taste
1 teaspoon cayenne pepper

Directions
Press the "Sauté" button to heat up your Instant Pot. Heat the coconut oil and sweat the onion for 2 minutes.
Add the other ingredients.
Secure the lid. Choose "Manual" mode and High pressure; cook for 2 minutes. Once cooking is complete, use a quick pressure release; carefully remove the lid. Bon appétit!

373. Winter One-Pot-Wonder

(Ready in about 15 minutes | Servings 4)

Is there anything better than a big bowl of creamy soup? Be generous with seasonings and watch the magic happens.

Per serving: 157 Calories; 12.3g Fat; 9.4g Carbs; 3.4g Protein; 4.7g Sugars

Ingredients
10 ounces coconut milk
10 ounces vegetable stock
1 garlic cloves, minced
1 teaspoon fresh ginger root, grated
4 tablespoons almond butter
Sea salt and ground black pepper, to taste
1/2 teaspoon turmeric powder
A pinch of grated nutmeg
1/2 teaspoon ground coriander
10 ounces pumpkin, cubed
1/3 cup leek, white part only, finely sliced

Directions
Place the milk, stock, garlic, ginger, almond butter, salt, black pepper, turmeric powder, nutmeg, coriander, and pumpkin in your Instant Pot.
Secure the lid. Choose "Manual" mode and High pressure; cook for 10 minutes. Once cooking is complete, use a natural pressure release; carefully remove the lid.
Now, blend your soup with a stick blender. Ladle your soup into serving bowls and top with leeks. Bon appétit!

374. Vegan Cream of Tomato Soup

(Ready in about 15 minutes | Servings 4)

A perfect, velvety soup that will warm you up immediately! An instant Pot simplifies everything!

Per serving: 136 Calories; 9.8g Fat; 5.8g Carbs; 7.2g Protein; 4.3g Sugars

Ingredients
2 tablespoons olive oil
1 shallot, chopped
1 celery, diced
3 ripe medium-sized tomatoes, puréed
4 cups roasted vegetable stock
1 teaspoon granulated garlic
1/2 teaspoon rosemary
1/2 teaspoon lemon thyme
Himalayan salt and ground white pepper, to taste
1 bay leaf
4-5 whole cloves
1/2 cup almond milk, unsweetened
2 heaping tablespoons fresh parsley, roughly chopped

Directions
Press the "Sauté" button to heat up your Instant Pot. Heat the olive oil and sauté the shallot and celery until softened.
Now, add tomatoes, stock, garlic, rosemary, lemon thyme, salt, black pepper, bay leaf, cloves, and milk; stir to combine well.
Secure the lid. Choose "Manual" mode and High pressure; cook for 8 minutes. Once cooking is complete, use a natural pressure release; carefully remove the lid.
Ladle into individual bowls and top each serving with fresh parsley. Serve hot and enjoy!

375. Zucchini and Leek Soup

(Ready in about 15 minutes | Servings 4)

This ketogenic soup recipe is very nutritious, high in essential vitamins and minerals. This is a great way to get more vegetables into your diet.

Per serving: 90 Calories; 7.4g Fat; 4.9g Carbs; 2g Protein; 1.5g Sugars

Ingredients
2 tablespoons coconut oil
1 medium-sized leek, thinly sliced
1 zucchini, chopped
2 garlic cloves, crushed
Sea salt and ground black pepper, to your liking
1/2 teaspoon cayenne pepper
4 cups vegetable stock
1/4 cup coriander leaves, chopped

Directions
Press the "Sauté" button to heat up your Instant Pot. Heat the coconut oil and sauté the leeks, zucchini, and garlic.
Next, stir in the salt, black pepper, cayenne pepper, and stock.
Secure the lid. Choose "Manual" mode and High pressure; cook for 8 minutes. Once cooking is

complete, use a natural pressure release; carefully remove the lid.
Serve warm garnished with coriander leaves. Bon appétit!

376. Cabbage Medley with Tempeh
(Ready in about 10 minutes | Servings 3)
Tempeh is an excellent source of vitamin K and calcium. Not to mention this will be the quickest and easiest way to make it.
Per serving: 172 Calories; 11.9g Fat; 8.9g Carbs; 10.1g Protein; 2.1g Sugars
Ingredients
2 tablespoons sesame oil
1/2 cup scallions, chopped
2 cups cabbages, shredded
6 ounces tempeh, cubed
1 tablespoon coconut aminos
1 cup vegetable stock
2 garlic cloves, minced
1 tablespoon lemon juice
Salt and pepper, to taste
1/4 teaspoon paprika
1/4 cup fresh cilantro, roughly chopped
Directions
Press the "Sauté" button to heat up your Instant Pot. Heat the sesame oil and sauté the scallions until tender and fragrant.
Then, add the cabbage, tempeh, coconut aminos, vegetable stock, garlic, lemon juice, salt, pepper, and paprika.
Secure the lid. Choose "Manual" mode and Low pressure; cook for 3 minutes. Once cooking is complete, use a quick pressure release; carefully remove the lid.
Press the "Sauté" button to thicken the sauce if desired. Divide between serving bowls, garnish with fresh cilantro, and serve warm. Bon appétit!

377. Easy Brussels Sprouts with Peppers
(Ready in about 10 minutes | Servings 4)
Make the best Brussels sprouts ever in a fraction of the time using a revolutionary electric pressure cooker. Brussels sprouts pair wonderfully with peppers and tomato paste!
Per serving: 107 Calories; 7.4g Fat; 9g Carbs; 2.6g Protein; 3.1g Sugars
Ingredients
2 tablespoons canola oil
1 white onion, chopped
1 garlic clove, minced
1 cup water
1 vegetable bouillon cube
1 teaspoon fennel seeds
1 tablespoon coconut aminos
1 red bell pepper, seeded and chopped
1 habanero pepper, chopped
3/4 pound Brussels sprouts, trimmed and halved
2 tablespoons tomato paste
1/2 teaspoon paprika
2 bay leaves
Sea salt and freshly ground black pepper, to your liking
Directions
Press the "Sauté" button to heat up your Instant Pot. Heat the oil and sauté the onion until it is softened. Add the other ingredients. Secure the lid. Choose "Manual" mode and Low pressure; cook for 4 minutes.
Once cooking is complete, use a quick pressure release; carefully remove the lid. Discard bay leaves and serve warm. Bon appétit!

378. Superb Teriyaki Mushrooms
(Ready in about 10 minutes | Servings 4)
Saucy, melt-in-your-mouth button mushrooms. You can play around with spices to match your preference.
Per serving: 110 Calories; 7.9g Fat; 6.8g Carbs; 5.9g Protein; 4.5g Sugars
Ingredients
1/4 cup port wine
1/4 cup coconut milk
1 tablespoon tamari sauce
2 tablespoons sesame oil
1 teaspoon ginger-garlic paste
1 ½ pounds button mushrooms
Sea salt and ground pepper, to taste
1 teaspoon red pepper flakes
2 tablespoons fresh chives, roughly chopped
Directions
Add wine, coconut milk, tamari sauce, sesame oil, ginger-garlic paste and mushrooms to a ceramic bowl; cover and let it marinate in your refrigerator for 40 minutes.
Add the mushrooms along with their marinade to the Instant Pot. Add salt, black pepper, and red pepper flakes.
Secure the lid. Choose "Manual" mode and High pressure; cook for 5 minutes. Once cooking is complete, use a quick pressure release; carefully remove the lid.
Serve garnished with fresh chives. Enjoy!

379. Broccoli Bake with Vegan Béchamel
(Ready in about 20 minutes | Servings 4)
Nothing says holiday dinner like a vegetable bake! You can try a combo of different low-carb vegetables here.
Per serving: 130 Calories; 7.9g Fat; 9.2g Carbs; 8.4g Protein; 3.8g Sugars
Ingredients
1/2 cup sunflower seeds, soaked overnight
2 tablespoons sesame seeds
1 cup water
1 cup almond milk, unsweetened
1/4 teaspoon grated nutmeg
1/2 teaspoon sea salt
1 tablespoon nutritional yeast
2 tablespoons rice vinegar

1 pound broccoli, broken into florets
1/2 cup spring onions, chopped
10 ounces white fresh mushrooms, sliced
Sea salt and white pepper, to taste
1 tablespoon cayenne pepper
1/4 teaspoon dried dill
1/4 teaspoon bay leaf, ground
Directions
Add sunflower seeds, sesame seeds, water, milk, nutmeg, 1/2 teaspoon of sea salt, nutritional yeast, and vinegar to your blender.
Blend until smooth and uniform.
Spritz a casserole dish with a nonstick cooking spray.
Add broccoli, spring onions and mushrooms.
Sprinkle with salt, white pepper, cayenne pepper, dill, and ground bay leaf. Pour the prepared vegan béchamel over your casserole.
Add 1 cup of water and a metal rack to your Instant Pot. Place the dish on the rack.
Secure the lid. Choose "Manual" mode and High pressure; cook for 3 minutes. Once cooking is complete, use a quick pressure release; carefully remove the lid.
Allow the dish to stand for 5 to 10 minutes before slicing and serving. Bon appétit!

380. Sunday Sweet Porridge
(Ready in about 10 minutes | Servings 2)
Here's a good idea for a romantic Sunday breakfast! This porridge is full of comforts that will warm you during the winter season.
Per serving: 308 Calories; 30.6g Fat; 7.9g Carbs; 5.6g Protein; 1.1g Sugars
Ingredients
2 tablespoons flaxseed meal
4 tablespoons coconut flour
1 tablespoon pumpkin seeds, chopped
1 tablespoon raw almonds, ground
1 cup unsweetened almond milk
1 cup water
1/8 teaspoon Monk fruit powder
Directions
Add all ingredients to the Instant Pot.
Secure the lid. Choose "Manual" mode and High pressure; cook for 5 minutes. Once cooking is complete, use a quick pressure release; carefully remove the lid.
Divide between two bowls and serve hot. Bon appétit!

381. Everyday Italian Pepperonata
(Ready in about 15 minutes | Servings 4)
Rustic, light and colorful, Italian Pepperonata will win your heart. When it comes to white wine, you can use Verdicchio or Pinot Grigio for this recipe.
Per serving: 308 Calories; 30.6g Fat; 7.9g Carbs; 5.6g Protein; 1.1g Sugars
Ingredients
2 tablespoons grapeseed oil
1/2 cup onions, chopped
2 green bell peppers, seeded and chopped
1 red bell pepper, seeded and chopped
1 yellow bell pepper, seeded and chopped
1 red chili pepper, seeded and minced
2 tomatoes, pureed
2 garlic cloves, crushed
1 tablespoon balsamic vinegar
1 teaspoon dried basil
1 teaspoon dried oregano
1 teaspoon dried thyme
1/4 cup Italian dry white wine
3/4 cup vegetable broth
Sea salt and ground black pepper, to taste
1 teaspoon paprika
2 tablespoons fresh Italian parsley, roughly chopped
Directions
Press the "Sauté" button to heat up your Instant Pot.
Heat the oil and sauté the onion until it is softened.
Add the other ingredients, except for Italian parsley.
Secure the lid. Choose "Manual" mode and High pressure; cook for 3 minutes. Once cooking is complete, use a quick pressure release; carefully remove the lid.
Press the "Sauté" button again to thicken the cooking liquid; let it simmer for 3 to 4 minutes.
Divide between four serving bowls and garnish with fresh parsley. Bon appétit!

382. Luxurious Cauliflower Parmigiana
(Ready in about 10 minutes | Servings 4)
Cauliflower is a real miraculous food. Cauliflower can protect your heart, boost your brain health and improve your digestive health.
Per serving: 209 Calories; 18.6g Fat; 8.3g Carbs; 6.1g Protein; 2.3g Sugars
Ingredients
1 pound cauliflower, broken into florets
Kosher salt and freshly ground black pepper, to taste
2 garlic cloves, chopped
1 teaspoon rosemary
1 teaspoon dried basil
2 tablespoons sesame oil
Vegan Parmesan:
1/2 cup sesame seeds
1/2 teaspoon sea salt
1/2 teaspoon oregano
1/4 teaspoon cumin seeds
1/4 teaspoon ground fennel seeds
Directions
Add 1 cup of water and a steamer basket to your Instant Pot.
Now, arrange cauliflower florets on the steamer basket. Add salt, black pepper, garlic, rosemary, basil, and sesame oil.
Secure the lid. Choose "Manual" mode and Low pressure; cook for 3 minutes. Once cooking is complete, use a quick pressure release; carefully remove the lid.

Thoroughly combine the remaining ingredients in your food processor until the mixture has the texture of Parmigiano-Reggiano granular cheese.
Top your cauliflower with Vegan Parmesan and serve immediately. Bon appétit!

383. Favorite Winter Noatmeal

(Ready in about 10 minutes | Servings 2)
Wow your beloved one with this nut-free, dairy-free, keto-friendly, vegan porridge – noatmeal! It will change the way you think about food!
Per serving: 352 Calories; 34.8g Fat; 8.3g Carbs; 5.5g Protein; 2.4g Sugars
Ingredients
3 tablespoons pumpkin seeds
1 tablespoon chia seeds
1 tablespoon sunflower seeds
Himalayan salt, to taste
2 tablespoons coconut oil
1/2 cup coconut milk
1/2 cup water
1 teaspoon ground cinnamon
1 teaspoon vanilla paste
1/2 teaspoon granulated stevia
Directions
Place all ingredients in your Instant Pot.
Secure the lid. Choose "Manual" mode and High pressure; cook for 5 minutes. Once cooking is complete, use a quick pressure release; carefully remove the lid.
Divide between two bowls and serve hot. Bon appétit!

384. Green Beans with Scallions and Mushrooms

(Ready in about 10 minutes | Servings 4)
Green beans are a powerhouse of vitamin C, K, A, and B6, as well as valuable minerals such as iron, manganese, calcium, and potassium. Incredible!
Per serving: 106 Calories; 7.7g Fat; 7g Carbs; 3.5g Protein; 1.7g Sugars
Ingredients
2 tablespoons olive oil
1/2 cup scallions, chopped
2 cloves garlic, minced
1 cup white mushrooms, chopped
3/4 pound green beans
1 cup vegetable broth
Sea salt and ground black pepper, to taste
1 teaspoon red pepper flakes, crushed
Directions
Press the "Sauté" button to heat up your Instant Pot. Heat the oil and sauté scallions until softened or about 2 minutes.
Then, add garlic and mushrooms; continue to cook an additional minute or so.
Add the other ingredients; gently stir to combine.
Secure the lid. Choose "Manual" mode and Low pressure; cook for 3 minutes. Once cooking is complete, use a quick pressure release; carefully remove the lid.

Serve warm and enjoy!

385. One-Pot Mushroom and Tofu Curry

(Ready in about 10 minutes | Servings 4)
Thanks to the Instant Pot, you can create this traditional spicy vegetarian dish with mushrooms in less than 10 minutes.
Per serving: 157 Calories; 9.5g Fat; 9.3g Carbs; 12.4g Protein; 3.2g Sugars
Ingredients
1 tablespoon coconut oil
1 ½ cups button mushrooms, sliced
1 garlic clove, minced
8 ounces firm tofu, pressed and cubed
8 ounces coconut milk
2 tablespoons curry paste
1 tablespoon Garam Masala
Sea salt and ground black pepper, to taste
2 tablespoons tomato paste
1 shallot, chopped
1 cup vegetable stock
2 heaping tablespoons coriander, chopped
Directions
Press the "Sauté" button to heat up your Instant Pot. Heat the oil and sauté mushrooms and garlic about 2 minutes or until fragrant.
Add cubed tofu to your Instant Pot.
In a food processor, blend the milk, curry, Garam Masala, salt, pepper, tomato paste, and shallot. Add this mixture to the Instant Pot.
Pour in vegetable broth and secure the lid.
Choose "Manual" mode and High pressure; cook for 5 minutes. Once cooking is complete, use a quick pressure release; carefully remove the lid.
Afterwards, press the "Sauté" button one more time and let it simmer until the sauce has reduced. Serve warm.

386. Croatian Blitva with Dry Sherry

(Ready in about 5 minutes | Servings 4)
Swiss chard is an excellent source of antioxidants, dietary fiber, iron, magnesium, vitamins C, K, and A. Serve with baked tofu for the full vegan keto experience.
Per serving: 109 Calories; 7.1g Fat; 8g Carbs; 2.8g Protein; 2.8g Sugars
Ingredients
2 tablespoons olive oil
1 teaspoon garlic, minced
1 cup scallions, chopped
1 ripe tomato, puréed
1 pound Swiss chard, torn into pieces
1/4 cup dry sherry
2 tablespoons dried parsley
1/4 teaspoon basil
Directions
Press the "Sauté" button to heat up your Instant Pot. Heat the oil and sauté garlic approximately 40 seconds or until aromatic.

Add the remaining ingredients and stir to combine well.
Secure the lid. Choose "Manual" mode and Low pressure; cook for 2 minutes. Once cooking is complete, use a quick pressure release; carefully remove the lid.
Serve in individual bowls and enjoy!

387. Broccoli, Artichoke and Spinach Dip

(Ready in about 10 minutes | Servings 10)
Broccoli is a powerhouse of many valuable nutrients. It fights cancer, boosts your immune system, and reduces many allergic reactions. Spinach is loaded with fiber, iron, calcium, copper magnesium and vitamins (C, K, E, A).
Per serving: 176 Calories; 13.7g Fat; 9g Carbs; 7g Protein; 1.5g Sugars
Ingredients
1 pound broccoli, broken into florets
1 cup vegetable stock
1/2 cup white onions, chopped
2 garlic cloves, chopped
4 ounces almond milk
1 teaspoon fennel seeds
1 teaspoon mustard seeds
1 tablespoon fresh lime juice
Sea salt and freshly ground black pepper, to taste
4 tablespoons olive oil
1 pound fresh spinach
10 ounces canned artichokes, drained and chopped
1/4 cup vegan mayonnaise
Directions
Add all ingredients, except for vegan mayonnaise, to your Instant Pot.
Secure the lid. Choose "Manual" mode and High pressure; cook for 3 minutes. Once cooking is complete, use a quick pressure release; carefully remove the lid.
Add vegan mayonnaise, stir and serve warm. Bon appétit!

388. Indian Peppers with Coconut Flour Naan

(Ready in about 20 minutes | Servings 6)
These naans are a little bit crunchier than classic flour flatbread. They pair wonderfully with Indian-inspired peppers.
Per serving: 348 Calories; 38.7g Fat; 3.2g Carbs; 0.6g Protein; 1.7g Sugars
Ingredients
3 teaspoons canola oil
1/3 teaspoon cumin seeds
2 red bell pepper, seeded and sliced
1 green bell pepper, seeded and sliced
1 garlic clove, minced
1 teaspoon dhania
1 teaspoon chili powder
1/2 teaspoon haldi
Sea salt and ground black pepper, to taste
1 tablespoon fresh lemon juice
Coconut Flour Naan:
1/2 cup coconut flour
1/2 teaspoon baking powder
1 ½ tablespoons ground psyllium husk powder
1/2 teaspoon salt
1/4 cup coconut oil, melted
1 ½ cups boiling water
1 tablespoon coconut oil, for frying
Directions
Press the "Sauté" button to heat up your Instant Pot. Heat the canola oil until sizzling. Once hot, sauté cumin seeds for 40 seconds.
Now, add peppers, garlic, and spices.
Secure the lid. Choose "Manual" mode and Low pressure; cook for 4 minutes.
Once cooking is complete, use a quick pressure release; carefully remove the lid. Add lemon juice.
To make naan, in a mixing bowl, combine coconut flour with baking powder, psyllium and salt; mix to combine well.
Add 1/4 cup of coconut oil; add the hot water to form a dough; let it rest for 10 minutes at room temperature.
Now, divide the dough into 6 balls; flatten the balls on a working surface.
Heat up a pan with 1 tablespoon of coconut oil over a medium-high flame. Fry naan breads until they are golden.
Serve these naans with Indian peppers and enjoy!

389. Tofu with Zhoug Sauce

(Ready in about 10 minutes | Servings 4)
Delicious tofu cubes with a homemade tangy sauce fitting for light dinner or a party appetizer. Zhoug sauce goes wonderfully with many vegan delicacies.
Per serving: 308 Calories; 28.3g Fat; 4.5g Carbs; 12.3g Protein; 1.4g Sugars
Ingredients
1 tablespoon grapeseed oil
1 (12-ounce) block extra-firm tofu, pressed and cubed
1/2 cup vegetable stock
1 teaspoon dried rosemary
Herby Sauce:
1 Hungarian wax pepper, stemmed and chopped
2 cloves garlic, chopped
1/2 cup fresh cilantro leaves
Kosher salt and ground black pepper, to taste
1/2 teaspoon ground cumin
1/3 cup extra-virgin olive oil
1 teaspoon sherry vinegar
Directions
Press the "Sauté" button to heat up your Instant Pot. Heat the oil until sizzling. Once hot, cook tofu until it has begun to brown.
Add vegetable stock and rosemary.
Secure the lid. Choose "Manual" mode and High pressure; cook for 3 minutes. Once cooking is

complete, use a quick pressure release; carefully remove the lid.
Then, mix all ingredients for the sauce in your food processor. Store in your refrigerator until ready to use.
Serve tofu with Zhoug sauce on the side. Enjoy!

390. Classic Vegan Cauliflower Soup

(Ready in about 15 minutes | Servings 4)
Is there anything better than thick and creamy soup during winter weekdays? Serve warm with kale chips. So good, right?
Per serving: 144 Calories; 11.4g Fat; 9.2g Carbs; 3.3g Protein; 3.5g Sugars
Ingredients
3 teaspoons sesame oil
1 shallot, chopped
2 cloves garlic, minced
1 celery stalk, chopped
3/4 pound cauliflower, broken into florets
4 cups water
4 vegan bouillon cubes
1 teaspoon fresh coriander, chopped
1/2 teaspoon ground cumin
1 teaspoon paprika
Himalayan salt and freshly ground black pepper, to taste
1/2 cup almond milk, unsweetened
2 tablespoons fresh parsley, chopped
Directions
Press the "Sauté" button to heat up your Instant Pot. Heat the oil and sauté the shallot until tender or about 2 minutes.
Add garlic and continue to cook for 30 seconds more, stirring frequently.
Add celery, cauliflower, water, bouillon cubes, fresh coriander, cumin, paprika, salt, and black pepper.
Secure the lid. Choose "Manual" mode and Low pressure; cook for 3 minutes. Once cooking is complete, use a quick pressure release; carefully remove the lid.
Then, add almond milk, press the "Sauté" button again and let it simmer an additional 4 minutes or until everything is heated through.
Afterwards, purée the soup with an immersion blender until smooth and uniform; then, return the soup to the Instant Pot.
Ladle into soup bowls, garnish with fresh parsley, and serve warm. Bon appétit!

391. Thai Cream of Celery Soup

(Ready in about 10 minutes | Servings 4)
Here's one of the easiest keto dishes to make for a delicious, no-stress family lunch. We opted for Thai seasoning but you can toss in whatever spices and herbs you have on hand!
Per serving: 141 Calories; 11.1g Fat; 9.1g Carbs; 2.2g Protein; 4.2g Sugars
Ingredients
2 tablespoons olive oil
1/2 cup leeks, chopped
3 cups celery with leaves, chopped
2 cloves garlic, smashed
1 (2-inch) piece young galangal, peeled and chopped
1 teaspoon shallot powder
2 fresh bird chilies, seeded and finely chopped
4 cups water
2 tablespoons vegetable bouillon granules
1/2 teaspoon Thai white peppercorns, ground
Sea salt, to taste
1 bay leaf
1/4 cup coconut cream, unsweetened
2 sprigs cilantro, coarsely chopped
Directions
Press the "Sauté" button to heat up your Instant Pot. Heat the oil and sauté the leeks until tender or about 2 minutes.
Add celery, garlic, and galangal; continue to cook an additional 2 minutes.
Next, add shallot powder, bird chilies, water, vegetable bouillon granules, Thai white peppercorns, salt, and bay leaf.
Secure the lid. Choose "Manual" mode and High pressure; cook for 2 minutes. Once cooking is complete, use a quick pressure release; carefully remove the lid.
Afterwards, purée the soup with an immersion blender until smooth and uniform; then, return the soup to the Instant Pot.
Add the coconut cream and press the "Sauté" button again. Let it simmer until everything is heated through.
Ladle into soup bowls, garnish with cilantro, and serve hot. Enjoy!

392. Ranch Broccoli Dip

(Ready in about 10 minutes | Servings 8)
Love vegetable dips? Yes, of course! This keto, Instant Pot version goes perfectly with veggies and other keto dippers.
Per serving: 74 Calories; 6.1g Fat; 3.5g Carbs; 1.7g Protein; 1.5g Sugars
Ingredients
2 cups broccoli, cut into florets
2 ripe tomatoes, diced
1 yellow onion, chopped
2 garlic cloves, sliced
1 teaspoon fresh coriander, chopped
Seasoned salt, to taste
1/2 teaspoon ground black pepper
1/2 teaspoon cayenne pepper
1/2 teaspoon dried dill weed
1 teaspoon Ranch seasoning mix
1/2 cup vegan mayonnaise
Directions
Prepare your Instant Pot by adding 1 cup of water and a steamer basket to its bottom.
Place broccoli florets in the steamer basket.

Secure the lid. Choose "Manual" mode and Low pressure; cook for 5 minutes. Once cooking is complete, use a quick pressure release; carefully remove the lid.
Add the broccoli florets along with the remaining ingredients to your food processor. Process until everything is well incorporated.
Serve well chilled with vegetable sticks. Bon appétit!

393. Spanish-Style Carrot Dip

(Ready in about 10 minutes | Servings 8)
Are you looking for a party dip that takes 10 minutes from start to finish? Serve this easy-to-make, inexpensive and delicious dip with keto flatbread.
Per serving: 89 Calories; 7.1g Fat; 6.4g Carbs; 0.7g Protein; 3.1g Sugars

Ingredients
1 pound carrots, trimmed, peeled, and chopped
1/4 cup sesame oil
1/2 teaspoon ground cumin
2 garlic cloves, crushed
1/4 teaspoon dried dill weed
1/2 teaspoon dried basil
1 teaspoon smoked Spanish paprika
Salt and ground white pepper, to your liking
1 tablespoon apple cider vinegar

Directions
Add all ingredients to your Instant Pot.
Secure the lid. Choose "Manual" mode and High pressure; cook for 1 minute. Once cooking is complete, use a quick pressure release; carefully remove the lid.
Transfer to a serving bowl and serve. Bon appétit!

394. Onion and Tofu Dipping Sauce

(Ready in about 10 minutes | Servings 8)
Get ready for this fabulous combination of ingredients! Fresh yellow onions, cashews, and tofu are definitely a match made in heaven!
Per serving: 195 Calories; 16.3g Fat; 7.8g Carbs; 7.1g Protein; 2.1g Sugars

Ingredients
3 tablespoons olive oil
2 yellow onions, peeled and sliced
1/2 teaspoon dried basil
1/2 teaspoon dried oregano
1 teaspoon dried thyme
2 garlic cloves, minced
1 cup tofu, pressed and cubed
1 tablespoon coconut aminos
Celery salt and ground black pepper, to taste
1 teaspoon smoked paprika
1/2 cup water
1/2 cup raw cashews, soaked overnight, drained

Directions
Press the "Sauté" button to heat up your Instant Pot. Heat the oil and sauté the onions until tender or about 2 minutes.
Add the other ingredients, except for cashews, and stir to combine well.
Secure the lid. Choose "Manual" mode and High pressure; cook for 3 minutes. Once cooking is complete, use a quick pressure release; carefully remove the lid.
Transfer the mixture to a food processor; stir in the cashews.
Purée this mixture in your food processor, working in batches. Transfer to a nice serving bowl and serve with veggies for dipping. Bon appétit!

395. Summer Veggie Kabobs

(Ready in about 10 minutes | Servings 5)
You don't have to heat up your grill to make tasty vegetable skewers. Trust us, an Instant Pot is really amazing kitchen appliance and it does wonders in the kitchen.
Per serving: 126 Calories; 9.5g Fat; 9.1g Carbs; 3.7g Protein; 4.4g Sugars

Ingredients
1/2 head of broccoli, broken into florets
1/2 head of cauliflower, broken into florets
1 red bell pepper, seeded and diced
1 green bell pepper, seeded and diced
1 orange bell pepper, seeded and diced
9 ounces button mushrooms
2 cups cherry tomatoes
1 teaspoon ground coriander
1 teaspoon cayenne pepper
Coarse sea salt and ground black pepper, to taste
1/4 cup olive oil

Directions
Prepare your Instant Pot by adding 1 cup of water and a metal rack to its bottom.
Thread your broccoli, cauliflower, bell peppers, mushrooms, and cherry tomatoes onto small bamboo skewers.
Sprinkle them with coriander, cayenne pepper, salt and black pepper. Drizzle with olive oil and transfer the skewers to the rack.
Secure the lid. Choose "Manual" mode and High pressure; cook for 3 minutes. Once cooking is complete, use a quick pressure release; carefully remove the lid. Bon appétit!

396. French-Style Broccoli Rabe Soup

(Ready in about 10 minutes | Servings 4)
It's going to be the best French soup ever! Try it and enjoy its wonderful taste!
Per serving: 121 Calories; 7.6g Fat; 8.5g Carbs; 4.3g Protein; 1.1g Sugars

Ingredients
2 tablespoons grapeseed oil
1 white onion, thinly sliced
2 garlic cloves, minced
1 bird chili, minced
1 (1-inch) piece fresh ginger root, peeled and grated
1 pound broccoli rabe, cut into pieces
4 cups warm water
2 tablespoons vegetable bouillon granules

1 celery, trimmed and diced
1 carrot, trimmed and sliced
3/4 cup acorn squash, peeled and cubed
1/4 cup dry white wine
Celery salt and ground black pepper, to taste
Directions
Press the "Sauté" button to heat up your Instant Pot. Heat the oil and sauté the onions, stirring frequently, until caramelized.
Add the remaining ingredients and gently stir to combine.
Secure the lid. Choose "Manual" mode and Low pressure; cook for 5 minutes. Once cooking is complete, use a quick pressure release; carefully remove the lid.
Lastly, purée the soup with an immersion blender until smooth and uniform; then, return the soup to the Instant Pot. Ladle into soup bowls and serve hot. Bon appétit!

397. Traditional Sunday Ratatouille
(Ready in about 35 minutes | Servings 4)
This simple but endlessly crave-worthy dish is both sophisticated and rustic. The secret lies in the simple approach – fresh eggplant, bell peppers, and herbs.
Per serving: 102 Calories; 7.1g Fat; 9.1g Carbs; 1.7g Protein; 5.9g Sugars
Ingredients
1 eggplant, peeled and sliced
2 teaspoons of table salt
2 tablespoons olive oil
1 purple onion, thinly sliced
3 garlic cloves, chopped
1 teaspoon hot paprika
1 red bell pepper, seeded and sliced
1 yellow bell pepper, seeded and sliced
2 large-sized tomatoes, chopped
1/4 teaspoon freshly ground black pepper
1/3 teaspoon cayenne pepper
1/3 teaspoon dried basil
1/4 teaspoon tarragon
Sea salt, to taste
Directions
Place the eggplant cubes with 2 teaspoons of table salt in a ceramic dish. Let it sit for 25 to 30 minutes. Drain and rinse the eggplant.
Press the "Sauté" button to heat up your Instant Pot. Heat the oil and sauté the eggplant until tender.
Add the remaining ingredients and gently stir to combine.
Secure the lid. Choose "Manual" mode and High pressure; cook for 3 minutes. Once cooking is complete, use a quick pressure release; carefully remove the lid.
Serve warm and enjoy!

398. Piri-Piri Tofu
(Ready in about 1 hour 10 minutes | Servings 4)
Here is the perfect blend of savory flavors that will delight your taste buds! If you don't have African bird's eye chili peppers on hand, feel free to substitute them with jalapeño peppers.
Per serving: 185 Calories; 13.8g Fat; 6.2g Carbs; 12.7g Protein; 2.1g Sugars
Ingredients
1 (15-ounce) block firm tofu, pressed, drained, and cubed
1/2 cup vegetable stock
1 tablespoon dark vinegar
Himalayan salt, to taste
1/4 teaspoon ground black pepper, or more to taste
1/2 teaspoon cayenne pepper
2 tablespoons coconut oil, melted
2 garlic cloves, crushed
1/2 teaspoon ground cumin
1/2 teaspoon dried marjoram
2 fresh African bird's eye chili peppers, seeded and finely chopped
1/2 cup scallions, chopped
Directions
Purée all ingredients, except for tofu and vegetable stock, in a food processor until creamy and uniform.
Transfer this mixture to a ceramic container; add tofu, cover your container and place in the refrigerator for 1 hour.
Transfer the mixture to your Instant Pot. Pour in vegetable stock and stir to combine.
Secure the lid. Choose "Manual" mode and High pressure; cook for 2 minutes. Once cooking is complete, use a quick pressure release; carefully remove the lid.

399. Party Cauliflower Balls
(Ready in about 15 minutes | Servings 8)
If you are new to the ketogenic diet, you might be wondering what type of appetizers you could serve at a party. This recipe offers an answer!
Per serving: 60 Calories; 4.8g Fat; 4g Carbs; 1.5g Protein; 1.1g Sugars
Ingredients
1 pound cauliflower, broken into florets
2 teaspoons vegan margarine
1/3 cup coconut cream
Sea salt, to taste
1/3 teaspoon ground black pepper
A pinch of freshly grated nutmeg
2 cloves garlic, peeled
3 tablespoons Kalamata olives, pitted
2 tablespoons smoked paprika
Directions
Add 1 cup of water and a steamer basket to the bottom of your Instant Pot.
Then, arrange cauliflower and kohlrabi in the steamer basket.
Secure the lid. Choose "Manual" mode and High pressure; cook for 2 minutes. Once cooking is complete, use a quick pressure release; carefully remove the lid.
Purée your cauliflower along with the remaining ingredients in a food processor.

Form the mixture into balls and roll each ball into smoked paprika powder. Arrange on a nice serving platter. Bon appétit!

400. Sriracha Carrot and Chard Purée

(Ready in about 15 minutes | Servings 4)
The next-level purée your family will love! This purée carries some of the flavors of Mexican cuisine, so you can increase or reduce the spiciness by controlling the amount of Sriracha chili sauce.
Per serving: 140 Calories; 11.3g Fat; 9.1g Carbs; 2.3g Protein; 4.4g Sugars

Ingredients
2 cups carrots, peeled and chopped
10 ounces fresh or frozen (and thawed) chard, torn into pieces
Sea salt, to taste
1/4 teaspoon ground black pepper, to taste
1/2 teaspoon garlic powder
1/2 teaspoon shallot power
1/2 teaspoon fennel seeds
1 teaspoon cayenne pepper
1 teaspoon Sriracha chili sauce
2 tablespoons coconut oil
3/4 cup vegetable broth
1/3 cup coconut cream

Directions
Add all ingredients, except for coconut cream, to your Instant Pot.
Secure the lid. Choose "Manual" mode and High pressure; cook for 2 minutes. Once cooking is complete, use a quick pressure release; carefully remove the lid.
Transfer the vegetable mixture to your food processor; add coconut cream and purée the mixture until uniform, creamy, and smooth. Serve warm. Bon appétit!

DESSERTS

401. Raspberry Upside-Down Cake
(Ready in about 35 minutes | Servings 5)
Check out this fabulous keto dessert for your Instant Pot and wow your family on the next weekend.
Per serving: 193 Calories; 17.9g Fat; 9.1g Carbs; 1.2g Protein; 3.4g Sugars

Ingredients
1/2 pound raspberries
1 ½ tablespoons lemon juice
1 cup coconut flour
2 tablespoons cassava flour
1/2 teaspoon baking powder
1/8 teaspoon sea salt
1/4 cup coconut oil, melted
1 tablespoon monk fruit powder
1/2 teaspoon ground cinnamon
1/4 teaspoon grated nutmeg
1/2 teaspoon orange zest
1 teaspoon vanilla paste
1 ½ teaspoons powdered agar

Directions
Add 1 ½ cups water and a metal rack to the Instant Pot.
In a mixing bowl, thoroughly combine raspberries and lemon juice. Spread raspberries in the bottom of the pan.
In another mixing bowl, thoroughly combine coconut flour, cassava flour, baking powder, and sea salt.
In the third bowl, mix the coconut oil, monk fruit powder, cinnamon, nutmeg, orange zest, and vanilla. Add powdered agar and mix until everything is well incorporated.
Pour the liquid ingredients over dry ingredients and mix to form a dough; flatten it to form a circle.
Place this dough in a baking pan and cover the raspberries. Cover the pan with a sheet of aluminum foil.
Lower the pan onto the metal rack.
Secure the lid. Choose "Manual" mode and High pressure; cook for 27 minutes. Once cooking is complete, use a natural pressure release; carefully remove the lid.
Finally, turn the cake pan upside down and unmold it on a platter. Enjoy!

402. Chocolate Dream Cheesecake
(Ready in about 25 minutes + chilling time | Servings 10)
Chocolate lovers will love this fabulous low-carb dessert. This recipe is pretty adaptable so you can add shredded coconut or chunks of sugar-free chocolate too.
Per serving: 351 Calories; 35.6g Fat; 7.8g Carbs; 4.3g Protein; 1.7g Sugars

Ingredients
Crust:
1/3 cup coconut flour
1/3 cup almond flour
2 tablespoons arrowroot flour
2 tablespoons cocoa powder, unsweetened
2 tablespoons monk fruit powder
1/4 cup coconut oil, melted
Filling:
10 ounces cream cheese, softened
8 ounces heavy cream, softened
1 teaspoon monk fruit powder
1/2 cup cocoa powder, unsweetened
3 eggs yolks, at room temperature
1/3 cup sour cream
4 ounces butter, melted
1/2 teaspoon vanilla essence

Directions
Prepare your Instant Pot by adding 1 ½ cups of water and a metal rack to its bottom.
Coat a bottom of a baking pan with a piece of parchment paper.
In mixing bowl, combine coconut flour, almond flour, arrowroot powder, 2 tablespoons of cocoa powder, and 2 tablespoons of monk fruit powder; now, stir in melted coconut oil.
Press the crust mixture into the bottom of the prepared baking pan.
To make the filling, mix the cream cheese, heavy cream, monk fruit powder, and cocoa powder.
Now, fold in the eggs, sour cream, butter, and vanilla; continue to blend until everything is well incorporated,
Lower the baking pan onto the rack. Cover with a sheet of foil, making a foil sling.
Secure the lid. Choose "Manual" mode and High pressure; cook for 18 minutes. Once cooking is complete, use a natural pressure release; carefully remove the lid.
Place this cheesecake in your refrigerator for 3 to 4 hours. Bon appétit!

403. Grandma's Orange Cheesecake
(Ready in about 35 minutes + chilling time | Servings 10)
This fancy cheesecake can be served on any occasion. In addition, it takes 35 minutes to put together. Serve with frozen raspberries if desired.
Per serving: 188 Calories; 17.2g Fat; 4.5g Carbs; 5.5g Protein; 1.3g Sugars

Ingredients
Crust:
1/2 cup almond flour
1/2 cup coconut flour
1 ½ tablespoons powdered erythritol
1/4 teaspoon kosher salt
3 tablespoons butter, melted
Filling:
8 ounces sour cream, at room temperature
8 ounces cream cheese, at room temperature

1/2 cup powdered erythritol
3 tablespoons orange juice
1/2 teaspoon ginger powder
1 teaspoon vanilla extract
3 eggs, at room temperature
Directions
Line a round baking pan with a piece of parchment paper.
In a mixing bowl, thoroughly combine all crust ingredients in the order listed above.
Press the crust mixture into the bottom of the pan. Then, make the filling by mixing the sour cream and cream cheese until uniform and smooth; add the remaining ingredients and continue to beat until everything is well combined.
Pour the cream cheese mixture over the crust. Cover with aluminum foil, making a foil sling.
Place 1 ½ cups of water and a metal trivet in your Instant Pot. Then, place the pan on the metal rack.
Secure the lid. Choose "Manual" mode and High pressure; cook for 30 minutes. Once cooking is complete, use a natural pressure release; carefully remove the lid. Serve well chilled and enjoy!

404. Star Anise Raspberry Curd
(Ready in about 20 minutes + chilling time | Servings 4)
You can keep this curd in the refrigerator for about a month and add it to other desserts as a great, creamy topping.
Per serving: 334 Calories; 32.9g Fat; 7.6g Carbs; 2.9g Protein; 6.6g Sugars
Ingredients
4 ounces coconut oil, softened
3/4 cup Swerve
4 egg yolks, beaten
1/2 cup blueberries
1 teaspoon grated lemon zest
1/2 teaspoon vanilla extract
1/2 teaspoon star anise, ground
Directions
Blend the coconut oil and Swerve in a food processor. Gradually mix in the eggs; continue to blend for 1 minute longer.
Now, add blueberries, lemon zest, vanilla, and star anise. Divide the mixture among four Mason jars and cover them with lids.
Add 1 ½ cups of water and a metal rack to the Instant Pot. Now, lower your jars onto the rack.
Secure the lid. Choose "Manual" mode and High pressure; cook for 15 minutes. Once cooking is complete, use a natural pressure release; carefully remove the lid. Serve
Place in your refrigerator until ready to serve. Bon appétit!

405. Yummy and Easy Chocolate Mousse
(Ready in about 20 minutes + chilling time | Servings 6)

This mousse mixes up fast and easy in your Instant Pot. It has a sophisticated flavor and lighter-than-air texture.
Per serving: 205 Calories; 18.3g Fat; 9.2g Carbs; 3.2g Protein; 6.6g Sugars
Ingredients
1 cup full-fat milk
1 cup heavy cream
4 egg yolks, beaten
1/3 cup sugar
1/4 teaspoon grated nutmeg
1/4 teaspoon ground cinnamon
1/4 cup unsweetened cocoa powder
Directions
In a small pan, bring the milk and cream to a simmer. In a mixing dish, thoroughly combine the remaining ingredients. Add this egg mixture to the warm milk mixture.
Pour the mixture into ramekins.
Add 1 ½ cups of water and a metal rack to the Instant Pot. Now, lower your ramekins onto the rack.
Secure the lid. Choose "Manual" mode and High pressure; cook for 10 minutes. Once cooking is complete, use a natural pressure release; carefully remove the lid. Serve
Serve well chilled and enjoy!

406. Luscious Tropical Dream Dessert
(Ready in about 15 minutes + chilling time | Servings 4)
If you like a richer flavor, you can replace the vanilla essence with a pure room extract. In addition, serve topped with shredded coconut.
Per serving: 118 Calories; 8.2g Fat; 7.6g Carbs; 3.7g Protein; 2.6g Sugars
Ingredients
3 egg yolks, well whisked
1/3 cup Swerve
1/4 cup water
3 tablespoons cacao powder, unsweetened
3/4 cup whipping cream
1/3 cup coconut milk
1/4 cup shredded coconut
1 teaspoon vanilla essence
A pinch of grated nutmeg
A pinch of salt
Directions
Place the egg in a mixing bowl.
In a pan, heat the Swerve, water and cacao powder and whisk well to combine.
Now, stir in the whipping cream and milk; cook until heated through. Add shredded coconut, vanilla, nutmeg, and salt.
Now, slowly and gradually pour the chocolate mixture into the bowl with egg yolks. Stir to combine well and pour into ramekins.
Add 1 ½ cups of water and a metal rack to the Instant Pot. Now, lower your ramekins onto the rack.

Secure the lid. Choose "Manual" mode and High pressure; cook for 8 minutes. Once cooking is complete, use a quick pressure release; carefully remove the lid.
Place in your refrigerator until ready to serve. Bon appétit!

407. Almond and Chocolate Crème
(Ready in about 15 minutes | Servings 4)
Many store-bought desserts contain an added sugar so be careful or make your homemade one.
Per serving: 401 Calories; 37.1g Fat; 9.2g Carbs; 9.1g Protein; 2.7g Sugars
Ingredients
2 cups heavy whipping cream
1/2 cup water
4 eggs
1/3 cup Swerve
1 teaspoon almond extract
1 teaspoon vanilla extract
1/3 cup almonds, ground
2 tablespoons coconut oil, room temperature
4 tablespoons cacao powder
2 tablespoons gelatin
Directions
Start by adding 1 ½ cups of water and a metal rack to your Instant Pot.
Blend the cream, water, eggs, Swerve, almond extract, vanilla extract and almonds in your food processor. Add the remaining ingredients and process for a minute longer.
Divide the mixture between four Mason jars; cover your jars with lids. Lower the jars onto the rack.
Secure the lid. Choose "Manual" mode and High pressure; cook for 7 minutes. Once cooking is complete, use a natural pressure release; carefully remove the lid. Bon appétit!

408. Vanilla Rum Flan
(Ready in about 15 minutes | Servings 6)
This is a great idea for the next family gathering. Just be sure to make a double batch!
Per serving: 263 Calories; 21.2g Fat; 3.2g Carbs; 10.5g Protein; 2.8g Sugars
Ingredients
6 eggs
1 cup Swerve
1 ½ cups double cream
1/2 cup water
3 tablespoons dark rum
A pinch of salt
A pinch of freshly grated nutmeg
1/4 teaspoon ground cinnamon
1 teaspoon vanilla extract
Directions
Start by adding 1 ½ cups of water and a metal rack to your Instant Pot.
In a mixing bowl, thoroughly combine eggs and Swerve. Add double cream, water, rum, salt, nutmeg, cinnamon, and vanilla extract.

Pour mixture into a baking dish. Lower the dish onto the rack.
Secure the lid. Choose "Manual" mode and High pressure; cook for 10 minutes. Once cooking is complete, use a natural pressure release; carefully remove the lid.
Serve well chilled and enjoy!

409. Navel Orange Cheesecake
(Ready in about 30 minutes + chilling time | Servings 5)
Creamy and flavorful, this is the perfect dessert for a hot summer day. Serve well chilled!
Per serving: 268 Calories; 22.7g Fat; 6.6g Carbs; 9.5g Protein; 5.2g Sugars
Ingredients
9 ounces cream cheese
1/3 cup Swerve
1/2 teaspoon ginger powder
1 teaspoon grated orange zest
1 teaspoon vanilla extract
3 eggs
4 tablespoons double cream
1 tablespoon Swerve
1 navel orange, peeled and sliced
Directions
Start by adding 1 ½ cups of water and a metal rack to your Instant Pot. Now, spritz a baking pan with a nonstick cooking spray.
Beat cream cheese, 1/3 cup of Swerve, ginger, grated orange zest, and vanilla with an electric mixer.
Now, gradually fold in the eggs, and continue to mix until everything is well incorporated. Press this mixture into the prepared baking pan and cover with foil.
Secure the lid. Choose "Bean/Chili" mode and High pressure; cook for 25 minutes. Once cooking is complete, use a natural pressure release; carefully remove the lid.
Mix the cream and 1 tablespoon of Swerve; spread this topping on the cake. Allow it to cool on a wire rack.
Then, transfer your cake to the refrigerator. Garnish with orange slices and serve well chilled. Bon appétit!

410. Sunday Butterscotch Custard
(Ready in about 20 minutes + chilling time | Servings 4)
Serve this dessert well chilled. Keep it in your refrigerator up to three days. It scoops well after freezing too.
Per serving: 201 Calories; 17.7g Fat; 6.2g Carbs; 4.2g Protein; 1.2g Sugars
Ingredients
5 egg yolks
1/3 cup coconut milk, unsweetened
1/2 teaspoon vanilla extract
1 teaspoon monk fruit powder
1 tablespoon butterscotch flavoring
1/2 stick butter, melted

Directions
Blend the egg yolks with coconut milk, vanilla extract, monk fruit powder, and butterscotch flavoring.
Then, stir in the butter; stir until everything is well incorporated. Divide the mixture among four Mason jars and cover them with lids.
Add 1 ½ cups of water and a metal rack to the Instant Pot. Now, lower your jars onto the rack.
Secure the lid. Choose "Manual" mode and Low pressure; cook for 15 minutes. Once cooking is complete, use a natural pressure release; carefully remove the lid. Serve
Place in your refrigerator until ready to serve. Bon appétit!

411. Fabulous Blackberry Brownies

(Ready in about 30 minutes | Servings 8)
The hardest part of this recipe will be keeping your kids away from this attempting dessert. Yes, it's difficult to wait for it to harden, but it is worth waiting for.
Per serving: 151 Calories; 13.6g Fat; 6.7g Carbs; 4.1g Protein; 1.1g Sugars
Ingredients
4 eggs
1 ¼ cups coconut cream
1 teaspoon Stevia liquid concentrate
1/3 cup cocoa powder, unsweetened
1/2 teaspoon grated nutmeg
1/2 teaspoon cinnamon powder
1 teaspoon espresso coffee
1 teaspoon pure almond extract
1 teaspoon pure vanilla extract
1 teaspoon baking powder
A pinch of kosher salt
1 cup blackberries, fresh or frozen (thawed)
Instructions
Start by adding 1 ½ cups of water and a metal rack to your Instant Pot. Now, spritz a baking pan with a nonstick cooking spray.
Now, mix eggs, coconut cream, Stevia, cocoa powder, nutmeg, cinnamon, coffee, pure almond extract vanilla, baking powder, and salt with an electric mixer.
Crush the blackberries with a fork. After that, fold in your blackberries into the prepared mixture.
Pour the batter into the prepared pan.
Secure the lid. Choose "Bean/Chili" mode and High pressure; cook for 25 minutes. Once cooking is complete, use a natural pressure release; carefully remove the lid. Bon appétit!

412. Blueberry Dessert Porridge

(Ready in about 10 minutes | Servings 4)
An Instant Pot dessert porridge must be one of the most popular desserts in the world. The reason is obvious – it is simple to make and just irresistible!
Per serving: 219 Calories; 18.2g Fat; 9.2g Carbs; 5.6g Protein; 4.9g Sugars
Ingredients
6 tablespoons golden flax meal
6 tablespoons coconut flour
2 cups water
1/4 teaspoon freshly grated nutmeg
1/4 teaspoon Himalayan salt
3 egg, whisked
1/2 stick butter, softened
4 tablespoons double cream
4 tablespoons monk fruit powder
1 cup blueberries
Directions
Add all ingredients to the Instant Pot.
Secure the lid. Choose "Manual" mode and High pressure; cook for 5 minutes. Once cooking is complete, use a quick pressure release; carefully remove the lid.
Serve garnished with some extra berries if desired. Enjoy!

413. Coconut and Lemon Squares

(Ready in about 25 minutes | Servings 6)
These squares are simply amazing! Spice extracts lend an extra depth to the cake base, while fresh lemon juice and shredded coconut add a hint of tanginess and crunch to the filling.
Per serving: 173 Calories; 15.6g Fat; 2.5g Carbs; 6.2g Protein; 1.6g Sugars
Ingredients
Crust:
3/4 cup coconut flour
1/4 cup coconut oil
2 tablespoons Swerve
1/2 teaspoon pure lemon extract
1/2 teaspoon pure coconut extract
1/2 teaspoon pure vanilla extract
1/2 teaspoon baking powder
A pinch of grated nutmeg
A pinch of salt
Filling:
4 eggs
1/2 cup Swerve
3 tablespoons freshly squeezed lemon juice
3 tablespoons shredded coconut
1/4 teaspoon cinnamon powder
Directions
Start by adding 1 ½ cups of water and a metal rack to your Instant Pot. Now, spritz a baking pan with a nonstick cooking spray (butter flavor).
Then, thoroughly combine all crust ingredients in your food processor. Now, spread the crust mixture evenly on the bottom of the prepared pan. Do not forget to prick a few holes with a fork.
Lower the baking pan onto the rack.
Secure the lid. Choose "Manual" mode and High pressure; cook for 8 minutes. Once cooking is complete, use a quick pressure release; carefully remove the lid.
Meanwhile, thoroughly combine all filling ingredients in your food processor. Spread the filling mixture evenly over top of the warm crust.

Return to the Instant Pot.
Secure the lid. Choose "Manual" mode and High pressure; cook for 15 minutes. Once cooking is complete, use a quick pressure release; carefully remove the lid.
Cut into squares and serve at room temperature or chilled. Bon appétit!

414. Zucchini and Peanut Cake

(Ready in about 30 minutes | Servings 6)
You can bake this delicious dessert in the oven, but you'll get an extra-moist cake in your Instant Pot.
Per serving: 121 Calories; 7.3g Fat; 7.9g Carbs; 6.5g Protein; 4.3g Sugars

Ingredients
1/2 cup peanut butter
1 pound zucchini, shredded
1/4 cup Swerve
2 eggs, beaten
1/2 teaspoon ground star anise
1 teaspoon ground cinnamon
1/4 teaspoon grated nutmeg
1/2 teaspoon rum extract
1/2 teaspoon vanilla
1/2 teaspoon baking powder

Directions
Start by adding 1 ½ cups of water and a metal trivet to your Instant Pot. Now, spritz a baking pan with a nonstick cooking spray.
In a mixing dish, thoroughly combine all ingredients until uniform, creamy and smooth. Pour the batter into the prepared pan.
Lower the pan onto the trivet.
Secure the lid. Choose "Bean/Chili" mode and High pressure; cook for 25 minutes. Once cooking is complete, use a natural pressure release; carefully remove the lid.
Allow your cake to cool completely before cutting and serving. Bon appétit!

415. Sophisticated Lavender Brownies

(Ready in about 30 minutes | Servings 6)
No special equipment needed to whip up this magnificent dessert! Coconut oil is the best option, but you can use grapeseed oil or another neutral oil in these brownies.
Per serving: 384 Calories; 36.6g Fat; 7.2g Carbs; 7.7g Protein; 1.3g Sugars

Ingredients
4 ounces chocolate, sugar-free
1/2 cup coconut oil
2 cups Swerve
4 eggs, whisked
1 teaspoon vanilla paste
1/4 teaspoon sea salt
1/4 teaspoon grated nutmeg
1/2 teaspoon dried lavender flowers
1/4 cup almond flour
1/2 cup whipped cream

Directions
Start by adding 1 ½ cups of water and a metal trivet to your Instant Pot. Now, spritz a baking pan with a nonstick cooking spray.
Thoroughly combine the chocolate, coconut oil, and Swerve. Gradually, whisk in the eggs. Add the vanilla paste, salt, nutmeg, lavender flowers and almond flour; mix until everything is well incorporated.
Secure the lid. Choose "Bean/Chili" mode and High pressure; cook for 25 minutes. Once cooking is complete, use a natural pressure release; carefully remove the lid.
Top with whipped cream and serve well chilled. Bon appétit!

416. Romantic Rosewater Dessert Porridge

(Ready in about 10 minutes | Servings 2)
Sweet enough to work as a dessert but healthy enough to replace your afternoon snack, this porridge is made with common ingredients such as coconut, seeds, coconut milk, and Stevia.
Per serving: 363 Calories; 36.4g Fat; 9.2g Carbs; 4.9g Protein; 4.8g Sugars

Ingredients
1/2 cup coconut shreds
1 tablespoon sunflower seeds
2 tablespoons flax seeds
2 cardamom pods, crushed slightly
1 teaspoon ground cinnamon
1 teaspoon Stevia powdered extract
1 teaspoon rosewater
1/2 cup water
1 cup coconut milk

Directions
Add all ingredients to the Instant Pot.
Secure the lid. Choose "Manual" mode and High pressure; cook for 5 minutes. Once cooking is complete, use a quick pressure release; carefully remove the lid.
Ladle into two serving bowls and serve warm. Enjoy!

417. Coconut and Raspberry Cupcakes

(Ready in about 35 minutes | Servings 6)
Life is a festival! Coconut and almond flour combine with double cream and butter to create these light, festive cupcakes. Topped with a frosting and frozen raspberries, they are irresistible.
Per serving: 403 Calories; 42.1g Fat; 4.1g Carbs; 4.2g Protein; 2.1g Sugars

Ingredients
Cupcakes:
1/2 cup coconut flour
1/2 cup almond flour
1/2 teaspoon baking soda
1 teaspoon baking powder
A pinch of salt
A pinch of grated nutmeg
1 teaspoon ginger powder

1 stick butter, at room temperature
1/2 cup Swerve
3 eggs, beaten
1/2 teaspoon pure coconut extract
1/2 teaspoon pure vanilla extract
1/2 cup double cream
Frosting:
1 stick butter, at room temperature
1/2 cup Swerve
1 teaspoon pure vanilla extract
1/2 teaspoon coconut extract
6 tablespoons coconut, shredded
3 tablespoons raspberry, puréed
6 frozen raspberries
Directions
Start by adding 1 ½ cups of water and a rack to your Instant Pot.
In a mixing dish, thoroughly combine the cupcake ingredients. Divide the batter between silicone cupcake liners. Cover with a piece of foil.
Place the cupcakes on the rack.
Secure the lid. Choose "Manual" mode and High pressure; cook for 25 minutes. Once cooking is complete, use a natural pressure release; carefully remove the lid.
In the meantime, thoroughly combine the frosting ingredients. Put this mixture into a piping bag and top your cupcakes.
Garnish with frozen raspberries and enjoy!

418. Mixed Berry Mini Cheesecakes
(Ready in about 25 minutes | Servings 6)
Mini cheesecakes? It might sound complicated, but you'd be surprised how easy it is to make them in your Instant Pot.
Per serving: 232 Calories; 22.1g Fat; 4.8g Carbs; 5.7g Protein; 1.9g Sugars
Ingredients
1/4 cup sesame seed flour
1/4 cup hazelnut flour
1/2 cup coconut flour
1 ½ teaspoons baking powder
A pinch of kosher salt
A pinch of freshly grated nutmeg
1/2 teaspoon ground star anise
1/2 teaspoon ground cinnamon
1/2 stick butter
1 cup Swerve
2 eggs, beaten
1/2 cup cream cheese
1/3 cup fresh mixed berries
1/2 vanilla paste
Directions
Start by adding 1 ½ cups of water and a rack to your Instant Pot.
In a mixing dish, thoroughly combine all of the above ingredients. Divide the batter between lightly greased ramekins. Cover with a piece of foil.
Place the ramekins on the rack.
Secure the lid. Choose "Manual" mode and High pressure; cook for 20 minutes. Once cooking is complete, use a natural pressure release; carefully remove the lid.

419. Chocolate and Hazelnut Birthday Cake
(Ready in about 35 minutes + chilling time | Servings 8)
This moist chocolate cake is topped with a homemade ganache and serve well chilled for the best keto birthday party ever!
Per serving: 230 Calories; 18.8g Fat; 9.1g Carbs; 8.9g Protein; 1.4g Sugars
Ingredients
Batter:
1 cup hazelnut flour
2 tablespoons arrowroot starch
1/2 cup cocoa powder
1 ¼ teaspoons baking powder
1/4 teaspoon kosher salt
1/4 teaspoon freshly grated nutmeg
6 eggs, whisked
8 tablespoons coconut oil, melted
1 teaspoon pure vanilla extract
1/2 teaspoon pure hazelnut extract
2/3 cup Swerve
1/3 cup full-fat milk
Hazelnut Ganache:
1/2 cup heavy cream
5 ounces dark chocolate, sugar-free
2 tablespoons coconut oil
Directions
Start by adding 1 ½ cups of water and a metal rack to your Instant Pot. Now, lightly grease a baking pan with a nonstick cooking spray.
In a mixing bowl, thoroughly combine dry ingredients for the batter. In another bowl, mix wet ingredients for the batter.
Add wet mixture to the dry mixture; mix to combine well. Pour the mixture into the prepared baking pan.
Secure the lid. Choose "Bean/Chili" mode and High pressure; cook for 30 minutes. Once cooking is complete, use a natural pressure release; carefully remove the lid.
Now, place the cake pan on a wire rack until it is cool to the touch. Allow it to cool completely before frosting.
Meanwhile, make your ganache. In a medium pan, bring the heavy cream to a boil. Turn the heat off as soon as you see the bubbles.
Add chocolate and coconut oil and whisk to combine well. Frost the cake and serve well chilled.

420. Party Blueberry Cobbler
(Ready in about 20 minutes | Servings 6)
This ketogenic blueberry cobbler is easy to make in the Instant Pot and it takes less than 20 minutes to prepare.

Per serving: 240 Calories; 20.5g Fat; 9.4g Carbs; 4.8g Protein; 5.1g Sugars
Ingredients
1 cup almond flour
3 tablespoons sunflower seed flour
1/2 cup Swerve
1/2 teaspoon baking soda
1 teaspoon baking powder
1/4 cup coconut cream
1/4 cup water
1/4 cup coconut oil, softened
2 tablespoons dark rum
1/2 teaspoon vanilla
1/2 cup blueberries
Directions
Start by adding 1 ½ cups of water and a metal trivet to your Instant Pot.
Mix all ingredients, except blueberries, until everything is well incorporated. Spoon the mixture into a lightly greased baking pan.
Fold in blueberries and gently stir to combine. Lower the baking dish onto the trivet.
Secure the lid. Choose "Bean/Chili" mode and High pressure; cook for 15 minutes. Once cooking is complete, use a natural pressure release; carefully remove the lid.
Allow the cobbler to cool slightly before serving. Bon appétit!

421. Easy Mexican-Style Flan
(Ready in about 15 minutes | Servings 4)
Take things up a notch and make your flan more exciting and interesting with common Mexican spices!
Per serving: 217 Calories; 16.8g Fat; 4.9g Carbs; 11.4g Protein; 3.7g Sugars
Ingredients
4 eggs, beaten
1 teaspoon liquid Stevia
1/4 cup coconut cream
1/4 cup hot water
1 cup coconut milk
1/8 teaspoon kosher salt
1/2 teaspoon cardamom, ground
1/2 teaspoon Jamaican allspice
1/4 teaspoon grated nutmeg
1/2 teaspoon vanilla extract
1 teaspoon orange rind, grated
Directions
Start by adding 1 ½ cups of water and a metal rack to your Instant Pot.
In a mixing bowl, thoroughly combine eggs and Stevia. Add coconut cream, water, coconut milk, salt, cardamom, allspice, nutmeg, vanilla, and orange rind. Pour mixture into a baking dish. Lower the dish onto the rack.
Secure the lid. Choose "Manual" mode and High pressure; cook for 10 minutes. Once cooking is complete, use a natural pressure release; carefully remove the lid.
Serve well chilled and enjoy!

422. Almond and Blackberry Crisp
(Ready in about 15 minutes | Servings 4)
If you're following a ketogenic diet, you can run out of ideas for dessert. Do not worry, we've got you covered. You can use blueberries, raspberries or cherries too.
Per serving: 255 Calories; 24.6g Fat; 8.6g Carbs; 3.4g Protein; 3.5g Sugars
Ingredients
1/2 pound blackberries
1 teaspoon ground cinnamon
1/4 teaspoon grated nutmeg
1/2 teaspoon ground cardamom
1/2 teaspoon vanilla paste
1/2 cup water
1/4 cup Swerve
5 tablespoons coconut oil, melted
1/2 cup almonds, roughly chopped
1/4 cup coconut flour
1/4 teaspoon Stevia
A pinch of salt
Directions
Place blackberries on the bottom of your Instant Pot. Sprinkle with cinnamon, nutmeg, and cardamom. Add vanilla, water and Swerve.
In a mixing bowl, thoroughly combine the remaining ingredients. Drop by the spoonful on top of the blackberries.
Secure the lid. Choose "Manual" mode and High pressure; cook for 10 minutes. Once cooking is complete, use a natural pressure release; carefully remove the lid.
Serve at room temperature and enjoy!

423. Mom's Red Velvet Cheesecake
(Ready in about 40 minutes | Servings 6)
Here's the perfect dessert to impress your guests or family. Throw some extra berries on top as a bonus.
Per serving: 373 Calories; 36.7g Fat; 5.1g Carbs; 8g Protein; 2.6g Sugars
Ingredients
1/2 cup almond flour
1/2 cup coconut flour
4 tablespoons coconut oil, melted
3/4 pound cream cheese, at room temperature
3/4 cup Swerve
3 eggs
A pinch of salt
A pinch of grated nutmeg
1/2 teaspoon ground cinnamon
1/2 teaspoon ground star anise
1 teaspoon vanilla extract
1 teaspoon red food coloring
Directions
Start by adding 1 ½ cups of water and a metal rack to your Instant Pot.
In a mixing bowl, thoroughly combine almond flour, coconut flour, and coconut oil. Press this mixture into a lightly greased cheesecake pan.

In another mixing bowl, beat the cream cheese together with Swerve. Fold in the eggs, one at a time, and continue to beat until well mixed.
Then, add the spices and extract; mix until everything is well incorporated. Spread the filling over the top of your cheesecake. Lower the pan onto the rack.
Secure the lid. Choose "Bean/Chili" mode and High pressure; cook for 35 minutes. Once cooking is complete, use a natural pressure release; carefully remove the lid. Bon appétit!

424. Traditional Carrot Cake
(Ready in about 35 minutes | Servings 8)
Sophisticated, airy and delicious, Instant Pot carrot cake is a big hit on any occasion. A cheesecake frosting shines in this amazing dessert recipe!
Per serving: 381 Calories; 35.1g Fat; 8.4g Carbs; 10.3g Protein; 3.7g Sugars
Ingredients
Carrot Cake:
2 cups carrots, grated
1 cup almond flour
1/2 cup coconut, shredded
1/4 cup hazelnuts, chopped
1/4 teaspoon ground cloves
1/4 teaspoon grated nutmeg
1/2 teaspoon ground cinnamon
1/2 teaspoon baking soda
1 teaspoon baking powder
4 tablespoons Swerve
1 teaspoon pure vanilla extract
4 eggs, beaten
1 stick butter, melted
Cream Cheese Frosting:
1 cup cream cheese
2 tablespoons Swerve
1/2 teaspoon pure vanilla extract
Directions
Start by adding 1 ½ cups of water and a metal rack to your Instant Pot. Now, spritz a cheesecake pan with a nonstick cooking spray.
In a mixing bowl, thoroughly combine dry ingredients for the cake. Then, mix the wet ingredients until everything is well combined.
Pour the wet mixture into the dry mixture and stir to combine well. Spoon the batter into the cheesecake pan.
Cover with a sheet of foil. Lower the pan onto the rack.
Secure the lid. Choose "Bean/Chili" mode and High pressure; cook for 30 minutes. Once cooking is complete, use a quick pressure release; carefully remove the lid.
Meanwhile, mix the frosting ingredients. Frost the carrot cake and serve chilled. Enjoy!

425. Brownie Squares with Blackberry-Goat Cheese Swirl
(Ready in about 30 minutes | Servings 8)
These brownies will be a great addition to your dessert table. They are eye-catching, impressive and oh so delicious!
Per serving: 309 Calories; 27.6g Fat; 7.4g Carbs; 10.8g Protein; 2.1g Sugars
Ingredients
Brownies:
5 tablespoons coconut oil, melted
1 cup Swerve
1/4 cup cocoa powder, unsweetened
3 teaspoons water
1/2 teaspoon vanilla extract
3 eggs, beaten
1/4 cup golden flax meal
3/4 cup almond flour
1/2 teaspoon baking soda
1/2 teaspoon baking powder
A pinch of salt
A pinch of grated nutmeg
1/4 cup chocolate chunks, sugar-free
Blackberry Goat Cheese Swirl:
2 tablespoons unsalted butter, softened
4 ounces goat cheese, softened
2 ounces cream cheese, softened
1 cup blackberries, fresh or frozen (thawed)
1 tablespoon Swerve
1/2 teaspoon almond extract
A pinch of salt
Directions
Start by adding 1 ½ cups of water and a metal rack to your Instant Pot. Now, spritz a square cake pan with a nonstick cooking spray.
Mix the coconut oil with Swerve, cocoa powder, water, and vanilla until well combined. Mix in the eggs, flour, baking soda, baking powder, salt, and nutmeg.
Mix until smooth and creamy. Add the chocolate and mix one more time. Add the batter to the prepared pan.
Secure the lid. Choose "Manual" mode and High pressure; cook for 25 minutes. Once cooking is complete, use a quick pressure release; carefully remove the lid.
Invert your brownie onto a platter. Allow it to cool to room temperature.
Meanwhile, make the blackberry-goat cheese swirl. Beat the butter and cheese with an electric mixer; add blackberries, Swerve, almond extract and salt and continue to beat until light and fluffy.
Drop this mixture on top of your brownie in spoonfuls; then swirl it with a knife. Bon appétit!

426. Triple-Berry and Bourbon Granola Crisp
(Ready in about 20 minutes | Servings 8)
This sophisticated granola crisp screams summer, but it's delicious year-round. You can use puréed fresh berries if desired.
Per serving: 236 Calories; 20.5g Fat; 9g Carbs; 7.3g Protein; 2.9g Sugars

Ingredients
2 cups mixed raspberries, blueberries and blackberries, fresh
2 ounces hazelnuts, chopped
2 ounces almonds, chopped
1 tablespoon sunflower kernels
1 tablespoon sesame seeds
3 ounces shredded coconut, unsweetened
1 teaspoon liquid Stevia
1/4 cup cocoa powder
5 tablespoons coconut oil, melted
1 teaspoon hazelnut extract
1 teaspoon vanilla extract
3 tablespoons bourbon
1/2 teaspoon ground cloves
1 teaspoon ground cinnamon
1/8 teaspoon sea salt
3 eggs

Directions
Place fresh berries on the bottom of a lightly greased Instant Pot.
In a mixing bowl, thoroughly combine the remaining ingredients. Place this granola mixture over the top of the raspberries.
Secure the lid. Choose "Manual" mode and High pressure; cook for 10 minutes. Once cooking is complete, use a natural pressure release; carefully remove the lid.
Serve warm or at room temperature. Bon appétit!

427. Coconut and Chocolate Fudge

(Ready in about 10 minutes + chilling time | Servings 6)

What about fudge recipes in an Instant Pot? This recipe is so easy to make but the hardest part of this recipe will be keeping your family away from this dessert. However, it is worth waiting for.

Per serving: 189 Calories; 19.8g Fat; 5.8g Carbs; 2.1g Protein; 1.6g Sugars

Ingredients
1/2 cup melted coconut oil
1/2 cup coconut milk
1/2 cup coconut flour
1/2 cup cocoa powder
1/2 cup Swerve
1/4 teaspoon ground cinnamon
1/4 teaspoon ground cloves
1 teaspoon vanilla paste
1 teaspoon coconut extract
A pinch sea salt
A pinch of grated nutmeg

Directions
Place coconut oil, milk, flour, cocoa powder, and Swerve in the Instant Pot.
Add the remaining ingredients and mix until everything is well incorporated.
Press the "Sauté" button and let it simmer stir until thoroughly heated.
Now, spoon the mixture into a baking sheet lined with a piece of foil. Transfer to your refrigerator for 2 to 3 hours.
Cut into squares and serve. Bon appétit!

428. Orange-White Chocolate Mini Lava Cakes

(Ready in about 10 minutes | Servings 4)

The Instant Pot makes the best and fastest lava cakes ever, with the steam making them super moist, light and gooey.

Per serving: 409 Calories; 36.8g Fat; 9.2g Carbs; 11.9g Protein; 1.1g Sugars

Ingredients
Nonstick cooking spray
4 ounces white chocolate morsels, sugar-free
4 tablespoons coconut oil
4 eggs
1/8 teaspoon coarse salt
1/2 teaspoon ground cinnamon
1/4 teaspoon ground cloves
1/4 teaspoon freshly grated nutmeg
1/2 teaspoon vanilla paste
2 drops orange essential oil
1/3 cup confectioners' Swerve
2/3 cup almond flour

Directions
Start by adding 1 ½ cups of water and a metal rack to your Instant Pot. Now, spritz 4 ramekins with a nonstick cooking spray.
Melt the chocolate and coconut oil in a microwave. Then, whip the eggs with an electric mixer, adding the salt, cinnamon, cloves, cloves nutmeg, vanilla, orange essential oil and confectioners' Swerve.
Add the melted chocolate mixture and mix again until everything is well incorporated. Lastly, stir in almond flour and mix again.
Spoon the batter into the prepared ramekins. Secure the lid. Choose "Manual" mode and High pressure; cook for 6 minutes.
Once cooking is complete, use a natural pressure release; carefully remove the lid. Invert cakes onto the serving plates and serve warm. Enjoy!

429. Blueberry and Cinnamon Muffins

(Ready in about 30 minutes | Servings 6)

Here's a new go-to ketogenic muffin recipe! A blend of blueberries and lime juice brings a fruity flavor, while cinnamon brings a deep and oriental flavor to these muffins.

Per serving: 209 Calories; 18.3g Fat; 8.1g Carbs; 5.6g Protein; 3.3g Sugars

Ingredients
3/4 cup almond flour
1/4 cup coconut flour
1/2 teaspoon baking powder
A pinch of salt
A pinch of grated nutmeg
1 ½ teaspoons cinnamon, ground

3 whole eggs, beaten
1/4 cup coconut oil
1/4 cup granulated Swerve
A few drops vanilla butternut flavor
1/2 teaspoon grated lemon peel
Topping:
1 cup blueberries
4 tablespoons water
1/2 tablespoon freshly squeezed lime juice
1/2 cup Swerve
1 teaspoon arrowroot, mixed with 1 teaspoon water
Directions
Start by adding 1 ½ cups of water and a rack to your Instant Pot.
In a mixing dish, thoroughly combine all ingredients for the muffins. Divide the batter between silicone cupcake liners. Cover with a piece of foil.
Place the cupcakes on the rack.
Secure the lid. Choose "Manual" mode and High pressure; cook for 25 minutes. Once cooking is complete, use a natural pressure release; carefully remove the lid.
In the meantime, place the blueberries, water, lime juice and Swerve into a saucepan over moderate heat; let it simmer until thoroughly heated.
Now, stir in the arrowroot slurry and simmer until the sauce is reduced. Place this topping over your muffins and serve at room temperature.

430. Zucchini Bundt Cake with Cream Cheese Frosting

(Ready in about 40 minutes | Servings 6)
Delicate zucchini, fresh eggs, nuts, and cocoa powder. You just can't get enough of this cake recipe!
Per serving: 352 Calories; 32.1g Fat; 9.1g Carbs; 9.2g Protein; 3.7g Sugars
Ingredients
Bundt Cake:
1 cup almond flour
1 cup Swerve
2 ounces cacao powder
1 teaspoon baking soda
1 teaspoon baking powder
1/4 teaspoon ground cinnamon
1/8 teaspoon grated nutmeg
A pinch of salt
4 eggs plus 1 egg yolk
1 stick butter, softened
1/2 pound zucchini, puréed
1 teaspoon vanilla extract
Frosting:
3 ounces cream cheese, softened
1/2 stick butter, softened
1 tablespoon milk
1 ½ teaspoons liquid stevia
1 ounce walnuts, chopped
Directions
Start by adding 1 ½ cups of water and a metal trivet to your Instant Pot. Spritz a 6-cup bundt pan with a nonstick cooking spray (butter-flavored).
Beat all ingredients for the cake using an electric mixer; beat on low speed for 40 seconds. Then, mix on medium speed for 2 to 3 minutes longer.
Spoon the mixture into the prepared pan. Cover tightly with a piece of foil. Lower the pan onto the trivet.
Secure the lid. Choose "Manual" mode and High pressure; cook for 25 minutes. Once cooking is complete, use a natural pressure release; carefully remove the lid.
Allow your cake to cool for 5 to 10 minutes before inverting onto a platter.
In a mixing bowl, combine cream cheese, butter, milk, and stevia using an electric mixer. Frost the cake, sprinkle with chopped walnuts, and serve well chilled. Enjoy!

431. Peanut and Chocolate Chip Cupcakes

(Ready in about 30 minutes | Servings 8)
Here is the recipe for true chocoholics! Double chocolate, peanut butter and sugar-free cupcakes sound like a dream.
Per serving: 185 Calories; 15.7g Fat; 7.2g Carbs; 6.6g Protein; 1.1g Sugars
Ingredients
1/4 cup almond flour
1/4 cup peanut flour
1/3 cup cocoa powder
2 ounces chocolate chunks, sugar-free
1/4 cup Xylitol
1/3 cup heavy whipped cream
2 tablespoons peanut butter
3 eggs, beaten
1/2 teaspoon baking powder
1/2 teaspoon baking soda
3 tablespoons coconut oil, softened
1/2 teaspoon vanilla paste
1/4 teaspoon ground cinnamon
A pinch of salt
Directions
Start by adding 1 ½ cups of water and a metal trivet to your Instant Pot.
In a mixing dish, thoroughly combine all ingredients for the cupcakes. Divide the batter between silicone cupcake liners. Cover with a piece of aluminum foil.
Place the cupcakes on the trivet.
Secure the lid. Choose "Manual" mode and High pressure; cook for 25 minutes. Once cooking is complete, use a natural pressure release; carefully remove the lid. Bon appétit!

432. Crêpe with Cinnamon-Cream Cheese Topping

(Ready in about 45 minutes | Servings 6)
The Instant Pot makes fantastic crepes, cooking them equally all the way through! The steam will make it extra light and fluffy.
Per serving: 252 Calories; 22.7g Fat; 6.8g Carbs; 8.3g Protein; 2.6g Sugars

Ingredients
3 eggs
1 cup coconut milk
1 cup almond flour
1/2 cup coconut flour
1 teaspoon baking soda
1 teaspoon baking powder
A pinch of kosher salt
1/4 cup granulated Swerve
Cinnamon-Cream Cheese Topping:
2 ounces ricotta cheese, at room temperature
2 tablespoons Swerve
1/2 teaspoon vanilla extract
1 teaspoon cinnamon powder
2 teaspoons ghee, melted
Directions
In a mixing dish, thoroughly combine the eggs and coconut milk.
Then, add the flour, baking soda, baking powder, salt, and Swerve.
Spritz the bottom and sides of your Instant Pot with a nonstick cooking spray. Add the crepe mixture and secure the lid.
Choose "Multigrain" mode and Low pressure; cook for 40 minutes. Cook until golden brown and crispy on the top. Once cooking is complete, use a natural pressure release; carefully remove the lid.
In the meantime, thoroughly combine all ingredients for the topping. Spread the topping over your crêpe and serve warm. Bon appétit!

433. White Peanut Butter and Chocolate Fudge

(Ready in about 10 minutes + chilling time | Servings 6)
Everyone will love this fancy white chocolate fudge. Every bite will melt in your mouth thanks to its creaminess.
Per serving: 259 Calories; 24.2g Fat; 7.6g Carbs; 3.3g Protein; 3.8g Sugars
Ingredients
1 stick butter, melted
1/2 cup coconut milk
1/2 cup Swerve
1/2 cup white chocolate chips, unsweetened
1/3 cup melted peanut butter
1/4 teaspoon ground cloves
1/4 teaspoon ground cinnamon
1 teaspoon vanilla extract
1/8 teaspoon kosher salt
1/8 teaspoon grated nutmeg
Directions
Place the butter, milk, and Swerve in your Instant Pot. Press the "Sauté" button and let it simmer until thoroughly heated.
Stir in the chocolate chips; stir until the chocolate is completely melted. Add the other ingredients and continue to stir until everything is well incorporated.
Now, spoon the mixture into a square cookie sheet lined with a piece of foil. Transfer to your refrigerator for 2 to 3 hours.
Cut into squares and serve. Bon appétit!

434. Key Lime Curd

(Ready in about 15 minutes + chilling time | Servings 3)
The curd is an easy but impressive dessert that you can prepare up to two days ahead of time. Key lime will add a touch of glamour and sophistication to your dessert.
Per serving: 414 Calories; 42.3g Fat; 8.2g Carbs; 3.8g Protein; 0.8g Sugars
Ingredients
1/2 cup coconut oil, softened
3/4 cup Swerve, granulated
3 large eggs
1 egg yolk
2 key limes, freshly squeezed
1/2 tablespoon key lime zest
1/8 teaspoon kosher salt
Directions
Start by adding 1 ½ cups of water and a metal rack to your Instant Pot.
Thoroughly combine the coconut oil and Swerve in a food processor. Gradually fold in the eggs and egg yolk; continue to mix for 1 minute longer.
Now, add the other ingredients. Divide the mixture among three Mason jars and cover them with lids. Secure the lid. Choose "Manual" mode and High pressure; cook for 12 minutes. Once cooking is complete, use a natural pressure release; carefully remove the lid.
Place in your refrigerator until ready to serve. Bon appétit!

435. Chunky Walnut Mini Cheesecakes

(Ready in about 20 minutes + chilling time | Servings 6)
Cream cheese, chocolate morsels, chunky walnut butter, creamy chocolate topping... these mini cheesecakes will blow your mind!
Per serving: 322 Calories; 29.9g Fat; 7.2g Carbs; 6.9g Protein; 2.2g Sugars
Ingredients
10 ounces cream cheese
2 ounces sour cream
1 egg, beaten
3 tablespoons walnut butter, chunky
1/4 cup chocolate morsels, sugar-free
1/2 teaspoon pure almond extract
1/2 teaspoon pure vanilla extract
1 teaspoon liquid Stevia
Topping:
2 ounces baker's chocolate, sugar-free
1/2 cup whipping cream
Directions

Start by adding 1 ½ cups of water and a metal rack to your Instant Pot. Line muffin cup holes with liners. Blend all of the above ingredients in your food processor until everything is well incorporated. Divide the batter among muffin cups. Lower the muffin cups onto the rack.
Secure the lid. Choose "Manual" mode and High pressure; cook for 15 minutes. Once cooking is complete, use a natural pressure release; carefully remove the lid.
Allow these mini cheesecakes to cool completely. Then, transfer them to your freezer and freeze until solid.
Now, microwave baker's chocolate in a glass dish. Fold in the cream and beat to combine well. Add a splash of water if needed.
Pour the cream over the top of frozen cheesecakes. Bon appétit!

436. Mint and Coconut Mousse
(Ready in about 30 minutes + chilling time | Servings 4)
This totally yummy mousse is loaded with coconut milk, eggs, and mint aromas. Serve with a dollop of sugar-free vanilla ice cream if desired.
Per serving: 271 Calories; 25.4g Fat; 5.9g Carbs; 7.5g Protein; 3.2g Sugars
Ingredients
1 ¼ cups coconut milk, unsweetened
4 eggs
1/2 cup Swerve, powdered
4 tablespoons coconut, shredded
4 drops mint extract
Directions
Start by adding 1 ½ cups of water and a metal rack to your Instant Pot.
In a mixing bowl, thoroughly combine all of the above ingredients. Pour the mixture into four Mason jars. Cover with their lids.
Secure the lid. Choose "Manual" mode and High pressure; cook for 25 minutes. Once cooking is complete, use a natural pressure release; carefully remove the lid.
Serve well chilled and enjoy!

437. Espresso Molten Cake
(Ready in about 10 minutes | Servings 6)
Espresso powder and cocoa powder are superstars of this easy, yummy dessert recipe. It will definitely impress all coffee lovers.
Per serving: 152 Calories; 12.1g Fat; 8.8g Carbs; 7.3g Protein; 1.6g Sugars
Ingredients
1/2 cup cocoa powder, unsweetened
1 teaspoon liquid Stevia
1/2 teaspoon baking soda
1/2 teaspoon baking powder
1/8 teaspoon sea salt
2 teaspoons espresso powder
2 eggs
1/2 cup double cream
1/4 teaspoon cinnamon powder
1/4 teaspoon grated nutmeg
1/2 teaspoon vanilla extract
Directions
Start by adding 1 ½ cups of water and a metal rack to your Instant Pot. Now, spritz a heatproof bowl with a nonstick cooking spray.
Now, whip all ingredients with an electric mixer.
Secure the lid. Choose "Manual" mode and High pressure; cook for 6 minutes. Once cooking is complete, use a natural pressure release; carefully remove the lid.
Invert your cake onto the serving platter and serve at room temperature. Bon appétit!

438. Cherry Baby Cakes
(Ready in about 25 minutes | Servings 6)
You no longer need to preheat an oven to bake a fruit cheesecake – you just need an Instant Pot! In this recipe, you can use fresh or frozen and sour or sweet cherries.
Per serving: 255 Calories; 21.6g Fat; 6.1g Carbs; 9.7g Protein; 2.8g Sugars
Ingredients
4 eggs, beaten
1/3 cup granulated Swerve
2 tablespoons coconut oil, melted
1/2 cup cream cheese
1/2 cup Greek-style yogurt
1 teaspoon vanilla extract
1/2 cup almond flour
1/2 cup coconut flour
A pinch of grated nutmeg
A pinch of salt
1 teaspoon baking powder
1/2 teaspoon baking soda
1/2 cup cherries, pitted
Directions
Start by adding 1 ½ cups of water and a metal rack to your Instant Pot. Now, spritz 6 ramekins with a nonstick cooking spray.
Whip the eggs and Swerve until uniform and smooth. Add the coconut oil, cheese, yogurt, and vanilla; mix until everything is well incorporated.
In another bowl, thoroughly combine the flour, nutmeg, salt, baking powder, and baking soda. Add this mixture to the egg/cheese mixture.
Fold in the cherries and gently stir to combine. Pour the batter into the prepared ramekins.
Secure the lid. Choose "Manual" mode and High pressure; cook for 20 minutes. Once cooking is complete, use a natural pressure release; carefully remove the lid.
Transfer your ramekins to a cooling rack. Loosen the sides of your cakes from the ramekins and turn them over onto plates. Serve well-chilled.

439. Raspberry and Chocolate Lava Muffins

(Ready in about 15 minutes | Servings 6)
Ooey-gooey, berry lava muffins are an impressive dessert that you will make over and over again. You can use blackberries or blueberries as well.
Per serving: 180 Calories; 17.6g Fat; 7.4g Carbs; 3.2g Protein; 1.2g Sugars
Ingredients
1 cup chocolate, sugar-free
1 stick butter
3 eggs
1 cup Swerve
1 cup almond flour
A pinch of salt
1/2 teaspoon vanilla extract
1/2 teaspoon ground star anise
1/2 teaspoon ground cinnamon
1 ½ cups raspberries, mashed with a fork
1/4 cup confectioner's Swerve
Directions
Start by adding 1 ½ cups of water and a metal rack to your Instant Pot. Now, spritz muffin cups with a nonstick cooking spray.
Melt the chocolate in a microwave. Add butter and whip with an electric mixer. Fold in the eggs and mix with the machine running.
Gradually mix in Swerve and flour. Then, add the salt, vanilla, star anise, and cinnamon. Lastly, fold in raspberries and gently stir to combine well.
Divide the mixture among muffin cups.
Secure the lid. Choose "Manual" mode and High pressure; cook for 6 minutes. Once cooking is complete, use a natural pressure release; carefully remove the lid.
Dust your muffins with confectioner's Swerve. Serve warm and enjoy!

440. Hazelnut and Cranberry Cookies

(Ready in about 20 minutes | Servings 6)
It's tea time! This cookie recipe is easy to follow and quick to prepare. You can add mixed berries to the batter.
Per serving: 213 Calories; 20.7g Fat; 4g Carbs; 3.7g Protein; 2.2g Sugars
Ingredients
1/2 cup almond flour
1/2 cup Swerve
1/2 teaspoon baking powder
A pinch of salt
1/2 teaspoon ground cinnamon
1/2 teaspoon ground cardamom
2 eggs, whisked
1/2 cup hazelnut butter
1 teaspoon vanilla extract
1/2 teaspoon hazelnut extract
1/3 cup cranberries, chopped
Directions
Mix almond flour, Swerve, baking powder, salt, cinnamon, and cardamom until well combined.
In a separate mixing dish, thoroughly combine eggs, hazelnut butter, vanilla and hazelnut extract. Add wet mixture to dry mixture.
Fold in cranberries and mix to combine well.
Add 1 ½ cups of water to the Instant Pot. Now, add this batter to well-greased idli molds and lower it onto the bottom of your Instant Pot.
Secure the lid. Choose "Manual" mode and Low pressure; cook for 12 minutes. Once cooking is complete, use a natural pressure release; carefully remove the lid.
Store in an airtight container. Bon appétit!

441. Slow Cooker Cranberry Delight

(Ready in about 3 hours 35 minutes | Servings 6)
Using fresh cranberries as the base, this old-fashioned yet elegant fruit dessert is easy to pull off in the Instant Pot. However, each ingredient in this dessert plays a part in its rich and memorable flavor.
Per serving: 223 Calories; 20.6g Fat; 8.4g Carbs; 2.5g Protein; 2.3g Sugars
Ingredients
9 ounces cranberries
1/2 cup Swerve
1 tablespoon tapioca starch
1/2 teaspoon vanilla extract
Topping:
2/3 cup almond flour
1 teaspoon baking powder
1 stick butter, melted
1/2 teaspoon ground cardamom
1/2 teaspoon star anise, ground
1/4 cup Swerve
Directions
Arrange cranberries on the bottom of the Instant Pot. Sprinkle with Swerve, tapioca starch, and vanilla extract.
In a mixing bowl, thoroughly combine the remaining ingredients for the topping. Drop by the spoonful on top of the cranberry mixture.
Secure the lid. Choose "Slow Cook" mode and Low pressure; cook for 3 hours 30 minutes. Once cooking is complete, use a quick pressure release; carefully remove the lid.
Serve at room temperature. Bon appétit!

442. Cappuccino Chocolate Pudding

(Ready in about 30 minutes | Servings 4)
Here is an easy and stress-free way to make a family dessert. In addition, pudding is one of the most popular dessert recipes for the Instant Pot.
Per serving: 319 Calories; 31.9g Fat; 8.6g Carbs; 6.5g Protein; 0.9g Sugars
Ingredients
2/3 cup double cream
1/2 stick butter, cut into pieces
1 ½ ounces grated chocolate, unsweetened

1 teaspoon ground cinnamon
1/2 teaspoon vanilla extract
3 tablespoons cocoa powder, unsweetened
1 tablespoon instant coffee granules
1/4 cup almond flour
A pinch of salt
2 whole eggs plus 2 egg yolks
1/2 cup granulated Swerve
Directions
Start by adding 1 ½ cups of water and a metal rack to your Instant Pot. Now, spritz a soufflé dish with a nonstick cooking spray.
In a small pan, heat the cream; add the butter and chocolate and stir to combine.
In a mixing bowl, whisk the other ingredients. Slowly fold in the hot chocolate/cream mixture, mixing constantly to combine well.
Pour the batter into the prepared soufflé dish.
Secure the lid. Choose "Manual" mode and Low pressure; cook for 20 minutes. Once cooking is complete, use a natural pressure release; carefully remove the lid.
Serve garnished with low-carb topping, if desired. Bon appétit!

443. Peanut Butter and Chocolate Mousse

(Ready in about 10 minutes | Servings 4)
Try a luscious, elegant, and beautiful mousse that features peanut butter, cocoa powder, vanilla and chocolate chips. It would make a great addition to any family meal.
Per serving: 372 Calories; 34.5g Fat; 8.7g Carbs; 8.4g Protein; 3.3g Sugars
Ingredients
2 eggs plus 2 egg yolks
1 teaspoon liquid Stevia
1/4 cup creamy peanut butter
1/4 cup cocoa powder
1 ½ cups whipping cream
1 teaspoon pure vanilla extract
1/2 teaspoon pure almond extract
A pinch of salt
A pinch of grated nutmeg
2 ounces chocolate chips, sugar-free
Directions
Whisk the eggs in a bowl. Then, in a saucepan over a moderate heat, cook Stevia, peanut butter, and cocoa powder. Mix until everything is well incorporated and heated through.
Then, mix in the cream, vanilla extract, almond extract, salt, and grated nutmeg.
Gradually add the cream mixture to the bowl with the eggs; whisk to combine well. Divide the mixture among four ramekins.
Add 1 ½ cups of water and a metal rack to your Instant Pot. Place the ramekins on the rack.
Secure the lid. Choose "Manual" mode and High pressure; cook for 8 minutes. Once cooking is complete, use a quick pressure release; carefully remove the lid.
Serve well chilled, topped with chocolate chips. Enjoy!

444. French-Style Pots de Crème

(Ready in about 15 minutes | Servings 4)
Oh là là! Camembert, a soft-ripened cheese from the Normandy region, is the star of this French dessert.
Per serving: 233 Calories; 20.3g Fat; 7.1g Carbs; 12.2g Protein; 0.2g Sugars
Ingredients
3/4 cup double cream
1 cup Swerve, powdered
1/3 cup espresso strong coffee, at room temperature
2 eggs, beaten
1 (8-ounce) container Camembert cheese, at room temperature
1/2 teaspoon vanilla extract
1/4 teaspoon cinnamon, ground
4 ounces chocolate chunks, sugar-free
Directions
In a small saucepan, bring the cream and Swerve to a simmer.
In a mixing dish, thoroughly combine the remaining ingredients. Add this egg mixture to the warm cream mixture.
Pour the mixture into ramekins.
Add 1 ½ cups of water and a metal rack to the Instant Pot. Now, lower your ramekins onto the rack.
Secure the lid. Choose "Manual" mode and High pressure; cook for 10 minutes. Once cooking is complete, use a natural pressure release; carefully remove the lid. Serve
Serve well chilled. Bon appétit!

445. Exotic Coconut Idli

(Ready in about 20 minutes | Servings 6)
This stunning cookie recipe features a mild and silky cream cheese, super-healthy almond flour and versatile coconut.
Per serving: 257 Calories; 24.9g Fat; 6.1g Carbs; 4.3g Protein; 3.3g Sugars
Ingredients
1/2 cup almond flour
1/2 cup coconut flour
1 teaspoon baking powder
1/2 cup powdered Swerve
A pinch of kosher salt
1/4 teaspoon ginger powder
1/2 teaspoon cardamom powder
1 teaspoon vanilla essence
2 tablespoons coconut oil
1 cup cream cheese, room temperature
1/4 cup lukewarm water
1/4 cup coconut flakes
Directions
Start by adding 1 ½ cups of water to the Instant Pot. Mix almond flour, coconut flour, baking powder, Swerve, salt, ginger powder, and cardamom powder, and vanilla until well combined.

Mix in the coconut oil, cream cheese, and water; mix until everything is well incorporated.
Now, spread your batter onto the prepared idli molds; lower it onto the bottom of your Instant Pot.
Secure the lid. Choose "Manual" mode and Low pressure; cook for 12 minutes. Once cooking is complete, use a natural pressure release; carefully remove the lid.
Allow your idlis to cool completely. Sprinkle with coconut flakes and enjoy!

446. Orange Dessert with White Chocolate

(Ready in about 20 minutes | Servings 4)
Try a refreshing, citrusy dessert in jars. An Instant Pot works wonders with easy-to-find ingredients and makes the best desserts you can imagine.
Per serving: 422 Calories; 39.8g Fat; 9.1g Carbs; 7.5g Protein; 1.8g Sugars
Ingredients
1/2 cup Swerve, granulated
4 tablespoons coconut oil
2 eggs
2 tablespoons fresh orange juice
1 cup heavy whipping cream
1/4 teaspoon star anise, ground
1/2 teaspoon vanilla essence
4 ounces shaved white chocolate, sugar-free
Directions
Start by adding 1 ½ cups of water and a metal rack to the Instant Pot.
Blend Swerve and coconut oil in your food processor until well combined. With the machine running, fold in the eggs and continue to blend until well combined. Stir in orange juice and mix again. Spoon the mixture into the jars; cover with the lids.
Secure the lid. Choose "Manual" mode and Low pressure; cook for 12 minutes. Once cooking is complete, use a natural pressure release; carefully remove the lid. Refrigerate overnight.
On an actual day, beat the cream with star anise and vanilla using an electric mixer on high speed.
Add the cream mixture to the orange curd mixture. Divide mousse among serving glasses. Top with shaved chocolate and serve well chilled.

447. Grandma's Zucchini Cake

(Ready in about 35 minutes | Servings 6)
This old-fashioned cake is definitive proof that zucchini and walnuts belong together! Your family will gobble up this beautiful and moist dessert!
Per serving: 359 Calories; 35.1g Fat; 6.6g Carbs; 8g Protein; 1.9g Sugars
Ingredients
1 cup almond flour
A pinch of table salt
1 ½ teaspoons baking powder
1 teaspoon pumpkin pie spice
2/3 cup Swerve, powdered
2 eggs, beaten
3 tablespoons coconut oil
1/2 cup double cream
1/2 pound zucchini, shredded, drained and squeezed dry
1 teaspoon vanilla paste
1/4 cup walnuts, chopped
Frosting:
4 ounces mascarpone cheese, room temperature
1/4 cup coconut oil, softened
1 ½ cups Swerve powdered
Directions
Start by adding 1 ½ cups of water and a metal rack to the Instant Pot. Now, lightly grease a cake pan with a nonstick cooking spray.
In a mixing bowl, thoroughly combine almond flour, salt, baking powder, and pumpkin pie spice.
Then, thoroughly combine Swerve, eggs, coconut oil, cream, zucchini and vanilla using an electric mixer
With the machine running on low, gradually add the prepared dry mixture; mix until everything is well combined.
Fold in the chopped walnuts. Spoon the batter into the prepared cake pan. Cover the pan with paper towels; then, top with a piece of aluminum foil making a foil sling.
Lower the pan onto the rack.
Secure the lid. Choose "Manual" mode and Low pressure; cook for 30 minutes. Once cooking is complete, use a natural pressure release; carefully remove the lid.
In the meantime, beat the cheese, 1/4 cup of coconut oil, and Swerve until well combined. Frost the cake and serve well chilled. Enjoy!

448. Peanut and White Chocolate Chip Cookies

(Ready in about 20 minutes | Servings 6)
There is a reason that old-fashioned recipes call for eggs every time. Eggs are a key ingredient and crucial part of traditional cookie recipes.
Per serving: 295 Calories; 26.3g Fat; 8.6g Carbs; 7.7g Protein; 2.5g Sugars
Ingredients
1/2 cup almond flour
1/2 cup coconut flour
1 ½ teaspoons baking powder
A pinch of salt
1/2 cup Swerve
1 stick butter, melted
2 eggs, beaten
4 tablespoons full-fat milk
1/2 teaspoon ground cinnamon
1/4 teaspoon ground cardamom
1/2 teaspoon vanilla essence
1/3 cup white chocolate chunks, sugar-free
1/4 cup peanuts, chopped
Directions
Start by adding 1 ½ cups of water and a metal rack to the Instant Pot. Line a cake pan with a piece of parchment paper.

Mix almond flour, coconut flour, baking powder, salt, and Swerve until well combined.
Mix in the melted butter, eggs, milk, and spices; fold in the chocolate and peanuts and mix until everything is well incorporated.
Now, grab your dough, smoothen a little bit and roll it to 1/2-inch thickness. Then, cut down the cookies with a cookie cutter.
Arrange the cookies on the prepared cake pan and lower it onto the rack in your Instant Pot.
Secure the lid. Choose "Manual" mode and Low pressure; cook for 15 minutes. Once cooking is complete, use a natural pressure release; carefully remove the lid. Bon appétit!

449. Fudge with Nuts and Neufchatel

(Ready in about 10 minutes + chilling time | Servings 6)
The only thing better than a classic fudge dessert is a cheesy Instant Pot fudge! Neufchâtel cheese will add special charm to this fudge.
Per serving: 404 Calories; 39.5g Fat; 6.1g Carbs; 8.7g Protein; 3.2g Sugars
Ingredients
10 ounces Neufchâtel cheese, room temperature
2 sticks butter
3/4 cup hazelnut butter
1/2 teaspoon vanilla extract
1/2 teaspoon star anise, ground
1/2 cup almond flour
1 ½ teaspoons stevia powder
Directions
Place the cheese, butter, and hazelnut butter in your Instant Pot.
Press the "Sauté" button and let it simmer until thoroughly heated.
Stir in the other ingredients and continue to stir until everything is well incorporated.
Now, spoon the mixture into a square cookie sheet lined with a piece of foil. Transfer to your refrigerator for 2 to 3 hours.
Cut into squares and serve well chilled. Bon appétit!

450. Light and Fluffy Lemon Cookies

(Ready in about 20 minutes | Servings 8)
This dessert makes itself! You can also customize the flavor by adding a mint, coconut, hazelnuts, or berries.
Per serving: 129 Calories; 13g Fat; 2.6g Carbs; 1.8g Protein; 0.9g Sugars
Ingredients
1/2 cup coconut, shredded
1/2 cup almond flour
1/4 teaspoon coarse salt
1 teaspoon baking powder
1/4 cup coconut oil, softened
1 cup Swerve
1 tablespoon lemon juice
1 teaspoon lemon rind
Directions
Start by adding 1 ½ cups of water and a metal rack to the Instant Pot. Line a cake pan with a parchment paper.
Then, thoroughly combine the coconut, almond flour, salt, and baking powder; mix until well combined.
Mix in the oil, Swerve, lemon juice, lemon rind; mix until everything is well incorporated.
Now, grab your dough, smoothen a little bit and roll it to 1/2-inch thickness. Then, cut down the cookies with a cookie cutter.
Arrange the cookies on the prepared cake pan and lower it onto the rack in your Instant Pot.
Secure the lid. Choose "Manual" mode and Low pressure; cook for 15 minutes. Once cooking is complete, use a natural pressure release; carefully remove the lid. Bon appétit!

OTHER KETO FAVORITES

451. Apple Pie Granola
(Ready in about 1 hour 35 minutes | Servings 4)
This granola will give you more than you could expect! Bear in mind that pecans, macadamia and Brazil nuts have fewer carbs than cashews, almonds and pistachios.
Per serving: 234 Calories; 22.2g Fat; 9.5g Carbs; 2.5g Protein; 5.3g Sugars
Ingredients
3 tablespoons coconut oil
1 teaspoon stevia powder
1 cup coconut, shredded
1/4 cup walnuts, chopped
1 ½ tablespoons sunflower seeds
1 ½ tablespoons pumpkin seeds
1 teaspoon apple pie spice mix
A pinch of salt
1 small apple, sliced
Directions
Place coconut oil, stevia powder, coconut, walnuts, sunflower seeds, pumpkin seeds, apple pie spice mix, and salt in your Instant Pot.
Secure the lid. Choose "Slow Cook" mode and High pressure; cook for 1 hours 30 minutes. Once cooking is complete, use a quick pressure release; carefully remove the lid.
Spoon into individual bowls, garnish with apples and serve warm. Bon appétit!

452. Spinach and Cheese Muffins
(Ready in about 15 minutes | Servings 6)
When you need a protein hit, prepare these muffins. Prepare a big batch as they freeze well.
Per serving: 236 Calories; 18.8g Fat; 3.3g Carbs; 13.2g Protein; 2.2g Sugars
Ingredients
6 eggs
1/3 cup double cream
1/4 cup cream cheese
Sea salt and freshly ground black pepper, to taste
1/2 teaspoon cayenne pepper
1 ½ cups spinach, chopped
1/4 cup green onions, chopped
1 ripe tomato, chopped
1/2 cup cheddar cheese, grated
Directions
Start by adding 1 cup of water and a metal rack to the Instant Pot. Now, spritz a muffin tin with a nonstick cooking spray.
In a mixing dish, thoroughly combine the eggs, double cream, cream cheese, salt, black pepper, and cayenne pepper.
Then, divide the spinach, green onions, tomato, and scallions among the cups. Pour the egg mixture over the vegetables. Top with cheddar cheese.
Lower the cups onto the rack.
Secure the lid. Choose "Manual" mode and High pressure; cook for 10 minutes. Once cooking is complete, use a natural pressure release; carefully remove the lid. Serve immediately.

453. Shirred Eggs with Peppers and Scallions
(Ready in about 10 minutes | Servings 4)
If you have never had shirred eggs, here is the perfect recipe to try out. You can add fresh chives, parsley or cilantro as well.
Per serving: 208 Calories; 18.7g Fat; 3.9g Carbs; 6.7g Protein; 2.3g Sugars
Ingredients
4 tablespoons butter, melted
4 tablespoons double cream
4 eggs
4 scallions, chopped
2 red peppers, seeded and chopped
1/2 teaspoon granulated garlic
1/4 teaspoon dill weed
1/4 teaspoon sea salt
1/4 teaspoon freshly ground pepper
Directions
Start by adding 1 cup of water and a metal rack to the Instant Pot.
Grease the bottom and sides of each ramekin with melted butter. Divide the ingredients among the prepared four ramekins.
Lower the ramekins onto the metal rack.
Secure the lid. Choose "Manual" mode and High pressure; cook for 5 minutes. Once cooking is complete, use a natural pressure release; carefully remove the lid. Bon appétit!

454. Homemade Blueberry Yogurt
(Ready in about 24 hours + chilling time | Servings 12)
Creamy and flavorsome, this homemade fruit yogurt is the perfect breakfast or dessert for a hot summer day. It scoops well after freezing too.
Per serving: 92 Calories; 0.6g Fat; 6.6g Carbs; 14.7g Protein; 5.4g Sugars
Ingredients
3 quarts raw milk
15 grams probiotic yogurt starter
1 teaspoon stevia powder
1 cup blueberries, fresh or frozen (and thawed)
Directions
Add the milk to the Instant Pot.
Secure the lid. Choose "Yogurt" mode; now, press the "Adjust" button until you see the word "Boil". Turn off the Instant Pot.
Use a food thermometer to read temperature; 115 degrees is fine; stir in the starter.
Press the "Yogurt" button again and then, press the "Adjust" button to reach 24 hours.

Place in your refrigerator for a few hours to set up. Add stevia and blueberries; serve well chilled. Bon appétit!

455. Breakfast Meatloaf Cups

(Ready in about 40 minutes | Servings 8)
These cups promote the best of a low-carb diet – ground meat, eggs and sharp cheese. Therefore, they are obviously perfect for your diet!
Per serving: 375 Calories; 22.2g Fat; 6.5g Carbs; 35.4g Protein; 4.5g Sugars

Ingredients
1 pound ground pork
1 pound ground beef
1/2 cup onion, chopped
2 garlic cloves, minced
Salt and ground black pepper, to taste
1/3 cup Romano cheese, grated
1/4 cup pork rinds, crushed
4 eggs, whisked
2 ripe tomatoes, puréed
1/4 cup barbecue sauce, sugar-free

Directions
Start by adding 1 cup of water and a metal trivet to the bottom of your Instant Pot.
In a mixing bowl, thoroughly combine ground meat, onion, garlic, salt, black pepper, cheese, pork rinds, and eggs.
Mix until everything is well incorporated. Divide the mixture among muffin cups.
In a small mixing bowl, whisk puréed tomatoes with barbecue sauce. Lastly, top your muffins with the tomato sauce.
Secure the lid. Choose "Manual" mode and High pressure; cook for 25 minutes. Once cooking is complete, use a quick pressure release; carefully remove the lid.
Allow them to cool for 10 minutes before removing from the muffin tin. Bon appétit!

456. Breakfast Casserole with Zucchini and Bacon

(Ready in about 25 minutes | Servings 8)
Energize your morning with this delicious, protein breakfast! Serve with some extra cheese, if desired.
Per serving: 320 Calories; 24.3g Fat; 5.3g Carbs; 19.7g Protein; 2.9g Sugars

Ingredients
1/2 pound zucchini, grated and squeezed dry
1 white onion, chopped
1 clove garlic, minced
6 slices bacon, chopped
1 cup Colby cheese, shredded
1 cup Cottage cheese, room temperature
8 eggs, beaten
1/2 cup Greek yogurt, room temperature
Sea salt and ground black pepper, to taste
1/4 teaspoon dried marjoram
1/4 teaspoon dried rosemary
1 teaspoon dried parsley flakes

Directions
Start by adding 1 cup of water and a metal trivet to the bottom of your Instant Pot.
Mix the ingredients until everything is well incorporated. Spoon the mixture into a lightly greased casserole dish.
Lower the casserole dish onto the trivet.
Secure the lid. Choose "Manual" mode and High pressure; cook for 20 minutes. Once cooking is complete, use a quick pressure release; carefully remove the lid. Bon appétit!

457. Spicy and Cheesy Chard Quiche

(Ready in about 35 minutes | Servings 6)
Enjoy this fresh, spicy quiche, inspired by Swiss chard and freshly grated Pepper-Jack cheese.
Per serving: 183 Calories; 14.4g Fat; 5.6g Carbs; 8.1g Protein; 2.8g Sugars

Ingredients
10 large eggs
1/2 cup double cream
Seasoned salt and ground black pepper, to taste
1 teaspoon cayenne pepper
2 cups chard, roughly chopped
1 habanero pepper, seeded and chopped
1 tomato, chopped
1/2 cup red onion, thinly sliced
1/2 cup Pepper-Jack cheese, freshly grated

Directions
Start by adding 1 ½ cups of water and a metal trivet to the bottom of your Instant Pot. Now, lightly grease a baking dish with a nonstick cooking spray.
In a mixing bowl, thoroughly combine the eggs with double cream, salt, black pepper, and cayenne pepper. Now, stir in the chard, habanero pepper, tomato, and onion. Spoon the mixture into the prepared baking dish.
Cover with a piece of aluminum foil, making a foil sling.
Secure the lid. Choose "Manual" mode and High pressure; cook for 20 minutes. Once cooking is complete, use a quick pressure release; carefully remove the lid.
Top with cheese and cover with the lid; allow it to sit in the residual heat for 10 minutes.
Serve immediately and enjoy!

458. Bacon Frittata Muffins

(Ready in about 15 minutes | Servings 6)
Loaded with meaty bacon, fresh eggs, two kind of cheese, and extraordinary spices, these Instant Pot frittata muffins are sure to please.
Per serving: 226 Calories; 20.1g Fat; 2.3g Carbs; 9.3g Protein; 1.3g Sugars

Ingredients
6 thin meaty bacon slices
1 large-sized zucchini, grated
1 red bell pepper, chopped

1 green bell pepper, chopped
4 teaspoons butter, melted
1/2 cup Colby cheese, shredded
3 egg, beaten
2 tablespoons cream cheese, room temperature
1 teaspoon shallot powder
1/2 teaspoon dried dill weed
1/2 teaspoon cayenne pepper
Salt and black pepper, to taste
Directions
Start by adding 1 ½ cups of water and a metal trivet to the bottom of your Instant Pot.
Place bacon slices in 6 silicone cupcake liners. Add zucchini and bell peppers.
Now, mix the butter, Colby cheese, eggs, cream cheese, shallot powder, dried dill weed, cayenne pepper, salt, and black pepper. Spoon this mixture into the liners.
Put the liners into an oven-safe bowl. Cover with a piece of foil. Lower the bowl onto the trivet.
Secure the lid. Choose "Manual" mode and High pressure; cook for 10 minutes. Once cooking is complete, use a natural pressure release; carefully remove the lid. Bon appétit!

459. Hungarian Hot Pot

(Ready in about 15 minutes | Servings 4)
This recipe calls for Hungarian smoked sausage so consider using Csemege Kolbasz, Gyulai Kolbasz or Debrecener.
Per serving: 292 Calories; 21.6g Fat; 8.4g Carbs; 15.7g Protein; 3.5g Sugars
Ingredients
1 tablespoon grapeseed oil
9 ounces Hungarian smoked sausage, casing removed and sliced
1 carrot, cut into thick slices
1 celery stalk, diced
2 bell peppers, cut into wedges
2 cups roasted vegetable broth
1/2 cup shallot, peeled and diced
Sea salt and ground black pepper, to taste
1/2 tablespoon hot pepper flakes
1 bay leaf
1/4 cup fresh cilantro leaves, roughly chopped
Directions
Press the "Sauté" button to heat up the Instant Pot. Now, heat the oil and brown the sausage for 2 to 3 minutes.
Stir in the other ingredients.
Secure the lid. Choose "Manual" mode and High pressure; cook for 10 minutes. Once cooking is complete, use a natural pressure release; carefully remove the lid. Bon appétit!

460. Spring Avocado Eggs

(Ready in about 25 minutes | Servings 5)
Here's an all-time favorite! Delicious deviled eggs with fresh and creamy filling. Yummy!
Per serving: 138 Calories; 10.2g Fat; 6.2g Carbs; 6.8g Protein; 1.7g Sugars
Ingredients
5 eggs
1 avocado, pitted, peeled and mashed
1 tablespoon fresh lemon juice
1 ripe tomato, chopped
1/2 teaspoon cayenne pepper
Kosher salt and white pepper, to taste
1/2 teaspoon chili powder
3 tablespoons spring onions, roughly chopped
Directions
Pour 1 cup of water into the Instant Pot; add a steamer basket to the bottom.
Arrange the eggs in a steamer basket.
Secure the lid. Choose "Manual" mode and High pressure; cook for 5 minutes. Once cooking is complete, use a natural pressure release; carefully remove the lid.
Allow the eggs to cool for 15 minutes. Peel the eggs, slice them into halves, and separate egg whites from yolks.
To make a filling, mix the avocado, lemon juice, tomato, cayenne pepper, salt, white pepper, and chili powder; stir in the reserved egg yolks. Now, stuff the egg whites with this mixture.
Garnish with green onions. Arrange on a nice serving platter and serve.

461. Dilled Cauliflower Purée with Au Jus Gravy

(Ready in about 20 minutes | Servings 4)
Use a grass-fed butter in this recipe if you are able; it would be a great way to add a quality fat to your keto diet.
Per serving: 291 Calories; 26.6g Fat; 8.1g Carbs; 7.1g Protein; 4.5g Sugars
Ingredients
Cauliflower Purée:
1 head of fresh cauliflower, broken into florets
1/4 cup double cream
2 tablespoons butter
3 cloves garlic minced
4 tablespoons Romano cheese, grated
1 teaspoon dried dill weed
Kosher salt and ground black pepper, to taste
Gravy:
1 ½ cups beef stock
1/2 cup double cream
3 tablespoons butter
Directions
Add 1 cup of water and a steamer basket to the bottom of your Instant Pot.
Then, arrange cauliflower in the steamer basket.
Secure the lid. Choose "Manual" mode and Low pressure; cook for 3 minutes. Once cooking is complete, use a quick pressure release; carefully remove the lid.

Now, puree the cauliflower with a potato masher. Add the remaining ingredients for the purée and stir well.
Press the "Sauté" button to heat up the Instant Pot.
Now, combine the ingredients for the gravy and let it simmer for 10 minutes.
Stir until the gravy thickens down to a consistency of your liking. Serve cauliflower purée with the gravy on the side. Bon appétit!

462. Aromatic Cheesy and Kale Bake

(Ready in about 30 minutes | Servings 6)
Need a last-minute dinner for a family gathering? Serve this cheese and kale bake with a spicy mayo sauce.
Per serving: 473 Calories; 43g Fat; 5.9g Carbs; 16.6g Protein; 3.2g Sugars
Ingredients
2 tablespoons olive oil
1/2 cup leeks, chopped
2 garlic cloves, minced
2 cups kale leaves, torn into pieces
7 eggs, whisked
2 cups cream cheese, shredded
1 cup Colby cheese, shredded
Sea salt and ground black pepper, to taste
1/4 teaspoon paprika
1/4 teaspoon dried rosemary
1/2 teaspoon dried thyme
Directions
Start by adding 1 cup of water and a metal trivet to the Instant Pot. Grease a baking pan with a nonstick cooking spray.
Simply mix all of the above ingredients until everything is well combined.
Spoon the batter into the prepared baking pan. Now, lower the baking pan onto the trivet.
Secure the lid. Choose "Meat/Stew" mode and High pressure; cook for 25 minutes. Once cooking is complete, use a quick pressure release; carefully remove the lid. Serve warm.

463. Coconut Porridge with Berries

(Ready in about 10 minutes | Servings 2)
This recipe is so versatile. You can experiment with spices and seeds.
Per serving: 242 Calories; 20.7g Fat; 7.9g Carbs; 7.6g Protein; 2.8g Sugars
Ingredients
4 tablespoons coconut flour
1 tablespoon sunflower seeds
3 tablespoons flax meal
1 ¼ cups water
1/4 teaspoon coarse salt
1/4 teaspoon grated nutmeg
1/2 teaspoon ground cardamom
2 eggs, beaten
2 tablespoons coconut oil, softened
2 tablespoons Swerve
1/2 cup mixed berries, fresh or frozen (thawed)
Directions
Add all ingredients, except for mixed berries, to the Instant Pot.
Secure the lid. Choose "Manual" mode and High pressure; cook for 5 minutes. Once cooking is complete, use a quick pressure release; carefully remove the lid.
Divide between two bowls, top with berries, and serve hot. Bon appétit!

464. Cauliflower "Mac and Cheese"

(Ready in about 20 minutes | Servings 6)
Here's a new twist on an old favorite – a cauliflower baked with cheese and spices in your Instant Pot! You won't be disappointed.
Per serving: 306 Calories; 25.7g Fat; 5.4g Carbs; 14.4g Protein; 3.5g Sugars
Ingredients
1 medium head of cauliflower, broken into florets
2 tablespoons butter, melted
2/3 cup cream cheese
1/2 cup milk
1/2 teaspoon cumin powder
1/2 teaspoon mustard seeds
1/2 teaspoon fennel seeds
Salt and black pepper, to taste
2 cups Monterey-Jack cheese, shredded
Directions
Add 1 cup of water and a metal rack to the bottom of your Instant Pot.
Then, place cauliflower in a casserole dish that is previously greased with melted butter.
In a mixing bowl, thoroughly combine cream cheese, milk, cumin powder, mustard seeds, fennel seeds, salt, and black pepper.
Pour this mixture over the cauliflower.
Secure the lid. Choose "Manual" mode and High pressure; cook for 7 minutes. Once cooking is complete, use a quick pressure release; carefully remove the lid.
Top with shredded Monterey-Jack cheese. Return to the Instant Pot, cover with the lid, and let it sit in a residual heat for 10 minutes. Bon appétit!

465. Zucchini Sloppy Joe's

(Ready in about 10 minutes | Servings 2)
Here's a fantastic way to get the taste of Sloppy Joes without extra calories and carbs! In addition, it can be ready in 10 minutes and store well in the refrigerator!
Per serving: 159 Calories; 9.8g Fat; 1.5g Carbs; 15.5g Protein; 0.7g Sugars
Ingredients
1 tablespoon olive oil
1/2 pound ground beef
Salt and ground black pepper, to taste
1 medium-sized zucchini, cut into 4 slices lengthwise
1 tomato, sliced
4 lettuce leaves
2 teaspoons mustard

Directions
Add olive oil, ground beef, salt, and black pepper to your Instant Pot.
Secure the lid. Choose "Manual" mode and High pressure; cook for 5 minutes. Once cooking is complete, use a natural pressure release; carefully remove the lid.
Divide the ground meat mixture between 2 zucchini slices. Add tomato slices, lettuce, and mustard. Top with the second slice of zucchini. Bon appétit!

466. Delicious Homemade Burgers

(Ready in about 35 minutes | Servings 4)
Who doesn't love burgers? These fantastic burgers can be done so easily in the Instant Pot. They might become a staple menu item in your keto diet.
Per serving: 410 Calories; 30.1g Fat; 1.4g Carbs; 31.7g Protein; 0.5g Sugars
Ingredients
Keto Buns:
3 tablespoons butter, softened
3 eggs, whisked
1/2 teaspoon sea salt
1/4 teaspoon cayenne pepper
1/2 teaspoon freshly ground black pepper
1 cup almond flour
1 teaspoon baking powder
1/2 teaspoon granulated garlic
1/2 teaspoon onion powder
Burgers:
1/3 pound ground pork
1/2 pound ground beef
Salt and ground black pepper, to taste
2 garlic cloves, minced
1/2 teaspoon cumin powder
Directions
Start by preheating your oven to 420 degrees F. Beat the butter and eggs until well combined. Add the remaining ingredients for the buns and continue to mix until the batter is smooth and uniform.
Divide the batter between muffin molds. Bake for 25 minutes and reserve.
Meanwhile, mix the ingredients for the burgers. Now, shape the mixture into four equal sized patties.
Add 1 cup of water and a steamer basket to the Instant Pot. Place the burgers in the steamer basket. Secure the lid. Choose "Manual" mode and High pressure; cook for 6 minutes. Once cooking is complete, use a quick pressure release; carefully remove the lid.
Assemble your burgers with the prepared buns. Bon appétit!

467. Fluffy Berry Cupcakes

(Ready in about 30 minutes | Servings 6)
A delicious way to kick off the day! Alternatively, a fantastic afternoon snack! It's up to you. Serve these cupcakes and wow your family.
Per serving: 238 Calories; 21.6g Fat; 4.1g Carbs; 7.5g Protein; 2.2g Sugars
Ingredients
1/4 cup coconut oil, softened
3 ounces cream cheese, softened
1/4 cup double cream
4 eggs
1/4 cup coconut flour
1/4 cup almond flour
A pinch of salt
1/3 cup Swerve, granulated
1 teaspoon baking powder
1/4 teaspoon cardamom powder
1/2 teaspoon star anise, ground
1/2 cup fresh mixed berries
Directions
Start by adding 1 ½ cups of water and a metal rack to your Instant Pot.
Mix coconut oil, cream cheese, and double cream in a bowl. Fold in the eggs, one at a time, and continue to mix until everything is well incorporated.
In another bowl, thoroughly combine the flour, salt, Swerve, baking powder, cardamom, and anise.
Add the cream/egg mixture to this dry mixture. Afterwards, fold in fresh berries and gently stir to combine.
Divide the batter between silicone cupcake liners. Cover with a piece of foil. Place the cupcakes on the rack.
Secure the lid. Choose "Manual" mode and High pressure; cook for 25 minutes. Once cooking is complete, use a natural pressure release; carefully remove the lid. Enjoy!

468. Mediterranean-Style Savory Tart

(Ready in about 35 minutes | Servings 6)
One of the easiest tart recipes to make for a delicious, no-stress family lunch. This is the recipe you will be making again and again.
Per serving: 353 Calories; 32.1g Fat; 4g Carbs; 12.6g Protein; 2.5g Sugars
Ingredients
10 ounces cream cheese
4 eggs, whisked
1 cup almond flour
1 tablespoon flaxseed meal
1 teaspoon baking powder
Coarse sea salt and ground black pepper, to taste
1/2 stick butter, melted
1 ½ cups zucchini, grated
1 clove garlic, pressed
1/4 teaspoon dried rosemary
1/4 teaspoon dried basil
1/2 cup Cheddar cheese, shredded
Directions
Begin by adding 1 cup of water and a metal rack to your Instant Pot. Then, spritz a heatproof bowl with a nonstick cooking spray and set aside.
In a mixing dish, thoroughly combine the cream and eggs. Gradually stir in the flour. Add the remaining ingredients, except for Cheddar cheese.

Spoon the mixture into the prepared heatproof bowl; cover with a piece of aluminum foil, making a foil sling.
Secure the lid. Choose "Manual" mode and High pressure; cook for 25 minutes. Once cooking is complete, use a quick pressure release; carefully remove the lid.
Add Cheddar cheese to the top of your tart and cover with the lid. Let it sit in a residual heat an additional 7 to 10 minutes. Bon appétit!

469. Salmon and Ricotta Fat Bombs

(Ready in about 15 minutes | Servings 6)
These fat bombs are a great idea for a party or afternoon snack. The flavor will knock your socks off!
Per serving: 130 Calories; 9.1g Fat; 1.7g Carbs; 10.2g Protein; 0.5g Sugars
Ingredients
1/2 pound salmon fillets
Salt and ground black pepper, to taste
1/4 teaspoon smoked paprika
1/4 teaspoon hot paprika
2 tablespoons butter, softened
4 ounces Ricotta cheese, room temperature
1/4 cup green onions, chopped
1 garlic clove, finely chopped
2 teaspoons fresh parsley, finely chopped
Directions
Start by adding 1 ½ cups of water and a metal rack to the bottom of your Instant Pot.
Place the salmon on the metal rack.
Secure the lid. Choose "Manual" mode and Low pressure; cook for 8 minutes. Once cooking is complete, use a quick pressure release; carefully remove the lid.
Chop the salmon. Add the salt, pepper, paprika, butter, cheese, onions, and garlic. Shape the mixture into balls and roll them in chopped parsley.
Arrange fat bombs on a serving platter and enjoy!

470. Pork and Green Bean Casserole

(Ready in about 30 minutes | Servings 6)
Here is a classic family recipe that you can prepare for any occasion! Habanero pepper and Colby cheese push this recipe over the edge.
Per serving: 348 Calories; 23.1g Fat; 8.6g Carbs; 26.3g Protein; 4.4g Sugars
Ingredients
1 pound ground pork
1 yellow onion, thinly sliced
2 garlic cloves, smashed
1 green bell pepper, thinly sliced
1 red bell pepper, thinly sliced
1 habanero chili pepper, thinly sliced
1 cup green beans
3 ripe tomatoes, chopped
1/2 teaspoon cumin, ground
Salt and ground black pepper, to taste
1/2 teaspoon cayenne pepper
1 cup Colby cheese, shredded
2 tablespoons fresh chives, chopped
Directions
Start by adding 1 ½ cups of water and a metal rack to the bottom of your Instant Pot.
Mix the pork, onion, garlic, pepper, green beans, tomatoes, cumin, salt, black pepper, and cayenne pepper until well combined.
Pour the mixture into a lightly greased casserole dish that will fit in your Instant Pot. Then, lower the dish onto the rack.
Secure the lid. Choose "Manual" mode and Low pressure; cook for 20 minutes. Once cooking is complete, use a quick pressure release; carefully remove the lid.
Top with Colby cheese and cover with the lid. Let it sit in a residual heat an additional 7 to 10 minutes. Serve garnished with fresh chives. Bon appétit!

471. Greek-Style Mushroom Muffins

(Ready in about 10 minutes | Servings 6)
This is a kid-friendly recipe as well as a picnic favorite. It is delicious either hot or cold.
Per serving: 259 Calories; 18.9g Fat; 6.7g Carbs; 15.7g Protein; 3.9g Sugars
Ingredients
6 eggs
1 red onion, chopped
2 cups button mushrooms, chopped
Sea salt and ground black pepper, to taste
1 ½ cups Feta cheese, shredded
1/2 cup Kalamata olives, pitted and sliced
Directions
Start by adding 1 ½ cups of water and a metal rack to the bottom of the Instant Pot. Spritz each muffin liner with a nonstick cooking spray.
In a mixing bowl, thoroughly combine the eggs, onions, mushrooms, salt, and black pepper. Now, pour this mixture into the muffin liners.
Secure the lid. Choose "Manual" mode and Low pressure; cook for 7 minutes. Once cooking is complete, use a quick pressure release; carefully remove the lid.
Sprinkle cheese and olives on top of the cups; cover with the lid for a few minutes to allow it to melt. Enjoy!

472. Pancakes with Cottage Cheese Topping

(Ready in about 1 hour 15 minutes | Servings 4)
This recipe is perfect for anyone bored of classic pancakes. It features cream cheese, eggs, and mayo.
Per serving: 372 Calories; 31.7g Fat; 8g Carbs; 14.6g Protein; 4.8g Sugars
Ingredients
Pancakes:
2 tablespoons coconut oil
4 eggs
8 ounces cream cheese
1/4 teaspoon kosher salt

1 teaspoon granulated Swerve
1 teaspoon ground psyllium husk powder
Topping:
6 ounces Cottage cheese, room temperature
4 tablespoons low-carb mayonnaise, preferably homemade
1 small shallot, minced
Sea salt and ground black pepper, to taste
Directions
Thoroughly combine the ingredients for the pancakes.
Spritz the bottom and sides of your Instant Pot with a nonstick cooking spray. Add 1/2 of the pancake mixture and secure the lid.
Choose "Multigrain" mode and Low pressure; cook for 35 minutes. Cook until golden brown and crispy on the top.
Once cooking is complete, use a natural pressure release; carefully remove the lid.
Repeat with the remaining 1/2 of the pancake mixture.
In the meantime, thoroughly combine all ingredients for the topping. Spread the topping over your pancakes and serve warm. Bon appétit!

473. Sichuan-Style Duck Breast
(Ready in about 2 hours 15 minutes | Servings 4)
A homemade broth makes everything better! Reserve the broth after cooking the chicken and store in your refrigerator or freeze for later use.
Per serving: 256 Calories; 13.7g Fat; 1g Carbs; 29.1g Protein; 0g Sugars
Ingredients
1 pound duck breast, boneless, skinless and cut into 4 pieces
1/2 teaspoon coarse sea salt
1/4 teaspoon Sichuan peppercorn powder
1/2 teaspoon cayenne pepper
2 garlic cloves, minced
2 tablespoons peanut oil
1/2 cup dry red wine
1 tablespoon sake
1/2 cup chicken broth
Directions
Place all ingredients, except for the broth, in the ceramic dish; place the dish in your refrigerator and let it marinate for 1 to 2 hours.
Then, transfer the meat along with its marinade to the Instant Pot. Pour in the chicken broth.
Secure the lid. Choose "Manual" mode and High pressure; cook for 10 minutes. Once cooking is complete, use a quick pressure release; carefully remove the lid.
Serve warm and enjoy!

474. Classic Chicken Gumbo
(Ready in about 20 minutes | Servings 6)
Looking for a hearty and satisfying chicken recipe? A warm, flavorful gumbo might be a perfect family meal!
Per serving: 233 Calories; 13.8g Fat; 8.7g Carbs; 19.6g Protein; 4.3g Sugars
Ingredients
2 tablespoons grapeseed oil
2 pork sausages, smoked, sliced
3 chicken legs, boneless and skinless
1 cup onion, chopped
1 cup bell peppers, finely chopped
3 cloves garlic, finely minced
1/2 teaspoon salt
1/4 teaspoon black pepper
1 teaspoon cayenne pepper
1 teaspoon Cajun spice mix
1 teaspoon filé powder
5 cups chicken broth
2 tomatoes, pureed
1 ½ cups fresh or frozen (thawed) okra
1/4 cup fresh coriander leaves, chopped
Directions
Press the "Sauté" button to heat up the Instant Pot. Now, heat the oil and cook the sausage and chicken until browned; reserve.
Add the onion, bell peppers, and garlic and sauté in pan drippings until they are softened.
Add the salt, black pepper, cayenne pepper, Cajun spice mix, filé powder, chicken broth and tomatoes. Secure the lid. Choose "Manual" mode and High pressure; cook for 12 minutes. Once cooking is complete, use a natural pressure release; carefully remove the lid.
Stir the okra into the Instant Pot; press the "Sauté" button one more time and let it simmer until the okra is tender, for 5 to 8 minutes.
Serve in individual bowls, garnished with fresh coriander. Enjoy!

475. Chia and Blackberry Jam
(Ready in about 10 minutes | Servings 12)
A berry jam turns out great in the Instant Pot. In addition, chia seeds improve the nutritional value of this homemade condiment.
Per serving: 38 Calories; 1.1g Fat; 8.2g Carbs; 1.2g Protein; 4.7g Sugars
Ingredients
10 ounces fresh blackberries, rinsed
1/2 cup Swerve, powdered
3 teaspoons chia seeds
1/2 cup water
Directions
Add blackberries to your Instant Pot.
Sprinkle with Swerve and chia seeds. Pour in 1/2 cup of water.
Secure the lid. Choose "Manual" mode and High pressure; cook for 2 minutes. Once cooking is complete, use a natural pressure release; carefully remove the lid.
Process the mixture with an immersion blender. Store your jam in a mason jar or serve immediately. Bon appétit!

476. Mushroom and Cream Cheese Pâté

(Ready in about 10 minutes | Servings 8)

If you're out of ideas for dinner or appetizer, give this recipe a try! Mushrooms are an excellent source of plant-based protein, B vitamins, antioxidants, vitamin E, fiber, potassium and selenium.

Per serving: 162 Calories; 14.4g Fat; 3.6g Carbs; 3.9g Protein; 2.4g Sugars

Ingredients
3 tablespoons olive oil
1 pound brown mushrooms, chopped
1/2 yellow onion, chopped
2 garlic cloves, minced
2 tablespoons cognac
Sea salt, to taste
1/3 teaspoon black pepper
1/2 teaspoon cayenne pepper
1 cup cream cheese, at room temperature

Directions
Press the "Sauté" button to heat up the Instant Pot. Now, heat the oil and cook the mushrooms with onions until softened and fragrant.
Stir in the garlic, cognac, salt, black pepper, and cayenne pepper.
Secure the lid. Choose "Manual" mode and High pressure; cook for 5 minutes. Once cooking is complete, use a quick pressure release; carefully remove the lid.
Transfer the mixture to a food processor. Add cream cheese and continue to mix until everything is well incorporated. Serve with veggie sticks. Bon appétit!

477. Japanese-Style Savory Custard

(Ready in about 10 minutes | Servings 4)

Dashi is a type of stock used in Japanese cooking. If you don't have dashi on hand, simply replace it with a homemade chicken stock.

Per serving: 206 Calories; 15.3g Fat; 5.5g Carbs; 11.1g Protein; 2.2g Sugars

Ingredients
4 eggs
3/4 cup dashi, cold
1/4 sour cream
2 teaspoons light soy sauce
1 tablespoon sesame oil
1 tablespoon mirin
1/2 yellow onion, minced
2 garlic cloves, minced
Salt and pepper, to taste
1/2 cup scallions, chopped

Directions
Prepare the Instant Pot by adding 1 ½ cups of water and a metal rack to its bottom.
Whisk the eggs, dashi, sour cream, soy sauce, sesame oil, and mirin in a mixing bowl. Now, strain this mixture over a fine mesh strainer into a baking dish. Add the onions, garlic, salt, and pepper; stir to combine well. Lower the cooking dish onto the rack.
Secure the lid. Choose "Steam" mode and High pressure; cook for 6 minutes. Once cooking is complete, use a natural pressure release; carefully remove the lid.
Serve garnished with chopped scallions. Enjoy!

478. Zucchini Cardamom Bread

(Ready in about 35 minutes | Servings 8)

Here is a perfect recipe when you're hosting a weekend brunch! This zucchini bread is sweetened with stevia. Enjoy!

Per serving: 205 Calories; 19.1g Fat; 4.3g Carbs; 6.1g Protein; 0.9g Sugars

Ingredients
4 eggs
1/3 cup olive oil
1 cup almond flour
2 tablespoons coconut flour
1 teaspoon stevia, liquid
A pinch of salt
A pinch of grated nutmeg
1 teaspoon baking powder
1 teaspoon ground cardamom
1 cup zucchini, grated

Directions
Prepare the Instant Pot by adding 1 ½ cups of water and a metal rack to its bottom. Lightly grease a baking pan with a nonstick cooking spray.
In a mixing dish, thoroughly combine dry ingredients. Then, in another bowl, thoroughly combine wet ingredients.
Add wet mixture to the dry mixture; continue to mix until uniform, creamy and smooth. Pour the batter into the prepared pan.
Lower the pan onto the trivet.
Secure the lid. Choose "Bean/Chili" mode and High pressure; cook for 25 minutes. Once cooking is complete, use a natural pressure release; carefully remove the lid.
Allow the zucchini bread to cool completely before cutting and serving. Bon appétit!

479. Creamy Breakfast "Cereals"

(Ready in about 15 minutes | Servings 4)

Prepare to become totally addicted to this delicious breakfast porridge! Almond and coconut flour, milk, and berries make it easy to give every dish a little something extra.

Per serving: 185 Calories; 14.4g Fat; 9.2g Carbs; 5.9g Protein; 6.8g Sugars

Ingredients
1/4 coconut flour
1/4 cup almond flour
1 tablespoon flaxseed meal
1/4 teaspoon kosher salt
1/2 cup milk
1/2 cup water
2 eggs, beaten

1/4 stick butter
4 tablespoons Swerve, granulated
2 tablespoons double cream
2 ounces raspberries
1 ounce blueberries
Directions
Add all ingredients to the Instant Pot.
Secure the lid. Choose "Manual" mode and High pressure; cook for 5 minutes. Once cooking is complete, use a quick pressure release; carefully remove the lid.
Serve garnished with some extra berries if desired. Enjoy!

480. Old-Fashioned Cherry Jam
(Ready in about 10 minutes | Servings 8)
The ultimate in freshness and deliciousness, this jam works great with desserts, breakfasts and snacks.
Per serving: 33 Calories; 0.1g Fat; 6.8g Carbs; 0.4g Protein; 3.6g Sugars
Ingredients
2 cups cherries, pitted
1/2 cup Swerve, granulated
1 tablespoon vanilla extract
1 teaspoon rum extract
1/2 teaspoon ground cardamom
2 teaspoons arrowroot powder
1 cup water
Directions
Add cherries to your Instant Pot.
Sprinkle with Swerve, vanilla, rum extract, and cardamom. Now, add arrowroot powder and water.
Secure the lid. Choose "Manual" mode and High pressure; cook for 2 minutes. Once cooking is complete, use a natural pressure release; carefully remove the lid.
Process the mixture with an immersion blender. Store in a mason jar or serve immediately. Bon appétit!

481. Spicy Mushroom Hot Pot
(Ready in about 10 minutes | Servings 4)
If you love mushrooms, give this recipe a try. When cooking is done, top the mushrooms with sharp cheese and let it sit for 10 minutes. Enjoy!
Per serving: 195 Calories; 14.3g Fat; 6.8g Carbs; 11.7g Protein; 3.5g Sugars
Ingredients
1 tablespoon olive oil
1 pound white mushrooms, thinly sliced
1/2 onion, chopped
1 cup water
Sea salt and ground black pepper, to taste
1 bay leaf
1 cup Colby cheese, shredded
Directions
Press the "Sauté" button to heat up the Instant Pot.
Now, heat the oil and cook the mushrooms with onions until softened and fragrant.
Add the water, salt, black pepper, and bay leaf.
Secure the lid. Choose "Manual" mode and High pressure; cook for 5 minutes. Once cooking is complete, use a quick pressure release; carefully remove the lid.
Add cheese, cover with the lid and let it sit in the residual heat until the cheese is melted. Serve warm.

482. Egg Balls in Marinara Sauce
(Ready in about 15 minutes | Servings 6)
Egg balls loaded with cheese and pork rinds, and then, cooked in a tangy marinara sauce. The flavors are fantastic!
Per serving: 395 Calories; 26.2g Fat; 8.6g Carbs; 29.4g Protein; 5.1g Sugars
Ingredients
1 ½ cups low-carb marinara sauce
8 eggs, whisked
1 ½ cups Romano cheese, grated
1 cup pork rinds, crushed
2 cloves garlic, finely chopped
2 tablespoons fresh parsley, chopped
Sea salt and ground black pepper, to your liking
1 tablespoon olive oil
Directions
Press the "Sauté" button to heat up the Instant Pot.
Add marinara sauce and bring it to a boil.
Now, in a mixing bowl, thoroughly combine the remaining ingredients. Form the mixture into balls. Then, drop the balls into the hot marinara sauce.
Secure the lid. Choose "Manual" mode and High pressure; cook for 8 minutes. Once cooking is complete, use a quick pressure release; carefully remove the lid. Bon appétit!

483. Lobster and Cheese Dip
(Ready in about 20 minutes | Servings 10)
This dipping sauce is definitely one of the best options to make you snack a delicious pleasure. Doubtless, it's easy to add plenty of seafood to your diet!
Per serving: 291 Calories; 20.7g Fat; 4.9g Carbs; 21.2g Protein; 3.2g Sugars
Ingredients
2 tablespoons butter
1 onion, chopped
1 celery, chopped
2 garlic cloves, minced
2 tomatoes, puréed
1 cup chicken broth
1 teaspoon Old Bay seasoning
Salt and ground black pepper, to taste
1/2 teaspoon paprika
30 ounces frozen lobster
2 cups cream cheese
1 cup Cheddar cheese, shredded
Directions
Press the "Sauté" button to heat up the Instant Pot.
Now, melt the butter and sauté the onion and celery until softened.
Then, add garlic and continue to cook an additional minute or until aromatic.

Add tomatoes, chicken broth, spices, lobster and cream cheese.
Secure the lid. Choose "Manual" mode and Low pressure; cook for 12 minutes. Once cooking is complete, use a quick pressure release; carefully remove the lid.
Using an immersion blender, puree the mixture to your desired consistency. Return the mixture to the Instant Pot.
Press the "Sauté" button and add Cheddar cheese. Let it simmer until everything is melted and incorporated. Bon appétit!

484. Party-Style Cheeseburger Dip
(Ready in about 10 minutes | Servings 10)
Quick cook time and versatility are just a few of the things that make cooking of dipping sauce in an Instant Pot so easy!
Per serving: 224 Calories; 13.6g Fat; 4.4g Carbs; 19.9g Protein; 2.2g Sugars
Ingredients
1 tablespoon olive oil
1 onion, chopped
1/3 pound ground pork
2/3 pound ground beef
2 ripe tomatoes, puréed
10 ounces Ricotta cheese
1/2 cup chicken broth
5 ounces Cheddar cheese, shredded
Directions
Press the "Sauté" button to heat up the Instant Pot. Then, heat the oil and sauté the onion until translucent and fragrant.
Now, add ground meat, tomatoes, Ricotta cheese, and chicken broth.
Secure the lid. Choose "Manual" mode and High pressure; cook for 6 minutes. Once cooking is complete, use a quick pressure release; carefully remove the lid.
Top with Cheddar cheese and serve warm.

485. Cauliflower Breakfast Cups
(Ready in about 15 minutes | Servings 6)
Cheesy cauliflower bites in elegant muffin liners. This is such a brilliant idea! Your family will be impressed with the deliciousness of these cups.
Per serving: 335 Calories; 25.9g Fat; 5.8g Carbs; 19.8g Protein; 2.6g Sugars
Ingredients
1/2 pound cauliflower, riced
Sea salt and ground black pepper, to taste
1/2 teaspoon cayenne pepper
1/2 teaspoon dried dill weed
1/2 teaspoon dried basil
1/4 teaspoon dried oregano
2 tablespoons olive oil
2 garlic cloves, minced
1/2 cup scallions, chopped
1 cup Romano cheese, preferably freshly grated
Salt and ground black pepper, to taste
7 eggs, beaten
1/2 cup Cotija cheese, grated
Directions
Start by adding 1 ½ cups of water and a metal rack to the bottom of the Instant Pot. Spritz each muffin cup with a nonstick cooking spray.
Mix the ingredients until everything is well incorporated.
Now, spoon the mixture into lightly greased muffin cups. Lower the cups onto the rack in the Instant Pot.
Secure the lid. Choose "Manual" mode and High pressure; cook for 10 minutes. Once cooking is complete, use a natural pressure release; carefully remove the lid. Bon appétit!

486. Mexican-Style Stuffed Peppers
(Ready in about 25 minutes | Servings 4)
These peppers with a Mexican flair are absolutely delicious! In addition, they can be prepared ahead of time.
Per serving: 407 Calories; 27g Fat; 8.3g Carbs; 32.4g Protein; 3.7g Sugars
Ingredients
1/2 pound ground beef
1/4 pound ground pork
4 eggs, whisked
2 garlic cloves, minced
1/2 cup onion, chopped
Salt and ground black pepper, to taste
1 (1-ounce) package taco seasoning mix
1 cup Cotija cheese, grated
4 bell peppers, remove seeds and cut the tops off
8 ounces canned tomato sauce
Directions
Start by adding 1 cup of water and a metal rack to the bottom of the Instant Pot. Spritz a casserole dish with a nonstick cooking spray.
In a mixing bowl, thoroughly combine the ground meat, eggs, garlic, onion, salt, pepper, taco seasoning mix, and Cotija cheese.
Fill the peppers with the cheese/meat mixture. Place the peppers on the rack in the Instant Pot. Pour the tomato sauce over the peppers.
Secure the lid. Choose "Manual" mode and High pressure; cook for 20 minutes. Once cooking is complete, use a natural pressure release; carefully remove the lid. Bon appétit!

487. Goat Cheese and Cauliflower Pancake
(Ready in about 35 minutes | Servings 4)
This giant pancake will become a hit with your family! Feel free to add another combo of seasonings.
Per serving: 198 Calories; 15.2g Fat; 4.9g Carbs; 11.2g Protein; 1.9g Sugars
Ingredients
3/4 pound cauliflower, riced
4 eggs, beaten
1/2 cup goat cheese, crumbled
1/2 teaspoon onion powder

1 teaspoon garlic powder
Sea salt and white pepper, to taste
2 tablespoons butter, melted
Directions
Simply combine all ingredients in a mixing bowl. Now, spritz the bottom and sides of your Instant Pot with a nonstick cooking spray. Pour the batter into the Instant Pot.
Secure the lid. Choose "Bean/Chili" mode and Low pressure; cook for 30 minutes. Once cooking is complete, use a natural pressure release; carefully remove the lid.
Serve with some extra butter or cream cheese if desired. Bon appétit!

488. Lasagna Cupcakes with Zucchini and Mozzarella

(Ready in about 20 minutes | Servings 6)
Use zucchini noodles and a low-carb pasta sauce to make delicious lasagna with only 4.2 grams of carbs per serving.
Per serving: 173 Calories; 8.7g Fat; 4.3g Carbs; 19.7g Protein; 2.5g Sugars
Ingredients
1 zucchini, thinly sliced
2 eggs, beaten
4 ounces cream cheese
10 ounces mozzarella cheese, grated
1/2 teaspoon dried dill weed
1 teaspoon cayenne pepper
1/2 cup pasta sauce
Directions
Add 1 ½ cups of water and a metal rack to the bottom of your Instant Pot. Spritz six cupcake molds with a nonstick cooking spray.
Line each cupcake mold with a zucchini slice.
In a mixing bowl, thoroughly combine eggs, cheese, dill, and cayenne pepper. Add 1/3 of this mixture to the cupcake molds; top with pasta sauce.
Repeat layers of zucchini, cheese mixture, and sauce, creating 3 layers in all, ending with pasta sauce. Lower the cupcake molds onto the rack.
Secure the lid. Choose "Manual" mode and High pressure; cook for 15 minutes. Once cooking is complete, use a quick pressure release; carefully remove the lid. Bon appétit!

489. Dad's Chorizo Dip

(Ready in about 15 minutes | Servings 12)
If you like Chorizo, you will love this appetizer. An Instant Pot makes it easy and fun to prepare food for the big game.
Per serving: 210 Calories; 16.6g Fat; 3.8g Carbs; 11g Protein; 1.5g Sugars
Ingredients
1 tablespoon olive oil
3/4 pound Chorizo, casings removed and crumbled
1 onion, peeled and chopped
15 ounces Ricotta cheese
1/2 teaspoon ground black pepper
2 tablespoons fresh parsley
2 tablespoons fresh chives, chopped
Directions
Press the "Sauté" button to heat up the Instant Pot. Now, heat the oil and brown Chorizo sausage for 2 to 3 minutes.
Add the onion, cheese and black pepper to the Instant Pot.
Secure the lid. Choose "Manual" mode and High pressure; cook for 10 minutes. Once cooking is complete, use a quick pressure release; carefully remove the lid.
Garnish with fresh parsley and chives. Bon appétit!

490. Easy Pizza Cups

(Ready in about 20 minutes | Servings 6)
Comforting and irresistible, these pizza cups are loaded with mozzarella, sauce, and olives. They are perfect for any occasion.
Per serving: 301 Calories; 22.1g Fat; 6.2g Carbs; 19.5g Protein; 2.5g Sugars
Ingredients
12 turkey bacon slices
1 cup pizza sauce
2 cups mozzarella cheese
1 teaspoon dried oregano
1 teaspoon dried basil
1/2 cup Kalamata olives, pitted and sliced
Directions
Start by adding 1 cups of water and a metal rack to the bottom of the Instant Pot.
Place two slices of bacon crisscrossed in each muffin cup. Divide the remaining ingredients among cups. Lower the muffin pan onto the rack.
Secure the lid. Choose "Manual" mode and High pressure; cook for 10 minutes. Once cooking is complete, use a quick pressure release; carefully remove the lid.
Allow these pizza cups to stand for 5 minutes before removing from the muffin pan. Bon appétit!

491. Favorite Lettuce Wraps

(Ready in about 15 minutes | Servings 6)
Looking for a perfect party appetizer? Make a double batch of these colorful, delicious bites and wow your guests!
Per serving: 301 Calories; 22.1g Fat; 6.2g Carbs; 19.5g Protein; 2.5g Sugars
Ingredients
2 chicken breasts
1 cup chicken stock
2 garlic cloves, minced
1/2 teaspoon black pepper
1 cup green onions, chopped
1 bell pepper, seeded and chopped
1 red chili pepper, seeded and chopped
1 cup cream cheese
1/2 cup mayonnaise
1 teaspoon yellow mustard
Sea salt, to taste

1 head of lettuce
Directions
Add chicken breasts, stock, garlic, and black pepper to your Instant Pot.
Secure the lid. Choose "Poultry" mode and High pressure; cook for 10 minutes. Once cooking is complete, use a quick pressure release; carefully remove the lid.
Then, shred the chicken and divide it between lettuce leaves. Divide the remaining ingredients between lettuce leaves and serve immediately. Bon appétit!

492. Classic Turkey Sandwiches

(Ready in about 25 minutes | Servings 6)
These classic turkey dish sandwiches are elegant enough to serve for a festive Thanksgiving dinner but simple enough for an everyday lunch.
Per serving: 299 Calories; 21.8g Fat; 2.9g Carbs; 22.8g Protein; 0.6g Sugars
Ingredients
Keto Buns:
2/3 almond flour
1/2 teaspoon baking soda
1 teaspoon baking powder
A pinch of salt
A pinch of grated nutmeg
4 tablespoons butter
2 eggs, whisked
Filling:
1 pound turkey breast, chopped
1 cup turkey stock
2 garlic cloves, smashed
1/2 teaspoon seasoned salt
1/4 teaspoon ground black pepper
Directions
Mix the dry ingredient for the buns. In another bowl, thoroughly combine the wet ingredients for the buns. Add the wet mixture to the dry mixture.
Pour the mixture into a lightly greased muffin pan. Secure the lid. Choose "Manual" mode and High pressure; cook for 10 minutes. Once cooking is complete, use a quick pressure release; carefully remove the lid.
Wipe down the Instant Pot with a damp cloth. Add the remaining ingredients and stir to combine. Secure the lid. Choose "Manual" mode and High pressure; cook for 10 minutes. Once cooking is complete, use a quick pressure release; carefully remove the lid.
Assemble your sandwiches and serve warm.

493. Tacos with Pulled Pork and Pico de Gallo

(Ready in about 55 minutes | Servings 4)
Here's an ideal, family dish for a weeknight! An exciting way to make and eat a pulled pork.
Per serving: 429 Calories; 26.7g Fat; 4.4g Carbs; 41g Protein; 2.3g Sugars
Ingredients
1 tablespoon lard, at room temperature
1 pound pork shoulder
1 cup broth, preferably homemade
Salt and black pepper, to taste
1/2 teaspoon cayenne pepper
1/2 pound sharp Cheddar cheese, shredded
1 cup Pico de Gallo
Directions
Press the "Sauté" button to heat up the Instant Pot. Melt the lard and sear the pork for 5 minutes, turning occasionally.
Use the broth to deglaze the pan. Season with salt, black pepper, and cayenne pepper.
Secure the lid. Choose the "Manual" setting and cook for 50 minutes at High pressure. Once cooking is complete, use a natural pressure release; carefully remove the lid.
Shred the prepared pork and reserve.
Place cheese in a large pile in a preheated pan. When the cheese is bubbling, top it with the meat. Add Pico de Gallo.
Afterward, fold over and place on a serving plate. Enjoy!

494. Canapés with a Twist

(Ready in about 10 minutes | Servings 8)
Tuna fish can protect your heart, regulate blood pressure and boost your immune system. Cucumbers can reduce cholesterol as well as improve your vision and digestion.
Per serving: 112 Calories; 5.8g Fat; 1.2g Carbs; 12.8g Protein; 0.7g Sugars
Ingredients
1 pound tuna fillets
1/4 cup mayonnaise, preferably homemade
1/2 teaspoon dried dill
1/2 teaspoon sea salt
1/4 teaspoon ground black pepper, or more to taste
2 cucumbers, sliced
Directions
Prepare your Instant Pot by adding 1 ½ cups of water and steamer basket to the inner pot.
Place the tuna fillets in your steamer basket. Secure the lid. Choose "Manual" mode and High pressure; cook for 4 minutes. Once cooking is complete, use a quick pressure release; carefully remove the lid. Flake the fish with a fork.
Add the mayonnaise, dill, salt, and black pepper. Divide the mixture among cucumber slices and place on a serving platter. Enjoy!

495. Egg Salad "Sandwich"

(Ready in about 25 minutes | Servings 4)
You won't be missing sandwich buns with this recipe. Dijon mustard adds an extra zing to every bite!
Per serving: 406 Calories; 37g Fat; 7.3g Carbs; 11.6g Protein; 4.2g Sugars
Ingredients
6 eggs
1/2 cup tablespoons mayonnaise
1 teaspoon Dijon mustard

1/2 cup cream cheese
1 cup baby spinach
Salt and ground black pepper, to taste
2 red bell peppers, sliced into halves
2 green bell pepper, sliced into halves
Directions
Place 1 cup of water and a steamer basket in your Instant Pot. Next, place the eggs in the steamer basket.
Secure the lid. Choose "Manual" mode and Low pressure; cook for 5 minutes. Once cooking is complete, use a quick pressure release; carefully remove the lid.
Allow the eggs to cool for 15 minutes. Chop the eggs and combine them with mayonnaise, Dijon mustard, cheese, and baby spinach.
Season with salt and pepper. Divide the mixture between four bell pepper "sandwiches". Serve well chilled and enjoy!

496. Mexican Beef Taco Lettuce Wraps

(Ready in about 15 minutes | Servings 4)
Make your taco night simpler and healthier with this easy Instant Pot recipe! When it comes to taco toppings, you can add sour cream, full-fat yogurt, cilantro, sliced avocado, shredded Mexican cheese, and so on.
Per serving: 219 Calories; 12.5g Fat; 2.7g Carbs; 24.1g Protein; 1.2g Sugars
Ingredients
1 tablespoon olive oil
1/2 red onion, chopped
1 pound ground chuck
1 bell pepper, seeded and sliced
1 teaspoon taco seasoning
1 cup beef stock
Salt and ground black pepper, to taste
Directions
Press the "Sauté" button to heat up the Instant Pot. Now, heat the oil and sauté the onion until tender and translucent.
Then, add ground chuck and cook an additional 2 minutes or until no longer pink.
Then, add bell pepper, taco seasoning, stock, salt, and black pepper.
Secure the lid. Choose "Manual" mode and High pressure; cook for 5 minutes. Once cooking is complete, use a natural pressure release; carefully remove the lid.
To assemble taco wraps, place a few lettuce leaves on each serving plate. Divide the meat mixture between lettuce leaves. Add toppings of choice and serve. Bon appétit!

497. Summer Picnic Fish Sandwiches

(Ready in about 30 minutes | Servings 3)
Are you looking for perfect picnic sammies? Prepare cod fillets in your Instant Pot and place them between keto oopsies.
Per serving: 280 Calories; 19.5g Fat; 4.1g Carbs; 22.3g Protein; 2.1g Sugars
Ingredients
1/4 cup fresh lemon juice
1 cup water
3 cod fillets
2 tablespoons butter, softened
1/2 teaspoon salt
1/4 teaspoon ground black pepper
1/4 teaspoon paprika
1/4 teaspoon dried dill weed
1 teaspoon Dijon mustard
8 lettuce leaves
1 cucumber, thinly sliced
Oopsies:
2 eggs, separated yolks and whites
1/4 teaspoon sea salt
3 ounces cream cheese
1/4 teaspoon baking powder
Directions
Place 1/4 cup of fresh lemon juice and water in the bottom of your Instant Pot. Add a steamer basket. Rub the cod fillets with softened butter. Season with salt, black pepper, paprika, and dill. Place the fillets in the steamer basket.
Secure the lid. Choose "Manual" mode and Low pressure; cook for 3 minutes. Once cooking is complete, use a quick pressure release; carefully remove the lid.
To make your oopsies, beat the egg whites together with salt until very firm peaks form.
In another bowl, thoroughly combine the egg yolks with cream cheese. Now, add the baking powder and stir well.
Next, fold the egg white mixture into the egg yolk mixture. Divide the mixture into 6 oopsies and transfer them to a silicon sheet.
Bake in the preheated oven at 290 degrees F for about 23 minutes. Serve fish fillets between 2 oopsies, garnished with mustard, lettuce and cucumber. Enjoy!

498. Mexican-Style Muffins

(Ready in about 10 minutes | Servings 6)
You can enjoy these hot and spicy, Mexican-inspired cupcakes all year long. Keep this recipe in your back pocket.
Per serving: 189 Calories; 13.4g Fat; 4.3g Carbs; 12.5g Protein; 2.8g Sugars
Ingredients
6 eggs
1/4 cup almond milk, unsweetened
1/2 teaspoon salt
A pinch of ground allspice
1/2 teaspoon Mexican oregano
1/4 cup green onions, chopped
1 tomato, chopped
1 ½ cups bell peppers, chopped

1 jalapeño pepper, seeded and minced
1/2 cup Cotija cheese, crumbled
Directions
Prepare your Instant Pot by adding 1 ½ cups of water to the inner pot.
Spritz six ovenproof custard cups with a nonstick cooking spray.
In a mixing dish, thoroughly combine the eggs, milk, salt, allspice, and Mexican oregano; mix to combine well.
Add green onions, tomato, bell peppers, and jalapeño pepper to the custard cups. Pour the egg mixture over them. Top with cheese.
Lower 3 custard cups onto a metal trivet; then, place the second trivet on top. Lower the remaining 3 cups onto it.
Secure the lid. Choose "Manual" mode and High pressure; cook for 7 minutes. Once cooking is complete, use a quick pressure release; carefully remove the lid. Serve at room temperature.

499. Savory Cheese Biscuits with Bacon

(Ready in about 20 minutes | Servings 6)
This is probably only savory biscuit recipe you'll ever need on a ketogenic diet! This is extremely versatile recipe because you can experiment with different flavors. Consider adding another combo of spices.
Per serving: 271 Calories; 23.8g Fat; 1.8g Carbs; 12.2g Protein; 1.2g Sugars
Ingredients
1 cup almond flour
1 teaspoon baking powder
1/2 teaspoon salt
1/4 teaspoon dried oregano
1/2 teaspoon dried basil
3 teaspoons butter, melted
3 eggs, whisked
1/2 cup double cream
6 ounces Colby cheese, grated
4 slices bacon, chopped
Directions
Start by adding 1 ½ cups of water and a metal rack to the Instant Pot. Line a cake pan with a piece of parchment paper.
Mix almond flour, baking powder, salt, oregano and basil until well combined.
Mix in the melted butter, eggs, and double cream; fold in the cheese and bacon; mix until everything is well incorporated.
Now, grab your dough, smoothen a little bit and roll it to 1/2-inch thickness. Then, cut down the cookies with a cookie cutter.
Arrange the cookies on the prepared cake pan and lower it onto the rack in your Instant Pot.
Secure the lid. Choose "Manual" mode and Low pressure; cook for 15 minutes. Once cooking is complete, use a natural pressure release; carefully remove the lid. Bon appétit!

500. Chicken Liver Mousse

(Ready in about 10 minutes | Servings 8)
Whit its lighter-than-air texture and rich flavor, this mousse will give you more than you could expect from a keto recipe!
Per serving: 143 Calories; 10.1g Fat; 2.2g Carbs; 10.4g Protein; 1.2g Sugars
Ingredients
1 pound chicken livers
1 Spanish onion, chopped
1/2 cup chicken stock
1/2 cup white wine
1 tablespoon olive oil
1 cup heavy cream
1/2 teaspoon dried basil
1/2 teaspoon dried oregano
1 sprig rosemary
1/4 teaspoon ground black pepper
A pinch of salt
A pinch of ground cloves
Directions
Simply mix all ingredients in your Instant Pot
Secure the lid. Choose "Manual" mode and High pressure; cook for 3 minutes. Once cooking is complete, use a quick pressure release; carefully remove the lid.
Afterwards, purée the mixture with an immersion blender until smooth and uniform. Serve with veggie sticks. Bon appétit!

www.ingramcontent.com/pod-product-compliance
Lightning Source LLC
Chambersburg PA
CBHW081113080526
44587CB00021B/3569